Advances in Meat Research – Volume 10

HACCP in Meat, Poultry and Fish Processing

The *Advances in Meat Research* series reviews recent advances in meat science and technology. Each volume concentrates on one specific topic and discusses it in depth. The chapter authors are recognized as authorities in their fields and are drawn from around the world providing an international perspective.

The following volumes are also available:

Volume 6   Meat and Health
Volume 7   Growth Regulations in Farm Animals
Volume 8   Inedible Meat By-Products
Volume 9   Quality Attributes and their Measurement in Meat, Poultry and Fish Products

Advances in Meat Research – Volume 10

HACCP
in Meat, Poultry and Fish Processing

Edited by

A.M. PEARSON
Courtesy Professor
Department of Animal Sciences
Oregon State University

and

T.R. DUTSON
Dean, College of Agricultural Sciences
Director of Agricultural Experiment Station
Oregon State University

BLACKIE ACADEMIC & PROFESSIONAL
An Imprint of Chapman & Hall

London · Glasgow · Weinheim · New York · Tokyo · Melbourne · Madras

Published by
Blackie Academic & Professional, an imprint of Chapman & Hall,
Wester Cleddens Road, Bishopbriggs, Glasgow G64 2NZ

Chapman & Hall, 2–6 Boundary Row, London SE1 8HN, UK

Blackie Academic & Professional, Wester Cleddens Road, Bishopbriggs, Glasgow G64 2NZ, UK

Chapman & Hall GmbH, Pappelallee 3, 69469 Weinheim, Germany

Chapman & Hall USA, 115 Fifth Avenue, Fourth Floor, New York NY 10003, USA

Chapman & Hall Japan, ITP-Japan, Kyowa Building, 3F, 2-2-1 Hirakawacho, Chiyoda-ku, Tokyo 102, Japan

DA Book (Aust.) Pty Ltd, 648 Whitehorse Road, Mitcham 3132, Victoria, Australia

Chapman & Hall India, R. Seshadri, 32 Second Main Road, CIT East, Madras 600 035, India

First edition 1995

© 1995 Chapman & Hall

Typeset in 10/12pt Times by Cambrian Typesetters, Frimley, Surrey

Printed in Great Britain by The University Press, Cambridge

ISBN 0 7514 0229 X

A catalogue record for this book is available from the British Library
Library of Congress Catalog Card Number: 95–76796

♾ Printed on permanent acid-free text paper, manufactured in accordance with ANSI/NISO Z39.48-1992 (Permanence of Paper).

Preface

The HACCP (hazard analysis critical control point) concept for food products was an outgrowth of the US space program with the demand for a safe food supply for manned space flights by the National Aeronautics and Space Administration (NASA). The original work was carried out by the Pillsbury Company under the direction of Howard E. Bauman, who as the author of chapter 1 describes the evolution of the HACCP system and its adaptation to foods.

The second chapter discusses the adoption of HACCP principles and explains how they fit into the USDA and FDA meat, poultry and seafood inspection systems. The next chapter discusses how HACCP principles can be extended to production of meat, poultry and seafoods, a most important area involved in producing a safe food supply. Chapter 4 deals with the use of HACCP in controlling hazards encountered in slaughtering and distribution of fresh meat and poultry, while chapter 5 discusses the problem – both spoilage and hazards – involved in processing and distribution of meat, poultry and seafood products.

Chapter 6 covers the entire area of fish and seafoods, including both fresh and processed products from the standpoints of spoilage and hazards. Chapter 7 discusses the concept of statistical quality control and acceptable risk levels. The next chapter discusses the concept of total quality management and how it dovetails with and extends information obtained by HACCP. Chapter 9 reviews and suggests how HACCP can be utilized by delicatessens and meat, poultry and fish retailers. Chapter 10 discusses how HACCP can be adapted to improving the safety of meat, poultry and fish products by restaurants and food service establishments.

Chapter 11 suggests how the HACCP program can be adopted by consumers to improve food safety in the home. Chapter 12 describes how HACCP should be organized and managed by the meat, poultry and fish industries. Chapter 13 discusses how predictive microbiology dovetails with the HACCP program. The final chapter covers national and international cooperation in governmental regulations and agreements for meat, poultry and fish inspection.

This book should be useful to anyone involved in production, slaughtering, processing and distribution of meat, poultry and fish products. The discussion herein should help in improving the safety and in preventing spoilage of these highly perishable products.

Although almost all the authors are from the USA the principles of

HACCP are internationally recognized. Hence, the information in this book is applicable to the meat, poultry and fish industries throughout the world. The information provided and its adoption may be useful to these industries regardless of their location.

A.M.P.
T.R.D.

Contributors

G.R. Acuff   International Meat and Poultry HACCP Alliance, Center for Food Safety, Texas A&M University, College Station, Texas 77843–2259, USA

H.E. Bauman   Consultant, 4580 Greenwood Drive, Hopkins, Minnesota 55343, USA
formerly of The Pillsbury Company

H.R. Cross   International Meat and Poultry HACCP Alliance, Center for Food Safety, Texas A&M University, College Station, Texas 77843–2259, USA

B.F. Dennis   24612 Lenah Road, Aldie, Virginia 22001, USA

T.R. Dutson   Agricultural Experiment Station, Oregon State University, Oregon 97331, USA

E.S. Garrett   Director, National Seafood Inspection Laboratory, National Marine Fisheries Service, 3209 Frederic Street, Pascagoula, Mississippi 39568, USA

J. Gillespie   Professor and Head, Veterinary Medicine Teaching Hospital, Department of Clinical Sciences, College of Veterinary Medicine, Kansas State University, Manhattan, Kansas 66506, USA

S.J. Goodfellow   Director of Technical Services, Deibel Laboratories, Inc., 10014 S.W. 56th Lane, Gainesville, Florida 32608, USA

K.B. Harris   International Meat and Poultry HACCP Alliance, Center for Food Safety, Texas A&M University, College Station, Texas 77843–2259, USA

M. Hudak-Roos   Vice President, Technical Food Information Spectrum, Atlanta, Georgia 30328, USA

T.A. McMeekin   University of Tasmania, PO Box 252-C, Hobart, Tasmania, Australia 7053

M.G. Manis   USDA-FSIS; 341E Administration Building, Washington, DC 20250, USA

J.L. Marsden   Department of Animal Science and Industry, Kansas State University, Manhattan, Kansas 65506, USA

B.I. Osburn   Professor and Associate Dean for Research, School for Veterinary Medicine, University of California – Davis, Davis, California 95616, USA

A.M. Pearson   Department of Animal Sciences, Oregon State University, Corvallis, Oregon 97331, USA

R.J. Price   Sea Grant Extension Program, Department of Food Science and Technology, University of California, Davis, California 95616, USA

M.R. Roberts   State of Florida, Florida Department of Agriculture, The Capitol, Tallahassee, Florida 32399, USA

T. Ross   University of Tasmania, PO Box 252-C, Hobart, Tasmania, Australia 7053

O.P. Snyder, Jr   Hospitality Institute of Technology and Management, 830 Transfer Road, Suite 35, St. Paul, Minnesota 55114, USA

D.M. Theno   Vice President of Quality Assurance and Product Safety, Foodmaker, Inc., 9330 Balboa Avenue, San Diego, California 92123, USA

R.B. Tompkin   Vice President Product Safety, Armour Swift-Eckrich, 3131 Woodcreek Drive, Downers Grove, Illinois 60515, USA

H.F. Troutt   Professor and Head, Department of Veterinary Clinical Medicine, College of Veterinary Medicine, University of Illinois, Urbana, Illinois 60801, USA

D.R. Ward   Professor and Associate Department Head, Department of Food Sciences, North Carolina State University, Raleigh, North Carolina 27695, USA

N.B. Webb   Webb Technical Group, Inc., Raleigh, North Carolina 27612, USA

Contents

3   Implementation of HACCP program on farms and ranches   36
H.F. TROUTT, J. GILLESPIE and B.I. OSBURN

4   Implementation of the HACCP program by meat and poultry slaughterers   58
S.J. GOODFELLOW

5   The use of HACCP for producing and distributing processed meat and poultry products   72
R.B. TOMPKIN

6 Implementation of the HACCP program by the fresh
  and processed seafood industry   109
  E.S. GARRETT, M. HUDAK-ROOS and D.R. WARD

7 Risk analysis, HACCP and microbial criteria in meat and poultry systems 134
K.B. HARRIS, H.R. CROSS, G.R. ACUFF and N.B. WEBB

8 Relationship of the HACCP system to Total Quality Management 156
N.B. WEBB and J.L MARSDEN

11   The HACCP program and the consumer   **300**
M.R. ROBERTS

12   Organization and management of HACCP programs   **319**
D.M. THENO

1 The origin and concept of HACCP

H.E. BAUMAN

1.1 Introduction

The concept and reduction to practice of the Hazard Analysis Critical Control Point (HACCP) system is directly related to The Pillsbury Company's projects in food production and research for the United States space program. The basics were developed by The Pillsbury Company with the cooperation and participation of The National Aeronautics and Space Administration (NASA), The Natick Laboratories of the US Armed Forces, and the US Air Force Space Laboratory Project Group.

The beginning of the HACCP system occurred in 1959 when the author was contacted by The Quartermaster Food and Container Institute, now known as the Natick Laboratories, and asked whether Pillsbury would participate in the Space program effort to produce a food that could be used under zero gravity conditions by astronauts. No one knew how foods, especially particulates might act in zero gravity, and the initial conservative approach to solving this problem was to produce bite-sized foods covered with a flexible edible coating to prevent crumbling and consequent atmospheric contamination.

The main problem, however, was to come as close to 100% assurance as possible that the food products being produced for space use would not be contaminated with pathogens (either bacterial or viral), toxins, chemicals or physical hazards that could cause an illness or injury that might result in an aborted or catastrophic mission.

It was quickly determined that the techniques of quality control in use at that time could not give a high level of assurance that there would not be a problem. Further, the amount of testing needed to statistically arrive at a reasonable decision point as to whether a food was acceptable was extremely high. In actual fact, during early production, a large part of each batch of food had to be utilized for testing, leaving only a small portion available for the space flights.

1.2 Development of the HACCP concept

This raised two questions. First, 'What could we do using new techniques that would help us approach the 100% assurance level?' Second, since food companies 'for good reason' did not practice this type of destructive testing, 'How much in the way of hazards was the industry missing by minimal tests of the raw materials, and in-line and end product tests?' The latter question brought into serious doubt the prevailing system of quality control that was being used in Pillsbury's plants and by the food industry as a whole. The studies showed that most quality assurance programs were based on what the current quality assurance manager believed was a good program. There was no uniformity of approach or even understanding in the food industry as to what constituted an excellent program.

In the search for answers, the zero defects program utilized by NASA was examined and was found to be designed for hardware. The types of testing that were used for hardware, using for example x-ray and ultrasound, were nondestructive and therefore suitable for that purpose, but not for food testing.

1.2.1 HACCP – a new approach

In looking for a better system, it was decided to try a new approach to the problem. It was concluded after extensive evaluation that the only way to succeed would be to develop a preventative system. This would require control over the raw materials, the process, the environment, personnel, storage and distribution beginning as early in the system as possible.

It was felt certain that if this type of control could be established, along with appropriate record keeping, that a product that could be said to be safe with a high degree of assurance should be able to be produced. For all practical purposes, if it was done correctly, it should not require any testing of the final packaged product other than for monitoring purposes.

It should also be noted that the type of record keeping required under NASA rules not only furnished a clue as to how to approach the new system, but also facilitated the experimentation with this approach, and it is still a basic part of the HACCP system as it now exists. Pillsbury were required by NASA contract to keep records that allowed traceability of the raw materials, the plant where the food was produced, the names of people involved in the production and any other information that might contribute to the history of the product; in other words, a mechanism for tracing problems back to the source. This required that a familiarity with the raw materials had to be developed, which was not being done at that time, in the normal process of food product development. For instance, in development of the HACCP system the latitude and longitude where the salmon used in salmon loaf were caught was known, as well as the name of the ship. It was by using this approach that the Hazard Analysis Critical Control Point System (HACCP) was developed.

1.2.2 *HACCP – A preventative system*

HACCP is a preventative system of food control. The system when properly applied can be used to control any area or point in the food system that could contribute to a hazardous situation, whether it be from contaminants, pathogenic microorganisms, physical objects, chemicals, raw materials, a process, user directions for the consumer or storage conditions. The hazard analysis portion of HACCP involves a systematic study of the ingredients, the food product, the conditions of processing, handling, storage, packaging, distribution and consumer use.

This analysis allowed the identification in the process flow of the sensitive areas that might contribute to a hazard. From this information the Critical Control Points (CCP) in the system that had to be monitored could be determined. The definition of a CCP is any point in the chain of food production, from raw materials to finished product, where loss of control could result in an unacceptable food safety risk.

The first problem using this approach was that while it was known what needed to be found it was not known how to do an adequate hazard analysis. While searching for a method, it was found that the US Armed Forces Natick Research and Development Center had developed a system of analysis called 'modes of failure', which was used for medical supplies. After evaluating this method, Pillsbury adopted the modes of failure technique as their model with modifications. It was also found that to do an adequate analysis each ingredient and product and its production system had to be broken down into its components and each segment analyzed for its potential contribution to safety. When this was completed, it was then necessary to connect them all together in order to develop the overall interrelationship. This is critical, because whenever changes are made in an approved interrelated system, the system must be reevaluated since any change in the system, even though it may appear innocuous, could have a major effect downstream in the system. Although this appears to be an onerous task, for anyone experienced in food technology, it is mainly a matter of utilizing the knowledge they already have, supplemented by information from suppliers and the literature.

1.2.2.1 *Raw materials and ingredients.*
The problem was approached by starting with the raw materials. Specific ingredients were looked at as well as each stage of processing as it moved from the field through the food chain. This was done to determine what might happen to it and what might be expected in the way of problems when it appeared at the plant. It was from these analyses, including searches of the literature, discussions with suppliers, and of course, Pillsbury's own extensive history of ingredients, that they were able to select out those sensitive ingredients and sensitive

areas that must be monitored and controlled in order to ensure that a hazard would not be brought into the plant.

1.2.2.2 Contaminants and handling. The areas of concern ranged from the potential presence of pathogens, heavy metals, toxins, physical hazards and chemicals, to the type of treatments the ingredients might have received such as pesticide applications or a pasteurization step. The next segment required an analysis of the manufacturing process, the building, the general environment and method of people control to ensure that all of the points or areas in the facilities and process that might contribute to a hazard were completely understood. It also included determining those procedures that would prevent a hazard. Another segment of investigation required the examination of the storage, transportation and distribution to be used for the product and the abuses it might receive. Finally, an analysis was conducted to determine what the consumer might do to the product that could cause unsafe conditions. The above is a rather simplified sketch of what must be done. It does, however, show that detailed knowledge of the total system for the production of any food must be developed.

1.3 Acceptance of HACCP by the food industry

Although started in 1959 and used in The Pillsbury Company production plants for several years, the HACCP system was first formally presented to the general public in the 1971 National Conference of Food Protection (Dept. Health Educ. Welfare, 1972).

Following this conference, Pillsbury was granted a contract by the Food and Drug Administration (FDA) to conduct classes for FDA personnel on the HACCP system. The first comprehensive document on HACCP was published by The Pillsbury Company (1973) and was used for training FDA inspectors in HACCP principles. A special session was also held with FDA personnel involved in acidified and low acid canned food regulations. This group developed the necessary information for the promulgation of the acidified and low acid canned food regulation (FDA, 1973), which resulted in a successful HACCP system.

1.3.1 Establishment of HACCP by other companies

During the 1970s and early 1980s a number of companies requested and were given information and help in establishing their own HACCP programs. It was not until 1985 that the HACCP system was seriously considered for broad application nationally in the food industry. In that year, the HACCP system was recommended by the National Academy of Science (NAS, 1985) in a publication entitled *An Evaluation of the Role of Microbiological Criteria for Foods and Food Ingredients*. The NAS committee (Subcommittee on Microbiological Criteria for Foods and Food Ingredients) concluded that a preventative system (HACCP) was essential for control of microbiological hazards (NAS, 1985). Their conclusion was that end product testing was not adequate to prevent foodborne diseases. In 1987, the National Oceanic and Atmospheric Administration (NOAA) was charged by the United States Congress:

'to design a program of certification and surveillance to improve the inspection of fish and seafood consistent with the HACCP system'. (*Congressional Record*, 1987)

This effort has been carried out by the National Marine Fisheries Service.

1.3.2 Role of various agencies

The National Academy of Science publication also recommended that a National Advisory Committee on Microbiological Criteria for Foods be established.

This committee was established and has been active, not only in developing microbiological criteria, but has embraced the total HACCP concept. The committee has further refined HACCP by adding to the principles of HACCP appropriate descriptions of what each principle involves. They have also developed a glossary of terminology used. The HACCP document of this committee is intended to be a guide for maintaining a uniform system through the use of the principles and definitions. This approach would make possible a universal system of food safety that should facilitate the movement of foods internationally as well as providing a high level of assurance that the foods are safe. Recently the Codex Committee on HACCP has published in draft form a HACCP document to be used internationally in conjunction with ISO 9000. At a 1993 International Life Sciences symposium in Atlanta, Ga the Associate Commissioner of the US Food and Drug Administration stated in a speech that the FDA is considering making HACCP mandatory for food processors.

There will undoubtedly be refinements in the future as more experience with the system is gained. It is easy to modify a HACCP system, which will be important as new pathogens or other safety issues may arise. However changes should be made with care, and only if there is general agreement that the modifications will add to the reliability and not degrade the system.

1.4 Summary

HACCP is a systematized, documented method of food safety control utilizing rules and guidelines designed to prevent, eliminate and/or detect hazards through all stages of growing, harvesting, production and distribution to the final use of the product by the consumer. The HACCP system is based on a four way partnership between:

- top management
- the plant manager
- the quality assurance manager
- the people working in the plant

Further, the people working at a particular monitoring station are responsible for the monitoring and logging of the data and to see that immediate action is taken if a problem occurs. This partnership ensures that a team approach is used to produce safe food.

The HACCP system has been proven to be a cost effective system and will result in savings over standard quality control procedures based primarily on 'after the fact' detection of a hazard rather than prevention. The benefits to the manufacturer are substantial, many of which can be documented. The consumer, of course, is the ultimate beneficiary in that safer foods are produced. Of further benefit to the consumer is the fact that in determining hazards and their control, the HACCP system takes into account the effect of any hazard on target groups within the population, such as infants, the elderly, those with compromised immune systems, those undergoing antibiotic treatments and the unique situations existing in nursing homes and hospitals.

One of the important factors to the management of a company, besides those mentioned above, is the monetary and publicity effects of loss of control resulting in a hazard to the consumer. This can result in the tremendous costs and effects of a recall. The costs of a recall in most instances have to be estimated, since much more than the loss of product is involved, including the following:

(a) The cost of the product and its likely destruction.
(b) The diversion of management time during this period.
(c) The loss of sales while the sales force is locating and picking up product.
(d) The loss of future sales because of publicity about the product.
(e) Possibility of legal action and/or financial responsibility.
(f) Other intangible costs, such as the loss of company reputation with the consumers and government agencies and the effects on sales of other products.

Obviously HACCP may not only be of benefit to consumers, but may also be a good business practice.

References

Dept. Health, Educ. Welfare (1972) *Proc. of 1971 National Conference on Food Protection.* Dept. of Health, Education and Welfare, US Government Printing Office, Washington, DC.

FDA (1973) *Acidified Foods and Low Acid Foods in Hermetically Sealed Containers.* Code of US Federal Regulations, Title 21, 1, Parts 113 and 114 (renumbered since 1973). FDA, Washington, DC.

NAS (1985) *An Evaluation of the Role of Microbiological Criteria for Foods and Food Ingredients.* Food Protection Committee, Subcommittee on Microbiological Criteria. National Academy of Science (NAS), National Research Council. National Academy Press, Washington, DC.

Pillsbury Company (1973) *Food Safety Through the Hazard Analysis and Critical Control Point System.* Contract No. FDA 72–59. Research and Development Department, The Pillsbury Company, Minneapolis, Minnesota 55414.

2 The HACCP system and how it fits into FSIS programs
M.G. MANIS

2.1 Introduction

2.1.1 FSIS background

The Food Safety and Inspection Service (FSIS), an agency of the US Department of Agriculture, is responsible for ensuring that meat, poultry and meat and poultry products in interstate and foreign commerce are safe, wholesome, not adulterated and accurately labeled. FSIS administers and enforces the Federal Meat Inspection Act, the Poultry Products Inspection Act and the regulations by which these laws are implemented. Federal inspectors enforce the inspection laws in about 6500 meat and poultry plants. Livestock and poultry are inspected before slaughter and their carcasses and organs are inspected again after slaughter. Meat and poultry products are inspected during processing, handling and packing. Inspectors have authority to stop any aspect of an operation and demand correction of any deficiency that they find may adversely affect the safety and wholesomeness of the product.

FSIS also monitors state inspection programs, which inspect meat and poultry products that will be sold only within the state in which they were produced. The 1967 Wholesome Meat Inspection Act and the 1968 Wholesome Poultry Products Inspection Act require state inspection programs to be 'at least equal to' the federal inspection program. If states choose to end their inspection programs or cannot maintain this standard, FSIS must assume responsibility for inspection.

2.1.2 Industry responsibility and HACCP

Process control is not the responsibility of FSIS, or even a shared responsibility between the agency and industry. Each approved establishment must assume full responsibility for making safe and wholesome products, in compliance with the FSIS enabling legislation. Industry is responsible for producing safe products and FSIS is responsible for assuring that industry is using processes that are effective to accomplish this responsibility. From a regulatory perspective, the more that process controls, anticipates and prevents problems, the more likely there will be fewer problems for inspectors to detect. From a public health perspective, properly processed products are less likely to become adulterated.

Today's meat and poultry industries are facing new challenges, with more complex processes, ingredients and packaging. Consequently, controls are becoming more important as processes become more complex and as new ones are developed. To maintain an effective inspection system under these circumstances, FSIS needs a model for meat and poultry inspection that provides an ongoing, scientific system of intensive evaluation and verification, applicable to production processes in all inspected facilities.

The HACCP system provides such a model. HACCP is an internationally recognized process control system that identifies points in the food production process that are critical to the control of food safety hazards. It provides plant management with specific controls to operate their production process at these points. Controlling, monitoring and verifying a processing system is more effective than relying upon end product testing to ensure a safe product. HACCP is a proactive strategy that anticipates food safety hazards and solves problems in advance to help prevent unsafe products from being produced. Please refer to chapter 1 for more information on the background and development of the HACCP concept.

2.1.3 FSIS and HACCP

In May 1993 Secretary of Agriculture Espy directed FSIS to initiate rulemaking to require all inspected meat and poultry establishments to develop and maintain a HACCP system. HACCP would supplement, not replace, FSIS inspection. FSIS inspectors would still maintain a daily presence in establishments to determine whether product produced is unadulterated and properly labeled before permitting it to be distributed in commerce.

HACCP is not an inspection system, it is an industry process control system that can make inspection more effective. Currently, FSIS performs inspection by having inspectors generate information about the establishment's production process and environment to evaluate the conditions under which meat and poultry products are being produced. This activity produces just a 'snapshot' of establishment activity. In contrast to the relatively small amount of information that can be generated, HACCP records will enable inspectors to see how the establishment has operated over time. The inspector will be able to determine whether problems have occurred, and, if so, how they were addressed.

FSIS inspection activities under HACCP will not be conducted to the exclusion of other inspection responsibilities such as those associated with economic adulteration and misbranding. FSIS will continue to perform inspection tasks to determine whether an establishment is producing product which is unadulterated and properly labeled.

2.2 HACCP study

2.2.1 Background

In 1990 FSIS initiated a HACCP study. The study consisted of four stages:

1. Consultations and public hearings.
2. Workshops.
3. In-plant testing.
4. Evaluation.

2.2.2 Consultations and public hearings

Between January and September 1990 FSIS initiated a series of consultations and public hearing. More than 100 meetings, involving over 3000 of the Agency's constituents, were held. Furthermore, over 30 individuals testified at five public hearings. At all of these sessions the Agency requested comments about:

- Selection of products/processes as subjects for workshops
- Workshops
- In-plant testing
- Evaluation of pilots
- Follow-up with interested parties
- Training
- Other topics

A summary of 46 oral and written comments, provided at the public hearings, conveys the following themes:

1. Limit critical control points *26 (57%)*

    - not economic fraud
    - not economic adulteration
    - not misbranding
    - not quality assurance

2. Develop HACCP with industry *23 (50%)*

    - be flexible, structure on a plant by plant or a product by product basis
    - treat large and small plants differently
    - use processing authorities, define qualifications of experts
    - minimize paperwork and record keeping requirements

3. Relation to inspection program   *21 (46%)*

- HACCP should augment present and future programs, not replace current inspection systems
- shift emphasis from final product to process control
- other mechanisms needed for economic adulteration
- should incorporate critical control point verification

4. Training   *20 (43%)*

- model after Better Process Control schools
- agency training should include industry employees
- should be certified by agency or an independent authority
- plant personnel require special qualifications

5. Testing   *19 (41%)*

- base program on: National Academy of Sciences HACCP recommendation, and National Advisory Committee on Microbiological Criteria for Foods seven principles
- develop generic models, and obtain industry and inspector consensus on models
- select cross section of plants, and test for 12 months

6. Program implementation   *17 (37%)*

- do not make mandatory until proven effective
- all plants not ready at one time, some near-HACCP now, some are not close
- gradually implement, change regulations gradually, two years is not enough time for a transition
- start with processing, before slaughter

7. Defining HACCP   *12 (26%)*

- HACCP is an effective process control tool, not a panacea for food safety
- not a fail-safe or zero-defect program
- be consistent with FDA

8. Plant responsibilities   *11 (24%)*

- plants should develop critical control points
- plant employees should take processing measurements
- extend agency statutory authority and extend HACCP from farm to table

9. Ensuring complete programs   *8 (17%)*

- incorporate: hazard analysis; prevention and detection; microbiological testing; records/process verification; end product testing; and product recall

2.2.3 Workshops

2.2.3.1 Background.

Five workshops were held between February 1991 and April 1992 to develop generic HACCP models for refrigerated foods, cooked sausage, poultry slaughter, ground beef and swine slaughter. The workshop participants represented industry, trade associations and FSIS. The workshops were open to the public for observation. Time was allotted for observer comments, but observers did not participate in the model development process.

The workshop objectives were:

1. To assure participants understood HACCP principles and their application.
2. To assist the industry participants in developing the generic models.
3. To provide information needed for the participants to develop plant specific HACCP plans.

FSIS facilitated the workshops by conducting all sessions, preparing all materials and leading the discussions. Five field inspection staff were chosen for each workshop to provide technical advice. A workshop steering committee of industry participants was established after each workshop. These committees were responsible for refining the generic models.

2.2.3.2 Workshop process.

The agency sought industry acceptance of HACCP by limiting its role to facilitating the session and focusing on industry participation. The models were restricted to the prevention of food safety hazards, e.g. microbiological, chemical and physical. The workshops consisted of both general and breakout sessions. In the general sessions discussion focused on issues relevant to the product/process and the overall model. Smaller working groups addressed specific details of the generic model. The small groups reassembled in general sessions to report their findings.

2.2.3.3 Model development.

The generic models were developed in accordance with the seven principles of the National Advisory Committee on Microbiological Criteria for Foods (NACMCF, 1989). This included:

2.2.3.3.1 Product category.

The participants developed product category descriptions by determining the product's: common name; use; type of package; length of shelf life, temperature; where it will be sold; labeling instructions; and possible special distribution control.

2.2.3.3.2 Process flow.

A process flow diagram was developed for

each product. In each model receiving was the first step in the process flow, and in the case of poultry slaughter, swine slaughter and refrigerated foods the process flow ended in storage. For ground beef and cooked sausage the process flow was extended to shipping.

2.2.3.3.3 Hazard analysis. In the first four workshops hazards were assessed by ranking each product according to six hazard characteristics, followed by the assignment of a risk category. This was conducted after the participants determined the types of raw materials and ingredients required for product preparation. The agency followed the guidelines established by NACMCF (1989) in their HACCP paper. In the final workshop, swine slaughter, a new method for conducting the hazard analysis was employed where a series of questions, appropriate to the specific food process, were asked. This approach reflected the NACMCF (1992) paper, and proved to be more effective. Furthermore, this revised paper is similar to the internationally agreed upon HACCP principles developed by the Food Hygiene Committee of the Codex Alimentarius Commission.

2.2.3.4 Workshop steering committees. During each workshop the industry participants were divided into five small breakout groups to focus on particular aspects of the generic model. In addition, each breakout group selected a steering committee representative. Each steering committee selected a chairperson to facilitate the transactions of the committee. These committees served to:

1. Enhance the generic model for consistency and readability.
2. Address any unresolved issues from the workshops.
3. Represent industry in amending the generic model following the development of plant specific HACCP plans.

Refining the generic models was the major role of each steering committee. In certain instances other activities were undertaken. The refrigerated foods steering committee developed new critical control points for 'receiving' after the plant specific plans were created. That committee was also charged with addressing the applicability of HACCP principle one. The committee recommended changing the first principle, and their recommendations were forwarded to the NACMCF. The poultry slaughter steering committee added several 'notes to industry' to the generic model. Finally, the swine slaughter steering committee added an addenda on pesticides, antibiotic residues and organic acid sanitizing systems to the generic model.

2.3 Critical control points for various models

Each generic model included critical control points (CCP) for chemical, microbiological and physical hazards at appropriate steps of production. The critical control points for each of the models are listed below.

2.3.1 Refrigerated foods (cooked and assembled) critical control points

1. Preparation: physical;
2. Cooking: microbiological;
3. Chilling: microbiological;
4. Assemble components: microbiological;
5. Gas flush: microbiological;
6. Package inspection: microbiological;
7. Labeling/code dating: microbiological, chemical;
8. Chilling: microbiological; and
9. Storage: microbiological.

2.3.2 Raw beef pattie critical control points

1. Sanitation: microbiological, chemical, physical;
2. Meat receiving: microbiological, physical;
3. Non-meat receiving: chemical;
4. Storage: microbiological;
5. Assemble/pre-weigh/pre-grind: microbiological, chemical, physical;
6. Final grind: physical;
7. Packaging/labeling: microbiological, chemical, physical;
8. Storage: microbiological; and
9. Shipping: microbiological.

2.3.3 Whole young chickens critical control points

1. Receiving: microbiological, chemical, physical;
2. Scalding: microbiological;
3. Venting/opening/eviscerating: microbiological;
4. Offline procedure: microbiological;
5. Neck/giblet chiller: microbiological, physical;
6. Final washer: microbiological;
7. Carcass chilling: microbiological, physical;
8. Packaging/labeling: microbiological, physical; and
9. Storage/distribution: microbiological.

2.3.4 Cooked sausage critical control points

1. Receiving: chemical;
2. Meat preparation: physical;
3. Non-meat ingredient compounding: microbiological, chemical;
4. Pre-blend/formulation/staging: microbiological, chemical;
5. Cook/smoke: microbiological;
6. Chill/storage: microbiological;
7. Peel: microbiological;
8. Packaging: microbiological, chemical, physical; and
9. Storage: microbiological.

2.3.5 Pork slaughter market hogs critical control points

1. Receiving/holding: microbiological;
2. Scalding: microbiological, chemical;
3. Dehairing: microbiological;
4. Trimming: microbiological, physical;
5. Neck breaker/head dropping/brisket opening: microbiological;
6. Splitting: microbiological;
7. Trim rail/final rail inspection: microbiological, physical; and
8. Cooler: microbiological.

2.4 In-plant testing of HACCP models

2.4.1 Background

Following the workshops nine volunteer plants were selected to test the refrigerated foods, cooked sausage and poultry slaughter generic models. The agency decided to test only these three because to test all five would have extended the HACCP study for at least another year. The agency assigned one HACCP Data Collector inspector, responsible for collecting the HACCP data, to each of the nine plants.

The test period was divided into three phases:

1. *Baseline period.* Baseline data was collected for three months, by the Data Collector. No changes in either production or inspection procedures occurred during this phase. Also, during this period the test plant developed its plant specific HACCP plan, based upon the workshop generic model.
2. *Implementation phase.* During this phase plant personnel and agency inspectors were trained in HACCP. The plant implemented their HACCP system for a minimum of three months. The plant used this

period to adapt the HACCP plan to its operation. The agency and plant management both had to agree that the HACCP plan was working properly before the test plant could enter the third phase.

3. *Operational phase*. This lasted for six months. During this period the HACCP plan was not altered, and the testing was considered fully operational.

2.4.2   Plant specific plan

Each test plant developed its own plant specific HACCP plan. These plans reflected the individual product, processing and distribution conditions of the plant. The generic models' identification of critical control points, the requirements for critical limits, monitoring, corrective action, record keeping and verification were designed to be broad. This flexibility allowed the generic models to be adapted to the unique circumstances of each test plant.

The distinction between a generic model and a plant specific plan can be illustrated by comparing the generic cooked sausage model for the microbiological critical control point 'cook/smoke' with a plant specific plan:

2.4.2.1   Critical limit.   Generic: Time and temperature sufficient to meet minimum USDA requirements for cooked sausage or an alternative process approved by a process authority.
Plant specific: Internal temperature of 68–71°C after cooking. Internal temperature of 32°C maximum after cold showering.

2.4.2.2   Monitoring.   Generic: Internal temperature by physical measurement in a timely manner or by an alternative procedure established by a process authority. Frequency to be determined by establishment based on processing system.
Plant specific: Smokehouse technician to check internal temperature after cooking from the coldest spots, determined to be the left and right side of the front rack. Record results on smokehouse product and temperature chart. Check internal temperature after showering from the warmest spots, determined to be the left and right side of the front rack. Record results on smokehouse product and temperature chart.

2.4.2.3   Corrective/preventive action.   Generic: Place product on hold and evaluate significance of the deviation. Disposition based on previously approved guidelines from quality assurance or process authority. Evaluate cause of deviation and take action to prevent recurrences.
Plant specific: Production manager to place items on hold and notify Quality Control (QC) manager of the deviation. Segregate the held

product if necessary. If internal temperature is not reached after cooking, return to smokehouse until temperature is reached. Notify QC manager of deviation from cook schedule. If internal temperature is not reached after showering, continue to shower until temperature is reached. Notify QC manager of deviation from cool schedule.

2.4.2.4 Verification. Generic: Periodic observation and/or measurement. Audit of relevant records, consumer contacts, and/or products to determine if monitoring is sufficient and critical limits are adequate for safety. Perform ongoing review of HACCP plan in response to deviations and/or system and product modifications. Document calibration of test equipment at intervals sufficient to meet critical limits.
Plant specific: QC manager to audit smokehouse product and temperature log daily. QC manager to calibrate digital thermometer weekly to a NBS traceable thermometer. Temperature controls are calibrated monthly by outside technician. Calibration to be verified by QC manager. All data is to be documented on the smokehouse product and temperature log.

2.4.3   Inspection during phases II and III

Once the baseline phase was completed, then the plant operated its HACCP system for at least nine months. The agency utilized the regularly assigned inspectors throughout the test period. The inspectors verified that compliance standards were met. Verification was defined as: methods, procedures and tests used to determine if the HACCP system is in compliance with the HACCP plan. While the plant designated employees to determine that monitoring and corrective/preventive actions were being carried out, FSIS inspectors also verified the HACCP plan apart from plant verification. The agency verification tasks were developed from the generic models.

   Also, FSIS inspectors performed evaluation tasks, which included checking records and looking for trends. Inspectors evaluated records for deviations or deficiencies on scheduled tasks to determine compliance with both critical limits identified in the HACCP plan as well as regulatory standards.

2.4.3.1 PBIS and HACCP. The Performance Based Inspection System (PBIS) is an automated management system that improves the documentation of inspection findings. PBIS includes:

1. A plant-specific monitoring plan developed from an Inspection System Guide (ISG).
2. A plant profile, an automated system to schedule inspection activity and record inspection findings.
3. A Corrective Action System.

PBIS enables the Agency to document findings on an inspector assignment schedule; document deficiencies and corrective action taken on a process deficiency record; and discuss deficient findings with plant management. Agency personnel maintain PBIS schedules and findings.

2.4.3.2 Procedures. The inspection activities during Phases II and III utilized PBIS, with certain modifications. The agency developed a supplemental ISG to incorporate HACCP tasks. A separate guide was developed for refrigerated foods, cooked sausage and poultry slaughter. The supplement identified the compliance standards applicable to the generic model critical control points. The supplement listed the HACCP plan as a regulatory reference, which represented a departure from the standard guide.

In addition to the standard tasks identified in the assignment schedule, HACCP tasks were assigned. HACCP tasks were limited to health and safety and were assigned the highest risk factor under PBIS. HACCP task times were established by applying the same procedures used to establish PBIS task times. Inspectors received a total of 6 to 7 hours of scheduled tasks, and 1 to 2 hours of unscheduled time per day.

2.4.3.3 Tests. Deficiency records were handled in a similar fashion during the in-plant testing. A deficiency is defined as a departure from FSIS regulatory requirements. Inspectors would first identify a deficiency and then classify it according to the deficiency guide. A deviation is defined as a departure from the plant specific plan where no deficiency is found, but established critical limits, record keeping and verification requirements are not met. Inspectors were responsible for noting all deviations, as well as plant management responses to the deviations.

During the in-plant tests inspectors utilized the following PBIS tools: plant profile; inspector assignment schedule; deficiency classification guide; process deficiency record; and the ISG. Inspectors performed evaluation and verification functions to provide an accurate measurement of the HACCP system in each test plant.

2.4.4 Phase II: Implementation

During Phase II the agency: determined the accuracy and availability of the plant specific plan, plant profile, and the supplemental ISG; established plant compliance with its HACCP plan; shared baseline and implementation data with plant management; conducted interviews with plant personnel and FSIS employees; and determined, along with plant management, when the plant was ready to commence Phase III.

Monthly on-site visits by either circuit, area, regional, or headquarters personnel were conducted. A check list was devised for these plant visits.

The checklist included:

- Reviewing the plant specific plan
- Reviewing the plant profile
- Observing plant personnel performing monitoring tasks at identified critical control points
- Observing corrective/preventive action by plant personnel
- Observing data recording
- Observing the performance of assigned verification tasks
- Reviewing all pertinent HACCP records

2.4.5   Phase III: Operational

During this phase the agency: established that all applicable HACCP plan procedures were followed; conducted reviews of process deficiency reports to determine the daily effectiveness of the plant's HACCP system; interviewed plant personnel; and encouraged open communication between the agency and the test plants.

A three part operational checklist was developed. In part one the plant specific HACCP plan was compared with the actual operation of the HACCP system. This included determining if any critical control points had been added, deleted or altered, and whether the HACCP plan procedures were followed at each critical control point. In part two observations of plant personnel performing monitoring tasks at each critical control point were conducted. Observations included determining if the plant: followed plant defect criteria; performed time/temperature checks; performed pre-operational sanitation inspections; followed employee hygiene practices; and performed verification inspections. In part three plant records were reviewed. The record review included determining if: limits were within prescribed parameters; critical limits were exceeded; corrective actions were recorded; deviations were detected; and calibration of temperature devices were checked.

2.5   Evaluation

2.5.1   Background

The final in-plant test was completed in September 1993, and the agency is in the process of evaluating the data. The evaluation tasks include: HACCP Model Checklist; National Profiles; Quantitative Plant Data; Qualitative Plant Data; Inspector and Plant Personnel Survey; Workshop Evaluation; Training; and Economic Impact.

The HACCP study is not designed to provide information on the value of HACCP. Its value has already been established by the scientific community. Rather, the study will provide the agency with tangible experiences in the implementation of HACCP in meat and poultry establishments.

2.5.2   Limitations

The HACCP evaluation is limited because the HACCP models were tested in only nine volunteer plants. These plants were not randomly selected, and they cannot be considered representative of the over 6500 meat and poultry plants regulated by FSIS. The replication of plants with similar characteristics was not possible given the numbers of plants involved in the study. Thus the data cannot be generalized to the total plant population because of the heterogeneity of the total plant population and the dynamic nature of the test program.

Quantitative baseline plant data were only collected for 3 months. It was not possible, during the time period of the in-plant testing, to conduct tests for seasonal variations or other variables for which controls cannot be provided. Testing was conducted on the normal production system of the plants. It was not possible to introduce anomaly batches or lots to ensure that all types of batches or lots were tested.

Only a limited number of on-site reviews were conducted. Therefore, it is possible that the analysis of qualitative plant data could be biased by day-to-day operational variability. While it would have been preferable that each plant was reviewed more than once during both 'pre-HACCP' and 'post-HACCP' data collection periods, resource constraints prevented more frequent visits.

2.5.3   HACCP model checklist

This task was intended to assess the conformance of both the generic HACCP models and the plant specific HACCP plans to the principles recommended by the NACMCF (1992). The NACMCF principles were used to develop a 50 question checklist. This task focuses on the plans, rather than the implementation of the plans. All applicable answers must be 'yes' for the HACCP plans and models to be regarded as in conformance with the NACMCF (1992) HACCP principles.

The refrigerated food model checklist is described below.

2.5.3.1   Description of product.

- Does the plan submitted include: the establishment and the product name; the ingredients and raw materials used; the production process; the packaging used; the temperatures at which the product is intended to be held, distributed and sold; and the manner in which the product will be prepared for consumption?

- Has a flow diagram for the production of the food been submitted?
- Is the flow diagram specific for the facility producing the food?

2.5.3.2 Hazard assessment.

- Has a hazard assessment been performed on all ingredients prior to any processing step, including: hazard ranking; and risk categorization?
- Does this assessment of ingredients include: physical hazards; chemical hazards; and microbiological hazards?
- Has a hazard assessment been performed on final product, including: hazard ranking; and risk categorization?
- Does this assessment of final product include: physical hazards; chemical hazards; and microbiological hazards?
- Have all identified hazards been specifically listed?

2.5.3.3 Determination of critical control points.

- Has the control of all identified physical, chemical and microbiological hazards been assigned to identified critical control points (CCPs)?
- Have these CCPs been entered in the flow diagram in numerical order?
- Is the manner of control defined for each identified hazard?

2.5.3.4 Establishment of critical limits.

- Have parameters necessary for control been identified for each CCP?
- Have critical limits been established for each parameter?

2.5.3.5 Establishment of monitoring requirements.

- Have monitoring procedures been provided to ensure that the parameters necessary for control at each CCP are maintained within the established critical limits?
- Are the monitoring procedures continuous or, where continuous is not possible, is the frequency of monitoring statistically based?
- Have procedures been developed for the systematic recording of monitoring data?
- Have the effectiveness of procedures for controlling chemical, physical and microbiological hazards been established through testing?
- Have persons responsible for monitoring been identified?
- Have signatures of responsible individuals been required on monitoring data?

2.5.3.6 Establishment of corrective actions.

- Have specific corrective actions been developed for each CCP?

- Do the corrective actions address: re-establishment of control; and disposition of affected product?
- Have procedures been established to record these data?

2.5.3.7   *Establishment of effective record keeping systems.*

- Have procedures been established to maintain the HACCP plan on file at the establishment?
- Have provisions been made to record information on ingredients when appropriate, such as: supplier certification documenting compliance with processor's specifications; processor audit records verifying supplier compliance; storage temperature record for temperature sensitive ingredients; and storage time records of limited shelf life ingredients?
- Have provisions been made to record information relating to product safety when appropriate such as: sufficient data records to establish the efficacy of barriers in maintaining product safety; sufficient data and records establishing the safe shelf life of the product; and documentation of the adequacy of the processing procedures from a knowledgeable process authority?
- Have provisions been made to record information on processing when appropriate such as: records from all monitored CCPs; and system records verifying the continued adequacy of the process?
- Have provisions been made to record information on packaging when appropriate such as: records indicating compliance with specifications of packaging materials; and records indicating compliance with sealing specifications?
- Have provisions been made to record information on storage and distribution when appropriate such as: temperature records; and records showing no product shipped after shelf life date on temperature sensitive product?
- Have provisions been made to record modifications to the HACCP plan file indicating approved revisions and changes in ingredients, formulations, processing, packaging, and distribution control as needed?

2.5.3.8   *Establishment of verification procedures.*

- Have procedures been included to verify that all hazards were identified in the HACCP plan when it was developed?
- Have procedures been included to verify that the HACCP system is in compliance with the HACCP plan?
- Has the frequency of verification inspection been established?
- Has provision been made for verification testing reports to include the following elements: existence of an approved HACCP plan and designation of person(s) responsible for administering and updating the HACCP plan; all records and documents associated with CCP monitoring

must be signed by the person monitoring and approved by a responsible official of the firm; direct monitoring data of the CCP while in operation; certification that all monitoring equipment is properly calibrated and in working order; deviation procedures; and any sample analysis for attributes confirming that CCPs are under control to include physical, chemical, microbiological or organoleptic methods?

2.5.4 National profiles

National profiles of plants producing refrigerated foods, cooked sausages, and young chickens were developed. These profiles provide an overview of the general plant population from which volunteer plants were selected.

The following data sources were used to develop the national profiles.:

2.5.4.1 Performance based inspection system (PBIS). Four major components of PBIS were utilized: plant profiles; the Inspection System Guide; Corrective Action System; and the schedules of inspection activity and records results of inspection.

2.5.4.2 Review and evaluation information system (REIS). The REIS records are derived from audits performed in slaughter, allied slaughter, and processing establishments.

2.5.4.3 Refrigerated foods survey. In 1990 the agency conducted a special survey to obtain information about refrigerated foods plants and the types of products produced.

2.5.4.4 Poultry inspection monthly production data. FSIS records the condemnation rates of slaughtered young chicken each month. These sources were used to determine: the population of plants; general characteristics of plant size and volume; and safety and health activities for each product category.

The data on safety and health activities are based on the following factors: maintenance of facilities, equipment, water supply and sewage disposal; sanitation and pest control; control of purchased materials; control of processing and production; finished product inspection; control of condemned and inedible materials; and handling, storage and shipping of finished products.

2.5.5 Quantitative plant data

This task involved the collection of physical, chemical and microbiological data for all nine test plants.

2.5.5.1 Microbiology. Microbiology samples were collected during and after completion of production to establish bacterial profiles for each product. The following data were collected:

2.5.5.1.1 Refrigerated foods and cooked sausage. Aerobic plate count @ 35°C; aerobic plate count @ 20°C; coliforms; *Escherichia coli*; *Staphylococcus aureus*; gas forming anaerobes; *Listeria* species; and other species.

2.5.5.1.2 Poultry slaughter. Aerobic plate count @ 35°C; coliforms; *Escherichia coli*; *Staphylococcus aureus*; gas forming anaerobes; and salmonellae.

2.5.5.2 Chemistry. The following chemistry data were collected, by product.

2.5.5.2.1 Refrigerated foods. Chlorine in processing water; salt concentration of in-process control points; pH; and unauthorized preservatives in finished product.

2.5.5.2.2 Cooked sausage. Type II protein calculations; nitrites/ nitrates; and salt concentration.

2.5.5.2.3 Poultry slaughter. Chlorine in processing water.

2.5.5.3 Physical processing. The physical factors included both plant performed activities and FSIS inspection activities.

2.5.5.3.1 Refrigerated foods and cooked sausage. Organoleptic wholesomeness; temperature; restricted ingredient control; time; sanitation; employee practices; heat treatment/internal temperature of product; separation of cooked and raw/finished and raw product; cooling treatment; environmental control; package integrity; finished product identity/date coding of product; and foreign material control.

2.5.5.4 Physical slaughter. The following poultry slaughter physical factors focus on the problem areas of sanitation, contamination, and product handling:

- Sanitation (overall slaughter facility and equipment)
- Product handling (condemned materials)
- Contamination (fecal)
- Sanitation (automatic eviscerating machine)
- Product handling (helper responses)

- Product handling (salvaged and reprocessed products)
- Product handling (salvage/reprocessed hangback rack or line carcasses)
- Contamination (carcasses before chillers)
- Contamination (salvage procedures in removing contamination)
- Contamination (reprocessing procedures)
- Contamination (fecal contamination on carcasses samples at prechill)
- Sanitation (removing debris from equipment, utensils and structures)

2.5.6 Qualitative plant data

This task addresses overall test plant regulatory compliance. Data were collected twice: in Phase I (baseline) and during the latter stages of Phase III (operational). Each plant was visited by a team of FSIS employees with expertise in both slaughter and processing inspection. The team that collected data in Phase I also returned to collect data in Phase III.

Data collection consisted of both reviewer observations and reviewer interviews with plant management. The review team was accompanied by one representative from plant management and one FSIS field employee. The following review factors were applied to all nine test plants.

1. *General housekeeping*: The general state of housekeeping and sanitation in the entire plant.
2. *Conditions of facilities*: Reflecting the commitment of plant management to provide and maintain adequate facilities in a safe, clean condition.
3. *Plant employee personal hygiene*: The level of hygiene practiced by all categories of company employees.
4. *Plant employee sanitary practices*: The level of employee sanitary practices while handling product.
5. *Plant employee attitudes about inspection*: Attitudes of company employees at all levels towards inspectors and conformance with inspection requirements.
6. *Plant employee training*: Management's commitment to provide plant employees with adequate training.
7. *Plant management attitudes toward employee supervision*: Management attitudes toward supervision and the methods used to achieve employee performance of work function.
8. *Plant management response to problems*: Management's methods for dealing with loss of process control, emergencies, or other difficult situations, i.e. carcasses on the floor, excessive contamination or pathology, and power outage.
9. *Plant management measures to protect product from contamination*: Management attitudes, strategies, and actions taken to prevent contamination and cross-contamination hazards in production.

10. *Product quality and safety*: Level of product quality according to health and safety attributes.
11. *Plant management programs and systems*: Management process control, organizational structure to assure quality control, and programs and systems operating to produce safe, wholesome foods under adequately controlled good manufacturing practices.

2.5.7 Inspector and plant personnel survey

This task was designed to obtain information about the implementation experience. FSIS inspectors and plant personnel were interviewed in each test plant. Interviews were conducted by FSIS headquarters and regional personnel midway through Phase II (implementation) and during the last month of Phase III (operational).

The following questions were posed to FSIS employees:

- Does the HACCP system as implemented control the process?
- Do you see an improvement in process control under HACCP?
- Have the plant staff responsible for monitoring been identified?
- Are corrective/preventive actions that are in accordance with the plant specific HACCP plan being used at each identified critical control point?
- What impact did HACCP have on your workload?
- How have your working relationships with plant personnel changed as a result of HACCP?
- How receptive was plant management to adopting HACCP?

The following questions were presented to plant personnel:

- Is the number of critical control points correct?
- Are the plant's record keeping procedures burdensome at any critical control point?
- How have your working relationships with FSIS personnel changed as a result of HACCP?
- To what extent, if at all, did you feel that you and your coworkers experienced difficulty in implementing HACCP?
- How flexible were FSIS officials in responding to corrective/preventive actions for HACCP violations?

2.5.8 Workshop evaluation

At the end of each workshop, participants and observers were asked to complete a questionnaire addressing workshop design; materials; generic model development; the workshop approach; and any suggested improvements. Furthermore, a separate questionnaire was developed for steering committee members and for FSIS employees and plant employees involved in the adaption of the generic model to the in-plant HACCP plan.

Workshop respondents were asked about the HACCP model development. This included: identifying critical control points; determining critical limits for each critical control point; developing monitoring plan activities; developing corrective action approaches; developing record keeping systems; and developing verification procedures.

Workshop respondents were asked to comment on the workshop design and operation, such as: rating the development of the process description; assessing the process flow diagram; and indicating whether there was sufficient opportunity for input. Respondents were asked to suggest other approaches for developing HACCP models.

In addition to questions about model development, workshop design and operation, workshop participants were asked whether: the HACCP model developed at the workshop was a viable framework for industry implementation; the workshop format offered a sound approach for producing other generic models; the presence of observers was beneficial to their workshop; and the generic HACCP model was useful.

2.5.9 Training

An understanding of HACCP principles, concepts and techniques is necessary for those responsible for developing, monitoring, and verifying HACCP plans. During the in-plant tests plant employees were provided with the knowledge necessary to develop their plant specific HACCP plans, and FSIS inspectors were trained to perform HACCP related inspection duties.

Headquarters and regional staff collected the training data by: observing the training sessions; administering a reaction survey instrument to trainees immediately after training; observing FSIS employees' performance during Phase II (implementation) and Phase III (operational); and informally interviewing FSIS employees. The evaluators observed one training session for each tested product.

The survey instrument addressed the usefulness and effectiveness of various training modules, including: the plant specific plan; the PBIS/HACCP relationship; inspector assignments; the Supplemental Inspection System Guide; the Process Deficiency Records; and monitoring and evaluating the HACCP plan.

2.5.10 In-plant changes

This evaluation task consists of identifying in-plant changes experienced by the test plants after implementing HACCP. These factors were: staffing; products; facilities; packaging; equipment; labeling; processing operations; and distribution. The agency developed a survey instrument which plant personnel used to record any changes during the testing period.

2.6   Current HACCP issues

In late 1993 the agency determined that it would be beneficial to allow all constituent groups greater access to the deliberative process prior to proposing a HACCP regulation. Thus, FSIS held the HACCP Round Table in March 1994. This meeting is viewed as an opportunity to allow free and frank discussion of the legitimate concerns of all constituents. What follows is a consideration of key regulatory issues, some of which were discussed at the Round Table.

2.6.1   Voluntary/mandatory

This issue is whether the agency should mandate HACCP. There are a variety of voluntary approaches.

1. Limit mandatory HACCP to those instances in which it is absolutely necessary, i.e. low acid canned foods.
2. A modified voluntary approach, where initially HACCP would be voluntary, then as data is gathered ultimately HACCP would become mandatory.
3. The agency would formulate mandatory critical control points, while industry adoption of HACCP systems would be encouraged rather than mandated.

These approaches assume that: regulators cannot mandate a commitment to quality; small producers do not have the resources for HACCP; and industry will accept greater ownership of HACCP if they are not compelled.

In the alternative, a mandatory HACCP program is suggested because some plants are less likely to have adequate controls without HACCP; HACCP must be mandated to ensure a level playing field; and a portion of industry will not take advantage of the most up-to-date technologies to control their manufacturing processes. They may skirt around the system, and may never be able to adopt and use it properly.

Some of the questions that will have to be addressed include:

Is there a sufficient basis for mandating HACCP?

How would a mandatory program impact small businesses?

Is there a reason and the means to encourage early adoption of HACCP?

Have sufficient pilot projects been attempted to gather data for mandating HACCP?

Will regulatory agencies have sufficient resources to mandate HACCP?

2.6.2 Review of HACCP plans

The agency must determine how it will verify HACCP plans. Normally verification would occur at the establishment. Verification may include review of any or all components of the HACCP plan, such as monitoring critical control point records; deviations and corrective actions; critical limits; and other pertinent HACCP records. Such verification presumes agency access to all HACCP plan information.

In addition to record review, verification activities may include assessing process controls at critical control points such as the use of microbiological techniques, i.e. equipment and on-line product sampling to measure bacterial levels.

Issues for agency consideration include: access to all relevant aspects of the HACCP records; extending verification beyond record review; and addressing potential conflict between agency verification and HACCP plan approval.

2.6.3 Transition period

It is anticipated that a transition period is needed for plants to incorporate HACCP. Plants will need time to: train their employees; obtain the necessary expertise to develop HACCP plans; operate under a HACCP plan to ensure that it functions properly; and possibly obtain plan approval.

A phased in approach, for mandatory HACCP, can be based on a combination of factors, such as length of time and type of product.

Possible options include: first implement HACCP for products associated with high risk; initially implement HACCP for products associated with low risk; or set a certain date where all plants must implement HACCP.

2.6.4 Plan approval

The question for the agency is what role, if any, it should play in approving plant generated HACCP plans. If HACCP plans are to be approved, then they should be approved either by the agency or a third party. The agency has experienced a lengthy headquarters approval process for about 500 Total Quality Control systems. There are questions about whether headquarters approval is more effective than field approval, and whether there is a sufficient number of technically proficient agency personnel available to provide timely HACCP plan approval.

Third party approval raises a different set of issues. Should third party approval include an on-site evaluation to determine the plan's adequacy and should third party approvers participate in plan development? Third party approval would place a financial burden on industry. Also, defining a third party, and determining their HACCP expertise would have to be decided. Further, the agency must explore its role in recognizing third parties, and determine how to identify a sufficient number of qualified individuals.

2.6.5 Critical limits

The agency needs to determine the relationship between current and future regulatory critical limits and the critical limits required for each HACCP plan. A critical limit is a criterion that must be met for each preventive measure associated with a critical control point. Plant management would be responsible for developing their HACCP plan, and ensuring that the critical limits control the identified hazards. In most instances critical limits would be plant specific.

Where a specific standard is prescribed by regulation, then HACCP plan critical limits must meet or exceed these requirements. If a plant's HACCP plan sets a critical limit that exceeds a regulatory requirement, then those limits would be met notwithstanding the regulatory standard. Finally, as regulatory agencies either add new requirements or amend current regulations, establishments would change their critical limits to reflect such agency action.

2.6.6 Generic models

The agency must decide what role it will play in the development of generic models and determine the relationship between generic models and plant specific HACCP plans.

There are a number of approaches to the development of generic models:

1. Government and industry develop the models, then have them approved by expert committees.
2. Regulatory agencies unilaterally develop the models.
3. Industry develops models and they are reviewed by an external group.
4. External groups develop generic models.

Regardless of how generic models are developed there is the additional question of how they should be applied. There are a variety of approaches:

1. The critical control points identified in the models would become mandatory. This, if a HACCP plan fails to address the generic critical control points, the plant would have to provide a justifiable reason for their absence.
2. The generic models could serve as suggested guidelines, rather than obligatory reference points.

3. Generic models would set the minimum standards for a particular process. Regardless of the authority of the generic models, the final responsibility for developing HACCP plans rest with industry.

In the alternative, it is argued that generic models should exist apart from any regulatory framework because generic models tend to result in plant specific HACCP plans that are not unique to each plant. Generic models may interfere with HACCP plans by not allowing the plans to capture the characteristics of each plant. An alternative may be for regulatory agencies to provide advice to industry on the development of HACCP plans in lieu of developing generic models.

2.6.7 Training

Training is an important component to the successful implementation of HACCP. The agency must define the groups of people, within the organization and industry, that need to be trained as well the performance outcomes expected at the conclusion of training. The agency should seek the advice of both experts in HACCP and education to help determine what type of training is necessary.

Industry training can include operating a HACCP system and developing HACCP plans. These are distinct activities. Ultimately, training to operate a HACCP system may be more beneficial than training to develop a HACCP plan. Also, there is the possible need to devise different levels of industry training, reflecting the reality that small operations are sufficiently dissimilar from large, complex operations.

The agency must determine the extent to which it intends to participate in industry training. The approaches include: direct government involvement and oversight of industry training; less direct involvement in which government approves course curriculum without participating in the process; joint government/industry determination of training needs and training participation; and no regulatory involvement in industry training.

Regardless of the approach it seems useful to consider standardizing training materials with respect to HACCP principles and application. This standardization can extend across commodity lines and may be applicable internationally.

2.6.8 Plan failure

The agency must examine its role in investigating the cause of HACCP plan failure, and what regulatory action is appropriate if a plan is flawed. Industry is ultimately responsible for any flaws or failures of the HACCP system, and must adjust their HACCP plans to re-establish control.

However, government has to ensure that the processor corrects short-comings, and ultimately the regulator has to determine if the HACCP system is in compliance with appropriate regulations.

Regulatory actions may include: increasing inspection intensity; increasing product testing; increasing reviews and audits; suspending or terminating an establishment's process; and reverting to pre-HACCP compliance requirements. Suspending or terminating an establishment's process is based on the assumption that a HACCP plan is intended to prevent the occurrence of food hazards. If a plan is not followed, then adulterated product may reach the consumer. If a plan is not being followed, and if the plan focuses solely on assuring food safety, then it is likely that the process covered by the plan is out of control and unsafe product will be produced.

2.6.9   Safety/economic

The agency must consider whether it should limit HACCP to safety, or expand HACCP to include economic factors. Limiting HACCP to safety reflects, in part, the view that at least in the early stages of HACCP implementation it is beneficial to limit its scope in order to help ensure successful adoption. Conversely, it can be argued that HACCP principles provide a logical approach for assuring compliance with all regulatory requirements. If the agency elects to limit HACCP to safety, then this does not negate or diminish agency responsibility to enforce its economic requirements. Rather, it means that the regulatory enforcement of economic considerations will occur outside the scope of HACCP.

2.6.10   Other quality systems

The agency must examine the relationship between HACCP and other quality programs, such as International Standards Organization (ISO) 9000. HACCP and ISO systems are compatible, and HACCP can be viewed as a subset of the ISO system, with HACCP's specialized emphasis on food microbiological, chemical, and physical hazards. The ISO system goes beyond regulatory food safety concerns, concentrating on clarifying standards of acceptability for all product features and requirements. ISO 9000 standards refer to compliance with reference standards, codes and quality plans for process control. HACCP is a method which can provide the necessary detail to ensure compliance with food safety requirements.

2.6.11   Scientific validity

While there is wide acceptance of the merits of HACCP, there appears to be a lack of empirical data demonstrating how well HACCP works in practice. It is difficult to obtain such data because each plant is unique, and finding comparable plants to conduct matched controls is problematic. Furthermore, certain outcome measures present challenges. For example, if the measure of the merits of HACCP is the contamination rate for certain pathogens, then because these pathogens may be present in very low numbers, detection and monitoring is uncertain. Thus, large trials, involving a high number of samples, would be required to produce meaningful results.

Evaluation of HACCP systems may best be accomplished on a plant by plant basis. The experience of a number of individual plants who have successfully employed HACCP could provide a cumulative assessment. Seeking industry data about their HACCP experiences would be useful.

2.7 Quadrilateral discussions on food safety

2.7.1 Introduction

Australia, Canada, New Zealand, and the USA established a dialogue on food safety issues when the four countries created the Quadrilateral Discussions on Food Safety. At the 1992 quadrilateral meeting in Canberra, Australia the USA presented a paper on HACCP principles and HACCP regulatory issues. The participants concluded, after consideration of the US paper, that there was a need to pursue an examination of HACCP in greater detail. Thus, a HACCP working group was established, and FSIS chaired the working group. The working group was charged with examining key concerns facing regulatory agencies in regard to HACCP.

2.7.2 HACCP working group

The working group was established in early 1993, and it focused its efforts on all salient HACCP regulatory issues. No direct consideration of either the theory of HACCP or the actual application of HACCP by industry was considered. The working group agreed to: identify and address regulatory issues; share information on the incorporation of HACCP within the group members' areas of responsibility; facilitate the identification of common approaches; and present a report on the status of HACCP regulatory issues at the 1993 Quadrilateral Discussions on Food Safety.

2.7.3 HACCP working group report

The working group report was presented in October 1993 in Maui, Hawaii. The report reflected the positions of all the working group participants. Different approaches were noted in the report because of the diverse regulatory perspective of the working group members.

The working group endorsed the principles of HACCP identified by the US National Advisory Committee on Microbiological Criteria for Foods and the Food Hygiene Committee of the Codex Alimentarius Commission. The working group stated that these principles form the basis for a proactive strategy which anticipates food safety hazards and solves problems in advance to help prevent the production of unsafe product.

The working group paper identified 12 key regulatory issues:

1. Voluntary/mandatory
2. Harmonize regulatory roles
3. Regulatory review of HACCP plans
4. Plan approval
5. Critical limits
6. Generic models
7. Training
8. HACCP plan failure
9. Safety/economic
10. Other quality systems
11. Costs
12. Scientific validity

Each issue was addressed by articulating a succinct issue statement, followed by background discussion and a series of discussion points.

The quadrilateral participants at the Hawaii meeting agreed to maintain the HACCP working group for at least another year. The working group was assigned the following tasks: exchange data, particularly for evidence of the beneficial implementation of HACCP; share generic models; examine the adequacy of documentation of existing process control systems; examine the role of government as an advisor assisting industry in the development of HACCP systems; and harmonize methods. The working group will present its findings to the quadrilateral participants in late 1994.

2.8 Summary

This chapter has discussed the status of HACCP in FSIS. Process control is industry's responsibility, and HACCP is a widely accepted process control system that anticipates food safety problems in advance to help prevent unsafe product from being produced. HACCP is not an inspection system, but it can make inspection more effective. Furthermore, FSIS inspection activities under HACCP will not be conducted to the exclusion of other regulatory responsibilities, and HACCP will not replace current inspection activities. Rather, HACCP will supplement the way FSIS conducts inspection.

In 1990 FSIS initiated a HACCP study. The agency sought input from its constituents prior to commencing the study. That input helped shape the entire process. The agency conducted five industry workshops in which FSIS facilitated the development of generic models based on the principles identified by the National Advisory Committee on Microbiological Criteria for Foods.

After the workshops nine test plants were selected to test three of the generic models for twelve months. Each plant developed its own plant specific HACCP plan based upon the applicable generic model. FSIS inspectors collected evaluation test data throughout the one year test period. The Performance Based Inspection System was modified to incorporate HACCP tasks for the regularly assigned in-plant inspectors. The HACCP tasks were limited to health and safety, and were assigned the highest risk factors.

The final in-plant test was completed in September 1993, and the agency is in the process of evaluating the test data. The evaluation tasks include: model checklist; national profiles; quantitative and qualitative plant data; in-plant surveys; workshop and training evaluation; and economic impact. The HACCP study is not designed to provide information about the value of HACCP. Rather, it will provide the agency with tangible experiences in the implementation of HACCP.

In late 1993 FSIS determined that it would be beneficial to provide its constituent groups with a forum to comment on the development of a mandatory HACCP regulation, and the HACCP Round Table was held in March 1994. This chapter identifies a number of key regulatory issues FSIS must address before it publishes a proposed HACCP regulation. Those issues are: mandatory/voluntary; plan review; transition; plan approval; critical limits; generic models; training; plan failure; safety/economic; quality systems; and scientific validity.

References

NACMCF (1989) *Hazard Analysis and Critical Control Point System.* Report, National Advisory Committee on Microbiological Criteria for Foods.
NACMCF (1992) Hazard analysis and critical control point system. *Intl. J. Food Microbiol.* **16**, 1.

3 Implementation of HACCP program on farms and ranches

H.F. TROUTT, J. GILLESPIE and B.I. OSBURN

3.1 Introduction

Outbreaks of foodborne illness, some with tragic consequences, have raised widespread concerns about the adequacy from farm to table of the food safety system in the USA. Numerous workshops, symposia, panel presentations and discussions, and other meetings have emphasized the need to involve Hazard Analysis Critical Control Point (HACCP) principles along the entire food chain as a means of increasing the safety of our foods of animal origin. The essential role of involving the entire food chain in preventive programs to reduce the risk of foodborne hazards has been recognized through the development of on-farm pre-harvest food animal food safety programs, and the maintenance of healthy animals (Food Animal Production Medicine Consortium, 1992; Heidelbaugh, 1992).

HACCP programs were developed in the 1960s through joint efforts of the US Army Natick Research and Development Laboratories, the National Aeronautics and Space Administration, and The Pillsbury Company (Sperber, 1991a) to assure the safety of foods for the US space program. Chapter 1 reviews the historical development of the HACCP program. The HACCP system is now widely used throughout the food processing industry as a quality control measure to assure the safety of food (Sperber, 1991a, b).

The HACCP system within the food processing industry focuses on the overall process – from growth and harvest to product utilization – and establishes an assessment of the risk of occurrence of specific hazards and how these can be functionally controlled at specific points throughout the process (Sperber, 1991b). Sperber (1991a) emphasizes that HACCP as a component of a total quality assurance effort does not rely on simply finished product testing. Rather, because HACCP focuses on control of hazards throughout the process, whatever that process may be, it is fundamentally preventive. In food animal production units, once a disease strikes or a production inefficiency occurs, economic loss of some magnitude is sustained. The HACCP system can provide an orderly means of implementing preventive medicine, including food safety programs on our food animal farms and ranches. Over the last several decades a variety of animal health programs, preventive in nature, have been implemented on livestock farms. Indeed, in many respects these programs have been or are based on either preventing or curtailing a hazard and the hazard was or is a specific disease process or production inefficiency. Specific examples of preventive medicine programs are presented in Table 3.1.

These programs are invariably constructed with the intent of preventing a specific management or medical problem. Thus, they are often 'hazard' based and formulated with some assessment of risk of occurrence. The program may be extensive and detailed outlining sub-programs. As an example a mastitis prevention or control program for a dairy operation may contain a number or all of the sub-programs presented in Table 3.2.

In addition to these sub-unit programs, specific medication and residue avoidance protocols can be added to the itemization. These efforts could be broadly categorized as HACCP based. In many regards the cornerstone of any control program is record keeping or the collection of meaningful information and data to provide the basis for logical judgments and decisions. The listing presented in Table 3.2 can be considered as rather detailed. However, the overall approach becomes even more detailed when all of the elements listed in Table 3.2 that are appropriate for the accomplishment of a mastitis prevention program are detailed for implementation. The key to the success of this program, or other livestock preventive medicine programs, is monitoring; monitoring to ascertain that program elements are actually implemented as specified and monitoring and review to assure that the program is accomplishing its purpose. Too frequently when even relatively non-complex preventive medicine programs are established on livestock farms, little if any effort is given to actively ascertaining that the program is implemented as designed.

Table 3.1 Examples of possible preventive medicine programs implemented on livestock farm and ranch production units[a]

Dairy	Beef	Swine
Neonatal management	*Cow-calf*	Reproductive efficiency
Colostrum management	Reproductive efficiency	Farrowing house program
Vaccination programs	Vaccination	Nursery programs
Young stock	Parasite and fly control	Medication protocols
Adult maintenance	Preconditioning	Vaccination protocols
Parasite control	*Feedlot*	Parasite control
Mastitis control-prevention	Arrival cattle protocols	Biosecurity
Reproductive efficiency	Vaccination protocols	
Dry cow health management	Medication protocols	

[a]There are wide varieties of preventive medicine programs that can be constructed.

Table 3.2 Components of a comprehensive mastitis control-prevention program for dairy cattle

Component	Use
Pre-milking teat/udder sanitation	Specify type of udder sanitation and preparation; use of single service towel; placement of milking equipment on dry teat
Use of strip cup/plate	Examine initial milk for abnormalities
Milking parlor and equipment sanitation and hygiene	Using clean equipment for milking, reduce risk of inducing infection
Milking procedures	Procedures facilitating proper milk let down; checking for under- and over-milking
Claw removal	Reduce risk of inappropriate vacuum to teat end; avoid liner slips
Post-milking teat dipping	Reduce risk of bacteria entry to teat canal
Milking equipment maintenance	Assure appropriate vacuum is consistently applied during milking process; assure cleanliness of milk delivery system
Disinfect teat cup liners between cows	Reduce risk of spread of infectious pathogens
Housing/environment management	Reduce risk of teat and udder contamination thus reducing risk of new intramammary infections
Bulk tank somatic cell counts	Assessment of possible level of subclinical mastitis within herd (*monitor*)
Cow somatic cell counts	To help define possible level of intra-mammary inflammation (*monitor*)
Microbiological culture of bulk tank milk Microbiological culture of individual quarters	To define causes of mastitis problem (*monitor*)
Dry cow treatment/dry cow management	Reduce incidence of new intramammary infections
Criteria for cow removal from the herd	Alleviate chronically infected cows to reduce risk of spread of infectious mastitis pathogens

Livestock operations in the USA will increase in size and complexity. Also, it is likely that there will be increasing emphasis on the on-farm implementation of what has been termed pre-harvest food safety programs (Food Animal Production Medicine Consortium, 1992). These programs will be directed to the elimination of on-farm sources for chemical residues, as well as the reduction of the risk of pathogenic microbiological contamination in foods of animal origin. These trends – increasing size and complexity of livestock operations and increasing emphasis on on-farm quality assurance programs – emphasize the need for on-farm HACCP based preventive medicine programs. HACCP provides the means for a systematic analytical approach to on-farm preventive medicine/quality assurance programs. This approach, or modifications of it, is likely to be essential in the overall health maintenance of our food animal production units in the future.

3.2 Livestock quality assurance programs

The concept of HACCP based programs for on-farm utilization is not novel. A number of livestock commodity organizations have or are in the process of developing HACCP based quality assurance programs. These programs have been focused on the avoidance of antimicrobial residues in meat and milk. Two examples are 'Pork Quality Assurance' (National Pork Producers Council, 1991) and 'Milk & Dairy Beef Quality Assurance Program' developed by the American Veterinary Medical Association and the National Milk Producers Federation (1991). These organizations have devised residue avoidance programs using 10 critical control points. In a detailed manner, for each effort, the rationale for the critical control point is explained and checklists, questions, or action plans are used to facilitate the implementation of the residue avoidance program. These programs are presented in Tables 3.3 and 3.4.

From the standpoint of general construction, these programs are similar. Each targets antimicrobial residues in meat or milk as the hazard, and each establishes a series of control points to reduce the risk of violative levels of residues occurring. Both programs are designed as general programs for national implementation, are strongly educational, are for on-farm implementation, emphasize appropriate record keeping as a critical control point, and in large measure rely on the veterinarian–client–patient relationship to establish monitoring and verification steps and processes. These programs are in use on farms. In addition to its primary focus, each is valuable in that it tends to increase the awareness and sensitivity of producers and veterinarians for the need for a more precise approach or system to alleviate the general hazard-drug residues. In the approach used

Table 3.3 Pork quality assurance program: ten critical control points for quality pork production

Step	Action	Step	Action
1.	Establish an efficient and effective herd health management plan	6.	Follow label instructions for use of food additives
2.	Establish a valid veterinarian–client–patient relationship	7.	Maintain proper treatment records and adequate identification of all treated animals
3.	Store all drugs correctly	8.	Use drug residue tests when appropriate
4.	Use only FDA[b] approved OTC[c] or Rx[d] drugs with professional assistance	9.	Implement employee/family awareness of proper drug use
5.	Administer all ingestible drugs and oral medications properly	10.	Complete quality assurance checklist annually

[a]With permission from the National Pork Producers Council (1991). [b]Food and Drug Administration. [c]Over the counter. [d]Refers to prescription.

Table 3.4 Critical Control Points for the Milk and Dairy Beef Residue Prevention Protocol: overview of the milk and dairy beef practitioner guidelines[a]

Critical Control Point	Objective

1. Practice healthy herd management
  a. Mastitis prevention program
  b. Animals maintained in clean, healthy environment
  c. Nutrition and reproductive program employed
  d. Vaccination and parasite control program
  e. Herd protected from introduction of diseases
  f. Newborn calves, replacement heifers and steers program
	Each dairy in a practice has a preventive herd health management program in place. A valid veterinarian/client/patient relationship is essential for the establishment of a drug use quality assurance program. Reduce costs of drug therapy by minimizing dependence on drug therapy. Conduct an annual herd health status review. Possibly consult with the National Dairy Database by contacting state extension veterinary specialist. Increase use of consultive services by a veterinarian.

2. Establish a valid veterinarian/client/patient relationship (VCPR):
  a. The veterinarian and producer have established a working relationship and understanding for making clinical judgments regarding the health of the animal(s) and the need for medical treatment
  b. Take into account all variables to assure absence of violative drug residues
	The veterinarian should be in control of the drug use and herd health management. Establish a valid VCPR relationship that permits prescription of drugs for 'extra-label' use as determined necessary and to prescribe drugs bearing the prescription legend. The veterinarian and producer agree on procedures for withholding the drug prescribed and the appropriate tests to be used.

3. Use only FDA-approved Over-the-counter (OTC) or Prescription (Rx) drugs with veterinarian's guidance:
  a. Understand difference between OTC and Rx drugs
  b. Understand 'extra-label' use restrictions
 	
  c. Determine that all Rx drugs prescribed are FDA approved
  d. Create an approved drug list
	Proper drug use is essential to residue avoidance
	
	Familiarity with common terms.
	
	Minimize legal liability, assure food safety, and assure drug effectiveness. See FDA compliance policy guidelines.
	Familiarity with FDA-approved Rx drugs.
	
	Limit the types of drugs used by creating a farm-specific list of drugs to be purchased.

4. Make sure all drugs used have labels that comply with state and/or federal labeling requirements	To comply with Grade 'A' Pasteurized Milk Ordinance and maintain survey ratings, all drugs must be properly labeled to assure proper use.
5. Store all drugs correctly	To comply with Grade 'A' Pasteurized Milk Ordinance and maintain survey ratings. Proper drug storage guards against improper drug use.
6. Administer all drugs properly and identify all treated animals	To assure proper withholding times, prevent transmission of infectious agents, and identify sick or treated animals.
7. Maintain and use proper treatment records on all treated animals	To keep an accurate farm-specific drug list, identify all cattle individually, and identify all treated animals.

Table 3.4 (contd.)

Critical Control Point	Objective
8. Use drug residue screening tests Test milk and urine by appropriate test(s) on and off farm	To prevent violative residues To provide additional certainty of residue absence in milk and meat and to corroborate findings by milk purchasers.
9. Implement employee/family awareness of proper drug use to avoid marketing adulterated products	To determine employee knowledge and awareness of proper drug use and methods to avoid marketing adulterated products.
10. Complete the milk and dairy beef residue prevention protocol annually	To prevent violative residues and assure consumers of pure and wholesome products.

[a]American Veterinary Medical Association, National Milk Producers Federation (1991). With permission from the American Veterinary Medical Association and Agri-Education, Inc.

by both programs, a common critical control point deals with the maintenance of health management or implementation of a herd health program. This critical control point in many respects serves as the foundation for the remainder of the program. Thus, it would be beneficial if an entire production medicine program was constructed around the HACCP concept and system.

3.3   Implementing HACCP on livestock units

When establishing production medicine/herd health programs, it must be remembered that each production unit is unique. Each unit will be different in terms of finances, management, labor, physical arrangement, animal population and genetics, nutritional programs, specific production methods, and the character of threats associated with infectious and/or metabolic disease. It is inappropriate to suggest that a comprehensive production medicine program established for Farm 'A' will function on Farm 'B'. It will not. Certainly, a generic program can serve as a template and with modification a program or elements of a program designed for Farm 'A' can be implemented successfully on Farm 'B', but the basis for success will be detailed modification. Contemporarily pre-harvest food safety programs for residue avoidance and selected microbial reduction or elimination should be incorporated into production medicine programs for livestock farms and ranches. The HACCP system serves as a very useful model for the construction and implementation of comprehensive production medicine programs that include pre-harvest food safety components. The food animal farm or ranch must be looked upon as a process, a process producing a healthy, safe, and as uniform product as possible for consumption. Hence, a HACCP based production medicine plan can be a significant component of a quality assurance, total quality management program for that farm or ranch and pre-harvest food safety should be incorporated into that plan as a clinically (preventive medicine) relevant entity.

3.3.1 Initiating on-farm HACCP preventive medicine programs

The concept and principles regarding HACCP have been discussed in Chapter 1 and have been recently presented by Sperber (1991a), Bryan (1992), and The National Advisory Committee on Microbiological Criteria for Foods (1992). These principles, however, have been largely applied to food processing and must be placed in the context of the food animal production unit. These production units can be complex in terms of the size and scope of the unit and the housing, feeding and movement and processing of animals within it. It has been pointed out (The National Advisory Committee on Microbiological Criteria for Foods, 1992; Bryan, 1992) that the HACCP approach can be used to help assure the safety of foods from production to consumption. As The National Advisory Committee on Microbiological Criteria for Foods has emphasized, it is simpler to institute HACCP in some elements of the food chain than others, however, HACCP should be adopted 'throughout the food chain to the fullest extent possible and reasonable.'

3.3.1.1 Implementing HACCP. For the farm and ranch it is necessary that the 'director' (the veterinarian) of the HACCP-based herd health program be capable of explaining the implications, including the benefits, of HACCP. HACCP is a very systematic approach to the prevention of hazards or animal health problems. It will take time and effort to construct a logical on-farm HACCP system and to consistently implement that system in as cost effective manner as possible. A great deal of research is needed to determine how HACCP can be best implemented on farms and ranches including what the expected costs and benefits will be.

To develop the program, it will be necessary for the veterinarian (HACCP director) to be able to fully explain HACCP and its implications. There is the possibility that ranch and farm management will be initially skeptical about the capabilities and value of the system. To make HACCP work, as with other animal health systems, management – from the top down – must understand HACCP and view it as a valued means of helping to assure a healthy and safe product and strongly endorse its implementation. Management will need to transmit its endorsement of HACCP throughout the labor force, not only verbally, but by demonstrating support actively through implementation of critical controls and timely corrective actions.

3.3.1.2 Involvement and training of staff.   From the outset, farm and
ranch labor must be involved in the design and development of the
HACCP program for 'their' farm or ranch. Before the implementation of
any HACCP program, educational or training sessions about HACCP and
its on-farm use should be developed and held for employees and family
members who work the production unit. These training sessions should
include instruction about HACCP principles, and how these can be used to
increase the safety of the product leaving the farm. Education about the
technical aspects of specific jobs can be covered in these training sessions
as well. Milkers on a dairy farm could receive information about the
function of milking equipment and the signs and signals of dysfunction,
about milking hygiene and how to determine the presence of mastitis. The
members of a vaccination or treatment crew at a beef feedlot would benefit
from receiving rudimentary information about the immune system, the
importance of vaccination, and how to properly maintain and inject
vaccines. Employees and family workers must be essential 'players' on the
HACCP 'team' and there must be an exchange of ideas within the team
about just how the program can be optimally implemented. Feedback from
the production unit's labor force especially about suitability of critical
controls must be solicited, encouraged, and taken seriously. This type of
involvement provides employee buy-in and promotes programmatic
success.

   To make the HACCP system for the farm and ranch work optimally, it is
likely that the effort be introduced strategically in increments establishing
priorities for any implementation. An early attempt at creating a system
that is all encompassing, that contends with a vast variety of perceived
hazards is likely to create an environment of frustration, apathy and
rejection of the concept.

3.3.2 Hazard identification

In general, a hazard in food processing is considered as a physical,
chemical, or biological entity that causes a food to be unsafe (The National
Advisory Committee on Microbiological Criteria for Foods, 1992; Bryan,
1992). This categorization of hazards also applies to farms and ranches.
However, the overall objective for the process we call a farm or ranch will
differ from the process that produces a finished food product. The farm
and ranch will be interested in residue avoidance and microbial reduction
efforts, and in animal health programs that reduce economic loss and
increase production. Table 3.1 presents categories of possible preventive
medicine programs for dairy, beef, and swine production operations. This
list is by no means inclusive. Animal health programs, depending on how
they are implemented, can directly relate to the implementation of pre-
harvest food safety efforts. These programs can use HACCP to provide an

overall systematic approach that facilitates the development and implementation of herd health programs. A presentation of general herd health
(production medicine) programs using HACCP is beyond the scope of this
chapter. We will confine our remarks to examples of HACCP constructed
pre-harvest food safety programs.

3.3.2.1 Identification of hazards.   Table 3.5 lists possible food safety
hazards that can exist on farms and ranches. A number of these such as
salmonellae and *Listeria monocytogenes* relate to animal well-being as
well. However, several such as *E. coli* 0157:H7, and *Yersinia enterocolitica*
cause no generally recognized clinical disease in the food animal and thus
present a challenge for on-the-farm HACCP preventive medicine programs.
This challenge is unlikely to be adequately countered until sufficient on-
farm research specifying the ecology and the epidemiology of these
organisms is accomplished. Table 3.6 lists on-farm conditions that can
contribute to food safety and food quality problems.
   For most pre-harvest food safety programs, the hazards will be known.
Programs to reduce the risk of violative antimicrobial residues in meat and
milk using critical control points have been worked out (Tables 3.3 and
3.4) and are widely implemented. The need for similar efforts that reduce
specific pathogenic microorganisms in animals and milk is becoming
increasingly apparent as a means of enhancing food safety in general. A
major problem for any pre-harvest food safety HACCP program will be

Table 3.5 Possible food safety hazards on farms and
ranches

Antimicrobial agents
 antibiotics
 sulfonamides
Heavy metals
 arsenic
 cadmium
 lead
 mercury
Pesticides
Acrobacter spp.
Campylobacter jejuni
Clostridium perfringens
Cryptosporidium parvum
Escherichia coli (0157:H7)
Other verocytotoxigenic *E. coli*
Listeria monocytogenes
Bacillus cereus
Salmonellae
Staphylococcus aureus
Yersinia enterocolitica
Taenia spp.
Toxoplasma gondii

Table 3.6 Conditions affecting carcass quality that can be controlled on the farm and ranch

---

Abscesses
  injection wounds
  wounds due to poor maintenance of facilities

Excessive bruising
  loading and unloading procedures
  truck design
  corral and chute design
  corral and chute animal handling protocols

Foreign objects
  injection protocols
  maintenance of needles and syringes

Filth
  feedlot design and drainage
  maintenance of walkways
  maintenance of holding pens and corrals
  sanitation protocols

---

how to reduce the risk from those foodborne pathogens that are carried by the food animal, but produce no detectable clinical illness in the animal. Until research works out the ecology and epidemiology of these organisms, as well as appropriate detection methods, critical control points will have to be based on an educated common sense approach.

3.3.2.2 Analysis of hazards. For a particular farm or ranch, the initial effort will be to conduct an analysis of the hazards that are to be controlled. This analysis should contain an assessment of the risk posed from a particular hazard and a determination of the hazard's severity. In other words, initiate a HACCP plan. The analysis should be accomplished by a HACCP team consisting of the veterinarian, a representative of farm management and representatives from the labor force for particular production or processing areas within the production unit. At times, it may be necessary to involve personnel from outside the farm or ranch who have special knowledge and expertise about the farm operation to help construct a HACCP plan. Depending on the scope and complexity of the operation, external members could include one or more of the following: an agricultural engineer, a nutritionist, an infectious disease expert, an epidemiologist, an animal health products sales representative and possibly a feed distributor. These personnel, some of whom can be drawn from cooperative extension programs, are brought into the planning on an as-needed basis. Various approaches can be used to bring the 'team' together on one farm; management meetings to discuss an initial draft with follow-up individual interviews of resource personnel can be appropriate. While on another production unit, it may be necessary to assemble several groups to construct a comprehensive plan. It is essential that the HACCP plan team have the capability of affirming the hazards (hazard identification) and can assign some level of risk and severity to the identified hazard. As the HACCP plan is constructed, this team will then specify critical controls to reduce the risk of occurrence, establish acceptable procedures for monitoring and verification of the controls, and specify corrective actions should critical control limits be exceeded. In order to facilitate the overall development of the HACCP plan, the team should develop a flow diagram or diagrams of the overall production units.

3.3.3   Flow diagrams

The operation of a food animal ranch or farm can be presented as a complicated process. In reality, the contemporary food animal production unit is composed of a series of interlocking processes that include gestational areas, the rearing and maintenance of the animals of concern, feed management and feeding, breeding management, housing and processing areas, waste disposal, and for a dairy farm, milking facilities, equipment and milking hygiene.

Flow diagrams or charts used to depict, initially, the food animal production unit as a process are useful in outlining and understanding the detailed on-farm animal-spatial interactions. The initial flow diagram is used to plot categories of animal activities and hazards that may be, or are known to be, present at various points or locations throughout the process. The flow diagram is then used to set in place critical control points (CCPs). The HACCP team can use the flow diagram to help decide what hazards are significant to pre-harvest food safety, and are to be controlled. This is the point where the assessment of the risk associated with a given hazard must be specified. It is not difficult for any food animal production unit to specify a large number of hazards that could threaten that unit.

The functional challenge for the HACCP team will be to decide which hazard or hazards are significant. And, as in food processing, hazards on the farm or ranch can be chemical, microbiological and/or physical (The National Advisory Committee on Microbiological Criteria for Foods, 1992).

Figure 3.1 is a HACCP on-farm flow diagram form that can be used to facilitate hazard analysis and the initial assessment of relevant critical control points. It was designed to provide space to outline the process and to list possible critical controls associated with a particular step in the product unit (process). The form is constructed so that the evaluator is prompted that monitoring and verification steps must be considered. The form is meant to be a component of a production medicine record. Space is provided for the farm name and address, identification of a particular processing step or unit within the farm – such as gestation barn, or a

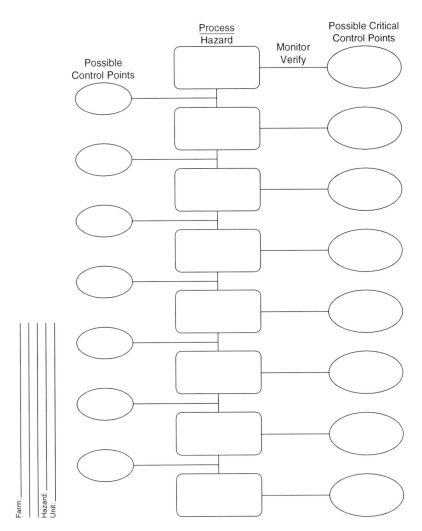

Figure 3.1 Flow diagram of HACCP on farm.

specific feedlot, or a calf-rearing facility – and the hazard to be controlled.
Figure 3.2 is a flow diagram depicting the various inter-related processes in
a generic dairy operation and listing possible chemical and microbiological
hazards at various steps within the overall operation. The diagram
demonstrates the possible food safety threats that can occur within a
relatively complex food animal production unit. The hazards that are listed
in the diagram can be tabulated to assess what preventive measure can be
applied to a relevant hazard as shown in Table 3.7.

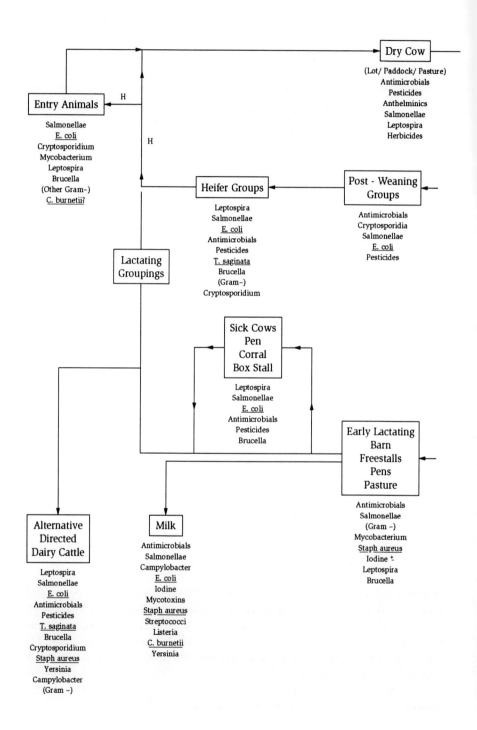

Dry Cow

(Lot/ Paddock/ Pasture)
Antimicrobials
Pesticides
Anthelminics
Salmonellae
Leptospira
Herbicides

Entry Animals

Salmonellae
E. coli
Cryptosporidium
Mycobacterium
Leptospira
Brucella
(Other Gram–)
C. burnetii?

H

H

Heifer Groups

Leptospira
Salmonellae
E. coli
Antimicrobials
Pesticides
T. saginata
Brucella
(Gram–)
Cryptosporidium

Post - Weaning Groups

Antimicrobials
Cryptosporidia
Salmonellae
E. coli
Pesticides

Lactating Groupings

Sick Cows Pen Corral Box Stall

Leptospira
Salmonellae
E. coli
Antimicrobials
Pesticides
Brucella

Early Lactating Barn Freestalls Pens Pasture

Antimicrobials
Salmonellae
(Gram –)
Mycobacterium
Staph aureus
Iodine ±
Leptospira
Brucella

Alternative Directed Dairy Cattle

Leptospira
Salmonellae
E. coli
Antimicrobials
Pesticides
T. saginata
Brucella
Cryptosporidium
Staph aureus
Yersinia
Campylobacter
(Gram –)

Milk

Antimicrobials
Salmonellae
Campylobacter
E. coli
Iodine
Mycotoxins
Staph aureus
Streptococci
Listeria
C. burnetii
Yersinia

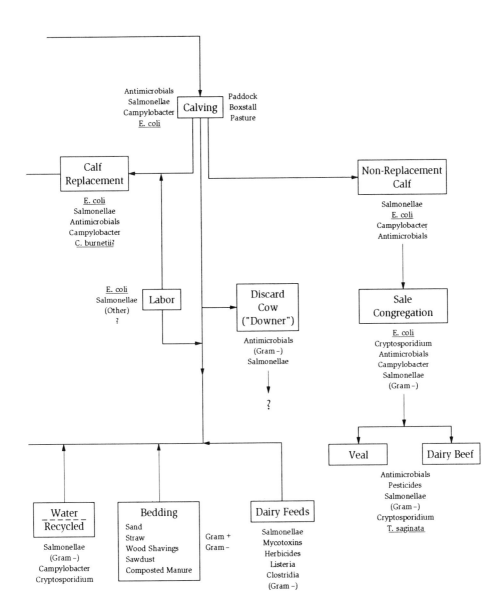

Figure 3.2 Flow diagram of dairy operation with listing of possible food safety hazards.

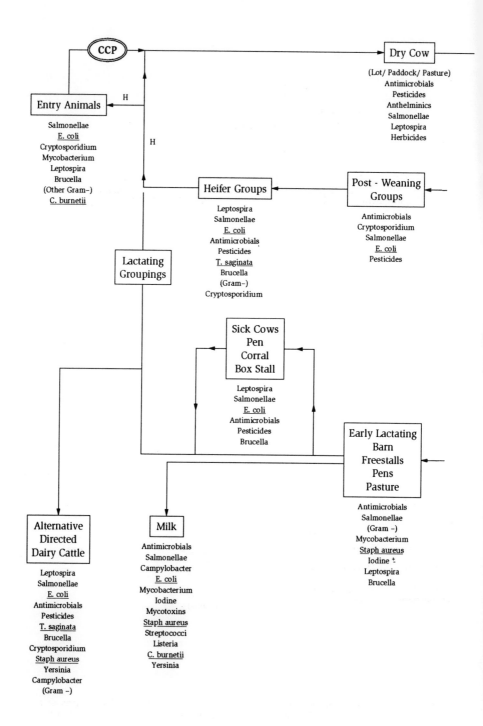

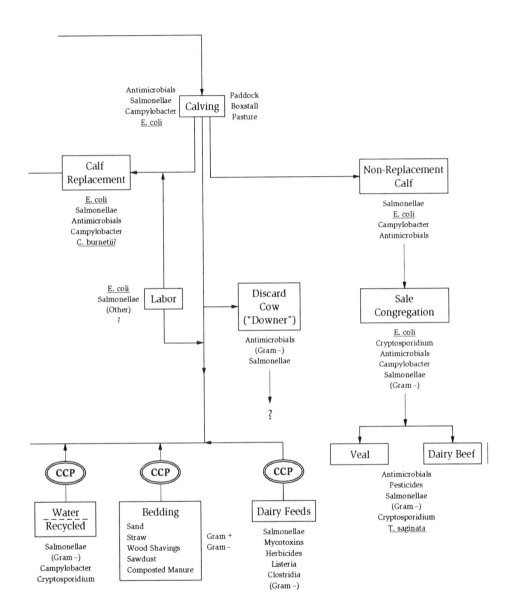

Figure 3.3 Flow diagram of dairy operation with listing of possible chemical and microbiological food safety hazards.

Table 3.7 Tabulation of hazards and possible preventive measures (examples)

Process step	Possible hazard	Possible preventive measures
Recycled water	Salmonellae	Do not flush alleys when cattle are present Air dry Do not flush with recycled water Redesign lagoon system – consider costs Chlorination – consider costs Scrape alleys – do not flush
Early lactating	Antimicrobial residue	Dairy Quality Assurance program ID treated cattle Observe withholding times Residue screening tests Maintain records

Figure 3.3 demonstrates the insertion of critical control points into the dairy operation when Salmonellae were identified as a foodborne hazard. The goal for this scheme is the reduction of the risk of salmonellae entry. Recycled flush water may play an important role in maintaining *Salmonella* infection cycles on large dairy operations (Gay and Hunsaker, 1993) and salmonellae can enter via carrier animals (Smith, 1990) and through contaminated feeds (Mitchell and McChesney, 1992). In addition to these critical controls, biosecurity procedures to protect contamination of feed stuffs from rodent and bird feces will need to be instituted. For this dairy example, limits for each critical control will need to be established and monitoring and verification procedures put in place.

Table 3.8 provides an illustration of a HACCP action plan for a swine production unit. This detailed action plan was devised by two veterinary graduate students who received an assignment to devise a HACCP-based program to reduce the prevalence of pathogenic *Yersinia* in a swine production unit. This program, perhaps too elaborate, illustrates the criteria or limits for the critical controls and reinforces the necessity of detailed monitoring and verification procedures.

3.4 Conclusion

The Hazard Analysis Critical Control Point system is a systematic approach that can be used to facilitate on-farm food safety programs to eliminate violative chemical residue and reduce the threat of foodborne pathogens. In many circumstances additional research is needed to

Table 3.8 HACCP action plan[a]

	Operation	Hazard	CCP	Control action	Criteria	Monitoring	Verification
Isolation	Transport vehicle	Contamination with *Yersinia*	CP	Disinfection (chlorhexidine) with high pressure steam pre-shipment Truck does not cross perimeter Transport personnel do not cross perimeter Request Monday shipments	No *Yersinia* contamination of transport vehicle No entry of transport driver into isolation facility	Managerial observation of unloading animals	Logs of shipment dates
	Small pen isolation	*Yersinia* contamination	CP	Disinfection (chlorhexidine) with high pressure steam (including pits) Rooms empty 1 week post-cleaning	No *Yersinia* contamination of pen areas Negative environmental swab	Managerial monitor of cleaning process Environmental swabs of rooms and pits post-cleaning Monthly adjustment and function test of high pressure steam equipment	Logs of cleaning and sampling dates Inventory monitor of disinfectant use Log of water usage at facility Inventory of sampling materials
	Observation for 45 days	*Yersinia* infection		Isolation rooms all-in, all-out: separate pits, ventilation Rodent control	All samples culture negative for *Yersinia*	Oral swabs of all imports on days 0, 15, 30 cultured onto CIN agar and PCR for pathogenicity Fecal samples on days 0, 15, 30 cultured as above	Logs of sampling dates and results Inventory of sampling materials
	Cull or dead animals	Source of *Yersinia* Attract wildlife which carry *Yersinia*		Dead animals placed outside perimeter in covered container for renderer pick-up within 24 hours of death Cull animals removed within 48 hours of cull decision, transport truck does not cross perimeter fence	Minimal exposure of dead animals to other imports No wildlife access to carcasses	Managerial monitoring of animal health Monitor of dead animal storage maintenance Alarm system for opening of dead animal container	Comparison of animal logs with bills and checks from renderer and cull buyer

Table 3.8 (contd.)

Operation	Hazard	CCP	Control action	Criteria	Monitoring	Verification
Water	*Yersinia* contamination		Groundwater source at a suitable distance from sewage of animal or human origin Chlorination of water	No *Yersinia* contamination in water pH<7 Temperature >20°C	Monitor pH and temperature of holding tank daily Manure dispersal needs to be a sufficient distance from well Weekly water culture	Inventory of chlorine Logs of daily measurements Water usage records
Perimeter control	Wildlife transmission of *Yersinia* to swine		Perimeter expanded wire fence with electric wire. Two foot deep cement slab base as fence foundation ½ inch hardware cloth across inlets and fan ports Feed spills cleaned immediately Entirely enclosed feed delivery system Feeder design and management to reduce feed spillage Keep grounds vegetation mowed No animals other than import swine allowed on premises	No access of wildlife into facility perimeter or buildings	Daily evaluation of fence integrity Alarm system that sounds when the gate is open Twice daily monitor for feed spills and appropriate feeder management Monitor for evidence of animals other than swine present Log of mowing dates	Feed efficiency data
Animal flow Transport from isolation	Contamination of trailer infecting import swine		Disinfection and high pressure steam cleaning of trailer between transport Trailer used only for import entry	No *Yersinia* contamination of trailer	Environmental swab and culture (as previously described) of trailer premovement	Managerial monitor Log of cleaning, movement and sampling Disinfectant inventory

	Hazard			Managerial monitor	
Dirt lot finishing	Contamination from environmentally present Yersinia and exposure to potentially infected wildlife	Discontinue use of dirt lots	No housing of swine outside environmentally controlled housing		
Cull or dead animals	Source of Yersinia. Attract wildlife which may carry Yersinia	Dead animals placed outside perimeter in covered container for renderer pickup within 24 hours of death. Cull animals removed within 48 hours of cull decision, transport truck does not cross perimeter force	Minimal exposure of dead animals to other imports. No wildlife access to carcasses	Managerial monitoring of animal health. Monitor of dead animal storage maintenance. Alarm system for opening of dead animal container	Comparison of animal logs with bills and checks from renderer and cull buyer
Water	Yersinia contamination	Groundwater source at a suitable distance from sewage of animal or human origin. Chlorination of water	No Yersinia contamination in water pH<7 Temperature >20°C	Monitor pH and temperature of holding tank daily. Manure dispersal needs to be a sufficient distance from well. Weekly water culture	Inventory of chlorine. Log of daily measurements. Water usage records
Perimeter control	Wildlife transmission of Yersinia to swine	Perimeter expanded wire fence with electric wire. Two foot deep cement slab base as fence foundation. ½ inch hardware cloth across inlets and fan ports. Feed spills cleaned immediately. Entirely enclosed feed delivery system. Feeder design and management to reduce feed spillage. Keep grounds vegetation mowed. No animals other than import swine allowed on premises	No access of wildlife into facility perimeter or buildings	Daily evaluation of fence integrity. Alarm system that sounds when the gate is open. Twice daily monitor for feed spills and appropriate feeder management. Monitor for evidence of animals other than swine present. Log of mowing dates	Feed efficiency data

Table 3.8 (contd.)

Operation	Hazard	CCP	Control action	Criteria	Monitoring	Verification
Transport to market	*Yersinia* infection from contaminated transport vehicle		Disinfection (as above) of trailer at a truck wash post delivery to slaughter and prior to farm return Used only transport for this farm Animals loaded at docks at perimeter fence, truck outside perimeter	No contamination of transport truck	Culture (as above) of truck post washing and preloading	Receipts from truck wash Managerial monitor of truck cleanliness

aFunk and Neumann (1994)

determine the on-farm epidemiology and ecology of foodborne pathogens before definitive critical controls can be established. This is especially important for those pathogens, such as *E. coli* 0157:H7, that cause no apparent illness in the animal. Also, the HACCP approach can be used to implement general animal health programs on a variety of food animal producing farms and ranches.

References

Agri-Education, Inc., 801 Shakespeare Ave., Stratford, Iowa 50249, USA.

American Veterinary Medical Association, National Milk Producers Federation (1991) Milk and Dairy Beef Quality Assurance Program. Milk and Dairy Beef Residue Prevention Protocol.

Bryan, F.L. (1992) *Hazard Analysis Critical Control Point Evaluations.* A guide to identifying hazards and assessing risks associated with food preparation and storage. World Health Organization, Geneva, Switzerland.

Food Animal Production Medicine Consortium (1992) *Providing Safe Food for the Consumer.* A blueprint for implementing preharvest food safety internationally. Proc. Workshop held November 19, 1992. Washington, D.C. USA.

Funk, J. and Neumann, E. (1994) Class project. Dept. Clinical Veterinary Medicine. University of Illinois. Urbana, Illinois 61801, USA.

Gay, J.M. and Hunsaker, M.E. (1993) Isolation of multiple salmonellae serovars from a dairy two years after a clinical salmonellosis outbreak. *J. Am. Vet. Med. Assoc.* **203**, 1314.

Heidelbaugh, N.D. (1992) Recommendations from the AVMA workshop on the safety of foods of animal origin. *J. Am. Vet. Med. Assoc.* **202**, 201.

Mitchell, G.A. and McChesney, D.G. (1992) A plan for salmonella control in animal feeds. In: *Proc. Symp. Diagnosis and Control of Salmonella. Oct. 29, 1991.* US Animal Health Association, San Diego. pp. 28–31.

The National Advisory Committee on Microbiological Criteria for Foods (1992) Hazard analysis and critical control point system. *Internat. J. Food Microb.* **16**, 1.

National Pork Producers Council (1991) *Pork Quality Assurance.* National Pork Producers Council, PO Box 10383, Des Moines, Iowa 50306, USA.

Smith, B.P. (1990) Salmonellosis. In: *Large Animal Internal Medicine* (B.P. Smith, ed), The C.V. Mosby Co., St. Louis, pp. 818–822.

Sperber, W.J. (1991a) The modern HACCP system. *Food Tech. No. 1* **45**(6), 116.

Sperber, W.H. (1991b) Use of the HACCP system to assure food safety. *J. Assoc. of Anal. Chem.* **74**, 433.

4 Implementation of the HACCP program by meat and poultry slaughterers

S.J. GOODFELLOW

4.1 Introduction

Implementation of HACCP programs in meat and poultry slaughter operations is no different than introducing HACCP into further processing plants or other types of food systems. The program must be designed by the individual company or plant for their respective operation(s). Each program, although individually tailored, must be based on the seven principles of HACCP including hazard assessment, critical control point (CCP) identification, establishing critical limits, monitoring procedures, corrective actions, documentation and verification procedures. Excellent overviews and background information on HACCP programs are presented in the AMI-NFPI HACCP workshop (1992), Tompkin (1990) and the USDA-FSIS, *HACCP Status Report* (1992).

4.2 Purpose of HACCP

The primary purpose of any HACCP program is the prevention of any problems that could contribute to or cause any threat to public health or safety. Health and safety issues are confined to microbiological, chemical and physical hazards. Regulatory, economic, operational or aesthetic issues, while necessary for business or legal purposes, are not related to public health or safety and should not be incorporated into a meat or poultry HACCP program.

4.2.1 Selection of team members

The initial phase for developing and implementing a HACCP plan for any meat or poultry slaughter operation is to assemble a multi-disciplinary HACCP team that consists of individuals who have specific knowledge or expertise on the operation's products and processes. It is not mandatory at this stage of development that team members have HACCP training. The most important factor(s) in selection of team members is that they have specific or esoteric knowledge of the plant(s) operations with responsibilities in different areas. The team may include personnel from maintenance, refrigeration, engineering, sanitation, quality assurance, laboratory, production or management. It is also recommended that outside experts in the areas of food microbiology and microbial pathogens as well as chemical and physical hazards be included in the team or closely associated with the development and implementation of the HACCP program.

4.2.2   Training of HACCP team

After selection of the HACCP team, the first priority is to ensure that all team members who are responsible for the design, implementation and operation of the program are trained in the principles of HACCP. This training should include imparting a working understanding of the hazards being monitored and controlled. Team members should be educated on microbial pathogens associated with meat and poultry products, at least to the level of what pathogens could be present, where they are and how can they be controlled or eliminated. This same approach should also be used for chemical and physical hazards.

Education and training of team members for microbial pathogens associated with meat and poultry products should include overviews of *Salmonella*, *Campylobacter*, *Listeria monocytogenes*, *Staphylococcus aureus*, *Yersinia*, *Clostridium botulinum*, *Clostridium perfringens*, *Bacillus cereus*, *Escherichia coli* 0157:H7, *Vibrio* and *Aeromonas*. The majority of the microbial pathogens are part of the gastrointestinal flora of warm blooded animals and birds. These organisms can also be associated with skin, hide, hair and feathers. Many of the bacterial pathogens can also be carried by plant employees. The critical point regarding implementation of HACCP programs into meat and poultry slaughter operations is that there is no defined 'kill' or bacteriocidal step in the process. The main emphasis of HACCP in slaughter operations, therefore, is to *minimize* the potential for contamination of the finished *raw* products. This can include sanitation, careful processing procedures and intervention strategies such as carcass washing. Current technology cannot assure a pathogen free product from any slaughter operation; therefore, the primary HACCP goal is to minimize contamination.

It should be mentioned that the main emphasis of the microbial training for the HACCP team will be on bacterial pathogens, but that other microbial pathogens associated with food animals, such as viruses and parasites should also be discussed.

Potential chemical hazards that should be addressed include agricultural chemicals, such as pesticides, herbicides, fungicides, fertilizers, antibiotics and hormones, and chemicals associated with the slaughter plant, such as cleaners, sanitizers, pesticides, lubricants and additives. Training should also include overviews of the potential physical hazards associated with slaughter operations including metal, glass, stones, paint, wood, equipment parts and personnel associated foreign material such as jewelry, buttons, pens, etc. that could be accidently incorporated into food products.

4.3   Development of the HACCP program

4.3.1   Selection of the HACCP team coordinator

Once the HACCP team has been selected and trained, one member of the team must be selected as the team coordinator. This individual must have organizational and communication skills, familiarity with the plant processes, and hopefully be in some position of authority in the company.

4.3.2   Development of the master HACCP program

The coordinator and HACCP team can then proceed to develop the master HACCP program. As with any food product, this development will consist of: (a) describing the food product(s) and their distribution (on a product by product basis), (b) identify the projected use and consumers of the product(s), (c) outlining a flow diagram, (d) verify the flow diagram, and (e) conducting a hazard analysis.

4.3.2.1   Product description.   The product description should include the product formulation, i.e. whole muscle, ground, marinated, etc., the form of distribution (refrigerated or frozen) and the potential for abuse through distribution or by the consumer.

4.3.2.2   Projected usage.   The projected use is primarily to identify any particular segment of the population that is at increased risk, such as infants, elderly, immunocompromised, etc.

4.3.2.3   Outlining and verifying flow diagram.   The flow diagram is designed to provide a complete description of all of the steps involved in the plant operations from raw material (live animals or birds) receiving through to shipment of finished product(s). An example of a flow diagram for beef slaughter and fabrication is presented in Figure 4.1. A flow diagram for a chicken slaughter operation is presented in Figure 4.2. The entire HACCP team should inspect the operation to verify that the flow diagram is complete and accurate.

4.3.2.4   Conducting a hazard analysis.   The next step in development of the HACCP program is to conduct a hazard analysis, which is the first of the seven HACCP principles (Principle #1). This analysis consists of

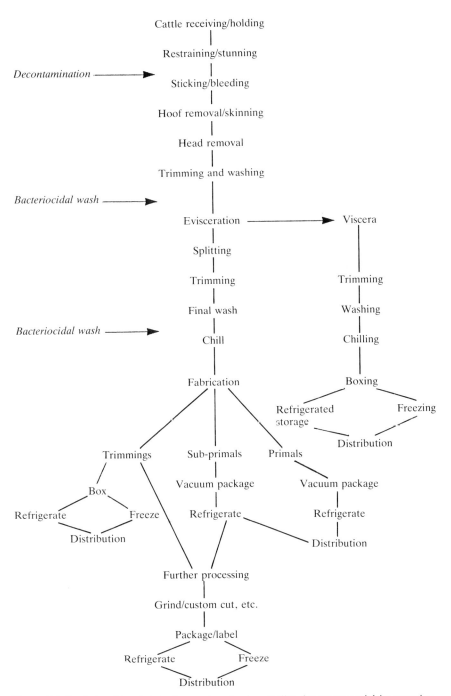

Figure 4.1 Beef slaughter, fabrication and packaging. Italics denote potential intervention steps.

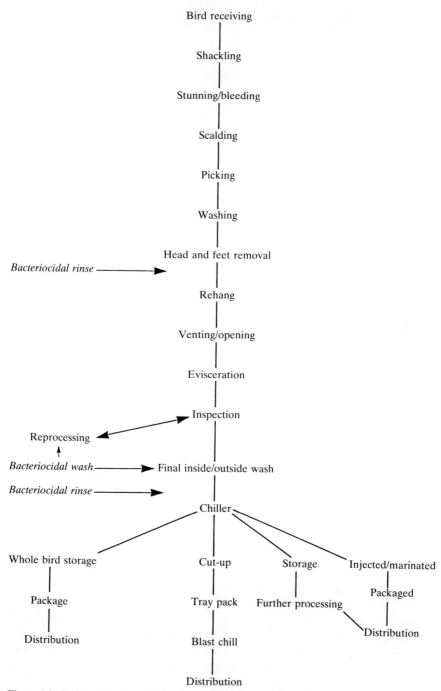

Figure 4.2 Chicken slaughter, fabrication and packaging. Italics denote potential intervention steps.

identifying the steps in the process where hazards can occur, the types of hazards involved (microbial, chemical or physical), the relative degree of risk by category, according to the National Advisory Committee of Microbiological Criteria for Foods (1990), and preventive measures to control the hazards; USDA-FSIS, NACMCF, HACCP Principles for Food Production (1990). A detailed format for this hazard analysis based on risk categories can be obtained from the National Advisory Committee mentioned above. This analysis serves as the basis for determining the critical control points (CCP) in the process, which is Principle #2 in the HACCP process. The CCPs are documented and critical limits or tolerances are set (Principle #3). Critical limits in slaughter operations where pathogen 'kill' steps are not available are set by establishing limits on times, temperatures, visual defects, concentration of bacteriocidal rinses, etc.

4.3.2.5 Documenting the seven principles of HACCP. After critical limits are set, the remainder of the seven principles are documented. These are monitoring procedures and frequency and designated personnel (Principle #4), deviation procedures and action/correction/disposal procedures (Principle #5), record keeping procedures (Principle #6) and documented verification procedures by designated personnel to assure compliance (Principle #7). Tabular formats for a HACCP control program can be found in many different references including Pierson and Corlett (1992) and Sperber (1991).

4.3.2.6 Modifying and updating HACCP plan. The final element in developing the HACCP plan is to establish formats and procedures for modification and updating of the plan any time that process changes or modifications are made. This is also necessary if new potential risks or hazards are documented.

4.4 Implementation of the HACCP program

4.4.1 Support of management

The phases described previously including the introduction, selection of a HACCP team and coordinator, training of the team in hazards and HACCP principles and development of a model program for each respective plant must be accomplished with the full commitment and support of upper management up to the highest corporate level. Attempts on the part of middle management and/or technical personnel to implement HACCP programs without complete upper management support will be ineffective. Upper management must be involved from the inception of HACCP in an operation, including defining policy and objectives as well as inputing into the selection of the HACCP team and coordinator.

4.4.2 Fitting HACCP plan into operations

Given this commitment and development, it must now be clearly established how the HACCP plan fits into company operations, programs and policies. It must also be established exactly how the model HACCP program and individual product HACCP programs to be developed fit into customer dictated requirements for HACCP programs and potentially mandated HACCP programs by the United States Department of Agriculture, Food Safety Inspection Service. HACCP programs are designed to address hazards, i.e. things that cause illness or damage to people. USDA regulations, Quality Assurance Departments, customer requirements and corporate policy are also concerned with these hazards. However, to a greater or lesser degree, all are also concerned with Good Manufacturing Practices (GMPs), sanitation, product quality issues, economic concerns, labeling issues and various aesthetic concerns that may or may not impact on public safety.

4.4.3 Focusing attention on hazards

HACCP programs *are not* designed to replace any current regulations or existing programs or personnel. HACCP programs *are* designed to focus attention and establish defined processes to prevent hazards to public health from occurring, using a prevention system to minimize hazards and eliminate them wherever possible.

4.4.3.1 Do not incorporate HACCP into standard operating procedures or customer requirements. One of the biggest problems that occurs with implementation of HACCP programs in meat and poultry operations is when companies attempt to incorporate all of their standard operating procedures into a HACCP plan. A second major problem has been when customers mandate that their suppliers incorporate all of the customer's requirements into the supplier's HACCP plan, including such things as fat content, size of the type on the shipping container, etc. Both of these problems have the same net effect: that is a HACCP plan that has dozens of critical control points per product and is impossible to administer as a true HACCP program. In similar manner, if USDA-FSIS mandates HACCP in meat and poultry plants, definitions will have to be established as to which regulations are economic, which tasks are PBIS, what issues are aesthetic, etc. Caution must be taken that legal requirements of various

USDA programs that involve aesthetics, economic adulteration or labor contracts do not dilute or misdirect the basics of the HACCP programs, which are in the food safety area.

4.4.3.2   Good Manufacturing Practices and sanitation – basis of the HACCP program.   In addition, two existing programs are required by USDA and are critical to meat and poultry operations. These are the basic Good Manufacturing Practice (GMP) and sanitation programs. Existing regulations are outlined in 21 CFR, 110 Good Manufacturing Practices, 9 CFR 308 Sanitation for Meat Products and 9 CFR 381, sub part H, Sanitation for Poultry Products. Both the sanitation and GMP programs are part of any effective HACCP program. In some cases they are directly related and intimately involved with product safety and critical control points. In other cases, they are associated with regulatory compliance and aesthetics and serve as a broad framework for the HACCP program.

4.4.3.2.1   Role of GMPs in HACCP.   The GMP regulations deal with employee hygiene practices, food handling procedures and plant/ equipment design. As mentioned previously, some specific GMPs do not have any direct bearing on product safety. Examples of this category of GMP would include locker size, slope of plant floors, adequate lighting (i.e. specific foot candle requirements), etc. However, many of the GMPs are directly related to product safety issues, and therefore, an integral part of the HACCP program. Some examples of this category of GMP are listed in Table 4.1. The relationship of the GMP program to HACCP must involve establishing which specifics of the GMP program are CCPs in regard to food safety. These points must be a part of the documented monitoring, corrective action, and verification format in HACCP.

4.4.3.2.2   Role of sanitation program in HACCP.   The sanitation program is multi-faceted involving pest control, equipment cleaning and maintaining the processing environment. All meat and poultry plants are required to maintain their operations in a sanitary manner at all times. The requirements for pest control programs are well documented in the regulations and will not be discussed in this chapter, except to state that pest management programs are basically a universal CCP, and part of any HACCP program because of the potential for spread of pathogenic microorganisms by insects, rodents and birds.

The cleaning/sanitizing portion of the sanitation program is also considered a universal CCP and includes sections for the equipment and the processing environment. This program will include a documentation of all clean up procedures employed in the plant, including chemicals used, application rate and method, contact time, rinse requirements and frequency. Maintaining equipment and the processing areas in a clean and

Table 4.1 Example of GMPs that are directly related to HACCP programs

GMP	Hazard	Control
A. Personnel		
1. Hygiene	Microbiological/pathogens	Hand washing, no open wounds, no infectious disease
2. Restroom	Microbiological/pathogens	Outer garments control, hand washing, hand and foot dips
3. Jewelry	Physical/foreign material	No watches, uncovered rings, earrings, nail polish, etc.
B. Plant		
1. Facility	Microbiological/pathogens	Plant construction – approved non-porous material
	Microbiological/pathogens	Water/sanitary sewer design – separate – trapped, no cross connections
	Physical/foreign material	Glass – not allowed or protected
2. Equipment	Microbiological/pathogens	Proper cleaning and sanitizing
	Chemical/lubricants, etc.	Approved materials
	Physical/foreign material	Proper construction, nuts, bolts, washers, gaskets, etc.
C. Food handling practices	Physical/foreign material	Inspection at receiving and at different processing stages
	Microbiological/pathogens	No raw to cooked product handling

sanitary condition is absolutely essential for control and elimination of microbial pathogens that are associated with any raw food of animal origin. As part of the HACCP program, daily pre-operational inspections are required with a Go/No Go decision made by the HACCP responsible employee (probably QA), based on visual inspection. The effectiveness of the clean up and the visual inspection will be verified with microbiological testing with swabs, rodoc plates, or other microbiological tests.

In summary, current GMP and sanitation programs have a direct relationship to HACCP principles and are part of a HACCP program. An overview of this relationship is presented in Table 4.2.

After the core team, together with upper management, has resolved how their HACCP plan 'fits' with customer requirements, USDA regulations, projected USDA mandates, existing departments such as QA and current GMP and sanitation programs, a format and schedule can be designed for implementation of the HACCP plan.

4.4.4 Product specific HACCP programs

A HACCP program for a meat or poultry operation is product specific. However, in many cases, individual product lines are so similar that they

Table 4.2 HACCP table for sanitation/GMPs

Process/procedure	Critical limit	Monitoring procedure	Corrective action	HACCP records	HACCP verification
Water quality	Chlorinated Zero coliforms	QA checks weekly	Chlorinate the source	QA records	QA supervisor review/ microbial plate counts
Sanitation – equipment	Meet GMP requirements	QA and operation supervisors check daily	Reclean and sanitize	QA records	Microbial plate counts
Sanitation – process environment	Meet GMP requirements	QA and operation supervisors check daily or weekly	Reclean and sanitize	QA records	Microbial plate counts
Personal hygiene	Meet GMP requirements	QA and operation supervisors check daily. Health care/ person monthly	Remove from processing environment. Correct problem	QA and health office records	QA supervisor and management review
External plant environment	Meet GMP requirements	Weekly QA checks	Reclean and treat as needed	QA records	QA manager and USDA requirements
Pest control	Meets USDA and plant plan	QA checks daily-insects. Weekly-bait stations.	Clean and treat according to problem	QA records	QA manager and USDA requirements

can be grouped together as one class for purposes of a HACCP plan. This grouping is necessary from a practical viewpoint since the size of cut, percentage of trim, etc. can result in a company selling 15 different products which from a HACCP standpoint are all the same product. The HACCP team should establish these product classes before proceeding with any additional implementation steps.

4.4.4.1 Product teams.   After product classes have been established, the HACCP coordinator and core team should select product team leaders and teams for each product class. These product teams should then be trained in the same manner as the core team. All members must be familiar with HACCP principles and potential hazards. They must also develop a working knowledge of the master HACCP plan developed by the core team. Frequently, at this stage in implementation, product team members, who have 'hands-on' knowledge of plant operations, may make very constructive suggestions for modifications in the master HACCP plan.

The next step is for the HACCP product teams to develop an individual HACCP plan for their respective product class. The product team plans should then be evaluated individually with the core team and collectively with other product teams. Suggestions and modifications can be made prior to testing the plan(s) at plant level.

4.4.4.2 Trial tests.   A trial test of one product team's HACCP plan for their product class should then be conducted under operating conditions. This plant trial run must include an evaluation of the entire HACCP plan for the product, including each process step, CCP, critical limit(s), monitoring procedure, corrective action, documentation and record keeping and verification. An evaluation of the results from the trial run should then be made by the core team and *all* product teams. Any problems encountered or inconsistencies noted must be openly discussed and necessary changes and modifications made for the HACCP product line tested *and* other HACCP product plans.

A second trial run should then be performed on the original product class evaluated. In conjunction with this pilot test, a second HACCP product class should be selected and evaluated at the same time. Preferably, the second product class will vary significantly from the first class in regard to processing steps, critical limits, etc. After the second trial runs are complete, results should be reevaluated by the HACCP core team and all the product teams and any final modifications or changes made to the HACCP product plans.

4.4.4.3 Training sessions.   At this stage plant management in conjunction with the HACCP core and product teams should provide a 2–4 hour training session for all employees giving an overview of HACCP principles, potential hazards and the HACCP plan formats. From an effectiveness standpoint, this training program should be conducted by a joint team of management, company HACCP team members and an outside expert in HACCP programs who has hands-on working knowledge of meat and poultry operations. This training is critical to the success of any HACCP program. Employee education, understanding and commitment are the keystones to product safety and public health.

4.4.4.4 Employee impact/modifying the HACCP plan.   At the stage of employee training and involvement in HACCP plans, additional changes or modifications for individual HACCP product plans may be suggested. The line employees in a meat or poultry plant frequently have the best knowledge of plant processes, effective procedures and potential problem areas. In many cases, they are best equipped to suggest practical operational procedures for monitoring CCPs and corrective action(s) for deviations from critical limits.

After employee input is integrated into the product plans, a set of effective operational procedures must be established for production supervisors, line personnel and operators. These procedures must include a detailed definition of accountability and responsibilities for specific portions of each HACCP plan for all involved personnel. In some cases, shared responsibilities will exist. However, specific accountability must be defined for the plans to function successfully.

4.4.4.5 Two week evaluation.   The HACCP product plans can now be implemented for all products. After initiation of the product plans, a two week operation should be performed before an extensive evaluation is conducted. It must be noted that in spite of all the training, expert advice, employee input and time and effort, unforeseen problems will develop. The two week operating time will allow the majority of these problems to appear so they can be corrected. This 'shakedown' period not only serves to refine the HACCP plans, but illustrates just how company/product specific HACCP plans are required. As part of the two week evaluation period, HACCP verification steps should be conducted for each product class. The verification procedures should be performed by the designated person(s) in the plan and an 'outside' individual such as the expert employed in training or a corporate QA supervisor.

Based on the two week trial period: changes, modifications and improvements will be made to all individual HACCP product plans. A second two week trial period should then be conducted and the individual HACCP product plans fine tuned for full time operation. As processes and product lines change, the HACCP plans can be revised and updated as needed.

4.4.4.6   Training new employees.   As a necessary on-going requirement, a 1–2 hour version of the employee training program should be designed and given to all new employees. This program should be administrated by personnel or employee relations departments in conjunction with the HACCP coordinator and core team. Employee turnover in meat and poultry plants is traditionally very high. It therefore almost mandates that

Table 4.3 Some microbial reduction procedures in meat and poultry slaughter operations

Procedure	Control
Pre-slaughter	
A. Meat animals	1. Clipping/trimming
	2. Washing/drying
B. Birds	1. Air clean/vacuum
Slaughter/dressing	
A. Meat animals	
1. Post sticking: initial treatments	
a. Cattle/sheep	1. Washing/scrubbing hide
	2. Reverse hide pullers
b. Swine	1. Scald tank water
	2. Dehairing/singeing
2. Pre-evisceration carcass treatments	
a. Rinse with approved solutions	1. Water
	2. Hot water: 160–180°F (71–82°C)
	3. Chlorinated water[a]
	4. Organic acids
b. Rinse with proposed[b] solutions	1. Phosphates
	2. Ozone/peroxide
	3. Chlorine dioxide
3. Post-evisceration treatments	1. Trimming
	2. Rinsing with bacteriocidal solutions (see 2 above)
B. Birds	
1. Scald tank treatments	1. Surfactants
	2. Sonication procedures
	3. Bacteriocidal chemicals
2. Pre-evisceration treatments	
a. Rinse with approved solution	1. Water
	2. Hot water: 160–180°F (71–82°C)
	3. Chlorinated water[a]
	4. Organic acids
	5. Phosphates
b. Rinse with proposed[b] solutions	1. Ozone/peroxide
	2. Chlorine dioxide
3. Post-evisceration treatments	
a. Pre-chill	1. Trimming
	2. Rinsing with bacteriodical solutions
b. Chill tank	1. Surfactants
	2. Sonication
	3. Incorporation of bacteriocidal chemicals in chill water

[a]Not approved for Canada. [b]USDA approval pending.

the new employee HACCP training be centralized and *not* consist of on-the-job training. This will require a monetary commitment from upper management. However, this type of training is essential to a successful HACCP program.

4.5 Summary

In summary, implementation of HACCP programs by meat and poultry slaughterers is very similar to that in other food operations. The main difference in slaughter operations is in the biological hazards area. In most cases, no lethal treatment is given to the raw meat and poultry products and complete elimination of microbiological hazards is impossible from a practical viewpoint. Therefore, this section of hazards for meat and poultry slaughters consists of minimizing or reducing, not eliminating hazards as is the case in cooking operations.

An entire series of microbial reduction or intervention strategies are available to red meat and poultry plants. These range from cleaning up the live animal/bird through modified evisceration procedures to final bacterio-cidal rinses. An overview of the types of reduction procedures employed by industry is presented in Table 4.3.

Monitoring and control of chemical and physical hazards in meat and poultry plants is very similar to other types of food operations.

Any HACCP program must have the commitment and support of upper management. Implementation must involve education and understanding as well as a corporate commitment to keep the program simplified to HACCP principles and not expanded to suit customer requirements. All plant employees must be involved, continuing education must be conducted and the HACCP product plans must be regularly updated and revised. A commitment to HACCP principles *will be* beneficial to companies and consumers.

References

American Meat Institute and National Food Processors Institute (1992) *HACCP Workshop.* March 17–19, 1992. Los Angeles, California.

National Academy of Sciences (1985) *An Evaluation of the Role of Microbiological Criteria for Food and Food Ingredients.* National Academy Press, Washington, D.C.

Pierson, M.D. and D.A. Corlett, Jr. (eds) (1992) *HACCP Principles and Applications.* Chapman & Hall, Inc., New York.

Sperber, W.H. (1991) The modern HACCP system. *Food Technol.* **45**(6), 116.

Tompkin, R.B. (1990) The use of HACCP in the production of meat and poultry products. *J. Food Prot.* **53**, 795.

USDA-FSIS, National Advisory Committee on Microbiology Criteria for Foods (1990) *HACCP Principles for Food Production.* USDA-FSIS Information Office, Washington, D.C.

USDA-FSIS (1992) *HACCP Status Report* February 1992, USDA-FSIS, Washington, D.C.

5 The use of HACCP for producing and distributing processed meat and poultry products
R.B. TOMPKIN

5.1 Introduction

This chapter discusses the use of HACCP to enhance the safety of processed meat and poultry products. It will be assumed that these products are produced under federal inspection by the US Department of Agriculture or its equivalent in a state inspected facility. The product categories described earlier will be used (Tompkin, 1986). Fermented products will not be discussed. Some information concerning fermented meats is available in an earlier volume of this series (Bacus, 1986).

The National Advisory Committee on Microbiological Criteria for Foods (NACMCF) report on HACCP is the recommended guide for developing HACCP plans for processed meat and poultry products (NACMCF, 1992). Additional information on the implementation of HACCP is available in a second report from the NACMCF (NACMCF, 1994). The term 'control', in this chapter, will mean:

(a) To manage the conditions of an operation to maintain compliance with established criteria.
(b) The state wherein procedures are being correctly followed and criteria are being met (NACMCF, 1992).

5.2 Reasons for using HACCP

Among the many reasons for using HACCP are the following:

- HACCP is a systematic, disciplined approach to process control that is based upon science.
- HACCP requires record keeping which provides an auditable document trail and a historical perspective of control. Traditional inspection provides only a snapshot view of control.
- HACCP avoids the use of statistically unreliable end product testing to assure food safety.
- Traditional inspection procedures are inadequate because many food safety hazards can not be detected by traditional means. HACCP

systems compensate for this weakness by incorporating appropriate controls to prevent or minimize their occurrence.
- Resources, which are often limited, are focused on and encourage improvements in food safety.
- Responsibility and accountability are clearly assigned.
- Timely adjustments are made to processes which will prevent loss of control and loss of product.
- If control is lost, it will be detected and appropriate actions can be taken to assure food safety and avoid costly product recalls.
- The HACCP concept is a logical, common sense approach that can be used to educate employees and the public in safe food handling procedures.
- HACCP is the most cost effective means to assure food safety.
- Successful implementation of HACCP maintains consumer confidence in product safety with no perceptible change in product cost.

Why not use HACCP? The most common objection is that the cost of implementation is too great. Commercial practice, however, indicates that the cost need not be excessive and can be manageable for most operations. Very small businesses may have more difficulty managing the cost due to the increased burden of record keeping and the need to seek outside assistance. Some flexibility should be permitted for the application of HACCP in small operations. The risk and severity of the potential hazards associated with the processes should determine the degree of flexibility when applying the principles of HACCP to very small businesses. All processes should be designed and managed to assure the production of safe products. Processors, large and small, must acquire the knowledge that is needed to correctly develop and implement HACCP. This will require a cooperative educational effort involving regulatory agencies, trade associations, universities, extension agents, and consultants.

5.3 Developing HACCP plans

Once it is decided who will be involved in developing the HACCP plan, the next step is to describe the products that will be produced, how they will be distributed, how the foods will be used, and who will be the intended consumer. All this information is helpful for assessing the potential problems that might develop during production, distribution and use of the products.

The next step requires developing a flow diagram for each process. A simple plant layout also is very helpful for assessing product flow, traffic patterns and separation of raw from ready-to-eat products. Having completed these tasks, it is necessary to walk through the facility and verify that the flow diagram(s) and plant layout are accurate.

Each company must decide what its HACCP plan(s) will look like. Experience has shown that a separate book devoted to the HACCP system tends to become outdated and merely used for visitors. An effective alternative is to combine the HACCP plan with the operating instructions. This approach assures that the HACCP plans will be updated with the operating instructions. When HACCP plans and operating instructions are combined there will be one document with common objectives for which everyone can strive.

For HACCP to be effective the HACCP plans must be incorporated into the actual operation. For example, it may be desirable for each person responsible for monitoring to have the pertinent portion of the flow diagram and control chart on their daily work sheet. This means that the pertinent information will be readily accessible to the person responsible for monitoring a critical control point (CCP). As much as possible the HACCP plan should be in the hands of the individuals responsible for monitoring, recording measurements and verifying. The work sheet could include the CCP, critical limits, how to avoid deviations, what to do if a deviation occurs, and space for recording the results of monitoring. The information must be available in a form that is understandable and usable to the operator as well as those responsible for verification.

The HACCP plan can exist in several forms such as in a notebook, folder or on file in the software of a computer. One HACCP plan can cover a process which is used for a number of similar products having different universal product codes (UPCs). It is not necessary to have a separate HACCP plan for each UPC if the hazard analysis shows that the products share the same potential hazards, risks, CCPs and critical limits. A guideline to facilitate the development of HACCP plans for processed meat and poultry products is provided as an addendum to this chapter. The guideline combines the operating instruction and HACCP plan for a process into one document.

5.4   Hazard analysis and risk assessment

Hazard analysis is the process of identifying the significant biological, chemical, and physical hazards in a process or product. The hazard analysis is critical to developing a complete HACCP plan because hazards which are overlooked may not be controlled. On the other hand, the tendency to be overly conservative and include too many potential hazards, however remote, also must be avoided. In Appendix A of the NACMCF report (NACMCF, 1992) examples of factors to consider when conducting a hazard analysis are listed. The list is very appropriate for processed meat and poultry products. The factors include the ingredients; intrinsic properties of the food during and after processing; processing procedures;

microbial content of the food during and after processing; facility design and layout; equipment design and location; packaging procedures; sanitation; employee health, hygiene, and education; how the food will be distributed and stored; how the food is intended to be prepared and used; and who will be the intended consumer.

It is strongly recommended that only Appendix A of the 1992 NACMCF report be used as a guide for conducting a hazard analysis. For a variety of reasons the abbreviated form of hazard analysis in Appendix B (Hazard Analysis and Assignment of Risk Categories) should not be used. For example, the rate at which cooked product is chilled is not considered. This means that the outgrowth of *Clostridium perfringens* and other sporeformers which can survive cooking and subsequently multiply in cooked meat and poultry products will be overlooked. Another point is that the issues of risk (an estimate of the likely occurrence of a hazard) and severity are not addressed when developing the 'risk categories'. The categories actually have little, if anything, to do with risk and are of no practical value to the HACCP plan.

Risk assessment is the process of estimating the probable a) occurrence of a hazard in a process or product and b) injury, illness or death among consumers of the food. Guidelines are being developed to facilitate the risk assessment of biological hazards. A NACMCF draft report of the elements of risk assessment is summarized in Table 5.1 (NACMCF, 1993). When a biological hazard is found to be associated with a process or product the information in Table 5.1 can be used to assess the risk and potential impact of the hazard on consumers of the product. This outline is intended for use by experts (e.g. epidemiologists, microbiologists, parasitologists). The outline also could be used to supplement the information listed in the aforementioned Appendix A.

5.4.1 Product recalls

Information on product recalls may be useful for the hazard analysis. Foods under federal inspection are subject to recall if found to be adulterated, contaminated with filth, or held under conditions whereby they may have been rendered injurious to health.

For meat and poultry products, the USDA has established a formal procedure which leads to a 'recall recommendation' (USDA, 1992a). The procedure consists of three parts: a) health hazard evaluation, b) recall classification, and c) recall strategy. The health hazard evaluation considers at least the following factors:

- Nature of the violation or defect
- Whether any illnesses or injuries have already occurred from the use of the product

Table 5.1 Components of risk assessment for biological hazards

---

I.   State reason for the assessment

II.   Hazard identification
      A. Likelihood of hazard(s) in the food
      B. Epidemiological data which identify the hazards associated with the product
      C. Clinical studies which determine the effect of a biological agent on humans
      D. Predictive modeling which predicts the development of a hazard and the conditions
         that may be important
      E. Fault tree – what happens if control is lost

III. Exposure assessment
      A. Population demographics – changing age patterns, immune deficiency of the exposed
         population
      B. Consumption patterns – who eats the food, how much
      C. Market basket surveys at retail level for the presence and number of the biological
         hazards
      D. Distribution patterns – local, regional, national, international
      E. Hazard characteristics – incidence, numbers, growth, death during distribution,
         storage and use

IV.   Dose–response assessment
      A. Estimate of how much is needed to cause disease among consumers
      B. Estimate of how many consumers will become ill based upon:
         ● Human volunteer studies
         ● Epidemiological data
         ● Animal test data
         ● Knowledge of the effect of the food
         ● Virulence or toxicity of the biological hazard
         ● Susceptibility of consumers

V.   Severity assessment
      A. Attack rate – estimate of the number of consumers that will become ill or those who
         may be exposed to the hazard
      B. Spectrum of disease – asymptomatic, death
      C. Sequelae – kidney failure, arthritis

VI.   Risk characterization
      ● A summary and interpretation of the available information, preferably in quantitative
        terms
      ● Include uncertainties and limitations of the data

Source: NACMCF (1993)

● Assessment of the risk or likelihood of occurrence of the hazard
● Assessment of the severity or consequences (immediate or long range)
  of the occurrences of the hazard

Product to be recalled is then classified according to the risk and severity
of the potential hazard as follows:

● Class I involves a health hazard situation where there is a reasonable
  probability that use of the product will cause serious, adverse health
  consequences or death
● Class II involves a potential health hazard situation where there is a
  remote probability of serious, adverse health consequences or death

- Class III involves a situation where use of the product is not likely to cause health consequences

The information obtained from the health hazard evaluation and the classification of the recall are then used to develop the recall strategy.

The first two steps of the overall recall procedure are very similar to the process of hazard analysis for a HACCP plan. When developing a HACCP plan an assessment is made of the potential hazards which might occur, the likelihood of their occurrence and their severity. In the circumstances leading to a recall, the hazard is known but an assessment of the risk and severity must still be made.

Will HACCP reduce product recalls? Yes, but the data are lacking to support this assumption for processed meat and poultry products. It would be accurate to state, however, that in the past when hazards have been identified with a process or product the USDA has responded with an appropriate regulation. This could be considered a form of corrective action by the agency. The risk of the hazards have been reduced, if not eliminated, by the agency's action and industry's reaction.

Product recalls occur when: a) control is lost in a process and a defect is not detected before the product leaves the establishment, b) available technology is not adequate to prevent or eliminate a hazard, and c) a processor violates existing regulations, either intentionally or through ignorance. Product recalls will more likely occur in establishments which do not have effective HACCP plans, because HACCP is designed to detect, to the extent that is technologically feasible, defects as they occur and prevent unacceptable product from leaving the plant. A review of the hazards involved in recalls will suggest the potential use of HACCP for reducing recalls.

During the seven years from 1987 through 1993 there were 206 Class I and II recalls involving meat and poultry products from USDA inspected establishments (Table 5.2). Class I and II recalls are concerned with food safety issues. Table 5.2 indicates that during the 7 years: 44 recalls involved physical hazards, 50 involved chemical hazards, and 112 involved micro-biological hazards. About 193 of the 206 recalls involved processed products as opposed to raw meat and poultry. Thus, processed meat and poultry products have been involved in more Class I and II recalls than raw meat and poultry products.

The data in Table 5.2 lists the classes of recall which were established for the various hazards. For example the agency's position on glass, sulfites, *L. monocytogenes* and *S. aureus* was that the potential severity of these hazards warranted a rating of Class I. The available information in each case led the agency to select either Class I or II for metal, plastic, certain chemicals, swollen containers/can defects, underprocessing/process devi-ations, salmonellae, and trichinae. Class II recalls were used for bone, species adulteration, sulfa drugs, mold and spoilage.

Table 5.2 Reasons for Class I and II recalls of meat and poultry products from 1987 through 1993

Reason	Class of recall	1987	1988	1989	1990	1991	1992	1993	Total
Physical									
Metal	I, II	1	2	2	1	3	5	5	19
Plastic	I, II		1	1	2		2	5	11
Glass	I				1		1	2	4
Bone	II				2	2			4
Other	I, II				1	2	3		6
Chemical									
Species	II	26	3	3	1	1		1	35
Sulfa drug	II		1			2			3
Sulfites	I			1	3				4
Chemicals	I, II	1		1					2
Other	I, II	1	1		1		3		6
Biological									
Swollen containers/can defects	I, II	4	2	1	2	1		1	11
Underprocessing/process deviation	I, II		3	6	2	5	5	1	22
L. monocytogenes	I			8	6	11	7	16	48
Salmonellae	I, II	1				1	1	1	4
Trichinae	I, II						3		3
S. aureus	I	2			1				3
Mold	II		2	1			3		6
Spoilage	II	1	1		2	5		2	11
Other	I, II		1	1	1			1	4
Totals		37	17	25	26	33	33	35	206

Source: Leslie (1994)

The data show several trends during the 7 year period. One is the high number (26) of recalls due to species adulteration in 1987 followed by the reduced number of violations as industry responded to new requirements established by the agency (USDA, 1987). Another trend is a decrease in the number of recalls involving swollen containers and can defects. A third trend is an increase in the number of recalls involving *L. monocytogenes*. Collectively, the data in Table 5.2 indicate that it would be beneficial to consumers, the agency, and producers if there were improved control of the processes for processed meat and poultry products.

The data in Table 5.2 indicate the types of hazards that can occur in processed meat and poultry products. The potential value of HACCP for preventing these hazards depends upon industry's ability to implement effective controls. The International Commission on Microbiological Specifications for Food (ICMSF) described two general types of CCP (ICMSF, 1988; Tompkin, 1990). One consists of a CCP which is effective and prevents or eliminates the identified hazard (CCP1). The other is a CCP which is less effective and minimizes or reduces, but cannot prevent or eliminate, the hazard (CCP2). This distinction also is reflected in the definition of CCP recommended by the NACMCF (NACMCF, 1992).

'A point, step, or procedure at which control can be applied and a food safety hazard can be prevented, eliminated, or reduced to acceptable levels'.

This is an honest recognition that the use of HACCP, *per se*, has its limitations and will not prevent all potential food safety hazards. Certain hazards are more preventable than others. Most chemical hazards of the nature listed in Table 5.2 can be prevented and, thus, CCP1 should apply. Of the biological hazards, can defects and swollen containers are normally due to microbial growth resulting from leaking containers or under-processing, both of which should be preventable. The measures used to prevent these deficiencies are effective and CCP1 should apply. Experience indicates that the preventive measures for salmonellae, trichinae and *S. aureus* are effective and controllable (CCP1). The potential risk of *L. monocytogenes*, however, can be minimized but not eliminated (CCP2). Finally, many processed meat and poultry products are perishable and even under optimum conditions spoilage is inevitable. For these products microbial spoilage can be minimized but not prevented (CCP2). It could be debated that spoilage of raw meat and poultry at refrigeration temperatures is not a food safety concern and that Class III would be more appropriate. The designations, CCP1 and CCP2, are generally not used by most proponents of HACCP today but they can be useful for assessing and communicating the potential success of a HACCP plan.

5.4.2 Epidemiological data

Another important source of information which may be useful for the hazard analysis is the reported outbreaks of foodborne illness attributable to meat and poultry products. The data in Table 5.3, which are the latest available at this time, do not differentiate raw meat and poultry from the commercial ready-to-eat products discussed in this chapter. It can merely be stated that these commercial products comprise some unknown portion of the total. The data also must be interpreted with caution. For example, an outbreak attributed to chicken salad, chicken à la king, or a chicken pot pie would likely be reported as 'chicken' whether or not the chicken was the source of the etiological agent. The data merely indicate that a food containing chicken was the vehicle of illness.

Approximately 73% and 27% of the outbreaks were attributed to red meat and poultry, respectively. The data show a trend toward fewer outbreaks of illness due to meat and poultry during the period 1969 through 1987 (Table 5.3). This favourable trend may be due to: a) actual improvements in preventing foodborne illness through education and efforts by the food industry; and/or b) a trend toward more underreporting of outbreaks. Limited evidence does exist for a reduction in the outbreaks of foodborne illness due to meat and poultry. For example, the reported cases of trichinosis has been declining (McAuley *et al.*, 1991; CDC, 1992). This decline can be attributed to several factors including laws which prohibit feeding garbage to hogs, increased use of home freezers, education which has led to the practice of thoroughly cooking pork, and regulations which assure the destruction of *Trichinella spiralis* in ready-to-eat pork products produced in federal establishments (McAuley *et al.*, 1991; USDA, 1992b–d). The major sources of trichinosis during the past ten years have been wild game (e.g. bear, walrus) which were inadequately cooked by consumers to destroy *T. spiralis* or pork products which were eaten raw. The latter has been a problem among recent immigrants from Southeast Asia. The decrease in trichinosis is an example of how a foodborne disease has been reduced by a farm-to-table approach through a combination of education and regulations.

Regulations implemented by the USDA also have been successful in preventing outbreaks of salmonellosis due to roast beef produced in federal establishments (USDA, 1982). Continuing emphasis by the agency has led to a reduction in the contamination of commercially produced roast beef and corned beef products as measured by tests for *E. coli* (Tompkin and Borchert, 1992). The presence of *E. coli* can be used to assess the effectiveness of sanitation procedures and to indicate the potential presence of enteric pathogens. The reduced incidence of *E. coli* in cooked beef products has been due to the cooperative effort of industry and the USDA to minimize contamination of these products with salmonellae and *L. monocytogenes*.

Table 5.3 Reported number of outbreaks of foodborne illness attributed to meat and poultry: 1969 through 1987[a]

Year	Beef[b]	Ham	Pork	Sausage	Chicken	Turkey	Other meats; stews	Total	All red meat[c]	All poultry
1969	72	↓	63	↑	23	47	–	205	135	70
1970	60	↓	37	↑	17	29	8	151	105	46
1971	43	↓	49	↑	11	16	5	124	97	27
1972	41	↓	45	↑	↓ 29	→	–	115	86	29
1973	28	15	12	4	↓ 19	→	3	81	62	19
1974	22	20	11	11	7	8	20	99	84	15
1975	54	23	11	11	14	13	20	146	119	27
1976	28	8	3	5	5	13	6	68	50	18
1977	27	10	8	10	6	8	9	78	64	14
1978	14	12	10	2	4	3	8	53	46	7
1979	20	10	10	0	8	3	7	58	47	11
1980	17	8	5	5	5	18	10	68	45	23
1981	34	9	7	6	18	16	2	92	58	34
1982	22	5	6	4	13	11	4	65	41	24
1983	9	3	5	2	6	3	7	35	26	9
1984	16	3	11	1	7	9	10	57	41	16
1985	11	4	5	1	5	6	8	40	29	11
1986	9	5	6	0	5	5	6	36	26	10
1987	6	1	4	0	8	1	4	24	15	9
								1595	1176	419

[a]Includes outbreaks of confirmed and unknown etiology. [b]Veal and lamb omitted from this tabulation. [c]Includes beef, pork, ham, sausage, and other meats; stews. *Source:* CDC (1970–73, 1974–77, 1979, 1979–82) and Bean *et al.* (1990).

5.4.3   Chemical hazards

One potential chemical hazard is an excess quantity of sodium nitrite. This potential hazard was recognized decades ago when controls were established by the USDA to minimize this risk. Other chemical hazards which should be considered include pesticide residues, antibiotics, sulfa drugs, cleaning and sanitizing agents, oils and greases. Information on the potential risk of chemical hazards in meat and poultry is available for use in the hazard analysis (NRC, 1985b, 1987; Katz and Brady, 1993).

Another potential hazard is failure to separate meat from different species of animals. A small number of consumers are sensitive (i.e. allergic) to the meat from certain species of animals. Also, a beef product which is contaminated with pork may not be heated adequately to destroy *Trichinella spiralis* and *Toxoplasma gondii*. For these reasons effective procedures must be in place to prevent errors in formulation or contamination with meat remaining in equipment during changeovers from one product to another (USDA, 1987). Specifically, the meat content of the product must agree with the ingredient statement so that sensitive consumers can avoid meats which may be hazardous to them. In general, this can be accomplished by removing residual meat from blenders, grinders, stuffers and other equipment and then rinsing the equipment thoroughly with water. Another effective option is to schedule the products in a manner that will avoid contamination. For example, an all beef product should be formulated using clean equipment at the start of an operation. This could then be followed by a product containing a blend of beef and pork.

5.4.4   Physical hazards

The major physical hazards include glass, metal, bone, wood, plastic, rubber, stones, shotgun pellets, needles used for injecting medications, and other foreign objects which can cause harm to the consumer. These hazards are best minimized by selecting suppliers with effective HACCP programs, monitoring incoming raw materials, and controlling the conditions of processing to minimize contamination. Controlling the risk of glass contamination begins with a strict policy of prohibiting unprotected glass in processing areas. For example, lights must be covered to prevent the glass from contaminating product. Metal detectors should be properly maintained, adjusted and located at strategic points in the process to reject raw materials or product with metal contamination.

Foreign objects, particularly bone fragments, are a chronic concern in processed meat operations. Their presence can be minimized in certain products but not prevented (e.g. coarse ground products). An effective control program will include following the trend of defects of this nature and responding to an increase in the number or percent of defects.

In the event a physical hazard is detected in a product then the suspect product can be tested with equipment which has been approved by the USDA. The equipment must be capable of detecting foreign particles (e.g. glass, metal, plastic) as small as 0.8 mm (1/32″) to be acceptable for sorting the product (USDA, 1933d). This suggests that particles of 0.8 mm (1/32″) or smaller are not a public health concern.

5.4.5 Biological hazards

The biological hazards of primary concern in raw meat and poultry are outlined in Table 5.4. It must be assumed that these hazards will be present in the raw materials and, therefore, the processing procedures must be designed to control them. Despite the potential presence of these and other biological hazards, a wide variety of processes and products have evolved over the years. A tabulation of the general categories of ready-to-eat meat and poultry products, major biological hazards, and CCPs for processing, storage and distribution appear in Table 5.5.

The biological hazards in foods can be categorized on the basis of the severity of the hazard (Table 5.6). The categories were developed to serve as the basis for recommending sampling plans for imported foods (ICMSF, 1986). The combined assessment of severity and risk were used to arrive at 15 cases, each of which represents a specific sampling plan (Table 5.7).

Table 5.4 Pathogens of primary concern in raw meat and poultry

Meat	Pathogen
Poultry:	Salmonellae *Campylobacter jejuni* *L. monocytogenes* *C. perfringens* *C. botulinum*
Pork:	Salmonellae *Yersinia enterocolitica* *L. monocytogenes* *C. perfringens* *C. botulinum* *Trichinella spiralis* *Toxoplasma gondii*
Beef:	Salmonellae *Escherichia coli* 0157:H7 *L. monocytogenes* *C. perfringens* *C. botulinum*

Table 5.5 Categories of ready-to-eat products, major biological hazards, and critical control points for processing, storage and distribution

Product category and examples	Processing		Storage, distribution	
	Major biological hazards	CCPs	Major biological hazards	CCPs
Raw salted cured: Country Ham, prosciutto	*T. spiralis, T. gondii,* enterics, *C. botulinum*	Salt, nitrite, time and temperature of curing and aging	Risk of *S. aureus* on cut or sliced product is very low due to other competing flora	None can be stored at ambient; refrigeration is recommended for sliced product
Perishable cooked uncured: Sliced roast beef, whole baked poultry, paté	Enterics, sporeformers, *L. monocytogenes*	Cooking, chilling, preventing recontamination	Sporeformers, recontaminants	Refrigerate
Patties, links, meatballs	*T. spiralis, T. gondii* (if pork is used), enterics, *L. monocytogenes*	Cooking, chilling, preventing recontamination	Sporeformers, recontaminants	Refrigerate or freeze
Cook-in-bag poultry breast or roast beef	Enterics, sporeformers	Cooking, chilling	Sporeformers	Refrigerate
Perishable cooked cured: Franks, sliced lunch meats, jellied meats, corned beef, smoked whole poultry	*T. spiralis, T. gondii* (if pork is used), enterics, sporeformers *L. monocytogenes*	Cooking, chilling, preventing recontamination	Sporeformers, recontaminants	Refrigerate
Prefried bacon	*T. spiralis, T. gondii,* enterics, *L. monocytogenes*	Cooking, chilling	Recontaminants	Refrigerate or freeze
Perishable canned cured: Canned ham, luncheon meat, ham patties	*T. spiralis, T. gondii,* enterics, sporeformers	Cooking, chilling	Sporeformers	Refrigerate

Shelf stable canned cured:			
Viennas, spreads, corned beef ($F_0 \geq 2.78$)	Sporeformers	Sealing, cooking, chilling	None
Canned ham, luncheon meat ($F_0 = 0.1–0.7$)	Sporeformers	Formulating, sealing, cooking, chilling	None
Sausages in lard, sliced dried beef, prefried bacon, bacon bits	T. spiralis, T. gondii (if pork is used), enterics, S. aureus	Formulating, cooking, and/ or drying to a specified water activity or other criteria, excluding oxygen from container	None
Pickled sausages, pigs feet	T. spiralis, T. gondii, enterics, sporeformers	Formulating, heating	None
Shelf stable canned uncured:			
Beef stew, whole chicken, chili, meat sauces, sloppy joe	Sporeformers	Formulating (high acid products), filling, sealing cooking, chilling	None
Dried:			
Jerky, snack meats	Enterics, S. aureus, T. spiralis, T. gondii (if pork is used)	Formulating, cooking and/ or drying to a specified water activity or other criteria	None
Freeze dried or dehydrated cooked meat or poultry	Enterics, T. spiralis, T. gondii (if pork is used)	Cooking, drying, preventing recontamination	None

Cases 1–3 involve the hazards of lowest severity; whereas, cases 13–15 involve the hazards of highest severity. The stringency of the sampling plan increases with the severity of the hazard and when the expected conditions of handling and preparing the food will increase the risk of the hazard. The rationale behind Tables 5.6 and 5.7 can be useful during the hazard analysis to address the issues of severity and the risk. The ICMSF also has published a reference manual for the biological hazards associated with foodborne illness. The manual is intended to facilitate the hazard analysis process and the development of HACCP plans (ICMSF, 1995).

When conducting a hazard analysis it should become evident that the biological hazards in cooked perishable processed meat and poultry products are of three types. One consists of pathogens (i.e. enteric pathogens, *S. aureus*, vegetative cells of sporeforming pathogens) which may be present in the ingredients and which are destroyed by the conditions of processing. Current USDA regulations for producing ready-to-eat products assure the destruction of these pathogens. As new issues have arisen the agency has responded with new or modified regulations to assure product safety. Since the non-sporeforming pathogens do not survive the conditions of processing, testing ingredients for these pathogens is not necessary.

Table 5.6 Severity of biological hazards which may be associated with meat and poultry

Effects of hazard	Species
Moderate, direct, limited spread, death rarely occurs	*Bacillus cereus* *Campylobacter jejuni* *Clostridium perfringens* *Staphylococcus aureus* *Yersinia enterocolitica* *Taenia saginata* *Toxoplasma gondii* ('normal' persons)
Moderate, direct, potentially extensive spread, death or serious sequelae can occur	Pathogenic *Escherichia coli* *Salmonella typhimurium* and other salmonellae which are not considered severe hazards Shigellae other than *Shigella dysenteriae* *Listeria monocytogenes* ('normal' persons)
Severe, direct	*Clostridium botulinum* types A, B, E, F Hepatitis A virus *Salmonella typhi* *Salmonella paratyphi A, B, C* *Shigella dysenteriae* *Listeria monocytogenes* (immune compromized persons) *Trichinella spiralis* *Toxoplasma gondii* (immune compromized persons)

Adapted from ICMSF (1986).

Table 5.7 Assessment of the severity of hazard and expected conditions of using a food to determine the stringency of the sampling plan or case

Type of hazard	Conditions in which food is expected to be handled, and consumed after sampling, in the usual course of events		
	Reduce risk of hazard	Cause no change in risk of hazard	May increase risk of hazard
No direct health hazard	Case 1	Case 2	Case 3
● Utility (e.g. general contamination, reduced shelf-life, and spoilage)			
Health hazard			
● Low, indirect (indicator)	Case 4	Case 5	Case 6
● Moderate, direct, limited spread, death rarely occurs	Case 7	Case 8	Case 9
● Moderate, direct potentially extensive spread, death or serious sequelae can occur	Case 10	Case 11	Case 12
● Severe, direct	Case 13	Case 14	Case 15

Source: Adapted from ICMSF (1986).

The second type of biological hazard consists of sporeformers (e.g. *C. botulinum*, *C. perfringens* and *B. cereus*) which can survive the processes used for producing perishable ready-to-eat meat and poultry products. Refrigeration below 10°C (50°F) will prevent multiplication of these pathogens. It should always be assumed that these pathogens may be present, no matter how low the risk, and that proper refrigeration of perishable products is essential for safety.

The third type consists of pathogens which may recontaminate products after processing to a ready-to-eat state. These pathogens (e.g. *L. monocytogenes*, salmonellae, *Yersinia enterocolitica*) must be controlled through a combination of: a) plant design to minimize the risk of cross contamination from the raw processing area to the cooked product handling area; b) an effective environmental sanitation program; and c) informed employees who follow procedures designed to protect exposed ready-to-eat product. Post process contamination will be addressed more fully later in this chapter.

5.5   Critical control points and critical limits

In this section of the chapter perishable cooked or canned products (Table 5.5) will be used to describe the establishment of critical control points and critical limits. The hazards associated with these products are similar and will be followed from formulating to distributing.

5.5.1   Formulating

The hazards of primary concern during formulating (e.g. preparing pickle solutions, boning, weighing, pumping, grinding, blending, mixing, tumbling) are chemical and physical in nature. The potential chemical hazards include adding excess sodium nitrite and inadvertent mixing of meat from different species of animals. The physical hazards include bone fragments, metal, glass and other foreign material. These physical hazards are best controlled by buying ingredients from suppliers with effective HACCP systems and verifying control by monitoring ingredients as they are received and used. The extent of monitoring should reflect the type of hazard, the level of risk associated with each ingredient, and confidence in the effectiveness of the suppliers HACCP system.

Commercial procedures for receiving and holding fresh meat ingredients should not result in uncontrollable biological hazards for these products. In addition, the procedures commonly used for thawing frozen meat ingredients (e.g. microwave, water immersion, holding under refrigeration and combinations of these methods) do not increase the potential hazards to uncontrollable levels. Errors in holding or thawing raw meats are of concern to product quality and spoilage, but not safety. Other ingredients (e.g. salt, phosphate, sugar, dextrose, starch, gelatin, hydrolysed protein) used in formulating these products are rarely a source of biological hazards for these products. An exception may be condiments or spices (e.g. salmonellae in pepper) which may be added after cooking. This potential hazard can be controlled by using treated (e.g. ethylene oxide, irradiation) spices.

The cleanliness of the equipment and the environment used for holding and formulating raw meat and poultry is an important concern for aesthetic reasons, but not for food safety. The procedures used for cleaning must be adequate to assure the production of clean, wholesome, unadulterated products. Only rarely is improper cleaning of formulating equipment a source of microbial spoilage for perishable cooked or canned products. The risk is even lower that improper cleaning will result in a micro-biologically unsafe product. The reasons for the low risk to safety include: a) low temperatures are used for holding and formulating the raw meat; b) there is a predominance of spoilage bacteria in the environment and the raw meat; c) most of the pathogens of concern are poor competitors in raw meat and poultry at low temperatures; d) the perishability of raw meat and poultry necessitates cooking in a timely manner to avoid deterioration of quality and loss of product; and e) the cooking procedures for perishable cooked or canned products provide a margin of safety which assures the destruction of the pathogens, except those which may be present as spores.

5.5.2 Cooking

A variety of batch and continuous cooking methods are used for perishable cooked ready-to-eat meat and poultry products. These methods include cooking in vats of water or oil or cooking in ovens for a specified time. The products may be cooked in pastic bags, cans, casings, molds and pans, or exposed with no protective covering. The method of cooking influences the rate of heat penetration and the variability of the thermal process. The cooking process must be controlled to achieve two food safety goals.

The first goal is to prevent excessive microbial multiplication during heating, before lethal temperatures are reached. Pathogens can multiply during very slow heating in the range of 10°C (50°F) to 52°C (126°F). Theoretically, this could result in an accumulation of heat stable toxin. When lethal temperatures are reached then the vegetative cells would be destroyed. The risk of this occurring is very low but must be considered. Another problem to consider is dehydration during the initial phase of heating, especially at a product's surface, which is not sealed in a container or plastic film. The reduction in water activity at the surface of the product can result in increased heat resistance and survival of pathogens (e.g. salmonellae).

The second goal is to heat the product to the required minimum internal temperature throughout the product. This also may require holding the product at a minimum internal temperature for a specified of time. This is the simplest approach to assuring microbiological safety.

In large diameter products the risk of non-sporeforming pathogens surviving the cooking process should be negligible. The minimum USDA temperature requirements for these products often exceed the minimum needed for microbiological safety. In addition, the slow penetration of heat results in substantial thermal destruction, particularly as temperatures exceed 60°C (140°F). Additional thermal destruction occurs during the relatively slow cooling of these products. Minor variations in heating and cooling that might occur from the location of the product in the oven or vat or other factors should be of relatively low risk to food safety.

In small diameter or thin products (e.g. links and patties) which are subjected to high temperatures for short times, the risk of non-sporeforming pathogens surviving is higher. Relatively minor variations in temperatures of meat or poultry products positioned across a moving belt can result in underprocessing. Two opposing factors exist for small products given high temperature short time processes. One is that the amount of weight loss during the cooking process often determines the economic viability of the process and product. The other is the necessity to achieve the minimum time and temperature required to assure product safety.

The American Meat Institute has developed a guideline for the production of cooked meat patties (AMI, 1992). The guideline describes options that could be available to industry when cooking patties, links and other small products using high temperature short time processes. The principles applied in the guideline could form the basis for cooking a variety of small products whether heated in air of controlled temperature and humidity, oil, water, microwave or other means. The present USDA requirements are based upon minimum holding times at certain internal temperatures (USDA, 1993a–c). Future consideration should be given to processes which are based upon the total thermal destruction achieved during both the heating and cooling phases of the cooking processes as described in the AMI guideline.

Cooking processes must be scientifically based upon data for the thermal destruction of pathogens. In perishable cured and noncured ready-to-eat products the enteric pathogens are of primary concern. Thus, data for salmonellae (Anellis et al., 1954; Osborne et al., 1954; Read et al., 1968; Garibaldi et al., 1969; Ng et al., 1969; Baird-Parker et al., 1970; Goepfert et al., 1970; Milone and Watson, 1970; Goodfellow and Brown, 1978; Gonzalez-Cabezas et al., 1983; Craven and Blankenship, 1983), E. coli 0157:H7 (Line et al., 1991), and L. monocytogenes (Farber, 1989; Mackey and Bratchell, 1989; Farber and Brown, 1990; Boyle et al., 1990; Harrison and Huang, 1990; Mackey et al., 1990; Bhaduri et al., 1991; Fain et al., 1991; Quintavalla and Campanini, 1991; Yen et al., 1991 and 1992; Sofos et al., 1992) should form the basis for deciding upon the cooking processes of perishable products. Cooking processes for perishable products could be based upon the destruction of 1×10^6/g of an enteric pathogen in the coldest area of the product. Raw meat which has been held under conditions which would permit multiplication of salmonellae or E. coli 0157:H7 to a level of 1×10^6/g would very likely be spoiled and rejected.

The minimum internal temperatures required by USDA often exceed those which are needed for food safety. For example, 62.8°C (145°F) or its equivalent in roast beef is based upon killing 10^6/g of salmonellae or E. coli 0157:H7 in the coldest area of the roast. It should be obvious then that the USDA requirements of 71.1°C (160°F) in uncured turkey breast is based upon product quality (i.e. doneness) and not food safety. This raises the question, should the critical limit be based upon the USDA requirement or the minimum required for safety? To avoid confusion and assure compliance, the USDA requirement should be specified as the critical limit. In addition, a corporate target level should be specified. Corporate target levels normally exceed USDA requirements and should be referred to as control points (CPs), not CCPS.

Corporate target levels may be higher than the USDA requirements for several reasons. One reason may be to minimize the risk that a lot will fail to meet a USDA requirement due to variability in heating. Other reasons may be to kill heat resistant spoilage bacteria (i.e. shelf life) or to achieve certain desirable product characteristics. For example, temperatures higher than 71.1°C (160°F) may help prevent pink discoloration of noncured poultry breast products.

5.5.3 Cooling

Cooling is important because initially it is a continuation of the cooking process. Cooling is also important because multiplication from germinated surviving spores must be controlled. The rate of cooling from 52°C (126°F), the upper limit for multiplication of *C. perfringens*, down to about 20°C (68°F) is important. Below 20°C (68°F) mesophilic sporeforming pathogens multiply slowly. The pathogenic mesophilic sporeformers which are likely to occur in cooked meat and poultry products do not multiply below 10°C (50°F).

Cooling can be achieved by a variety of methods (e.g. showering with water, vats of water or ice and water, cold air of various degrees of velocity, liquid nitrogen or carbon dioxide). The product may be exposed on racks, moving belts, or immersed in water. Products which are to be vacuum packaged must be chilled before packaging to avoid loose film.

Condensation is a common problem when warm moist air comes into contact with colder surfaces. Condensation can be a source of microbial contamination, but whether this is significant to public health is debatable and would depend upon the circumstances.

Cooling of products which have been cooked in cans, molds or impermeable plastic films is often accomplished in water baths or by showering water over the product. Imperfect seals can result in the uptake of water into the products, therefore, the cooling water must be controlled (e.g. potable, chlorinated) to minimize the risk of microbial contamination. Contamination through container seals and seams with potable water is a spoilage or quality issue, not a safety issue, for perishable products which are to be sold under refrigerated or frozen conditions.

5.5.4 Holding

Perishable cooked or canned products normally are held at refrigeration temperatures before packaging, storing or distributing. This is necessary to schedule product for packaging, to achieve optimum temperatures for slicing and/or to achieve minimal product temperatures for packaging, boxing and palletizing. These are all quality requirements established by a company and are not food safety concerns. The major food safety concern is to avoid contamination of exposed product with hazardous materials during refrigerated holding. This is a manageable concern and should be of low risk with a suitable environmental control program.

5.5.5   Packaging

Perishable canned or cook-in-bag products are placed into boxes for subsequent storing and distributing. Packaging other exposed perishable cooked products is an opportunity for product contamination. The risk of contamination with microbial pathogens is manageable with a suitable environmental control program and employee education. Package integrity is a quality, not a safety, issue for these products. Proper coding of the products is a CP because this is essential to successfully initiate, monitor, and then verify the effectiveness of a recall.

5.5.6   Preventing recontamination

Generally, current good manufacturing practices (CGMP) are supplemental to, but separate from, the HACCP plan. In specific situations, however, some aspects of CGMP are important preventive measures. Preventing recontamination of cooked products with enteric pathogens during cooling, holding, and packaging is an example. The specific aspects of CGMP which are important to prevent recontamination could be incorporated into the HACCP plan as requirements for the CCP, preventing recontamination.

Previously, it was stated that the cleanliness of the raw processing environment and equipment is not an important food safety concern. This is not true for the cooked product handling areas. The cleanliness of the environment and surfaces which contact the exposed cooked products can be a food safety concern, particularly for products in which L. monocytogenes can multiply.

To place this concern into perspective the production of a sliced lunch meat will be used as an example. A general flow diagram for producing the product is outlined in Figure 5.1. This process is typical of a variety of products consisting of pork, beef and/or poultry. The products may or may not be cured and may be cooked in a casing, flexible plastic film, or a can.

Since the presence of enteric pathogens (i.e. listeriae, salmonellae) in raw meat cannot be controlled, the steps prior to cooking cannot be CCPs for control of these pathogens. The minimum USDA requirements for cooking these products depends upon the formulation. A temperature of 64.4°C (148°F) is required for cured sausages, 68.3°C (155°F) for cured poultry products, 65.6°C (150°F) for perishable canned ham, and 71.1°C (160°F) for noncured poultry products. Industry will often target for a temperature that exceeds the USDA minimum. Considering the size of the products and the time for heating and cooling there is a substantial margin of safety. Salmonellae and listeriae cannot survive these commercial processes; thus, the cooking step is effective for eliminating these hazards (CCP1).

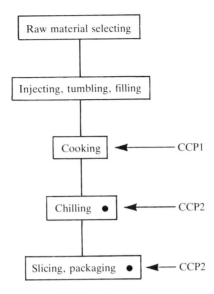

Figure 5.1. Flow diagram for producing sliced lunch meats from perishable cooked or canned processed meat and poultry products. Identification of contamination sites and CCPs for controlling *L. monocytogenes.* ● Sites of major contamination. CCP1, effective CCP. CCP2, not absolute.

After cooking, the products are chilled, sliced and then packaged. During these steps the product will be exposed to potential recontamination. An estimate of the risk of recontamination in USDA inspected facilities is evident from the data in Table 5.8. These data show that the risk of recontamination with salmonellae is very low. It is evident that the commercial conditions existing in federally inspected establishments have been effective for preventing recontamination of cooked products with salmonellae.

The data for *L. monocytogenes* are less favorable. For example, 19 out of 1049 analyses of ham sliced from cans were positive, an incidence of 1.81%. These data indicate that despite industry's efforts since 1986 there continues to be a low, but detectable, level of contamination in the products tested. The number of recalls each year provides additional evidence (Table 5.2). These data indicate that current procedures and regulations in place in federally inspected facilities can minimize, but not prevent, the presence of *L. monocytogenes* in these products (i.e. CCP2). This is because *L. monocytogenes* is naturally present in processed meat plants as part of the normal flora and can multiply in the environment and in or on equipment even at refrigeration temperatures. Control of *L. monocytogenes* requires specific procedures to minimize its presence and

Table 5.8 USDA results of monitoring for salmonellae and *L. monocytogenes* in ready-to-eat meat and poultry products from 1983 through May 1993[a]

	Salmonellae		*L. monocytogenes*	
	No. of analyses	No. of analyses positive	No. of analyses	No. of analyses positive
Cooked sausage	13 401	3	6688	107
Roast/corned beef	9324	14	3122	71
Cooked poultry	6606	4	4498	46
Salads/spreads	5739	1	3884	50
Sliced canned ham	1552	0	1049	19
Prosciutto	714	0	142	1
Cooked imports	1342	4	1643	15
Jerky	1008	0	548	0
Total	39 686	26	21 574	309
% of analyses positive		0.066		1.43

[a]The results exclude data for samples collected and analysed as a follow-up to a positive monitoring sample. Details of the USDA monitoring program are available (USDA, 1990). *Source*: Green (1994).

reduce the risk of product contamination (Tompkin *et al.*, 1992). New technology is needed to further reduce the risk of *L. monocytogenes* contamination.

There has been considerable discussion at an international level over appropriate criteria for *L. monocytogenes*. For example, the ICMSF has developed a recommendation for sampling foods for *L. monocytogenes* which considers the risk to the consumer and whether multiplication can occur (ICMSF, 1994). This information along with the recommendations of the NACMCF (1991), WHO (1988), and other information on listeriae control (Tompkin *et al.*, 1992; Lammerding and Farber, 1994) could be used as a scientific basis for future USDA policies (USDA, 1990). The HACCP plans established by industry and verified by the USDA through plant inspections and microbiological testing should reflect the experience gained with *L. monocytogenes* since 1986.

5.5.7 Storing and distributing

Perishable ready-to-eat meat and poultry products should be stored and distributed at 5°C (41°F) or below (FDA, 1993). The microbial changes which occur in these products during storage and distribution are influenced by a wide variety of factors (Table 5.9). The risk of biological hazards is determined by the combined effects of these factors and the subsequent conditions of storage and distribution.

Table 5.9 Factors influencing the microbial content of ready-to-eat meat and poultry products

Factor	Measurement(s)
Ingredients	Types and levels of microorganisms in ingredients which can survive the heating process
Heating	The conditions of heating (e.g. time, temperature, humidity)
Cooling	The method of cooling and potential for recontamination
Product composition	Brine content/water activity Type and amount of fermentable carbohydrate Product pH; type and level of acidulant Level of smoke, liquid or natural Phosphate content Level of residual nitrite Hot oil dipping or flaming to brown the surface Spices, condiments applied to the surface after heating Sodium lactate content
Packaging	Product temperature during packaging and palletizing Degree of vacuumization and leaker formation Rate of oxygen transmission through packaging materials Addition of oxygen scavengers Modified atmosphere content
Contamination after heating	Types and levels of microorganisms contaminating the product between heating and packaging.

Source: Adapted from Tompkin (1986).

5.6 Monitoring

The results of monitoring must become available in time to adjust a processing step and, thereby, prevent a deviation from occurring. This is the ultimate objective of HACCP (i.e. preventing deviations which lead to potential food safety hazards). This means that the methods for monitoring will usually involve a rapid measurement such as visual observation, temperature, time, pH or humidity. Ideally, monitoring should be performed continuously with the information being used to automatically adjust the conditions of the process and prevent a deviation from occurring. If continuous measurement is not possible then, ideally, the frequency of monitoring should be based upon statistics reflecting the variability of the process. The accuracy and reproducibility of the method of monitoring must be considered.

The effectiveness of the HACCP system depends upon the accuracy of the instruments and the education of the individuals who are involved in monitoring. These individuals are often production personnel who are responsible for specific steps in a process. They must be given the means and the training to correctly perform their task(s). They should understand the purpose of the steps in the process for which they are responsible and the importance of monitoring those steps. They should be unbiased in their monitoring and reporting, accurately report their results, and know what to do when the results indicate an unfavorable trend or when a critical limit is not met. They must know that they have front line responsibility for control of specific steps in the process and that the ultimate safety of the final product will depend upon their performance. These individuals must be supported by supervisors and others who are involved in verifying that the CCPs are under control.

5.7 Corrective action

The use of HACCP does not guarantee that food safety hazards will not occur. With an effective HACCP plan and the necessary resources to support the plan fewer problems should occur. Deviations will occur for a variety of reasons even with the best of plans and full implementation. Some deviations may be within the control of management and, perhaps, could be prevented. Just as we do not live in an accident free world we cannot operate totally deviation-free processes. Some deviations will be for natural causes. For example, severe storms can cause loss of electricity and loss of control throughout a facility. Truck accidents unfortunately will occur and the product may become unacceptable due to damage or, in the case of perishable product, loss of refrigeration. An important feature of HACCP is that the deviations will be detected. This then can trigger appropriate corrective actions.

When a deviation occurs a series of possible corrective actions may be required (Tompkin, 1992). The actions are listed in the chronological order that they would normally occur.

- If necessary, stop the operation
- Place all suspect product on hold
- Provide a short term fix so that production can be safely resumed and additional deviations will not occur
- Identify and correct the root cause for failure so that future deviations will not occur
- Dispose of the suspect product in an appropriate manner (see below)
- Record what happened and the actions taken
- If necessary, review and improve the HACCP plan

The options available for disposition of suspect product include:

- Release the product. This is not very wise since a question of safety is involved.
- Test the product to verify whether the product is safe to release. This is a fairly common approach to assess the acceptability of suspect product.

Sampling protocols are available to help decide the number of samples and the likelihood of detecting a defect.
- Divert the product to a safe use. For example, a cooked product which is contaminated with salmonellae could be safely used as an ingredient in a product which is to be retorted.
- Reprocess the product. This may require reworking the product as a raw ingredient or simply, recooking the product.
- Burn, bury, or otherwise destroy the product.

The appropriate disposition of noncompliance product is influenced by the following factors:

- The severity of the potential hazard (e.g. botulism *vs.* illness from *C. perfringens*).
- The risk, or likelihood, of the hazard (e.g. 50% chance *vs.* one in a million).
- Ability to detect the hazard (e.g. glass fragments *vs.* a lost bolt).
- How the food will be stored, shipped and prepared for serving.
- Who will prepare the food.
- Who is the intended consumer (e.g. infants *vs.* normal population).

It is necessary to maintain a record of the deviations that occur. This information should be collected in chronological order in a notebook, file or other means for ready access and review. The information should include what happened, why, the actions taken to prevent future occurrences, the disposition of the product and who had input into the product disposition.

5.8   Record keeping

An effective HACCP plan requires the use of record keeping procedures that will document the HACCP system (NACMCF, 1992). The type and amount of records that may be necessary should reflect the severity and risk of the potential hazards, the methods used to control the hazards, the controllability of the process and the method of recording measurements. A process involving hazards of low risk, low severity and a favorable history of controllability need not be burdened with excessive record keeping. On the other hand a process involving hazards of high risk, high severity and a history of poor control should require more extensive documentation. The type and amount of records can be a highly debatable issue.

The purpose of record keeping is to provide information that can be used to verify that the process has been under control. The records should be retained beyond the expected shelf life of the products. In the event HACCP becomes mandatory then regulatory personnel must have access to the records which pertain to CCPs, deviations, corrective actions and other information which is pertinent to the HACCP plan so the agency can fulfill its responsibilities (NACMCF, 1992, 1994). The specific records which will be available must be resolved. In addition, it will be essential that the records be considered proprietary and not released to the public.

5.9 Verification

Verification is an important aspect of HACCP. A common, simple, but very important, form of verification is for another person (e.g. supervisor, quality assurance personnel) to review the methods being used for monitoring to be sure that monitoring is being performed correctly and that the process is under control. The review also involves checking through the records for deviations and trends. This aspect of verification does not remove responsibility from the person who is responsible for monitoring. Instead, this activity is intended to supplement monitoring and, in a sense, provide a second layer of protection. Verification also involves verifying that critical limits at CCPs are satisfactory and that the facility's HACCP plan is complete, accurate and functioning as planned.

The primary role of regulatory agencies is to verify that HACCP plans are complete, effective and being followed correctly (NACMCF, 1994). Other aspects of verification include validation and revalidation (NACMCF, 1992). A checklist (Table 5.10) has been developed which can serve as a guide when verifying a plant's HACCP plans (Tompkin, 1994).

The sampling plans associated with the 15 cases in Table 5.7 are *not* recommended for routine sampling of finished product to verify the safety of a production lot or to verify that a HACCP plan is operating correctly. End product testing of processed meat and poultry products is not necessary, if the HACCP plans have been properly designed and are operating correctly. In fact, routine end product testing for pathogens should be discouraged since it is an unreliable means to ensure the microbiological safety of foods (NRC, 1985a; ICMSF, 1986, 1988, 1994b; IOM, 1991; NACMCF, 1992).

Recognition of the limitations of end product testing has been a major factor behind the movement to use HACCP to assure the safest possible foods. The sampling plans associated with the 15 cases, however, could be used for sampling finished product when a deviation has occurred and the disposition of a lot is in question. Under these circumstances it may be a matter of either testing or destroying a product. Since the product will be on hold, it will be possible to apply an appropriate sampling plan and collect all the data (e.g. processing records, test results, input from experts) that may be helpful for making a decision. For purposes of verification, appropriate chemical, physical and microbiological tests

Table 5.10 General questionnaire for use in HACCP verification

Name of plant:
Date of review:

- Who is the HACCP team leader?
- Who is responsible for the HACCP plans?
- Is there a HACCP plan for each process?
- Is there a flow diagram for each process?
- Is a simple plant layout available?
- Review the layout. Does the flow of product and people minimize the possibility of cross-contamination?
- Who was responsible for identifying the hazards and CCPs?
- Does that person qualify as an expert in hazard analysis for the type of foods and food processes in the facility?
- Was a generic HACCP plan used as the basis for the plant's HACCP plan?
- If so, which generic plan(s)?
- Have critical limits been established for each CCP in each HACCP plan?
- Who established the limits?
- What rationale was used for the critical limits?
- Who approves a change in a CCP? Is the change documented?
- Select a HACCP plan and review the current process flow. Does it agree with the HACCP plan?
- Who monitors the CCPs?
- Do they understand their role in the HACCP plan?
- Is the monitoring done according to the plan?
- Are the results recorded?
- Who verifies that the CCPs are being monitored correctly?
- Do the operators know the critical limits and when a deviation occurs?
- Do the operators know how to adjust the process to prevent a deviation or does this occur automatically?
- What happens when a deviation occurs?
- Is a plan in place to address deviations at each CCP?
- How is management notified of a deviation?
- Are corrective actions for deviations recorded?
- Is a deviation log book or similar central record being maintained?
- Who is responsible for making decisions on corrective actions?
- Where are the HACCP plan records maintained?
- Are the records available for verification (can they be seen and reviewed)?
- Are all records pertaining to CCPs available?
- Where and how long are they kept?
- Who is responsible for maintaining the records?
- Is the effectiveness of the HACCP plan verified by any physical, chemical or microbiological testing?
- Who collects and interprets the data from tests which are performed for verification?
- Who receives the test results?
- Do the plant manager and his/her staff understand the HACCP concept and support the plant's HACCP system?
- Are those who are directly involved with CCPs adequately trained?
- Who is responsible for training?
- Does the plant have someone on staff who has attended a course in HACCP?
- On the basis of your review is the HACCP plan complete, accurate and being correctly followed?
- Do you have any recommendation for correction or improvement?

Source: Tompkin (1994).

should be applied to verify that the HACCP plan is operating correctly. This may involve, for example, tests for indicator organisms (e.g. total count, coliform) rather than tests for pathogens.

5.10 Should HACCP be mandatory?

The National Research Council's subcommittee on microbiological criteria for foods (NRC, 1985a) recommended that HACCP be mandatory. This recommendation was reached after concluding that the use of micro-biological criteria would not assure food safety. Instead, the committee recognized that the use of HACCP would be more affective and, where appropriate, HACCP should be supplemented with microbiological criteria and testing. The committee provided very few examples of ready-to-eat meat and poultry products for which microbiological criteria would be beneficial.

As previously stated, microbiological testing can be helpful when dealing with suspect product resulting from a deviation. Otherwise, routine end product testing, particularly for pathogens, is not recommended.

The purpose of HACCP is to assure the safety of food to the extent that is possible with current technology. A modification of the Codex guidelines (Codex, 1989) established for determining whether microbiological criteria should be established for a food could be used to decide whether to make a HACCP plan mandatory for a specific food or process. As with microbiological criteria, HACCP should be mandatory when there is a definite need and it can be shown to be effective and practical. Keeping in mind that HACCP is to be used to control chemical, physical and biological hazards in food then the following should be considered (Tompkin, 1994):

- The evidence of hazard to health
- The expected hazards associated with raw materials
- The effect of processing on expected hazards
- The likelihood and consequences of food safety hazards during subsequent handling and storage
- The category of consumer at risk
- The cost benefit ratio associated with the application of HACCP

5.11 Summary

HACCP is an effective management tool for producing the safest possible products with current technology. If a preventable problem occurs, the problem should be detected and potentially hazardous product should be withheld from shipment until the appropriate information can be collected to make an informed decision. The use of HACCP is beneficial to consumers and to protect the business. The cost benefit ratio for HACCP is so favorable that industry should adopt its use independent of future regulatory activity.

References

AMI (1992) *Interim Guideline to Assure the Microbiological Safety of Precooked Meat Patties.* American Meat Institute, Washington, D.C.

Anellis, A., Lubas, J. and Ryman, M.M. (1954) Heat resistance in liquid eggs of some strains of the genus *Salmonella. Food Res.* **19**, 377.

Bacus, J.M. (1986) Fermented meat and poultry products, in Advances in Meat Research – Volume 2. *Meat and Poultry Microbiology* (A.M. Pearson and T.R. Dutson eds), AVI Publishing, Westport, Connecticut. pp. 123–164.

Baird-Parker, A.C., Boothroyd, M. and Jones, E. (1970) The effect of water activity on the heat resistance of heat sensitive and heat resistant strains of salmonellae. *J. Appl. Bacteriol.* **33**, 515.

Bean, N.H., Griffin, P.M., Goulding, J.S. and Ivey, C.B. (1990) Foodborne disease outbreaks, 5-year summary, 1983–1987. *J. Food Prot.* **53**, 711.

Bhaduri, S., Smith, P.W., Palumbo, S.A., Turner-Jones, C.O., Smith, J.L., Marmer, B.S., Buchanan, R.L., Zaika, L.L. and Williams, A.C. (1991) Thermal destruction of *Listeria monocytogenes* in liver sausage slurry. *Food Microbiol.* **8**, 75.

Boyle, D.L., Sofos, J.N. and Schmidt, G.R. (1990) Thermal destruction of *Listeria monocytogenes* in a meat slurry and in ground beef. *J. Food Sci.* **55**, 327.

CDC (1970–1973) *Foodborne Outbreaks* (Four separate reports consisting of annual summaries for 1969, 1970, 1971, and 1972). Centers for Disease Control, Atlanta, Georgia.

CDC (1974–1977) *Foodborne & Waterborne Disease Outbreaks* (Four separate reports consisting of annual summaries for 1973, 1974, 1975 and 1976). Centers for Disease Control, Atlanta, Georgia.

CDC (1979) *Foodborne & Waterborne Disease Surveillance.* Annual Summary for 1977. Centers for Disease Control, Atlanta, Georgia.

CDC (1979–1982) *Foodborne Disease Surveillance* (Five separate reports consisting of annual summaries for 1978 (revised), 1979, 1980, 1981 and 1982). Centers for Disease Control, Atlanta, Georgia.

CDC (1992) Summary of notifiable diseases, United States, 1992. Centers for Disease Control and Prevention. *Morbidity and Mortality Weekly Report*, **41**(55), 58.

Codex (1989) Principles for the establishment and application of microbiological criteria for foods. *CAC Procedural Manual*, 7th edn, Codex Alimentarius Commission, Food and Agriculture Organization, Rome.

Craven, S.E. and Blankenship, L.C. (1983) Increased heat resistance of salmonellae in beef with added soy proteins. *J. Food Prot.*, **46**, 380.

Fain, A.R., Line, J.E., Moran, A.B., Martin, L.M., Lechowich, R.V., Carosella, J.M. and Brown, W.L. (1991) Lethality of heat to *Listeria monocytogenes* Scott A: D-value and Z-value determination in ground beef and turkey. *J. Food Prot.*, **54**, 756.

Farber, J.M. (1989) Thermal resistance of *Listeria monocytogenes* in foods. *Intl. J. Food Microbiol.* **8**, 285.

Farber, J.M. and Brown, B.E. (1990) Effect of prior heat shock on heat resistance of *Listeria monocytogenes* in meat. *Appl. Env. Microbiol.* **56**, 1584.

FDA (1993) *Food Code*. 1993 Recommendations of the United States Public Health Service and Food and Drug Administration. National Technical Information Service, Springfield, Virginia.

Garibaldi, J.A., Straka, R.P. and Ijichi, K. (1969) Heat resistance of *Salmonella* in various egg products. *Appl. Microbiol.* **17**, 491.

Goepfert, J.M., Iskander, I.K. and Amundson, C.H. (1970) Relation of the heat resistance of salmonellae to the water activity of the environment. *Appl. Microbiol.* **19**, 429.

Gonzalez-Cabezas, M.P., Becker, H. and Terplan, G. (1983) Comparative study of the heat resistance of several *Salmonella* serovars from dry products and raw materials. *Arch. Lebensmittelhyg.* **34**, 122.

Goodfellow, S.J. and Brown, W.L. (1978) Fate of *Salmonella* inoculated into beef for cooking. *J. Food Prot.* **41**, 598.

Green, S. (1994) *Status of* L. monocytogenes *sampling program*. Microbiology Division, Science and Technology. Food Safety and Inspection Service, USDA (pers. commun.).

Harrison, M.A. and Huang, Y.-W. (1990) Thermal death times for *Listeria monocytogenes* (Scott A) in crabmeat. *J. Food Prot.* **53**, 878.

ICMSF (1986) *Microorganisms in Foods 2. Sampling for Microbiological Analysis: Principles and Specific Applications*. International Commission on Microbiological Specifications for Foods, 2nd edn. University of Toronto Press, Toronto, Ontario.

ICMSF (1988) *Microorganisms in Foods 4. Application of the Hazard Analysis Critical Control Point (HACCP) System to Ensure Microbiological Safety and Quality*. International Commission on Microbiological Specifications for Foods. Blackwell Scientific, Oxford.

ICMSF (1994) Choice of sampling plan and criteria for *Listeria monocytogenes*. *Intl. J. Food Microbiol.* **22**, 89.

ICMSF (1994) *Microorganisms in Food 5. Characteristics of Microbial Pathogens*. International Commission on Microbiological Specifications for Foods. Chapman & Hall, London.

IOM (1991) *Seafood Safety*. Committee on Evaluation of the Safety of Fishery Products, Institute of Medicine. National Academy Press, Washington, D.C.

Katz, S.E. and Brady, M.S. (1993) Antibiotic residues in food and their significance, in *Antimicrobials in Foods* (P.M. Davidson and A.L. Branen eds), Marcel Dekker, New York. pp. 571–595.

Lammerding, A.M. and Farber, J.M. (1994) The status of *Listeria monocytogenes* in the Canadian Food Industry. *Dairy Food Environ. Sanit.* **14**, 146.

Leslie, G. (1994) *Product Recalls*. Epidemiology and Emergency Programs Staff, Food Safety and Inspection Service, USDA, Washington, D.C. (pers. commun.).

Line, J.E., Fain, A.R., Moran, A.B., Martin, L.M., Lechowich, R.V., Carosella, J.M. and Brown, W.L. (1991) Lethality of heat to *Escherichia coli* 0157:H7: D-value and Z-value determinations in ground beef. *J. Food Prot.* **54**, 762.

Mackey, B.M. and Bratchell, N. (1989) The heat resistance of *Listeria monocytogenes*. *Lett. Appl. Microbiol.* **9**, 89.

Mackey, B.M., Prichet, C., Norris, A. and Mead, G.C. (1990) Heat resistance of *Listeria*: Strain differences and effect of meat type and curing salts. *Lett. Appl. Microbiol.* **10**, 251.

McAuley, J.B., Michelson, M.K. and Schantz, P.M. (1991) Trichinosis surveillance, United States, 1987–1990. *CDC Surveillance Summaries, Morbidity Mortality Weekly Report* **40** (SS-3), 35.

Milone, N.A. and Watson, B.S. (1970) Thermal inactivation of Salmonella senftenberg 775W in poultry meat. *Health Lab. Sci.* **7**, 199.

NACMCF (1991) *Listeria monocytogenes*. Recommendations by the National Advisory Committee on Microbiological Criteria for Foods. *Intl. J. Food Microbiol.* **14**, 185.

NACMCF (1992) Hazard analysis and critical control point system. *Intl. J. Food Microbiol.* **16**, 1.

NACMCF (1993) Principles of risk assessment for illness caused by foodborne biological agents (unpublished draft report). National Advisory Committee on Microbiological Criteria for Food.

NACMCF (1994) The role of regulatory agencies and industry in HACCP. *Intl. J. Food Microbiol.* **21**, 187.

Ng, H., Bayne, H.G. and Garibaldi, J.A. (1969) Heat resistance of *Salmonella*: the uniqueness of *Salmonella senftenberg* 775W. *Appl. Microbiol.* **17**, 78.

NRC (1985a) *An Evaluation of the Role of Microbiological Criteria for Foods and Food Ingredients*. Subcommittee on Microbiological Criteria, National Research Council. National Academy Press, Washington, D.C.

NRC (1985b) *Meat and Poultry Inspection. The Scientific Basis of the Nation's Program*.

Committee on the Scientific Basis of the Nation's Meat and Poultry Inspection Program, National Research Council, National Academy Press, Washington, D.C.

NRC (1987) *Poultry Inspection. The Basis for a Risk-Assessment Approach*. Committee on Public Health Risk Assessment of Poultry Inspection Programs, National Research Council, National Academy Press, Washington, D.C.

Osborne, W.W., Straka, R.P. and Lineweaver, H. (1954) Heat resistance of strains of *Salmonella* in liquid whole egg, egg yolk, and egg white. *Food Res.* **19**, 451.

Quintavalla, S. and Campanini, M. (1991) Effect of rising temperature on the heat resistance of *Listeria monocytogenes* in meat emulsion. *Lett. Appl. Microbiol.* **12**, 184.

Read, R.B., Bradshaw, J.G., Dickerson, R.W. and Peeler, J.T. (1968) Thermal resistance of salmonellae isolated from dry milk. *Appl. Microbiol.* **16**, 998.

Sofos, J.N., Schmidt, G.R., Boonmasiri, N. and Yen, L. (1992) Thermal destruction of *Listeria monocytogenes* in meat products, in *Volume 4, Proc. 38th Intl. Cong. Meat Sci. Technol. August 23–28*, Clermont, France.

Tompkin, R.B. (1986) Microbiology of ready-to-eat meat and poultry products, in Advances in Meat Research – Volume 2. *Meat and Poultry Microbiology* (A.M. Pearson and T.R. Dutson eds), AVI Publishing, Westport, Connecticut. pp. 89–121.

Tompkin, R.B. (1990) The use of HACCP in the production of meat and poultry products. *J. Food Prot.* **53**, 795.

Tompkin, R.B. (1992) Corrective action procedures for deviations from the critical control point critical limits, in *HACCP. Principles and Applications* (M.D. Pierson and D.A. Corlett eds), Van Nostrand Rheinhold, New York. pp. 72–89.

Tompkin, R.B. (1994) HACCP in the meat and poultry industry. *Food Control* **5**, 153–161.

Tompkin, R.B. and Borchert, L.L. (1992) Impact of microbiology on safety and shelf life of processed meats, in *44th Ann. Recip. Meat Conf., Am. Meat Sci. Assoc.*, National Livestock and Meat Board, Chicago. pp. 43–52.

Tompkin, R.B., Christiansen, L.N., Shaparis, A.B., Baker, R.L. and Schroeder, J.M. (1992) Control of *Listeria monocytogenes* in processed meats. *Food Australia* **44**, 370.

USDA (1982) Requirements for the production of cooked beef, roast beef, and cooked corned beef. 9 CFR 318.17. *Federal Register* **47**, 31854.

USDA (1987) Species identification sampling for cooked product. *FSIS Directive 10,230.1*, dated 10/14/87. US Department of Agriculture, Food Safety and Inspection Service, Washington, D.C.

USDA (1990) Microbiological monitoring program: sampling, testing procedures and actions for *Listeria monocytogenes* and *Salmonella*. *FSIS Directive 10,240.1, Rev. 1*, dated 8/30/90. US Department of Agriculture, Food Safety and Inspection Service, Washington, D.C.

USDA (1992a) Recall of inspected meat and poultry product. *FSIS Directive 8080.1 Rev. 2*, dated 11/3/92. US Department of Agriculture, Food Safety and Inspection Service, Washington, D.C.

USDA (1992b) Prescribed treatment of pork and products containing pork to destroy trichinae. US Department of Agriculture, Food Safety and Inspection Service. 9 CFR 318.10, *Code of Federal Regulations*, US Government Printing Office, Washington, D.C.

USDA (1992c) Prescribed treatment of pork and products containing pork to destroy trichinae. 9 CFR 318.10. *Federal Register* **57**, 27874.

USDA (1992d) Poultry products containing pork: trichinae treatment. 9 CFR 381.147. *Federal Register* **57**, 28083.

USDA (1993a) Heat processing procedures, cooking instructions, and cooling, handling, and storage requirements for uncured meat patties. 9 CFR 318.23. *Federal Register* **58**, 41138.

USDA (1993b) Performance based inspection system (PBIS) tasks for heat processed, uncured meat patties. *FSIS Notice 55–93*, dated 9/28/93. US Department of Agriculture, Food Safety and Inspection Service, Washington, D.C.

USDA (1993c) Instructions for verifying internal temperature and holding time of meat patties. *FSIS Directive 7370.1*, dated 9/28/93. US Department of Agriculture, Food Safety and Inspection Service, Washington, D.C.

USDA (1993d) Foreign particle contamination of meat or poultry products. *FSIS Directive 7310.4, Rev. 2*, dated 12/28/93. US Department of Agriculture, Food Safety and Inspection Service, Washington, D.C.

WHO (1988) *Foodborne Listeriosis*. Report of a WHO Informal Working Party. WHO/EHE/
FOS/88.5. World Health Organization, Geneva.
Yen, L.C., Sofos, J.N. and Schmidt, G.R. (1991) Effect of meat curing ingredients on
thermal destruction of *Listeria monocytogenes* in ground pork. *J. Food Prot.* **54**, 408.
Yen, L.C., Sofos, J.N. and Schmidt, G.R. (1992) Thermal destruction of *Listeria
monocytogenes* in ground pork with water, sodium chloride and other curing ingredients.
Lebensm.-Wiss. u.-Technol. **25**, 61.

Addendum Guideline for writing Operating Instructions/HACCP Plans for processed meat and poultry products[1]

This guideline for writing Operating Instructions/HACCP Plans is based upon the principles, definitions and procedures developed by the NACMCF (1992). The NACMCF report should be used to resolve questions that might arise and for additional information. This guideline can be adapted for use in a variety of processes (e.g. slaughtering) other than for making processed products. Operating instructions describe how a product is made and the factors that must be controlled to assure the product is safe and in compliance with product quality and regulatory requirements.

Previous experience has shown that a separate HACCP document is impressive for showing customers and inspectors, but the HACCP plans are seldom used by the plant and are often out of date. For this reason and others it is better to incorporate the HACCP plans into the operating instructions. It will then be possible to simultaneously verify and update the HACCP plans and the operating instructions. Also, the information will be more widely available to plant personnel.

Pertinent sections of the operating instructions can be transferred to work sheets for the operators in the plant. The work sheets can specify the factors that must be controlled, criteria that must be met, and information that must be recorded.

The criteria in the instruction define the parameters, limits or targets required for each step in the process. All the criteria are important for meeting the product requirements. In this guideline, the steps in the process which are critical to product safety (i.e. critical control points or CCPs) are capitalized and given a double asterisk (**). The steps which are especially important for product quality or regulatory compliance (i.e. control points or CPs) are capitalized and given a single asterisk (*).

The language and procedure for writing the Operating Instructions/ HACCP Plans has been standardized. In this guideline the process will begin with the first action step (e.g. grinding, blending) in the formulation room. Pickle formulating, where appropriate for the product, will have its own instruction. The receiving and holding of raw meat, other ingredients,

[1]Developed by M.E. Kenagy, F.J. Alexander, R.B. Tompkin *et al.* in the Armour Swift-
Eckrich Quality Assurance Department. © Armour Swift-Eckrich, 1994.

and packaging materials should be covered by a general operating procedure. An example of a form for the operating instruction/HACCP plan is as follows:

Operating Instruction/HACCP Plan

Product/description: Brand:
This covers the following UPCs:
EST. No: Plant:
Issue No: Date: Prepared by:

Approvals: Quality   Plant   Operations: R&D:
                  Assurance: Manager:

Meat ingredients:	pounds
Non meat ingredients:	pounds
	Total

Operation   *Procedure*   *Criteria*   *Freq.*   *Res.*   *Ver.*

                   Comments/
                   corrective action:

                   Comments/
                   corrective action:

                   Comments
                   corrective action:

Add additional operations as necessary to complete instruction.

A.1 Headings

After filling in the information at the top of the form, it is then necessary to describe the process, specify criteria, who is responsible for monitoring and verifying, and provide information on corrective actions and record keeping. The following information will serve as a guide for completing the form.

A.1.1 Operation. Use action verbs to describe the action at each step in the process. Collectively, the boxes constitute the flow diagram for the process.

A.1.2 Procedure. Describe the action(s) that occur at each step in the process.

A.1.3 Criteria. Specify critical limits for CCPs; other limits for control points. Temperatures, holding times, mixing times, vacuum settings, casing sizes, length, diameter, etc. fall under this heading. Reference QA procedures where applicable.

> *Freq.* (Frequency) State how often checks must be made.
> 1/ba   = 1/batch
> 1/hr   = 1/hour
> 1/sh   = 1/shift
> etc.

> *Res.* (Responsibility) State who is responsible for checking.
> OP   = Hourly line worker
> SUP   = Production Supervisor
> QA   = Quality Assurance Inspector
> QAM   = QA Manager
> MEC   = Mechanic

> *Ver.* (Verification) State who is responsible for verifying that a step in the process is under control.
> RECORDS MUST BE KEPT FOR ALL ACTIONS AND MEASUREMENTS MADE AT CRITICAL CONTROL POINTS

> *Comments.* Insert information that helps to clarify something or describes how to deal with a problem that may occur (i.e. corrective action).

A.2   Critical Control Point (CCP)

A CCP is a point, step or procedure at which control can be applied and a food safety hazard can be prevented, eliminated, or reduced to acceptable levels.

All steps in the process that are CCPs are identified with two asterisks (**), capitalized, and listed under the heading, Criteria.

A.2.1   Examples of CCPs:

> *Species of meat.* Some individuals are sensitive to certain species of meat. They can avoid this problem only if the meat in the product agrees with the ingredient statement. Also, beef products which become contaminated with pork may not be processed adequately to destroy *T. spiralis* or *T. gondii* which may be in the pork.
> ** IDENTIFY MEAT SPECIES FOR COMPATIBILITY WITH PRODUCT

Bone removal.   Bone fragments can cause injury to consumers.
   ** OPERABLE BONE COLLECTOR ADJUSTED TO MAXIMUM

Nitrite concentration.   Excessive levels of nitrite in a product can cause illness or death to consumers. The maximum amount permitted in cured meat is 156 ppm, except for bacon (120 ppm).
   ** VERIFY CURE BAG ADDITION
In comments section state
   ** EACH LOT OF CURE BAGS TESTED BY SUPPLIER
                              or
   ** TEST EACH LOT OF CURE UPON RECEIPT FOR PROPER NITRITE LEVEL BEFORE USE

Cooking temperature.   The minimum internal temperatures required by USDA often exceed what is needed for food safety. For example, 62.8°C (145°F) or its equivalent in roast beef is based upon killing 10^6/g of salmonellae or *E. coli* 0157:H7 in the coldest area of the roast. It should be obvious then that the USDA requirements of 71°C (160°F) in uncured turkey breast is based upon product quality (i.e. doneness) and not food safety. For uniformity throughout all procedures, the USDA requirement is specified as a CCP whether or not it is minimum required for safety. In addition, corporate target levels should be specified. The corporate target levels normally exceed the USDA requirement and are CPs, not CCPs. Thus, a single asterisk is used.
   Corporate target levels may be higher than USDA requirements for several reasons. One reason is to minimize the risk that due to variability in cooking none of a lot will fail to meet the USDA requirement (i.e. the critical limit). Other reasons may be for killing heat resistant spoilage bacteria (i.e. shelf life) or to achieve certain desirable product characteristics.
   ** INTERNAL TEMP: 68°C (155°F) (USDA) Cured turkey product
    * INTERNAL TEMP: 70°C (158°F) (Corp)
   ** INTERNAL TEMP: 71°C (160°F) (USDA) Noncured turkey product
    * INTERNAL TEMP: 73°C (164°F) (Corp)

Metal detection.   Metal fragments can cause injury to consumers.
   ** OPERABLE METAL DETECTOR SET FOR 1.5 mm FERROUS AND 2.5 mm
      NONFERROUS

If the adjustment size is not known state:
   ** OPERABLE METAL DETECTOR SET AT MAXIMUM FOR THE PRODUCT AND
      CONDITIONS

A.3   Control Point (CP)

A CP is a point, step or procedure at which biological, physical or chemical factors which are not harmful to consumers can be controlled. This differs from the definition for control point in the NACMCF report.
   All steps in the process that are control points are identified by a single asterisk (*), capitalized, and listed under the heading, Criteria.

A.3.1   Examples of CPS:

Temperature of raw meat ingredients. Incoming meat temperatures can influence product quality.
* MAX. MEAT TEMP: 2°C (36°F)

Rework. Improper handling of rework can cause quality problems due to microbial spoilage, color fading, rancidity, and other product defects. Always list information about how rework should be correctly handled.
* MAX. % REWORK: 5%
* MAX. AGE: 5 days
* MAX. TEMP: 4°C (40°F)

Time and temperature relationships. Time and temperature must be controlled at various steps to produce products of the desired quality (e.g. shelf life, sliceability). State product temperatures, cooler and blast freezer temperatures, holding times, required product temperatures, who is responsible for checking these and how often they are checked. State who verifies that this is being done and whether records are kept.
* COOLER TEMP: −2–0°C (28–32°F)
* MAX. HOLD TIME: 24 hours
* PRODUCT TEMP: 0–2°C (32–36°F)

Product touchers. If product touching is not considered a product safety issue, it may be a control point for quality.
* NO TOUCHERS

Yield checks. USDA requires these for certain products.
* YIELD CHECKS

Net Weight. Specify information required to satisfy net weight requirements.
* PROPERLY CALIBRATED, TARED SCALE

Leaker packages. Where applicable, list information about leakers.
* NO LEAKERS

Code dating. Code dating is a CP because this information is essential to successfully initiate, monitor, and then verify the effectiveness of a recall.
* JULIAN CODE DATE
     or (whichever is applicable)
* SELL BY CODE DATE

The instruction should include the pallet pattern for all UPCs.
——— boxes/layer
——— layers/pallet
——— boxes/pallet

End the procedure with shipping. The Operating Instructions/HACCP Plans do not need to explain the criteria for shipping. This information should be covered in a general operating procedure for shipping and holding packaged products.

6 Implementation of the HACCP program by the fresh and processed seafood industry

E.S. GARRETT, M. HUDAK-ROOS and D.R. WARD

6.1 Introduction

The United States seafood industry is among the nation's oldest industries and has many dynamic environmental, sociopolitical, and economic interactions. Within this interactive matrix is the additional challenge of producing a safe product in a system that comprises a complicated nesting of resource availability, harvesting, and global trade issues.

6.2 Significance of the seafood industry

6.2.1 Resources

From a domestic producer's perspective, a major underlying concern begins with the need for understanding and protecting fishery habitats to economically sustain a recurring fishery resource (Figure 6.1). Coastal estuaries serve as a breeding ground and habitat for over 75% of US commercial and 80–90% of the recreational catch of fish and shellfish. These coastal habitats annually produce hundreds of wild species. Nearly 300 000 fisherpersons using 94 000 vessels commercially harvest the US fishery resources (NMFS, NOAA, 1994). Unlike land-based food animal production systems, commercial seafood harvesters compete with a large recreational entity. One estimate indicates that wild species of US fishery resources are subject to 17 000 000 recreational anglers deploying millions of boats and vessels (NMFS, NOAA, 1994). In 1993 US per capita consumption of commercially harvested species averaged nearly 15.0 lbs (NMFS, NOAA, 1994). The US per capita consumption for 1993 of recreational harvested seafoods is not available but historically has been estimated to be 3 to 4 lbs (NMFS, NOAA, 1989).

Wild seafood resources are supplemented by species derived from aquaculture. In 1992, the estimated US aquaculture production was nearly 313 000 metric tonnes consisting of baitfish, catfish, salmon, trout, clams, crawfish, mussels, oysters, shrimp, and a number of miscellaneous species, such as ornamental fish, alligators, algae, tilapia, hybrid striped bass,

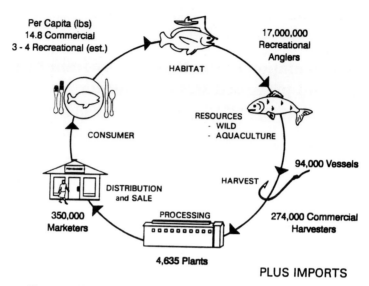

Figure 6.1 The US fisheries system. *Source*: NMFS, NOAA (1994).

numerous aquatic plants, etc. Interestingly, many of these species are produced and processed throughout the country, and not just in the coastal regions of the coastal states (NMFS, NOAA, 1994).

6.2.2 Fishery habitats

Fishery habitats may influence food safety due to concerns over pollution, agriculture run-off, sewage disposal, and natural marine organisms, such as dinoflagellates that produce toxins harmful to humans. These food safety concerns encompass long-term (chronic concerns) and short-term (acute) issues, both of which are not fully understood.

6.2.3 US imports of fishery products

Along with habitat, the US fishery system has significant resource concerns. US seafood businesses cannot rely solely on domestically produced products. For that matter, neither can any highly industrialized nation. For a number of years over 50% of the US consumption of seafoods has relied on foreign produced products. In 1993, the USA imported 53% of its total consumption of seafoods, which originated from 172 countries. The trend for economic reliance on seafood imports has been relatively stable for the past 10 years to the extent that the USA is now the world's second largest importer of seafoods. Figure 6.2 indicates

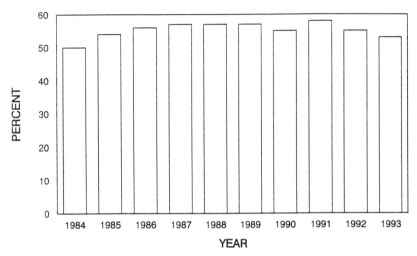

Figure 6.2 Seafood imports as a percentage of US per capita consumption. Percent figure based on calculated edible meat weight basis. *Source*: Koplan (1994).

the 10 year trend of reliance on foreign seafood products as a function of percentage of US consumption (Koplan, 1994).

Currently, the principal imported species are shrimp, tuna, lobster, groundfish, and salmon. It is estimated that seafoods exported to the USA are handled in 8125 processing facilities (FDA, 1994a). Seafood imports also include large volumes of aquacultured products. In 1993, it was estimated that the USA imported two billion dollars in cultured products, primarily shrimp and salmon.

When dealing with seafood imports, it can be difficult to determine the harvest waters. For example, Table 6.1 depicts the principal countries from which salmon was imported in 1988. Neither Switzwerland nor Panama possess salmon fishery resources, yet they appear as exporting countries. Transshipment of fishery products through several countries, often for value-added purposes, complicate the food safety chain.

6.2.4 Exports of fishery products

US participation in the international trading of seafoods is incredibly complex since not only is it the world's second largest importer of seafoods, but it is also the world's leading exporter of such commodities. For example, in 1993 the USA exported seafoods to 162 countries (Koplan, 1994). The increasing export trend has come about with the full development of the Northwest and Alaska fisheries and improved efficiencies in processing techniques. Major US exports include salmon, crabs, surimi, fishblocks, groundfish, flatfish, shrimp and lobsters. Instead of importing blocks of surimi, US labor rates and processing efficiencies

Table 6.1 Imports: salmon fresh

Country	Pounds (lbs)	Metric tonnes	US Dollars
Norway	16 843 368	7640.02	56 553 813
Canada	8 497 888	3854.56	19 750 777
United Kingdom	1 245 073	564.76	4 811 866
Switzerland	32 240	14.62	62 289
Panama	6244	2.83	25 163
Chile	1 838 259	833.82	3 990 825
Denmark	702 580	318.68	2 200 360
New Zealand	293 925	133.32	919 994
Total	29 459 557	13 362.61	88 315 087

are such that those items are now exported to Asia, representing a major breakthrough for US fishery exports. US exports of aquacultured products include Rainbow trout, Atlantic salmon, tilapia, catfish, freshwater crayfish and live mussels exported to 19 countries in Europe, North and South America, and Asia. The fascinating dichotomy of being the world's largest exporter of seafoods and the second largest importer of such commodities requires that US participation in international trading of seafoods be extremely complicated when developing marketing and import/export food control and inspection strategies, including Hazard Analysis and Critical Control Point (HACCP) concepts (Garrett and Jahncke, 1994).

6.2.5   Challenges facing the US seafood industry

The US fishery system's food safety program is further challenged by changes in the US corporate structure. Within the past 10 years, there has been an acceleration of changing industry conditions. For example, there have been numerous agribusiness mergers resulting from non-seafood oriented food companies purchasing seafood operations. Agribusiness consolidations, coupled with economic stress, have led to more sophisticated wholesale buying techniques of seafood products, particularly as many seafood firms have had to downsize their inventory operations. Many of the changes currently occurring within the seafood industry are leading to an increased business sophistication, particularly in the areas of (1) raw material acquisition, (2) processing and packaging methods, (3) inventory and shipping procedures, and (4) national and international regulatory interfaces.

6.2.6   Food safety in the US fishery system

Detailed understanding of the food safety issues faced by the fishery system have been obscured by the vocal public debate on the safety of the

US seafood supply. Apart from the recent focus on the need to reduce microbial pathogens on meat and poultry, the issue of seafood product quality and safety has been one of the more extensively debated legislative consumer topics. From a regulatory perspective, the debate represents the initiation of an evolutionary and large scale legislative effort to reexamine all regulatory food control and inspection systems. While the specific outcomes of the discussion are uncertain, change is inevitable. As the 21st century approaches and rapidly evolving technology allows microconstituents and minute levels of contaminants to be measured in foods, without a concurrent understanding of the public health relevance there must be change.

There are sophisticated and many seemingly unrelated, but complimentary factors such as increased consumer awareness; shrinking budgetary resources; changing product forms; the need to harmonize food standards internationally to facilitate trade; and increased reliance on imported food products which are forcing regulatory officials and legislators alike to reexamine the current levels of acceptable risk. Incumbent in the new examination of previously established acceptable risk levels is the need to search for new innovative control and inspection strategies to manage the public risk. These strategies must incorporate the changing scientific, technical, sociological, legal and institutional realities, without a diminution of current food control and risk management precepts. An introspection and review of the scientific, technical, sociopolitical, and institutional basis upon which the current food control strategies are based and their relevance to the current state of technology must be reformulated for the regulatory future of food safety (Garrett *et al.*, 1994).

As a non-integrated and independent function to this conclusion, the National Academy of Sciences (NAS) has recommended that regulatory agencies move away from traditional food inspection strategies and proceed rapidly toward a more science-based approach, namely the Hazard Analysis Critical Control Point (HACCP) system (NAS, 1985a,b, 1987, 1990, 1991).

6.3   HACCP in the seafood industry

6.3.1   Background

HACCP is an industry driven concept that provides a preventive system for hazard control. It is based upon a systematic approach to define hazards and critical control points within the system. It requires both industry and government participation, with the industry's role primarily being to design and execute the system and the government's role primarily that of approving the industry system design, verification and, in some cases, technical assistance. In 1985, NAS (1985a) indicated that while HACCP has worked well for the low-acid canned food industry, it had not been successfully transferred to other food commodities. They pointed out that HACCP must be an industry driven program with the role of the regulatory agency being that of approval of the industry's basic element design, on-site verification, and training.

In the USA, credit for the development of HACCP (for foods) is given to the 1971 *Food Protection Conference* (APHA, 1972), with its first industry application by The Pillsbury Company for astronaut feeding during the inception of the NASA Space Program. The basic concepts of HACCP, however, are found in the Hazard Opportunity Studies (HAZOP), which have been employed by the chemical and engineering industries for hazard controls dating back to the mid 1930s (Mayes and Kilsby, 1989).

6.3.2 Benefits of HACCP

A clear distinction must be made between HACCP, which is an industry driven and operated system, and HACCP-based inspectional techniques that are employed in regulatory control programs. As indicated by Bryan (1988), HACCP itself is not a regulatory inspection system and should not be viewed in that light. Rather, HACCP-based regulatory inspection systems have to be developed with 'new eyes', requiring more sophisticated understanding of the actual processes. From a regulatory perspective, one of the benefits of the HACCP concept is that, if properly implemented by industry, governmental inspection frequencies should be much lower in facilities employing HACCP than in those operating solely under Good Manufacturing Practices (GMPs). This should also be true when examining food products for which there is an unknown production history such as imports. HACCP is a system that focuses on hazards and their prevention, and in that light, can be viewed as non-traditional. HACCP truly separates the essential from the non-essential and allows for a systematic focusing of resources to prevent major errors. It is not a perfect system, however, even when applied in a HACCP-based regulatory inspection program. The system is unique, representing state-of-the-art industry hazard control techniques, and has applications in many other industries well beyond the food industry.

6.3.2.1 HACCP – two part system. HACCP is a two-part system. The first part requires that a flow diagram be developed which details each operational step in the process. Then a hazard analysis must be conducted to determine all significant hazards. The analysis is done relative to the end-use of the product and with a determination of the probability (likelihood) and severity of the hazard. Included in identifying hazards is the determination of preventive measures for each hazard. With the assistance of a decision tree, the best Critical Control Points (CCPs) for each significant hazard can be determined. Each CCP then has criteria developed: 'critical limits', for the preventive measure associated with the CCP; monitoring procedures to be in place to determine that hazards are being controlled; pre-planned 'corrective actions' to be followed when deviations occur from the critical limits; record keeping procedures to document that the HACCP system is working effectively; and, verification procedures conducted on a frequency sufficient to demonstrate that the entire HACCP system is operationally accurate, according to the written HACCP plan, and effectively implemented. These requirements are generally referred to as the seven principles of HACCP (NACMCF, 1992; CFPRA, 1992; CAC, 1993).

HACCP is a dynamic program that requires an active role by plant personnel and management. While the hazard analysis, CCP determination, and establishment of the critical limits appear to be 'done once', each must be verified to ensure that the HACCP plan is accurate and effective. If any process or product change occurs, an evaluation of the previous hazard analysis must be done. Process or product modifications can eliminate or add new hazards. The same reasoning follows for CCPs and critical limits. These important principles also should be verified if a product is implicated in a foodborne illness or injury.

Monitoring, corrective actions, and record keeping, usually considered the 'active components' of a HACCP system, must also be verified. These are usually verified on a more frequent basis than the hazard analysis, CCPs, or critical limits. Included in verification are the important steps of validating that the critical limits are suitable for their intended purpose, management review of records, calibration of equipment, confirmation of corrective actions and proper product dispositions (Hudak-Roos and Garrett, 1991).

6.3.3   History of HACCP in the seafood industry

Various aspects of HACCP have been explored for use in the seafood industry since the early 1970s. First to examine the HACCP principle of hazard analysis in terms of integrated numerically weighted product risk potential was the National Marine Fisheries Service's (NMFS) National Seafood Inspection Laboratory (NSIL) (Garrett et al., 1977). The laboratory examined risk potentials of seafood products through the design of a numerical risk potential index system. Such a system surrounds the HACCP principal hazard analysis, because the risk potential indices (values) were calculated from a detailed examination of the hazards associated with seafoods, such as harvest area, processing type, intended consumer group, etc. In this reference, the risk potential indices were aligned to the laboratory analytical priority that a NMFS inspected seafood end product should receive. The indices, however, also could apply to the amount of due diligence in terms of care, custody and control needed to produce a safe product.

Another look at HACCP applications for seafood was done by Lee (1977), who described some principles for analyzing hazards. One of his lasting contributions to seafood hazard analysis was the table on seafood hazard categories in order of decreasing risk (Table 6.2). This table defines the hazard analysis rule of thumb still used today. In general, the risk increases with more handling, higher storage temperatures, and if the product is not further cooked by the end user.

Lee (1977) applied a hazard analysis and outlined HACCP Critical Control Points (CCPs) for three US Northwest seafood industries: smoked fish, dungeness crab, and cooked shrimp processing. While concentrating on microbial hazards and their control, Lee (1977) also was one of the first to recognize the importance of influencing factors, such as harvesting, consumer abuse potential, plant layout and construction, sanitation, etc. in pinpointing CCPs. Later, Lee and Hilderbrand (1992) expanded on the earlier seafood HACCP work.

Except for low acid canned foods, such as canned fish, HACCP principles were virtually ignored by the seafood industry until the late 1980s. Low acid canned seafoods were produced under HACCP controls because of regulations promulgated in 1973 (CFR, 1992a,b,c). These regulations were instituted because of a *Clostridium botulinum* threat in canned mushrooms, which could endanger many consumers. Since the *Clostridium botulinum* concern, as well as other microbiological concerns, existed for other low acid canned food commodities, a more structured

Table 6.2 Seafood end product hazard analysis[a]

Category (Decreasing risk)	Description	Example
1	Heat-processed foods usually consumed without additional cooking	Cooked shrimp
2	Nonheat-processed raw foods often consumed without additional cooking	Shucked molluscan shellfish eaten raw
3	Formulated foods usually consumed after cooking	Fish sticks and breaded shrimp
4	Nonheat-processed raw foods usually consumed after cooking	Fresh or frozen fish fillets and cooked molluscan shellfish
5	Raw seafoods usually consumed after cooking	Live crustacean and molluscan shellfish

[a]Lee (1977)

mandatory regulatory control program based upon HACCP principles was created.

HACCP became a common term in the seafood industry in the late 1980s when Congress mandated the National Oceanic and Atmospheric Administration (NOAA) to conduct a study to design a new, improved system of seafood surveillance based on HACCP (US Congress, 1986, 1988). The study was directed by NOAA's National Marine Fisheries Service (NMFS) National Seafood Inspection Laboratory (NSIL).

6.3.3.1 Recommendations of the National Academy of Sciences. Already experienced in HACCP, NSIL based their study on recommendations made by the National Academy of Sciences (NAS, 1985a,b). In part, these recommendations included:

1. HACCP application requires technical expertise in the food product. The expertise must be used to analyze the hazards, identify CCPs, and establish effective monitoring. Therefore, a food industry should develop its own HACCP system, with just the minimum requirements and outline offered by the regulatory agency.

2. Training is required for regulatory officials as well as food processing personnel.

3. The use of HACCP for the food industry should be expanded beyond the low acid canned food industry and should be made mandatory.

6.3.3.2 Model Seafood Surveillance Project. In order to institute the NAS recommendations, NMFS designed a project to produce a description and associated costs for a new mandatory seafood inspection program based on HACCP. The project stressed industry involvement, training, and the use of the developed system as mandatory. The project was called the Model Seafood Surveillance Project, or MSSP for short (NMFS, 1987, 1989, 1990).

In order to provide for a new program that addressed the principal hazards in the consumption of seafood as well as their associated regulatory concerns at that time, the MSSP thoroughly examined the HACCP concept and its current applications. While the history of HACCP in the food processing arena was based on microbiological safety concerns at the processing level, HACCP had been successfully applied in other manufacturing concerns to cover areas other than safety. Also, emerging HACCP publications gave a clear indication of an evolutionary trend as more and more HACCP application experts were giving credence to the use of sanitation critical control points and the expansion of HACCP beyond microbiology and low acid canned foods to include chemical and physical hazards and other commodity processes.

Thus, the MSSP team came to the conclusion that for a new program to be effective, adequate, and cost resourceful, it must cover fishery products from harvest through consumption. The team also concluded that an expanded HACCP concept, one that covers and includes critical control points for not only food safety but wholesomeness (plant and food hygiene) and economic malpractice concerns, has value and should be researched through the study's operation (Garrett and Hudak-Roos, 1991).

6.4   HACCP and seafood safety

The MSSP began with an examination of seafood safety. Fueled by inflammatory media reports, the public's perception of seafood safety was degenerating quickly. Therefore, in order to focus a new mandatory HACCP-based seafood inspection program on real needs, the issues surrounding seafood safety had to be clarified. Through examination of seafood-borne illness data collected by the Centers for Disease Control (CDC) and analyzed for the years 1978–1986, the major seafood safety issues were determined to be: ciguatoxin, scombrotoxin (histamine poisoning) and the consumption of raw molluscan shellfish (bacterial pathogens, viruses and biotoxins such as Paralytic Shellfish Poison).

6.4.1   CDC seafood safety data

The CDC data indicated that these three major issues were not as widespread as perceived. For example, more than 80% of all the seafood-borne illnesses were reported from only nine states or territories and just under one-half of the reports came from four of these nine states or territories. It was recognized, however, that the nine states and territories in question were among the better reporting entities to CDC. Also, the three principal seafood-borne illness issues encompassed over 80% of all seafood-borne illness reports, but were found in less than 50 species of the 500 species in the US marketplace. Nonetheless, when compared to other foodstuffs, seafood safety raised certain questions. Seafood-borne illness data reported to CDC represented only about 5% of all foodborne illness cases. However, of the animal protein sources (beef, poultry, other meats), seafood was reported to be the etiological vehicle in over 50% of all illness outbreaks (CDC, 1979, 1981, 1983a,b, 1985, 1989, 1990).

6.4.1.1   Seafood surveillance system.   In order to more accurately define these seafood safety issues so that a focussed and comprehensive seafood HACCP surveillance system could be designed, MSSP contracted with the National Academy of Sciences (NAS). Specifically, NAS was asked to:

1. Meet with appropriate federal government personnel and selected state government agencies to determine perspectives on seafood safety, to learn about seafood safety control programs, and to hear the concerns and recommendations of these agencies. Control programs conducted by these agencies were to be evaluated and recommendations for improvement made.
2. Collect and examine data on seafood-borne illnesses in the USA.
3. Evaluate the efficacy of the current system(s) for reporting and documenting seafood-borne illnesses. Evaluate the adequacy of current mechanisms for advising the fishing industry and the public of desirable or necessary actions to ameliorate problems caused by seafood-borne illness.
4. Identify the cause of illness in nine targeted states and territories from consumption of either commercially or recreationally caught seafood in relation to the species and percentages of fishery products implicated in such illnesses, the demography of affected consumers, and the possible role of ethnic dietary habits or improper handling by the consumer. This task included a review of how the US food control system addresses major health hazards associated with fishery products, as well as recommendations for improvements.
5. Examine contemporary procedures for identifying, detecting, and quantifying etiological agents in seafood, along with the methods used, pertinent scientific research, and recommendations for improvement.
6. Review the role of imported fishery products in reports of seafood-borne outbreaks of illness in the USA and examine the relative prevalence and significance of imported and domestic seafoods as vehicles.
7. Conduct a statistical evaluation of FDA's acceptance sampling plans and associated decision criteria, with an evaluation of the quality assurance principles and procedures used by FDA to accept results of private testing laboratories for blocklisted imported products, and make recommendations for improvements.
8. Review contaminants associated with seafoods and assess how well the current regulatory framework protects public health.
9. Assess indices of health risk assessment already determined by FDA and EPA for selected environmental pollutants that have an impact on fisheries, and recommend future research directions.

The NAS Committee on Evaluation of the Safety of Fishery Products completed and reported on these nine tasks in *Seafood Safety* (NAS, 1991). The assessments and recommendations made within that text provide the basis for improved seafood safety in a new mandatory HACCP-based surveillance program, as described by the MSSP (NMFS, 1995).

6.5 Seafood industry workshops

The MSSP designed an operational approach that encompassed production (harvest, aquaculture) through consumption (retail, consumer education) with an expanded HACCP surveillance concept (safety, wholesomeness, economic malpractice). In cooperation with the National Fisheries Education Research Foundation (NFERF) of the National Fisheries Institute (NFI) under a Saltonstall-Kennedy grant, NMFS personnel assigned to the MSSP conducted 49 seafood industry workshops.

Workshops were held for the following commodities:

breaded shrimp
cooked shrimp
raw shrimp
blue crab
molluscan shellfish
smoked and cured fish
breaded fish and specialty items
scallops
lobsters (two)
raw fish (five regional)
West Coast crab products (two)
crawfish.

Special workshops were held for:

hazards of Pacific species
hazards of Caribbean species
imports (two)
aquaculture products (three)
sampling (two)
wholesaling and distributing (four)
vessels (16)

Multipurpose workshops covering all commodities, vessels, and distribution were also held in the Caribbean and Pacific. Workshops were attended by industry members, state regulatory agencies, and federal personnel.

6.5.1 Purpose of workshops

The purpose of the workshops was to provide for interactive risk communication with the seafood industry, as recommended by the 1985 NAS text. The workshop laid forth the 'bare bones' outline of a new HACCP-based mandatory surveillance program and let the industry determine the details. Each workshop was conducted in like fashion:

1. Basic HACCP theory was taught; two working groups were organized.
2. Each working group developed a portion of a HACCP plan for their industry.
3. Two portions were shared, discussed, and consensus reached with all participants.
4. The workshop participants nominated a steering committee to follow through the rest of the process to produce a generic HACCP regulatory model for their industry.

6.5.2   Outcome of workshops

The workshop deliberations, centered on the commodity topic, encompassed all aspects of producing that commodity including considerations before receipt of material and post-production/distribution. Participants examined safety, wholesomeness, and economic fraud hazards associated with their commodity, categorizing these hazards as perceived or actual. It was recognized that the HACCP system must deal with actual substantial risk hazards, but that perceived hazards must be encountered through other mechanisms such as research, marketing, education, training, etc. This preliminary hazard analysis then permitted participants to function in two groups, each using the hazard analysis as the basis for their discussions.

   Group A concentrated on product safety issues, determining the focus of effort needed for their commodity based on actual hazards. They defined the regulatory and research requirements for a new mandatory seafood surveillance program and also the plant and food hygiene (sanitation) requirements for a new program Group B focused on process critical control point identification with associated criteria, such as preventive measures, monitoring and records. The sanitation requirements from Group A and the process control requirements from Group B were incorporated into a generic model to be tested and refined as part of the MSSP process.

6.5.2.1   Testing the HACCP models.

The preliminary generic HACCP model developed at each commodity workshop was tested in randomly selected seafood plants producing that commodity. Using the NMFS statistical registry, plants were categorized by production volume to randomly select plants of all sizes. Selected plants were not necessarily involved in the workshops or participants of the NMFS voluntary inspection program. Each selected plant was visited by a testing team comprised of NMFS MSSP personnel and a representative of National Fisheries Education and Research Foundation (NFERF). The generic model was carefully screened against current plant practices, noting differences, similarities and deficiencies in either the plant or model. Additionally, economic information was solicited from plant management by NFERF to determine the cost of implementing the newly designed program. Results of the testing (both sanitation and process controls) were summarized and presented to the industry steering committee selected at the initial workshop. MSSP personnel made recommendations to change the model (where necessary) based on the results of the testing. These changes could include adding steps, preventive measures, monitoring, records, etc. or upgrading or downgrading critical control points. The industry steering committee then elected to change the model (or not) and determined which of the sanitation requirements would be critical control points, thereby finalizing the generic model for their commodity. Reports and implementation manuals were released by NFERF to all participants, detailing the results and conclusions for each industry. NMFS, utilizing most of the results of these industry models, created proposed HACCP regulatory models for each tested commodity as well as prototypes for retail, food service and non-state insular areas (Garrett and Hudak-Roos, 1990).

These different commodity HACCP regulatory models offer insight and direction for seafood industry firms contemplating HACCP and are available from the National Seafood Inspection Laboratory, Pascagoula, Mississippi. The models provide a HACCP and sanitation program outline for the specific commodity.

6.6   NMFS HACCP program

6.6.1   Program components

In part as a result of the MSSP, the National Marine Fisheries Service instituted a HACCP-based voluntary regulatory program in July of 1992 (NMFS, NOAA, 1992). The scope of the NMFS program covers seafood processing facilities, vessels, retail, food service operations, and training. This HACCP-based inspection system consists of:

• requesting service
• HACCP plan development, review and approval
• label review
• proposed participant production pre-validation activities
• HACCP certification of facility personnel
• NMFS on-site validation
• selected product laboratory analysis
• recurring NMFS on-site HACCP systems audit of facilities.

The scope of the NMFS on-site HACCP system audit is two fold: (1) to determine facility HACCP plan adherence; and (2) to formally rate the facility's sanitation program. In terms of the HACCP plan adherence, the

Table 6.3 NMFS HACCP systems audit frequency schedule processing establishments

Frequency rating	Systems audit frequency	Qualifying visits for next higher level
Level I	Once every six months	NA
Level II	Once every two months	3
Level III	Once every month	2
Level IV	Once every two weeks	2
Level V	Daily	NA

on-site system audit focuses on records, adherence to stated procedures, and other factors, such as execution of unapproved HACCP plans or procedure modifications. Facility sanitation audits focus on: pest control, structure and lay out, maintenance, cleaning and sanitizing, personnel, restrooms, water supply, ice, chemicals, ventilation, and waste disposal procedures. Deviations in any aspect of the on-site audit (HACCP plan adherence or facility sanitation) are rated as being either minor, major, serious, or critical; with allowable differences depending upon whether the facility is producing low or substantial risk products.

6.6.1.1 Facility rating and inspection frequency. The individual system audit facility rating level determines the amount of NMFS inspectional effort, ranging from a daily inspection to one visit every six months as indicated in Table 6.3 for processing establishments. These frequencies are different for vessels, retail, and food service establishments.

6.6.1.2 Examination of product lots. Also, during the NMFS HACCP system audit, fixed percentages of product lots are examined to determine whether such lots are in compliance with processing specifications and/or grade standards. A Level I or II firm would have 2% of the lots sampled, while a Level III firm would have 4% examined, and a Level IV firm 8% examined. Again, similar audit procedures are in place for vessel, retail and food sevice establishments.

6.6.2 Substantial and low risk products

Laboratory analysis is required for certain substantial and low risk products. Substantial risk products are defined as:

- ready-to-eat shrimp
- fully cooked and/or warm and serve fish
- crabmeat
- surimi
- uncooked molluscan shellfish.

Low risk products are:

- breaded shrimp
- near-shore and estaurine fish
- tuna
- shark
- swordfish
- mahi mahi.

Laboratory analysis for substantial risk products consists of both micro-biological and chemical analyses, while low risk products are subjected only to certain chemical analyses.

6.6.2.1 Laboratory analyses. The purpose of the product laboratory analysis is not for 'lot acceptance' purposes. Rather, the analyses are in the 'surveillance mode' to ensure that the in-plant HACCP system and federal verification role is functioning correctly. The laboratory analyses performed for system surveillance purposes are limited and equate to a maximum of six lots yearly per facility for all high risk products, and a maximum of three lots yearly for all low risk products. Sampling plans and product acceptance criteria for laboratory analysis are those recommended by FDA, Codex Alimentarius Commission, or the National Advisory Committee on Microbiological Criteria for Foods.

6.6.3 Differences between NMFS and FDA programs

It must be understood that the voluntary NMFS Seafood HACCP Inspection program operates on a user fee basis, and differs significantly from the proposed FDA mandatory seafood HACCP program. The major points of difference center on the NMFS program focusing on the full range of regulatory concerns dealing with product safety, wholesomeness and economic fraud issues. Additionally, the NMFS program requires preapproval of HACCP plans, labels and product specifications. Further, the NMFS program requires specified levels of federal audit frequencies, product examination and laboratory analysis. In addition to the afore-mentioned, NMFS on a user fee basis, offers HACCP training for the facility employees with a certification of the participants who successfully pass an examination. The NMFS training focuses on the HACCP theory and the NMFS HACCP program requirements. Additionally, on a user fee basis, NMFS offers HACCP consulting services to prepare facilities or individuals to participate in the NMFS HACCP program. Such consulting services include how to prepare an appropriate HACCP plan submission to participate in the NMFS program.

6.7 FDA's HACCP program

The success of HACCP in the seafood industry along with public pressure and tighter resources prompted FDA to issue proposed HACCP regulations. On January 28, 1994 the US Food and Drug Administration's 'Proposal to Establish Procedures for the Safe Processing and Importing of Fish and Fishery Products' was published in the *Federal Register* (FDA, 1994a). In many respects, this proposed rule marks a turning point in the history of regulatory food inspections in the USA. In the proposal's preamble, FDA recognizes the significance of HACCP with the statement, 'adoption of HACCP controls by industry, coupled with inspections by FDA based on the HACCP system will produce a more effective and more efficient system for ensuring the safety of seafood products than currently exists.'

FDA's previous experience with HACCP has been with the low acid canned food (LACF) regulations and the joint FDA/NOAA HACCP pilot. (NOAA, National Oceanic and Atmospheric Administration, is the parent agency for NMFS.) LACF regulations, while HACCP-based, apply HACCP controls to two hazards, botulism in canned foods and contamination because of poor container integrity. The FDA/NOAA pilot program involved the voluntary development and implementation of HACCP-based systems by seafood processors and HACCP-based inspections by the two agencies. Although both efforts offer only a limited perspective, FDA's experiences with these programs help frame the conclusion that implementation of HACCP would make a good system better.

At the time of writing, FDA is in the process of reviewing all the comments submitted on its proposed HACCP regulation. No doubt, this review will result in a substantial revision of the final regulation, scheduled to be published in the fall of 1995. While the authors are unable to comment on the final regulation, we can review a few of the more salient features of the proposed regulation.

6.7.1 HACCP-based system

The regulation is based on HACCP principles with industry being responsible for development and implementation of the system and FDA being responsible for verification that the system is adequate to control the food safety hazards and is properly implemented. A significant point of the proposed regulation is that the mandatory HACCP controls focus strictly on food safety hazards.

6.7.2 Seven or five HACCP principles?

The seven principles of HACCP become five in the proposed rule. Corrective actions and processor verification are not required but only suggested. It should be noted that this omission is expected to change when the final rule is published. Failure to mandate compliance to the scientifically accepted seven principles of HACCP are reported to be the consequence of the mandated Office of Management and Budget (OMB) review. The recommendation is unfortunate and points to the fact that OMB reviewers failed to see HACCP as an integrally linked system of preventive food control (Martin, 1994).

6.7.3   Mandatory training

Each processor or importer must have at least one individual in their employ who has successfully completed a HACCP training program, which has been approved by FDA. Although few question the need for industry training, given the small size of many seafood processing plants and the lack of technically trained employees, the training requirement could be a potential problem for some segments of the industry. To ensure that standardized training curriculum and formats will be used, a Seafood HACCP Alliance comprised of FDA, NMFS, USDA, AFDO, industry trade associations and faculty from Sea Grant Universities has been initiated. The materials produced by the Alliance will serve as the training model.

6.7.4   Records access

In order for HACCP to be effective, records associated with the monitoring of CCPs must be made available to regulatory agencies to allow the agencies to discharge their verification function. Moreover, if corrective actions and verification are ultimately required, records associated with these activities must also be made available to the agencies. The proposed rule, however, contains an interesting additional element: FDA would require that processors maintain records of consumer complaints 'that may be related to a critical limit deviation' and that these records be part of those made available to inspectors. This so called 'consumer complaint file' is extremely controversial, and mandates access to records not considered essential to regulatory verification as developed by the NACMCF.

6.7.5   Obligations of importers

Since the USA is a major importer of seafoods, the proposed requirements on imports are important. According to the proposed rule, an importer must develop and implement a HACCP plan for the seafood commodity while it is in control of the importer. The importer must also have on file HACCP plans of each of its foreign processors. Additionally, the importer must take affirmative steps to ensure that the fish and fishery products that it offers were produced under the HACCP plan that it has in its possession. Obviously, the import requirements are of interest to domestic processors who compete with imports. Domestic processors want a 'level playing field'. Vital to a level playing field, however, is not just the fact that paperwork is in place, but that the HACCP plan is executed properly and compliance is monitored. FDA addresses this issue by stipulating that importers must provide evidence that imported products have been produced under the conditions that comply with the HACCP plans on file. FDA then goes on to list several procedures that they would accept as appropriate evidence.

6.7.6 General sanitation control procedures

Although not intended as a part of the specific HACCP requirements, the proposed rule addresses 18 specific procedures that 'shall be in place'. While these requirements will not be discussed here, it is of interest to note that many of the procedures are currently part of the current Good Manufacturing Practices described in part 110 of the Code of Federal Regulations. The difference being the proposed HACCP rule uses the mandatory word 'shall' while the current GMPs use the permissive word 'should'. A small but immensely significant change.

As stated above, the authors are aware of the fact that the specifics of this discussion may not apply by the time this book is published. This is unfortunate. Nonetheless, irrespective of the specifics of the final regulation, the concerns and philosophy of the FDA, as revealed in the proposed regulation, are both instructive and illuminating.

6.8 Impact of FDA's proposed HACCP regulation – an example

Using the FDA proposed rule, HACCP plans would be different to the NMFS expanded HACCP-based program. For example, in the production of a fish steak, such as swordfish that will be packaged in bulk and distributed in a frozen state, there are certain process flow steps (Figure 6.3). At each process step there may be the opportunity to apply preventive measures to help control hazards that threaten the safety of the product. Some of these preventive measures are process controls, such as time and temperature parameters. Some hazards are sanitation related, such as microbial contamination of the fish from the personnel or equipment. Other preventive measures must be applied for such hazards. The HACCP program concentrates on the process control aspects of producing safe fish, although the sanitation aspects are just as important.

According to the recently released FDA *Fish and Fishery Products*

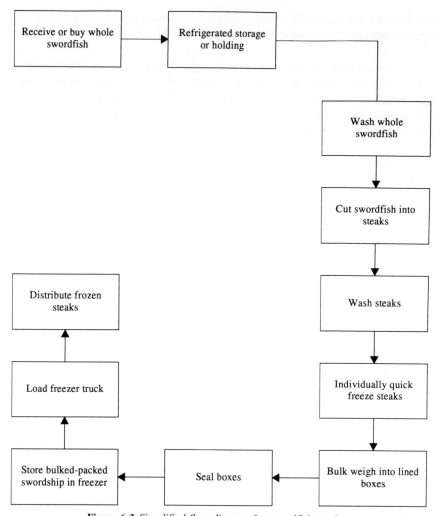

Figure 6.3 Simplified flow diagram for swordfish steaks.

Hazards and Controls Guide (FDA, 1994b), there are significant process hazards that must be controlled for the safety and wholesomeness of the product. For whole raw swordfish, the guide lists mercury contamination as one (FDA, 1990) and decomposition as another, which are controlled at a 'receiving' or 'buying,' CCP. Additionally, during holding and storage, temperature and time conditions could lead to decomposition. Finally, even if the distribution of the frozen swordfish is out of the producer's control, certain aspects of control during distribution to ensure a frozen state to prevent decomposition could be performed by the producer.

According to the guide, controlling methyl mercury contamination in whole swordfish requires historical data to develop a purchase specification and/or testing of suspect fish or lots of fish. By knowing the historical pattern of methyl mercury contamination related to size of the fish, location of catch, etc., the producer can control at the point of buying and receipt whether the fish will be accepted. Without a pattern of knowledge or if the fish are suspect, FDA indicates that the proper prevention would be to require testing at the point of receipt. The regulatory tolerance for methyl mercury is 1 ppm (part per million) in the edible portion of the fish. For the processing plant, the critical limit would be to have all fish meet the purchase specification (based on the historical information) for size and location or have 1 ppm or less methyl mercury based on analytical results. The plant would monitor each lot (or each fish) against the complied historical data and the purchase specification. Alternatively, the plant would have a laboratory test the fish for methyl mercury. If the fish did not meet the requirements of the purchase specification, then the plant could test the fish or reject it. If the fish had a concentration of methyl mercury greater than 1 ppm, the fish would be rejected. These are corrective actions. Finally, the plant would keep records of the decisions made for each lot of fish related to methyl mercury and schedule reviews of these records and the historical data for verification purposes.

Similarly, each principle of HACCP can be applied to the other significant process hazards. For decomposition at 'buying' or 'receiving,' decomposition during 'refrigerated storage' or 'holding,' and decomposition as a result of temperature abuse during 'distribution,' prevention, critical limits, monitoring, corrective actions, record keeping, and verification can be defined (Table 6.4).

In a HACCP system, each product and producer is different. For example, in the above HACCP outline, freezing was not considered a critical control point (CCP) for decomposition. However, for some plants that receive large quantities of fresh swordfish in a very short period of time, freezing the fish might greatly overwhelm the freezing capacity of the plant's freezer unit. If this was a chronic problem, some firms might choose 'freezing' as a CCP for the hazard decomposition. In other cases, some firms do not have a distribution problem and would not select 'distribution' as a CCP for decomposition.

6.9 Summary

HACCP has been successfully applied across the seafood industry, shellfish (molluscan and crustacean), finfish, and foodservice. The authors have personally interviewed processors who contend that implementation of HACCP has significantly improved their operations. While the prime

Table 6.4 HACCP plan simplified table* for whole swordfish

CCP	Significant hazard	Preventive measures	Critical limits	Monitoring	Corrective actions	Records	Verification
Buy and receive whole swordfish	Methyl mercury	Purchase specification that controls the size and location of catch	Must meet purchase specification requirements	Receiving manager checks each lot against specification and history	Hold and test each fish; dispose of those greater than 1 ppm; use others	Receiving	Sample for mercury at a set frequency
		Comparative history	Must be within history of size and location	Receiving manager checks each lot against history	Hold and test each fish; dispose of those greater than 1 ppm; use others	Receiving	Sample for mercury at a set frequency to collect more data
		Test lot or fish	1 ppm in the edible portion	A sample of each fish is sent to the laboratory for analysis	Dispose of fish greater than 1 ppm; use others	Analytical results	Send check sample to the laboratory
Refrigerated storage of whole swordfish	Decomposition	Provide adequate temperature control	45°F	QC checks recording thermometer chart three times a day	Check each fish temperature and sensory decomposition; dispose/use	Recorder chart and QC log	Calibrate recording thermometer; check with other thermometer
		Use first in first out rotation	Fish must be cut within 24 hours of receipt	Production manager checks inventory twice a day	Process older fish immediately	Refrigerated storage inventory control	Check that fish are processed within 24 hours

Distribution of frozen cut swordfish	Decomposition	Careful selection of carrier	Carrier must be on accepted list	Shipping manager checks each carrier against list	Do not load on unacceptable trucks	Shipping	Manager verifies adequacy of carrier once a year
		Require temperature charts	All vehicles must have temperature charts	Shipping manager checks each truck for temperature recorder	Do not load on unacceptable trucks	Shipping	Manager reviews records daily
		Label product and educate carrier	All boxes must be labeled 'Keep Frozen'; all carriers must receive written instruction	Shipping manager provides instruction to each trucker; purchasing confirms proper label on boxes	Call carrier with instructions; do not use unacceptable boxes	Shipping; purchasing	Manager reviews records daily; line supervisor verifies labels

*Based upon the proposed FDA Fish and Fishery Products Hazards and Controls Guide.

objective of HACCP is to prevent safety hazards, processors report enhanced product quality as well as cost savings due to better overall process control. For these processors, HACCP is not in the future – it is happening now.

References

APHA (1972) *Proc. National Conf. on Food Protection*. American Public Health Association, Food and Drug Administration, Washington, D.C.

Bryan, F.L. (1988) Hazard analysis critical control point: What the system is and what it is not. *J. Environ. Hlth.* **50**, 400.

CAC (1993) Codex Alimentarius Commission. Supplement One to Volume One, General Requirements, Section 7.5, *Guidelines for the Application of the Hazard Analysis Critical Control Point (HACCP) System*. Food and Agriculture Organization of the United Nations World Health Organization, Rome.

CDC (1979) *Annual Summary of Foodborne Diseases (1978)*. US Department of Health and Human Services, Atlanta, Georgia.

CDC (1981) *Annual Summary of Foodborne Diseases (1979)*. US Department of Health and Human Services, Atlanta, Georgia.

CDC (1983a) *Annual Summary of Foodborne Diseases (1981)*. US Department of Health and Human Services, Atlanta, Georgia.

CDC (1983b) *Annual Summary of Foodborne Diseases (1980 and 1981)*. US Department of Health and Human Services, Atlanta, Georgia.

CDC (1985) *Annual Summary of Foodborne Diseases (1982)*. US Department of Health and Human Services, Atlanta, Georgia.

CDC (1989) *Annual Summary of Foodborne Diseases*, unpublished data. US Department of Health and Human Services, Atlanta, Georgia.

CDC (1990) *Surveillance Summaries, Foodborne Disease Outbreaks, 1983–87*, Vol. 39. No. SS-1, US Department of Health and Human Services, Atlanta, Georgia.

CFPRA (1992) *HACCP: A Practical Guide*, Technical Manual No. 38, Campden Food and Drink Research Association, Gloucestershire, UK.

CFR (1992a) *Code of Federal Regulations*, Title 21, Part 108. US Govt. Print. Office, Washington, D.C.

CFR (1992b) *Code of Federal Regulations*, Title 21, Part 113. US Govt. Print. Office, Washington, D.C.

CFR (1992c) *Code of Federal Regulations*, Title 21, Part 114. US Govt. Print. Office, Washington, D.C.

FDA (1990) *Fish and Seafood Compliance Policy Guides: Fish, Shellfish, Crustaceans, and Other Aquatic Animals – Fresh, Frozen, or Processed – Methyl Mercury, CPG 7108.07*. Food and Drug Administration, Washington, D.C.

FDA (1994a) *Federal Register*, Vol. 59. No. 19, Friday, Jan. 28, 1994. Proposed Rules, p. 4187. Food and Drug Administration, Washington, D.C.

FDA (1994b) *Fish and Fishery Products Hazards and Controls Guide*. Food and Drug Administration, Washington, D.C.

Garrett, E.S. and Hudak-Roos, M. (1990) Use of HACCP for seafood surveillance certification. *Food Technol.* **44**, 159.

Garrett, E.S. and Hudak-Roos, M. (1991) US Seafood Inspection and HACCP. *Microbiology of Marine Food Products*. Van Nostrand Reinhold, New York, New York.

Garrett, E.S. and Jahncke, M. (1994) HACCP in aquaculture. Presented at the International Association of Milk, Food and Environmental Sanitarians Meeting, August 3, 1994. San Antonio, Texas.

Garrett, E.S., Haines, G.J., Brooker, J.R., Hamilton, R.W., Billy, T.J., Stocks, P.K. and Lima dos Santos, C.A. (1977) A new method to classify fishery products by microbial risks, in *Proc. Internat. Conf. Handling, Processing, and Marketing of Tropical Fish*, Tropical Products Institute, London.

Garrett, E.S, Hudak-Roos, M. and Jahncke, M. (1994) The international trading of seafoods – issues and opportunities. Presented at the Insittute of Food Technologists Annual Meeting Symposium *Blocks in Trading Blocks and Regulatory Opportunities*. June 25–29, 1994. Atlanta, Georgia.

Hudak-Roos, M. and Garrett, E.S. (1991) Monitoring, corrective actions and record keeping in HACCP. *Quality Assurance in the Fish Industry*. Proc. Internat. Conf., August 26–30, 1991. Copenhagen, Denmark.

Koplan, S. (1994) Personal communication. Fisheries Statistic Division, National Marine Fisheries Service, Silver Spring, Maryland.

Lee, J. (1977) *Hazard Analysis and Critical Control Point Applications to the Seafood Industry*. Dec. ORESU-H-77. Oregon State University, Sea Grant College Program, Corvallis, Oregon.

Lee, J. and Hilderbrand, Jr, K.S. (1992) *Hazard Analysis and Critical Control Point Applications to the Seafood Industry*. Oregon State University, Sea Grant College Program, Corvallis, Oregon.

Martin, Roy (1994) Personal communication. Vice President, Science and Technology, National Fisheries Institute, Inc., Arlington, Virginia.

Mayes, T. and Kilsby, D.C. (1989) The use of HAZOP hazard analysis to identify critical control points for the microbiological safety of food. *Food Quality and Preference* 1(2), 53.

NACMCF (1992) *Hazard Analysis and Critical Control Point System*. Adopted Report. US Department of Agriculture, Washington, D.C.

NAS (1985a) *An Evaluation of the Role of Microbiological Criteria for Foods and Food Ingredients*. National Academy of Sciences, National Academy Press, Washington, D.C.

NAS (1985b) *Meat and Poultry Inspection, The Scientific Basis of the Nation's Program*. National Academy Press, National Academy of Sciences, Washington, D.C.

NAS (1987) *Poultry Inspection, The Basis for a Risk-Assessment Approach*. National Academy of Sciences, Washington, D.C.

NAS (1990) *Cattle Inspection, Committee on Evaluation of USDA Streamlined Inspection System for Cattle (SIS-C)*. National Academy Press, Washington, D.C.

NAS (1991) *Seafood Safety, Committee on Evaluation of the Safety of Fishery Products*. National Academy of Sciences. National Academy Press, Washington, D.C.

NMFS (1987) *Plan of Operations – Model Seafood Surveillance Project*. National Marine Fisheries Service, Office of Trade and Industry Services, National Seafood Inspection Laboratory, Pascagoula, Mississippi.

NMFS (1989) *Plan of Operations – Model Seafood Surveillance Project*. National Marine Fisheries Service, Office of Trade and Industry Services, National Seafood Inspection Laboratory, Pascagoula, Mississippi.

NMFS (1990) *Plan of Operations – Model Seafood Surveillance Project*. National Marine Fisheries Service, Office of Trade and Industry Services, National Seafood Inspection Laboratory, Pascagoula, Mississippi.

NMFS (1993) *NMFS Fishery Products Inspection Manual*, Part I, Chapter 9, Section 02. National Marine Fisheries Service, Office of Trade and Industry Services, Silver Spring, Maryland.

NMFS (1995) *The Draft Report of the Model Seafood Surveillance Project. A Report to Congress*. National Marine Fisheries Service, Office of Trade and Industry Services, National Seafood Inspection Laboratory, Pascagoula, Mississippi. In review.

NMFS, NOAA (1989) US Department of Commerce. *Current Fishery Statistics No. 8800: Fisheries of the United States, 1988*. Silver Spring, Maryland.

NMFS, NOAA (1992) *Federal Register*, Vol. 57, No. 146, Wednesday, July 29, 1992. Rules and Regulations, pp. 33456–33458. Washington, D.C.

NMFS, NOAA (1994) US Department of Commerce. *Current Fishery Statistics No. 9300: Fisheries of the United States, 1993*. Silver Spring, Maryland.

US Congress (1986) Senate. Committee on Appropriations. *Report to accompany H.R. 5161*. Rept. 99–425, 99th Congress, 2nd Session, Sept. 3.

US Congress (1988) Senate. Committee on Appropriations. *Report 100–388*, 100th Congress, June 20.

7 Risk analysis, HACCP and microbial criteria in meat and poultry systems

K.B. HARRIS, H.R. CROSS, G.R. ACUFF and N.B. WEBB

7.1 Introduction

An effective food safety program must be based on strong risk analysis principles and on the concept of 'prevention' using the seven principles of HACCP. The program must support the concept that risk analysis and HACCP should be incorporated from the beginning to the end of the marketing chain – from farm to table. These concepts should be based on science, and all interventions and management decisions relating to food safety must have strong scientific documentation. The industry, the government regulators and the consumers must understand their individual roles to have an effective food safety program. The responsibility of having a safe food supply depends on everyone – no single individual or group can meet this responsibility alone. Therefore, all segments must work together to identify hazards and assess potential risk, develop science and technology for interventions, and communicate appropriately between industry, government regulators and consumers.

7.2 Risk analysis

Humans are constantly making decisions that are often based on the benefit of the outcome versus the risk of the process, like the benefit of saving time versus the risk of flying. We are faced with risks on a daily basis. Fortunately, technology continues to decrease many of the risks; however, other risks are often created in the process (Kindred, 1993). Risks are an inherent part of life, and it is important that they are identified and managed appropriately, especially in our food supply.

Risk analysis is a process that can be used to identify and manage risk. It actually involves three separate components – risk assessment, risk management and risk communication. Each component is needed to collect and interpret scientific data, make appropriate management decisions based on the scientific information and to communicate the findings and decisions as needed.

7.2.1 Risk assessment

Risk assessment is a scientific process that identifies and classifies potential hazards and the risks associated with them. It also interprets scientific information and documents the uncertainties in a manner that facilitates informed management decisions to be made. Risk assessment is a complex process, but it provides support for management decisions. According to the National Academy of Sciences (NRC, 1983) risk assessment has four components – hazard identification, dose-response assessment, exposure assessment and risk characterization.

1. *Hazard identification*
   This is the process of using scientific, epidemiological and other data to link biological, chemical or physical hazards to illness in consumers. The process should include the amounts, frequencies and locations of the agent(s) that cause human illness and disease.
2. *Dose-response assessment*
   This is an estimate on the basis of available information and the quantity of the hazard needed to cause illness.
3. *Exposure assessment*
   Exposure assessment determines the probability of contact or consumption of the hazard by a susceptible individual or population.
4. *Risk characterization*
   This integrates the results from the previous steps to estimate the incidence of disease under various conditions of human exposure, including uncertainties.

Kindred (1993) provided the following explanation of how the Environmental Protection Agency (EPA) employs risk assessment to control pesticide use. She noted that the EPA also determines the level of residues allowed in animal feeds and human food. First, the toxicity effect to humans is determined, then a dose-response assessment is used to determine potency. Safety factors are applied, and animals are used to identify the highest dosage possible without eliciting adverse effects, which is called the No Observable Effect Level (NOEL). Then the 'uncertainty factor' to account for differences in animals and humans is employed to set a 'Reference Dose' for the compound.

Risk assessments should be performed for each of the specific areas of the food system. All potential hazards in the specific areas need to be identified during the process to properly assess the risks. According to Kindred (1993):

'Information is limited and sometimes continually increasing for any given hazard; therefore, there are unknowns and/or uncertainties in risk assessments. It is crucial that uncertainties related to each part of the scenarios be expressed in risk estimates.'

Overall, the completed assessment must include all of the information used to identify the risk (scientific and other), the methods applied and descriptions of the unknowns/uncertainties that were used in the risk assessment. A detailed risk assessment of each specific area must be conducted before a food safety plan involving HACCP can be implemented effectively. Unfortunately, risk assessment is much more complex than it sounds, and extreme care should be taken to make sure the assessment is accurate before proceeding to risk management and risk communication. Risk assessment for pathogens is complicated by the fact that almost no infectious dose data is available to use in developing the risk assessment model.

7.2.2 Risk management

Risk management was defined by National Research Council (1989) as:

'The evaluation of alternative risk control actions, selection among them (including doing nothing), and their implementation; the responsible individual or office (risk manager) sometimes oversees preparation of risk assessments, risk control assessments, and risk messages. Risk management may or may not be open to outside individuals or organizations.'

Decision makers involved in risk management must consider the actual risk assessment and any social, political and economic concerns. The process of risk management must correctly utilize the information provided in the risk assessment and from other sources in order to improve food safety. Risk management would include the use of sequential interventions at critical control points (CCPs) in the HACCP plan.

7.2.3 Risk communication

Risk communication is the last but a critical step in risk analysis. It requires all interested parties to communicate with each other. They must exchange information relating to both the scientific data collected and the uncertainties. Each group must voice its concerns in order for risk communication to be successful. The National Research Council (1989) described risk communication as:

'An interactive process of exchange of information and opinion among individuals, groups, and institutions; often involves multiple messages about the nature of risk expressing concerns, opinions, or reactions to risk messages or to legal and institutional arrangements for risk management.'

It is important that all parties (industry, government regulators and consumers) involved in food safety openly communicate with each other about risks and ways to decrease them. All groups must work together and focus on all aspects of the food supply – from farm to table. Communication of risk to consumers is a very difficult task, and the sole use of technical information to accomplish this communication is generally not effective.

7.3   How risk analysis and HACCP contribute to food safety

Risk analysis and HACCP must be implemented throughout the entire chain to provide consumers with the safest food supply possible. Once the hazard analysis is completed, CCPs should be identified. Interventions included as CCPs in a HACCP plan must be based on science and may be applied in live animal production, through slaughter and processing, into distribution, retail, food service and even by the consumer. HACCP plans should address all hazards to public health – biological, physical and chemical.

7.3.1   *Interventions are required to reduce risk*

HACCP plans for every segment of the industry should include effective pathogen interventions. The meat and poultry industry has done a good job throughout the years of addressing the issues of physical and chemical hazards, by implementing metal detectors and testing for chemical residues, etc. However, little has been done to address the issue of developing interventions for pathogens. Unfortunately, lives were lost before pathogen interventions became a top priority. However, according to the Blue Ribbon Task Force Report (National Live Stock and Meat Board, 1994) and the *National Beef Safety Research Agenda: A Research Plan for Beef Safety Research* (National Cattlemen's Association, 1994) the industry is prepared to respond to the issue and has identified research priorities to develop the needed interventions. The following summarizes the recommendations issued by the Blue Ribbon Task Force:

- implement Hazard Analysis and Critical Control Point systems in each segment of the food production chain
- conduct research to identify the reservoirs of *E. coli* O157:H7
- encourage government approval and industry-wide adoption of anti-microbial rinses for beef carcasses
- encourage government approval and further research to optimize the irradiation process
- conduct research to develop new pathogen reduction/intervention technologies
- establish microbial guidelines to measure the effectiveness of HACCP plans
- implement national consumer education programs on food safety

As a follow-up to the Blue Ribbon Task Force report, the National Cattlemen's Association built on the Task Force recommendations to develop the following specific research priority recommendations (National Cattlemen's Association, 1994):

- risk factors and bacterial levels associated with the bovine during management and transportation prior to slaughter
- influence of beef cattle farm management practices on prevalence of human enteric pathogens
- influence of stress on prevalence of human enteric pathogens in the bovine
- identifying sources of human enteric pathogens contaminating beef carcasses
- developing intervention systems for reducing enteric pathogenic bacteria on beef carcasses
- developing science and technology to improve food safety of beef from packer to food service and retail
- sources of bacterial foodborne pathogens for raw beef products, carcass breakup, fabrication, food service and retail
- the influence of sources of raw beef on pathogens in ground beef
- the relationship of condensation and foodborne illness
- the influence of employee education and training on foodborne illness
- the impact of consumer knowledge and education on food safety
- improving the surveillance systems and public health concerns related to foodborne bacterial disease related to both human and animal surveillance systems
- evaluation of manufacturing and consumer practices related to foodborne illness

7.3.2 Appropriate use of interventions

Interventions need to be placed throughout the entire meat and poultry production process. However, there is currently only one fail-safe intervention in place (Figure 7.1) and that is proper cooking. Sequential interventions need to be in place throughout the system to minimize the risk. Therefore, as interventions are developed by the scientific community and approved by USDA, they should be used immediately by the appropriate segment of the industry. For example, anti-bacterial rinses could be implemented on the slaughter floor to reduce pathogen load (Barkate *et al.*, 1992; Prasai *et al.*, 1992). Once anti-bacterial rinses are approved by USDA, they should be part of the slaughter HACCP plan and put into use immediately. From that point on, HACCP plans should not be approved for slaughter operations unless at least one anti-bacterial rinse is included at the appropriate CCP(s). Points on the slaughter floor that should be considered for anti-bacterial rinses are post-hiding, post-evisceration and post-final washing. As other interventions are developed

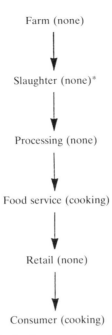

Figure 7.1 Interventions in the food safety continuum. *Anti-bacterial rinses (lactic acid, acetic acid, TSP, hot water, etc.) are effective, but have not been approved for use in meat.

along the food production chain, they too should be implemented. The more interventions that are applied, the greater the reduction in risk and the safer the food supply.

7.4   HACCP versus end-product microbial testing

Microbial testing must be applied appropriately. If misused, microbial testing can lead to a false sense of security in the safety of the food supply. Microbial testing around CCPs and for incoming raw materials can be effective methods to verify that the preventive systems are working. However, microbiological testing is not effective for end-product testing or 'test and hold' programs. Beneficial data for microbiological trend analysis can be accumulated over long periods of time. Microbial testing for HACCP verification and trend analysis usually includes non-pathogenic organisms (e.g. aerobic plate counts, coliforms, etc.), but may also include pathogens under specific circumstances. Test and hold programs for pathogens on raw materials or end-products are not effective components of a food safety program. The test and hold methods have the following problems:

(a) Pathogens occur in extremely small numbers and the distribution of bacteria within a food is not homogenous; therefore, a truly representative sample may not be possible. To accomplish a high level of confidence that a defective lot (containing a pathogen) will be detected an extremely large sample must be taken. For example, in order to properly test a 10 000 lb (4.5 tonnes) lot of ground beef for *E. coli* O157:H7 at the 0.20% level, over 2500 samples would have to be examined to be 99% confident that the lot is pathogen free. This is an unrealistic approach and the cost to the industry and ultimately the consumer would not be justified because risk to public health would not be completely reduced using this approach.

(b) HACCP is based on the concept of 'prevention' rather than the concept of trying to 'inspect out' the problem. Therefore, relying upon final product testing to ensure safety of foods is contrary to the principles of HACCP.

(c) Microbiological testing to ensure the safety of foods may give the industry and the consumer a false sense of security if no pathogens are found. It could send the wrong signal to the consumer and decrease the likelihood of careful handling and proper preparation. This could result in more outbreaks of foodborne illness.

(d) Test and hold procedures do not assure that the prevention process (HACCP) is working, and they do not assure that the product is safe. Microbiological testing cannot necessarily detect a process that is out of hygienic control.

(e) Test and hold procedures are very expensive, and the resources could be better spent in making certain that a strong, effective HACCP program with appropriate interventions is in place.

7.5 The role of microbiological criteria

According to the National Research Council (NRC, 1985), 'a criterion is a yardstick on which a judgment or decision can be made.' Therefore, microbiological criteria could be established to evaluate the presence of microorganisms in food. The NRC (1985) specifies that a microbiological criterion should include the following:

1. A statement describing the identity of the food or food ingredient.
2. A statement of the contaminant of concern, i.e., the microorganism or group of microorganisms and/or its toxin or other agent.
3. The analytical method to be used for the detection, enumeration, or quantification of the contaminant of concern.
4. The sampling plan.
5. The microbiological limits considered appropriate to the food and commensurate with the sampling plan used.

In a presentation to the World Congress on Meat and Poultry Inspection, Acuff (1993) emphasized that successful development and application of microbiological criteria requires a 'thorough understanding of the food production process and the significance of the presence of various microorganisms.' If developed and used appropriately, microbiological criteria could enhance the safety of food and consumer confidence in the food supply.

However, there are different types of microbiological criteria – standard, guideline and specification. Caution should be used to make sure their use is appropriate, and that the desired results are obtained. The Subcommittee on Microbiological Criteria for Foods and Food Ingredients (NRC, 1985), recommended the following definitions for the different types of criteria.

7.5.1 Microbiological standards

A microbiological standard is a microbiological criterion that is a part of a law, ordinance or administrative regulation. A standard is a mandatory criterion. Failure to comply constitutes a violation of the law, ordinance or regulation and will be subject to the enforcement policy of the regulatory agency having jurisdiction.

Since a standard is mandatory, any food that does not meet the criterion may be subjected to rejection, destruction, reprocessing or diversion. These are strict limits, and should be applied when epidemiological data show that a food is a frequent vehicle of disease. The implementation of specific standards could result in 'the recall or downgrading of significant quantities of what otherwise may be wholesome food' (NRC, 1985).

7.5.2 Microbiological guidelines

A microbiological guideline is a criterion that often is used by the food industry or a regulatory agency to monitor a manufacturing process. Guidelines function as alert mechanisms to signal whether microbiological conditions prevailing at critical control points or in the finished product are within the normal range. Hence, they are used to assess processing efficiency at critical control points and conformity with Good Manufacturing Practices.

Guidelines are advisory criteria; therefore, they allow judgments to be made on the product acceptability. If the food is out of compliance, immediate action may still be required by management or regulatory agencies. Individual companies may establish proprietary guidelines for their own control and to collect information on the microbiological condition of raw products or other areas in the processing line.

7.5.3   Microbiological specifications

A microbiological specification is used as a purchase requirement, whereby conformance becomes a condition of purchase between buyer and vendor of a food or ingredient. A specification can be either mandatory or advisory. Specifications are routinely used by buyers and vendors to establish acceptability criteria for a raw material or a finished product, and for governmental agencies to evaluate foods purchased for government programs.

7.5.4   Microbiological criteria and safety

Microbiological criteria could be used to help improve the safety of the food supply. However, there are limitations to their use, and these must be considered before establishing either standards, guidelines or specifications. Specific tests applied to see if a food meets certain criteria often only indicate the potential of a hazard because they most often test for indicator organisms rather than specifically for pathogens or their toxins.

Another consideration, is the fact that some microorganisms may be potentially dangerous but naturally occurring in raw products. However, they may be eliminated or reduced to low levels through normal processing and cooking procedures, which would make it unrealistic to set standards for the raw products. Microbiological criteria are not needed for every food product. From a safety standpoint, cooked, ready to consume products may have a greater need for microbial criteria than do uncooked products.

7.5.5   Sampling procedures

According to Acuff (1993), an effective sampling plan is one of the most essential components of a microbiological criterion. Sampling for the presence of microorganisms requires examining either the entire lot or a representative sample from the lot. Sampling of an entire lot, which is the quantity of product produced, handled and stored within a limited time period, under uniform conditions, is impractical. Therefore, the statistical concepts of population probability and sampling must be used to determine the appropriate sample size from the lot and to provide conclusions drawn from the analytical results. The lot is made up of sample units, and a sufficient number of units must be selected to determine the microbiological acceptability of a lot. The design of the sampling plan must allow for rejection of inferior lots within a set level of confidence. Detailed information regarding statistical concepts of population probabilities and sampling, choice of sampling procedures, decision criteria and practical aspects of application as applied to microorganisms in food can be found in a publication by the International Commission on Microbiological Specifications for Foods (ICMSF, 1986). The following discussion on sampling plans is taken from Acuff (1993).

7.5.5.1 Two-class plans.   A simple method for determining whether to accept or reject a food lot can be based upon a microbiological test conducted upon several randomly selected sample units (n) with a preset maximum number of sample units allowed to yield unsatisfactory results (c). The test will usually determine the presence or absence of an organism or it will determine whether the samples are above or below a preset concentration (m). Thus, in a two-class sampling plan designed to make a presence/absence decision on the lot, $n = 5$, $c = 2$ means that 5 sample units are obtained and examined; if more than 2 of the samples show the presence of the organism of concern, the lot is rejected.

7.5.5.2 Three-class plans.   Three-class plans were designed for situations in which the quality of the product can be divided into three attribute classes based upon the concentration of the organisms within the sample units, 0 to m, m to M, and greater than M. The level of the test organism which is acceptable in the food is denoted by m. M is a hazardous or unacceptable level of contamination. Any count above a concentration M is considered unacceptable; therefore, a count from any of the n sample units exceeding M will result in rejection of the lot. In the three-class plan, c indicates the number of sample units that can contain a concentration above m, but only up to and including M. This classification of sample units has been determined to be less than desirable, but a few of the sample units (c) will be allowed without rejecting the lot. Thus, in a three-class sampling plan, the food lot will be rejected if any one of the sample units exceeds M or if the number of sample units with contamination levels from m to M exceeds c.

The proposed system by ICMSF (1986) classifies foods into 15 hazard categories called cases, and it provides suggested sampling plans (Table 7.1).

7.5.6 Disposition of product

The action to be taken when a microbiological criterion is exceeded depends upon the purpose for establishing the criterion. Criteria may be established for purposes ranging from acceptability of raw materials to monitoring of critical control points to acceptability of the finished product. Willingness to accept the defined appropriate action will depend heavily upon the intelligent establishment of rational and defensible criteria. Foods determined to be a direct health hazard will require cautious consideration when alternatives other than total destruction are

Table 7.1 Plan for stringency (case) in relation to degree of health hazard and conditions of use[a]

Type of hazard	Conditions in which food is expected to be handled and consumed after sampling in the usual course of events[b]		
No direct health hazard	*Increase shelf life*	*No change*	*Reduce shelf life*
Utility (e.g. general contamination, reduced shelf life and spoilage)	**Case 1** 3-class $n = 5, c = 3$	**Case 2** 3-class $n = 5, c = 2$	**Class 3** 3-class $n = 5, c = 1$
Health hazard	*Reduced hazard*	*No change*	*Increased hazard*
Low, indirect (indicator)	**Case 4** 3-class $n = 5, c = 3$	**Case 5** 3-class $n = 5, c = 2$	**Case 6** 3-class $n = 5, c = 1$
Moderate, direct, limited spread	**Case 7** 3-class $n = 5, c = 2$	**Case 8** 3-class $n = 5, c = 1$	**Case 9** 3-class $n = 10, c = 1$
Moderate, direct, potentially extensive spread	**Case 10** 2-class $n = 5, c = 0$	**Case 11** 2-class $n = 10, c = 0$	**Case 12** 2-class $n = 20, c = 0$
Severe, direct	**Case 13** 2-class $n = 15, c = 0$	**Case 14** 2-class $n = 30, c = 0$	**Case 15** 2-class $n = 60, c = 0$

[a]Adapted from ICMSF (1986). [b]More stringent plans would generally be used for sensitive foods destined for susceptible populations. [c]n = number of sample units drawn from lot; c = maximum allowable number of positive results.

considered. However, destruction of a finished product is costly, and alternative actions should be sought and used whenever possible. Reliance placed upon monitoring of critical control points to give assurance that a process has been properly applied will reduce the probability that destruction of a product will be required based upon finished product testing. Evidence that a critical control point is not under control should generate immediate action, preventing future occurrences, and may provide immediate correction of the situation before destruction or re-routing of the product is required.

7.5.7 Establishment and implementation

Microbiological criteria are not needed for all foods. A criterion should be established and implemented for a food or food ingredient only when there is a recognized need and when the criterion can be shown to be effective and practical. The criterion must accomplish its objective. Additional factors to be considered include (NRC, 1985):

1. Evidence of a hazard to health based upon epidemiologic data or a hazard analysis.

2. The nature of the natural and commonly acquired microflora of the food and the ability of the food to support microbial growth.
3. The effect of processing on the microflora of the food.
4. The potential for microbial contamination and/or growth during processing, handling, storage and distribution.
5. The category of consumers at risk.
6. The state in which the food is distributed.
7. Potential for abuse at the consumer level.
8. Spoilage potential, utility and Good Manufacturing Practices.
9. The manner in which the food is prepared for ultimate consumption.
10. Reliability of the methods available to detect and/or quantify the microorganisms or toxin of concern.
11. The cost/benefit associated with the application of the criterion.

7.5.8   Cost of implementation

Implementation of reasonable and effective microbiological criteria can provide for enhanced food safety and efficient trade. The cost of implementing microbiological criteria is offset by the possible reduction in foodborne disease, the reduction in finished product destruction, and the more efficient movement of products through trade channels. Cost benefit studies are required to determine an accurate cost of implementation. Such studies will depend on the accuracy of costs in reducing a given illness, as well as the measures to be implemented.

7.5.9   Application to raw meat and poultry

The Codex 'General Principles for the Establishment and Application of Microbiological Criteria for Foods' (Codex, 1981) state that a microbiological criterion should be established and applied only where there is a definite need and where it is both practical and likely to be effective. The presence of various pathogenic bacteria on raw meats and poultry is primarily a result of their incidence in the live animal rather than a result of inferior hygiene. The occurrence of these pathogens in raw meat and poultry cannot be entirely prevented by the application of strict sanitary hygienic principles. In addition, the distribution of pathogens in raw products is extremely variable, severely limiting the degree of confidence of a sampling plan to indicate the absence of a particular pathogen in a lot.

Enterobacteriaceae have been frequently used in the industry as indicators of the degree of hygiene during slaughter/dressing procedures. These organisms do constitute part of the raw product microflora after slaughter and dressing. However, their presence is due to unavoidable fecal contamination, and they do not necessarily provide any information regarding the presence of pathogens. Even without examination for pathogens or indicator organisms, it is logical to assume, based upon the knowledge of conventional slaughter/dressing procedures, that some fecal contamination is inevitable and that pathogenic bacteria may be present on raw products. A Food and Agricultural Organization/World Health Organization working group on microbiological criteria for foods (FAO/ WHO, 1979) concluded that the number of indicator organisms in raw meat neither reflects adherence to a code of hygienic practice nor indicates presence or absence of pathogens. Therefore, criteria for raw meat and poultry products based upon indicator organisms were not considered to be justified by this group.

Microbiological quality control of meat and poultry processing involves development and use of processing methods which are designed to restrict microbial contamination and growth. Microbiological monitoring of the product and the processing environment can be used to determine the effectiveness of these procedures. Aerobic plate counts (APC) can be used to monitor these procedures and Good Manufacturing Practices, and criteria based upon such examinations are a valuable aid in establishing quality control programs. While these criteria may be effective for evaluating processing conditions in-house, because of the perishable nature of the product, it is probably not possible to set APC limits for criteria to be applied at the retail level or port of entry. In 1973, the State of Oregon set microbiological standards for fresh and frozen red meat at the retail level and revoked the standards four years later because:

1. The standards were unenforceable and created a general adverse reaction.
2. There was no evidence of reduction of foodborne disease or improvement in quality characteristics of the meat.
3. The standards may have created erroneous consumer expectations of improved quality and decreased hazard.

7.5.10 *Application to cooked meat and poultry*

Microbiological criteria can be appropriately used to evaluate the microbiological quality of raw materials, to evaluate the effectiveness of equipment sanitation and to determine the microbiological condition of the freshly processed product. Baseline information for these evaluations must be established by the processor if useful limits are to be established. In some instances, a particular cooked product may have been determined to be a significant vehicle for foodborne disease (i.e. *Salmonella* in cooked, uncured meats). Microbiological criteria are recommended in such situations. In most cases, application of microbiological criteria to any of these products after they have entered trade channels is of little value.

The safety and quality of commercially processed foods is primarily a result of the treatments they receive and the restriction of post-processing recontamination. The perimeter of safety provided through traditional processing methods is very wide and greatly reduces opportunities for survival or growth of microorganisms. Control of these processes through programs such as the Hazard Analysis Critical Control Point (HACCP) system is the only logical way to assure the safety of the food supply.

7.6 Statistical process control

Applied statistical procedures have become invaluable tools to many manufacturing industries. The application of statistical analysis has allowed better control of factors such as size, weight, thickness, temperature, etc., that are critical to production processes. Processes that utilize some type of statistical control generally yield products that are more consistent in their given attributes.

In the 1940s, the term Statistical Quality Control (SQC) was developed when the American Standards Association (ASA), acting on the request of the war department, became involved in the application of statistical quality control to manufacturing processes (Banks, 1989). SQC is the implementation of statistical techniques to measure and improve the quality of processes and includes Statistical Process Control (SPC). SPC analyzes a specific measurable process and determines which variations of the process are normal and acceptable and those which are not.

Juran and Gryna (1988) define a process as any specific combination of machines, tools, methods, materials and/or people used to attain specific qualities in a product or service. A process can also be described as a set of causes and conditions that repeatedly come together to transform inputs into outputs. In the food processing industry, the inputs include commodities, ingredients, information, facility equipment, equipment controls, heat environment and people. Outputs include products and services.

Measurements of acceptability are taken at periodic intervals during production and are used to determine whether the particular process in question is under control (within predetermined limits). Therefore, SPC results indicate to an operator when too much variation has occurred, and thus, signal the need for process adjustment. SPC enables a company to monitor products continuously and make prompt changes when deviations occur. Consequently, SPC application decreases operation costs by reducing the amount of defective product or increasing the efficiency of a process.

In addition to being incorporated for day-to-day monitoring and quality improvement, SPC may be used strategically over time. A company can enhance its competitive position by intelligently utilizing information generated by control charts and statistics to improve a process in such a manner that it not only increases the quality of a product, but also reduces production costs.

SPC utilizes preventive rather than detective procedures. It replaces older management techniques such as concentrating on quarterly profits, rigidly following a production schedule, observing the concept of quality control, and telling individuals what to do (Clements, 1988). Rather, the ideas of continuous improvement; taking time to monitor a process; empowering an operator to take corrective action; and allowing operators to meet, discuss, and plan better production methods are encouraged by SPC. Advanced planning rarely goes beyond the next 24 hours by old procedures.

The actual technique of SPC can be interpreted as 'stable, predictable, and capable' (Clements, 1988). A process is analyzed by sampling and examining critical characteristics of a product. Consistency in the desired product characteristics indicates *stability*, slight and consistent variation from day-to-day suggests that the process is *predictable*. If the variation is always less than the specified variation limits, it is always *capable* of meeting specifications.

To achieve the above, the operator stops the process at regular intervals and evaluates it. He/she records information and makes calculations. When the process is out-of-control, the operator takes action to correct the variation. The corrective action is noted and the process is checked soon after to ensure that the adjustment keeps the process in control.

In a HACCP program, a number of steps (CCPs) in a food process require monitoring. To reiterate, a CCP is any step, point or process at which control can be applied and a food safety hazard can be prevented, eliminated or reduced to acceptable levels (NACMCF, 1992). Critical limits are established at each CCP. Within the critical limits of a CCP (e.g. range of pH, temperature of cooking, level of water activity) the specific process is considered to be within a safe operating range.

Because the potential for food hazard exists at a CCP, these steps must be carefully monitored to ensure that the CCP does not become out of control. The application of SPC to evaluate certain CPPs represents a crucial procedure in HACCP.

7.6.1 Statistical process control measures critical control points

In a HACCP program, to monitor is to conduct a planned sequence of observations or measurements to assess whether a CCP is under control and to produce an accurate record for future use in verification (NACMCF, 1992). Monitoring can be done by observation or measurement. Whether a CCP will be evaluated by observation or measurement depends on the established critical limit, available methods, and/or cost (Hudak-Roos and Garrett, 1992). In general, observations generate qualitative data, whereas, measurements yield quantitative data. When feasible, continuous monitoring techniques are always preferred over interval monitoring procedures.

Monitoring serves three main purposes (NACMCF, 1992). (i) Monitoring tracks the food processing system's operation. If there is a trend towards the loss of control at a CCP, action can be immediately taken before a deviation occurs outside critical limits. (ii) Monitoring can determine when there is loss of control and deviation does occur at a CCP. At this point, corrective action must be taken. (iii) Monitoring provides written documentation for use in the verification of HACCP.

The appropriate statistical technique for monitoring a CCP will depend on what is desired relative to speed, ease of computation and accuracy. A variety of statistical methods are available for interpreting and summarizing data, as well as determining sample sizes (Zar, 1984; Taylor, 1987a; USDA, 1987).

7.6.2 Control charts

In 1924, Walter A. Shewhart of Bell Telephone Laboratories suggested the use of control charts to handle quality control problems during production (Puri *et al.*, 1979). Today, control charts are commonly employed during manufacturing or processing to allow workers to make intelligent and rapid decisions about processing variation. To many they are considered the basic tools of quality assurance.

Control charts provide a graphical means to monitor a measurement process, diagnose measurement problems, document measurement uncertainty and generally aid in methodology development (Taylor, 1987b). By employing control charts, operators can more effectively control a process because the charts can aid in the identification of variation causes, and therefore, improve the overall process.

Variation in a process is attributable to two types of causes: unassignable and assignable causes (Puri *et al.*, 1979; Nolan, 1990). Unassignable (chance) causes are minor fluctuations in a process that are due to random variation. These causes are beyond human control and cannot be completely eliminated. Environmental conditions or measurement errors may lead to unassignable variation. Assignable (special) causes induce major fluctuations in a process, many times leading to an out of control process. An assignable cause may be due to machine failure, inconsistency in raw materials or workmanship, new workers, contamination or deterioration. These causes can be identified and eliminated.

7.6.2.1 Planning control charts. Development of a control chart requires careful planning. Planning covers seven phases (Nolan, 1990):

1. Determining the objective of the chart.
2. Sampling, measurement, and sub-grouping.
3. Ascertaining most likely special causes.
4. Determining the notes required.
5. Formulating a reaction plan for out of control points.
6. Administration.
7. Setting a schedule for analysis.

The team must agree why the chart is being developed. Understanding the objective of the chart allows the team to remain focused on the intent of the control chart, giving the team a definite goal and permitting it to pursue new objectives once the initial objective is accomplished.

The sampling, measurement and sub-grouping step involves selecting a variable to be charted, the control chart type, the method of measurement, the magnitude of measurement variation, the point of sampling, the strategy for sub-grouping and the frequency of subgroups. Subgroups represent the number of samples taken at each sampling interval to obtain an average value. To determine the most likely causes one must be aware of all the possible factors that could cause variation in a process. A list of these should be included on the planning form.

Notes should be recorded on control charts to better determine what causes variation in a process. The most likely causes generally dictate what type of notes will be included. Notes should document information and activities about the process that will aid in the identification of these causes. Notes may include the name of suppliers, variable measurements, incorporation of new equipment or procedures, maintenance performed, environmental conditions, etc.

A reaction plan is developed to minimize disruptions when a process is out of control (assignable cause occurs). The reaction plan is either a checklist or flowchart that the operator uses to take corrective action and learn more about the assignable cause.

The administration step dictates that specific tasks should be handled by properly trained personnel. The team that plans the control chart should assign responsibilities. Tasks should be clearly identified on the planning form and the assigned people notified of their responsibilities. The tasks may include making measurements, recording data, computing statistics, plotting statistics, revising control limits, and filing forms.

Finally, a schedule to analyze the control chart at specified times should be established. All members involved with the control chart plan should be present.

7.6.3 Types of control charts

The type of control chart to be employed depends on the process to be evaluated, the number of levels of a variable to be monitored, the precision desired, etc. In SPC, two types of control charts are commonly used, Shewhart and cumulative summation (CUSUM) control charts.

7.6.3.1 Shewhart control charts. The Shewhart control chart is a graphical presentation of quality control efficiency (USDA, 1987). If the procedure is 'in control', the results will almost always fall within the established control limits.

Shewhart charts (also known as X and R charts) display the mean and range (standard deviation) values for a given process. To indicate boundaries of acceptable operation, control limits are drawn on the chart. Upper and lower control limits are often set at ±3 standard deviations from the mean (Shainin, 1990). New control limits must be ascertained for the process if there is any type of modification (e.g. new ingredient or equipment alteration).

Figure 7.2 is a typical example of a Shewhart chart. The center dark line indicates the mean value and the control limits are depicted by dashed lines. The range values are shown in the lower part of the graph. The Shewhart chart provides an effective method for determining whether variation is attributable to unassignable or assignable causes. It discloses trends and cycles that can lead to the diagnosis of problems created by assignable causes and promotes corrective action. Out of control situations

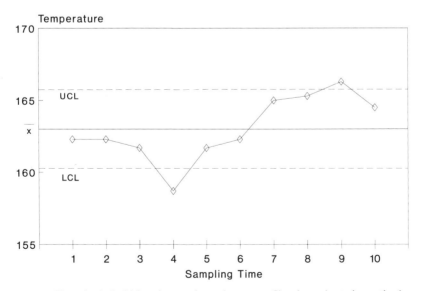

Figure 7.2 Hypothetical chicken breast thermal process. Shewhart chart shows the lower control limit (LCL), upper control limit (UCL), and average value (x). In this process, a drop below an internal temperature of 160°F (71°C) LCL represents underprocessing of chicken product and warrants a decision on product disposition (e.g. decision to reprocess). Processing temperatures above the UCL lead more to quality and energy concerns.

can be signaled by the occurrence of one or more points outside the control limits or seven or more consecutive points above or below the central mean line showing a trend or bias (USDA, 1987).

7.6.3.2 CUSUM control charts. The CUSUM control chart is a graphic plot of the running summation of process deviation from a control value (Webb and Price, 1987; USDA, 1987). Its underlying mathematical concepts are highly involved, but its construction is simple. The employment of CUSUM charts allows an operator to detect small changes in the process, giving a more accurate account of changes that might occur. Consequently, the CUSUM chart is more sensitive to process variation than the Shewhart control chart. CUSUM charts allow rapid detection of process deviation. However, their application is not practical on systems that drift over extended periods of time or have (comparing) multiple levels (USDA, 1987; Webb and Price, 1987).

Similar to Shewhart charts, they have a central line from which to judge process variation (Figure 7.3). However, the central line does not represent the actual mean of production samples, but rather zero deviation from a control value. Points that deviate from the central line result from summation of subsequent deviations. For more information on CUSUM charts and their construction, the reader should consult the *Chemistry Quality Assurance Handbook* (USDA, 1987).

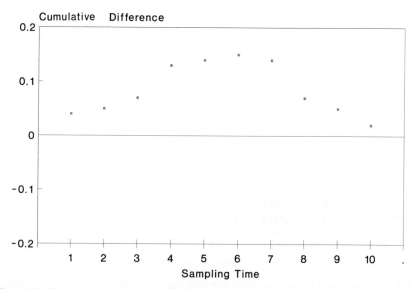

Figure 7.3 Cumulative summation (CUSUM) chart demonstrating a hypothetical pH trend analysis of a macaroni salad product. When points climb or fall, the pH is above or below the control value (central line). When the pH is near the control value, points run horizontal (middle section of graph) to the control value.

7.6.4 *Capability*

Capability studies compare results to original specification to determine if the variation expected in the process could be contained by specification limits (Clements, 1988). This is achieved by measuring variability, calculating control limits, and determining whether the process is stable and within designed specifications. The capability index or ratio (C_p) indicates how much of the tolerance range is consumed by the expected variation of the process. C_p can be calculated as follows:

$$C_p = \frac{\text{specified width}}{\text{process width}}$$

If the C_p is $\geqslant 1.0$, then the process variability is at or within the 3 standard deviations. Conversely, $C_p < 1.0$ indicates that the process variability exceeds 3 standard deviations, and adjustments must be made to improve the process. An ideal process will have a C_p of $\geqslant 1.33$ (Clements, 1988). At $\geqslant 1.33$, the process is using $\leqslant 75\%$ of the tolerance range.

7.6.4.1 *Sampling and monitoring CCPs.*

A sample is a portion of a population or lot. It may consist of an individual or groups of individuals (Taylor, 1987a). Carefully designed sampling plans are typically required to provide reliable samples. The plan should address the type and number of samples to be taken, the details of collection, and the procedures to be followed. In a HACCP system, samples taken at CCPs during monitoring should represent the population from which they are taken. Poor sampling (monitoring) can lead to a misrepresentation of conditions that truly exist and defeat the purpose of a HACCP system altogether. This could result in a breakdown in food safety.

Those involved in a HACCP program must determine how established CCPs will be monitored. Decisions such as: when to record the results of monitoring, whether continuous or interval monitoring will occur at a given CCP, and the type of measurement or instrument to be incorporated must be made. If the process is continuously monitored, how often will the data be processed?

An appropriate statistical analysis program is a basic requirement of SPC. In the development of sampling plans, statistics can allow determination of (i) the limits of confidence for a measured value of the population mean, (ii) the tolerance interval for a given percentage of the individuals in the population, and (iii) the minimum number of samples required to establish the above intervals with a selected confidence level (Taylor, 1987a). For additional information on sampling plans, the reader should refer to such sources as Taylor (1987a) and the *Chemistry Quality Assurance Handbook* (USDA, 1987).

7.7 Summary

To be effective, food safety programs of the future must have a foundation based on the principles of risk analysis and HACCP. Food safety reforms at the government and industry levels should result in the increased use of scientifically proven systems for controlling food safety hazards. Such systems will include HACCP programs that use effective interventions throughout slaughtering and processing, also with extensive employee and consumer education.

The present organoleptic system of inspection has done a very good job of preventing diseased animals and physical contaminants from entering the food chain, but the war on pathogens will only be won by spreading the risk-based HACCP safety net from the farm to the table. Parts of the present system should be retained, but inspection reform should significantly change the focus from just the slaughter/processing segment to include the entire food chain. Such a system will require the active participation of all segments – the industry, government regulators and consumers.

Acknowledgements

The authors express their sincere gratitude and appreciation to James Marsden and Kelly Karr of the American Meat Institute and James Ball, Pam Stachelek and Payton Pruett of Webb Technical Group, Inc. for their help and support.

References

Acuff, G.R. (1993) *Microbiological Criteria*. Paper presented at World Congress on Meat and Poultry Inspection. Oct. 10–14, 1993. College Station, Texas.
Banks, J. (1989) History and evaluation of quality control, in *Principles of Quality Control*. John Wiley & Sons, Inc., New York.
Barkate, M.L., Acuff, G.R., Lucia, L.M. and Hale, D.S. (1992) Hot water decontamination of beef carcasses for reduction of initial bacterial numbers. *Meat Sci.* **35**, 397.
Clements, R. (1988) *Statistical Process Control and Beyond*. Robert E. Krieger Publishing, Malabar, Florida.
Codex (1981) Codex Alimentarius Commission, 14th Session, 1981: *Report of the 17th Session of the Codex Committee on Food Hygiene, Washington, D.C. 17–21 Nov. 1980*. Food and Agricultural Organization, Rome.
FAO/WHO (Food and Agricultural Organization/World Health Organization) (1979) *Microbiological Criteria for Foods*. Report of a Joint FAO/WHO Working Group on Microbiological Criteria for Foods, Geneva, 20–26 February 1979. WHO, Geneva.
Hudak-Roos, M. and Garrett, E.S. (1992) Monitoring critical control points critical limits, in *HACCP: Principles and Applications*. M.D. Pierson and D.A. Corlett (eds), Van Nostrand, Reinhold, New York. pp. 62–71.
ICMSF (1986) *Microorganisms in Foods. 2. Sampling for Microbiological Analysis: Principles*

and Specific Applications. 2nd edn., International Commission on Microbiological Specifications for Foods. University of Toronto Press, Toronto.

Juran, J.M. and Gryna, F.M. (1988) *Juran's Quality Control Handbook*. 4th edn., McGraw Hill, New York.

Kindred, T.P. (1993) *An Overview of Risk Assessment*. Paper presented at Ninety-seventh Annual Meeting of the United States Animal Health Association, October 23–29, 1993. Las Vegas, Nevada.

NACMCF (1992) National Advisory Committee on Microbiological Criteria for Foods. *Hazard Analysis and Critical Control Point System*, March 20, 1992.

National Cattlemen's Association (1994) *National Beef Safety Research Agenda: A Research Plan for Beef Safety Research*. Englewood, Colorado.

National Live Stock and Meat Board (1994) *Solving the* E. coli *0157:H7 problem: A Blueprint for Industry Action*. Final Report of the Blue Ribbon Task Force. Chicago, Illinois.

NAS, National Research Council (1983) *Risk Assessment in the Federal Government: Managing the Process*. National Academy Press, National Academy of Sciences, Washington, D.C.

National Research Council (1989) *Improving Risk Communication*. National Academy Press, National Academy of Sciences. Washington, D.C.

Nolan, K.M. (1990) Planning a control chart. Quality Progress. American Society for Quality Control, Milwaukee, WI (23) Dec. pp. 51–55.

Prasai, P.K., Acuff, G.R., Lucia, L.M., Morgan, J.B., May, S.G. and Savell, J.W. (1992) Microbiological effects of acid decontamination of pork carcasses at various locations in processing. *Meat Sci.* **32**, 413.

Puri, S.C, Ennis, D. and Mullen, K. (1979) *Statistical Quality Control for Food and Agricultural Scientists*. G.K. Hall & Co., Boston, Massachusetts.

Shainin, P.D. (1990) The tools of quality part III: Control charts. Quality progress. American Society for Quality Control, Milwaukee, WI. **23**(8), 79.

Taylor, J.K. (1987a) Principles of sampling, in *Quality Assurance of Chemical Measurements*. Lewis Publishers, Inc., Chelsea, Michigan. pp. 55–74.

Taylor, J.K. (1987b) Control charts, in *Quality Assurance of Chemical Measurements*. Lewis Publishers, Inc., Chelsea, Michigan. pp. 129–146.

USDA (1987) *Chemistry Quality Assurance Handbook*. Vol. 1. United States Department of Agriculture; Food Safety and Quality Service, Washington, D.C.

Webb, N.B. and Price, J.F. (1987) Quality control concepts and systems, in *The Science of Meat and Meat Products*. 3rd edn. Food & Nutrition Press, Westport, Connecticut, pp. 587–623.

Zar, J.H. (1984) *Biostatistical Analysis*. 2nd edn. Prentice-Hall, Englewood Cliffs, New Jersey.

8 Relationship of the HACCP system to Total Quality Management

N.B. WEBB and J.L. MARSDEN

8.1 The importance of quality

8.1.1 What do we mean by quality?

Webster's Dictionary (1989) defines quality as 'a degree of excellence or superiority in kind'. The American Society for Quality Control (ASQC, 1987) specifies that quality is 'the totality of features and characteristics of a product or service that bear on its ability to satisfy stated or implied needs'. Crosby (1979) states that quality is 'conformance to requirements'. Juran (1993) suggests two simple definitions of quality: 'fitness for use' and 'quality is customer satisfaction'.

The term quality has come to embody stringent standards in industrial operations, products, and services. To consumers, quality implies that products will perform as stated by the vendor and that services will be reliable. To the meat, poultry, and seafood industries, quality can be interpreted as satisfying consumer expectations in terms of specific product quality attributes such as food safety, aesthetics, convenience and nutrition.

It is very important that modern food companies define the quality standards for the specific customers they serve. Customers are more demanding than ever and, in general, will seek products and services offered by companies that have a reputation for adhering to stringent quality standards. Therefore, companies that provide goods and services which are consistent in quality stand the greatest chance for growth and, ultimately, survival.

To remain profitable, meat, poultry and seafood processors must incessantly strive for quality improvement and more uniform products. If these industries are to realize customer confidence and long-term benefits in the future, quality must always be a top priority.

8.1.2 The need for a 'culture' change

Juran (1993) felt that two primary forces had a major impact on quality following World War II. The first was the Japanese revolution in quality, and the second was the prominence of product quality in the public mind.

These two forces caused a change in business conditions that are typically influenced by quality (e.g. competition and higher levels of customer satisfaction). Therefore, modifications of such business conditions are necessary for today's companies to survive.

To consistently compete on a quality basis in modern day markets, it is essential for a company to instill a positive attitude towards quality in each of its employees. In other words, there must be a 'culture' throughout the entire organization that emphasizes the importance of quality.

The 'culture' change can be interpreted as the ability to develop and foster a climate encompassing belief, assumption, supposition, wisdom, understanding, etc., that make up the psychological environment within the organization. The company culture encompasses the factors that deal with the minds of people, and environment that conditions attitudes, moderates behaviour and guides action (Price, 1990). To modify a company's performance, cultural factors have to be addressed and attitudes must be changed.

A cultural change requires tremendous effort and dedication from all employee levels, including top management personnel. However, once the commitment to quality is made, rewards are manifested by greater employee motivation, improved uniformity in finished products or services, greater profits and, usually, increased customer satisfaction. By setting precise goals, implementing positive preventive steps and corrective actions to problems, and continuously improving quality, a company will be prepared for future changes as dictated by economics and customer needs.

8.2 Total Quality Management (TQM): the key to continuous quality improvement

8.2.1 TQM defined

Total Quality Management (TQM) can be defined as an effort for continuously improving the quality of all processes, products, and services through universal participation of all employees, that leads to greater customer satisfaction and loyalty, and improved business results (Sarvandan, 1992). Sashkin and Kiser (1993) have stated:

'TQM means that the organization's culture is defined and supports the constant attainment of customer satisfaction through an integrated system of tools, techniques and training. This involves the continuous improvement of organizational processes, resulting in high quality products and services'.

The result of TQM is that companies supply products and services that are economical, useful, competitive, and of uniform quality (King, 1989).

In order to meet the modern day needs for quality control, many American corporations, governmental agencies and other groups have instituted TQM programs. In many cases, the TQM approach has produced remarkable changes in how management and employees envision and interpret quality.

The TQM approach requires a company to develop a strategy, involving all levels and functions of the company, that focuses on satisfying the customer. Everyone involved in TQM will have a new 'mind-set' towards quality. Consequently, there will be a drastic and permanent change in the 'culture' of the company, giving company personnel an entirely new focus on quality improvement.

8.2.2 TQM as a vehicle for corporate quality innovation

In the early- and mid-1980s, struggling American firms such as Ford Motor Company and Motorola, Inc. implemented TQM into their corporate frameworks. TQM programs changed the financial directions of these two corporations, as well as those of other struggling companies. As TQM infiltrated Ford, the company's commitment to quality began to be recognized by the motto 'Quality is Job 1'. Because of Ford's improved quality, this automobile manufacturer is now a leader in sales, profits and customer satisfaction.

Motorola, the American leader in the manufacture and sale of semiconductors, has been even more dramatic in its turnaround as a result of TQM. This company has been described as being 'fanatical about quality' by Hart and Bogan (1992), and for good reason. In 1990, Motorola's defect reduction and other quality strategies resulted in a savings of over $500 million in manufacturing costs. Customer rejections were reduced from approximately 40% to negligible levels in less than 10 years.

Because the TQM approach, in many respects, is foreign to current and past management procedures, management must undergo a transformation of philosophy in order to execute TQM, as outlined by Deming (1986). For example, a company operating with a TQM system will not award contracts to suppliers based solely on the lowest bid, but will alternatively develop a long term, mutually supportive relationship to assure that suppliers provide the stipulated quality. The company will utilize teamwork to build quality into its products or services, relying heavily on input from suppliers and customers in order to continuously improve all processes and services. Also, managers will not be evaluated solely by profits nor employees solely by production quotas; instead, quality will be emphasized over production throughput statistics.

Statistical process control procedures will be employed to determine product quality variation so that continuous quality improvement can be effectively measured. Employees at all levels need to be trained and empowered to correct problems on their own initiative, and barriers that typically rob workers of pride in their workmanship must be removed.

The TQM approach is the most consistent and best method to ensure that meat, poultry and seafood products are at a level of quality and safety that consumers have come to expect. Emphasis must be placed upon key factors dictated by customer needs such as shelf-life, convenience, packaging, nutritional attributes and safety.

8.3 The Hazard Analysis Critical Control Point (HACCP) system

The Hazard Analysis Critical Control Point (HACCP) system was jointly developed by The Pillsbury Company, the National Aeronautics and Space Administration, and the US Army Natick Research and Development Laboratories to assure safe foods for the US space program (Bauman, 1990; Sperber, 1991). The HACCP system was established to control and monitor every step of a food process to evolve as a preventive rather than as an inspection-oriented quality control system. As a result, HACCP was espoused as a zero defects approach to safe food processing.

HACCP is most widely defined as a sytematic preventive, seven-principle approach to food safety. The steps include (NACMCF, 1992):

1. Conducting a hazard analysis and risk assessment.
2. Determining critical control points (CCPs).
3. Establishing critical limits for CCPs.
4. Monitoring critical limits.
5. Correcting deviations from critical limits.
6. Establishing an effective record keeping system.
7. Verifying that the HACCP program is working correctly.

For the HACCP system to be successfully incorporated into a food process, all of the principles must be carefully implemented for the specific process. This is best accomplished within a TQM framework.

The objective of a HACCP program is to preclude problems associated with hazards (physical, chemical and microbiological) in food products. The essential preventive evaluations and corrective actions are controlled by the worker. In other words, quality control of potentially hazardous points is built into the process as production occurs versus evaluation or testing of final products (Sperber, 1991). This is how the TQM concept is applied in the implementation of a successful HACCP system.

The combination of TQM and HACCP provides a total systems approach to food processing, encompassing the elements of food safety, food quality and productivity (NFPA, 1992). This combined approach will stress commitment, education, preventive and corrective action, statistical control, record keeping, verification and teamwork.

The incorporation of effective statistical, record keeping and verification procedures are critical in making the HACCP system work effectively. Statistical procedures may include the utilization of cumulative summation (CUSUM) or Shewhart (X bar R) charts (USDA, 1987; Webb and Price, 1987) to monitor and maintain control of CCPs. Record keeping provides evidence that procedures and processes were followed in a manner that assures a safe process. HACCP records should include, but not be limited to HACCP team members and responsibilities, hazards associated with each CCP and corresponding preventive measures, critical limits, monitoring systems and corrective actions (NACMCF, 1992). To assure that the HACCP system is operating as outlined, verification procedures should include such activities as (NACMCF, 1992):

1. Scientific evaluation of critical limits to assure that these limits are adequate.
2. Random sample collection and analysis.
3. Frequent reviews of the HACCP plan to demonstrate its effectiveness.
4. Review of process deviations or product dispositions.
5. Revalidation of the HACCP plan.

TQM teams, responsible for developing and implementing HACCP, should comprise representatives from a variety of disciplines and workers from all levels. This type of diversity assures effective evaluation of all areas that may have an impact on safe food processing. TQM teams have been referred to as 'quality circles' (Juran, 1967; Taylor, 1987; Sashkin and Kiser, 1993), and these teams are necessary in making a TQM program successful. In addition, a sound HACCP operation requires a company to establish a strong, positive rapport with all vendors to ensure that consistent and safe raw materials and/or supplies are provided.

Those responsible for developing and implementing a HACCP system within a TQM program should not be complacent and believe that a simple HACCP approach is sufficient to prevent or solve all food safety problems. Rather, a HACCP system, within a TQM program, must entail a philosophy, culture, and discipline that educates everyone in the company to anticipate and solve even the most complex problems associated with food safety.

Archer (1990) has indicated that a HACCP program must be flexible. Management must recognize new microbiological, chemical or physical hazards as they emerge and adapt the HACCP plan to address these new safety issues. A company that effectively applies a flexible, adaptable HACCP program can consistently provide safe foods for its customers.

8.4 Modern quality management: striving for continuous quality improvement

Before the implementation of modern-day quality management, American philosophies centered on the containment of defective products (Crosby, 1989). American manufacturers viewed the occurrence of defects as an inevitable part of processing, and would resign themselves to the fact that losses would arise due to reworks.

The Japanese 'invasion' of American business in the 1970s initiated rethinking of the quality procedures and policies practiced in the USA (Crosby, 1989). Initially, Americans accused Japan of 'price dumping'. However, careful examination of Japanese business procedures revealed that Japan had made a serious commitment to quality, thus dramatically reducing costs. Ironically, the Japanese concepts of quality had been derived from the teachings of such American quality authorities as Deming and Juran (Doty, 1991). These experts stressed the importance of quality throughout the production system and the utilization of statistical methods for sustaining it. Consequently, the Japanese would capitalize on the concepts that Americans had initially ignored.

8.4.1 Steps for successful transition: philosophies of quality management leaders

Deming's (1986) philosophy on quality improvement is effectively paraphrased as 14 points of quality transformation. These points, paraphrased below, can be applied to all businesses: small-to-large, service, or manufacturing.

1. Create constancy of purpose toward improvement – Aim to become competitive and give consumers what they want.
2. Adopt a new philosophy – Management must awaken to the challenge of a new economic age.
3. Cease dependence on inspection – Eliminate mass inspection by building quality into the product.
4. Eliminate awarding business for the price of profitability – Move toward a single supplier for any one item, establishing a long-term relationship between purchaser and supplier.
5. Improve constantly.
6. Institute on the job training.
7. Institute supervisor leadership – Stress quality over productivity.
8. Drive out fear – Give employees the opportunity to express their ideas and eliminate fear of not reaching production quotas.
9. Eliminate barriers between departments – People from all departments must work as a team to anticipate problems and continuously improve processes.

10. Eliminate slogans, exhortations and targets – These devices do not consider that most problems are related to the system (process) and not the people.
11. Eliminate work standards, numerical goals and management objectives and numbers – Replace work standards with leadership.
12. Remove barriers that rob employees of pride – Management must listen to employees and give them the resources to perform well.
13. Institute education and self-improvement.
14. Transformation is everybody's job.

According to Juran (1993), customer satisfaction can be achieved through two components: (i) product features, and (ii) freedom from deficiencies. Product features (e.g. durability, performance, reliability, etc.) refer to the quality of design and have a major effect on market share and the ability to establish premium prices (i.e. product or service specifications). Freedom from deficiencies refers to conformance to product or service specifications (i.e. zero defects). Products that are free from deficiencies lead to cost reductions (e.g. less rework, fewer customer complaints, etc.). This component addresses the assurance of uniformity for customers.

Juran (1993) concluded that TQM is a systematic process which must be led by upper management. Quality goals must be developed and responsibilities be assigned to achieve established targets. Employee participation through quality circles is strongly recommended by Juran (1967).

In the early 1960s, Crosby (1979) began advocating a zero defects concept. He believed that management received what it requested. If managers expected a percentage of nonconforming products, then they would receive that percentage. Conversely, if managers emphasized prevention and trained employees accordingly, then defect-free products and services would result (Crosby, 1979, 1989).

Crosby (1979, 1984) has also described 14 steps to quality improvement, these being somewhat different from Deming's (1986) 14 points. The key elements of these steps include the ideas of commitment, teamwork, quality awareness, corrective action and zero defects. The final step suggested that a company repeat the entire 14-step procedure. This implies the dynamic nature of quality improvement, continuous enhancement through learning, monitoring, and participating.

Crosby (1984) emphasized 'do it right the first time' and clearly identify or define the 'it' for employees. 'It' can be interpreted as any task that an employee conducts in a job or during a process. The quality of the final product will depend on the successful execution of 'it'. Crosby (1986) also stressed the fact that quality is the 'price of nonconformance' or the price of doing things wrong. He stated that preventing a company from going to sleep, keeping the management team filled with dreams, offering customers new and improved products, and creating an enjoyable work environment make a company continually successful.

Peters and Waterman (1982) researched the problems of the effectiveness of management in creating a corporate quality improvement system. Their investigation helped raise the level of executive thinking about quality. Furthermore, they stipulated important changes that must occur in management philosophy in order to make quality improvement a reality.

In summary, quality management philosophers generally agree on a few basic principles that lead to successful programs, *viz.*:

1. The customer is the key. Products and services must be designed to meet customer needs, and thus, customer input is critical.
2. Quality involves the participation of everyone in the company, including all levels of management, line employees, as well as the participation of suppliers and distributors. Quality improvement must be a part of the company culture.
3. When quality is emphasized, tasks should be performed correctly the first time, while constantly striving for improvement.

8.4.2 *Quality leadership for the future*

According to an interview by Axland (1993), Juran has indicated that the quality leaders of the future can help their respective economies by aiding in the development of quality know-how for the society in general. These leaders must have a broad knowledge of the principles of successful quality management. Armand V. Feigenbaum, another modern quality authority, has characterized future quality leaders as people with broad quality backgrounds (Axland, 1993). These leaders should emphasize infrastructure leadership, and partnerships among the various sectors of business, government and education.

Although the principles of modern quality management were predominantly developed by the non-food industries, they can be effectively and practically applied in the meat, poultry and seafood industries. These industries must move faster in adopting the principles of modern quality management in order to meet the food safety and consumer quality issues in the near future and to develop a sound base for the long term.

8.5 The economics of quality

8.5.1 *The impact of quality on company finances*

The cost of quality is not easily definable. According to Deming (1986), there is a danger in relying solely on visible figures (e.g. production statistics, sales, overhead costs). Consequently, Crosby (1979) was very adamant about defining quality in economic terms. Although quality costs are sometimes hard to determine, the final value can be readily discerned in the profitability of the firm. Some of the less easily defined benefits from TQM are:

1. The multiplying effects on sales from satisfied customers or the negative effects on sales from dissatisfied customers.
2. The enhancement of productivity when a quality culture becomes effective.
3. The tremendous positive influence due to improved pride of workmanship and employee morale.

Sarvandan (1992) suggested that quality improvement has an impact on a company both internally and externally. Internally, when quality improves, there will be higher productivity, allowing the company to increase market share and usually increase profits. Externally, quality enhancement increases customer satisfaction and loyalty, with an increase in repeat purchases or services.

8.5.2   Quality audits

The concept of performing a periodic audit of quality assessment, quality control or quality management has been a part of TQM since its inception. A company should conduct periodic audits to determine the financial, as well as other, benefits of the quality program. According to Crosby (1979), ideally, the performance of a TQM program can best be expressed in terms of dollars realized from a quality improvement process.

The stepwise procedures for developing financial advantages and audits in meat processing operations have been defined by Webb (1979). Essentially, it involves the assessment and budgeting of a program of quality management and financially tracking each step to determine the benefits. This system stipulates that quality costs can be placed into three categories, viz.: failures, appraisals and prevention. Webb (1979) has outlined methods for accurately determining these costs. In most cases, these methods are appropriate in modern TQM systems.

Failures comprise such elements as rework, product damage, spoilage, liability losses and troubleshooting costs. Appraisals include testing, evaluation, laboratory operation, outside services (e.g. consultation) and USDA control requirements; in general, this is the verification component of HACCP. Finally, prevention will incorporate such activities as special training sessions, quality assurance programs, development of specifications, creation of testing procedures and quality circle activities.

Current emphasis on HACCP applications in the meat, poultry and seafood industries suggests that the best expenditure of resources is the implementation of a HACCP system within a TQM program. However, many HACCP systems have been developed for the specific purpose of avoiding or preventing catastrophes in food safety without considering TQM. This is not a financially sound basis for establishing a HACCP plan. HACCP should be viewed as a component of the overall quality improvement process by specifically targeting food safety. It is imperative that a TQM program be developed for the entire company and that a HACCP system be part of the TQM approach. Food safety should play a major role in the operation of TQM, but it should not be the only consideration in terms of a corporate approach to quality management. These costs should be viewed as an investment of resources within the preventive realm. However, HACCP can result in a poor return for the investment unless the benefits of TQM are realized.

Within this total approach to quality management, the economics of profitability will be realized for the HACCP food program. In order to sustain the system, management should install an ongoing financial auditing and tracking system for the HACCP and quality management programs. This type of plan must be clearly stipulated at the onset of the program so that those responsible for providing the resources are aware of the long-term benefits, as well as the measurement of effectiveness, losses, failures, etc.

Sarvandan (1992) indicated that even successful and profitable firms should implement TQM. TQM prevents complacency, instills pride in its employees and stockholders, increases competitiveness and keeps the company aware of customer requirements. Without a successful TQM program, today's successful company could be tomorrow's poor performer.

8.6 Implementation of TQM and HACCP

8.6.1 Phases of TQM implementation

According to Jablonski (1991), there are five phases necessary for the successful implementation of TQM. These include:

1. Preparation.
2. Planning.
3. Assessment.
4. Implementation.
5. Diversification.

The initial phase, preparation, is unique relative to other phases in that it has a definite beginning and end. The other phases evolve over time and are continuous. In the preparation phase, key executives of the company, with the aid of a professional facilitator, prepare a vision statement, set goals and write a policy that supports the strategic plan of the company. The preparation phase concludes with a commitment of resources necessary to plan for TQM implementation.

Planning lays the foundation for change within the organization. In this phase, the implementation plan is developed and resources are committed for specific objectives.

The assessment phase involves exchange of information necessary to support the preparation, planning, implementation, and diversification phases. It consists of surveys, evaluations, questionnaires and interviews throughout all levels of the company. Implementation entails training managers and workers with the intent of evaluating and improving processes and implementing change. Finally, diversification may be performed after successful completion of the previous stages. If TQM has had a favorable impact on the organization, an effort is made to include other company departments, subsidiaries and suppliers.

Within the diversification phase, a company should select the best suppliers, with the ultimate goal of developing a long-term, mutually supporting relationship with a limited number of suppliers (Deming, 1986). This allows the supplier to develop economy and innovative approaches, as well as better meet requirements for the company. Other advantages of this approach include: more uniform products and/or services, a continuous flow of products, inventory reduction, increased efficiency with price negotiations and more time working with the supplier on quality specifications. As a consequence, good supplier/company relationships will be developed because the company treats the supplier as a partner rather than as a vendor (NFPA, 1992). Ultimately, the long-term relationship between a company and a limited number of suppliers will result in greater productivity and profit.

Similar to the development of a new product or service, creation of a TQM program demands time, training, research and fine-tuning. Successful TQM programs require commitment and patience. It took the DuPont Polymers Division four years to realize positive results through TQM according to Gibson (1987). This company went back to the drawing board many times before it was able to create an effective quality framework. However, because of its hard work and commitment, DuPont is now reaping tremendous benefits from its efforts.

8.6.2 Crosby's Quality Improvement Process (QIP)

Crosby's (1984, 1985) Quality Improvement Process (QIP) is a sound approach for the perpetuation of TQM. The stages of QIP are described as the six Cs by Crosby, viz.:

Comprehension deals with understanding the basics of quality improvement. Once there is understanding, all employees can begin their *commitment* to quality improvement.

Competence involves implementation of quality improvement in a methodical way, ensuring that everyone understands and has an opportunity to participate in the improvement.

Communication requires two-way interaction and involves complete understanding and support of everyone in the corporate society, including customers and suppliers.

Correction eliminates errors by identifying problems and determining the causes of these problems. This involves employees from all levels and departments.

Continuance ensures that quality improvement will continue forever in a TQM company.

8.6.3 Quality circles

A TQM operation requires teamwork. Therefore, it is logical to develop teams which can effectively conduct process quality improvements. During the Japanese quality revolution, such teams became known as quality circles.

A quality circle is a small group of people doing similar work, meeting regularly to identify, analyze and solve product quality problems, as described by Amsden and Amsden (1976). The main objective of the circle is to prevent and solve problems related to the quality of outputs. Almost any process can benefit from a quality circle analysis. As a result, teamwork is highly beneficial for establishing and maintaining the seven principles of the HACCP approach. Quality circles can be an organizational resource for preventing problems, troubleshooting and training other employees (Taylor, 1987).

Quality circles give employees an opportunity to make constructive contributions to their jobs, causing workers to take more interest and pride in their jobs. The environment fostered by a quality circle can stimulate the creativity of employees and help defeat complacency. The quality circles concept is based upon the premise that management believes an employee performing a job can do more about controlling the quality for the specific process or service than anyone else.

It has been determined that the successful implementation of quality circles can best be achieved by first providing seminars, workshops, and/or videos for both supervisors and employees. These presentations must include detailed methods for establishing quality circles and the guidelines for their continued effectiveness. Managers and supervisors can then follow-up with effective application of this information with the employees.

Taylor (1987) recommended that a quality circle should operate by:

1. Clearly identifying problems, which are studied in relation to the total processes.
2. Generating ideas to solve problems, grouping similar ideas together and prioritizing them according to importance or urgency.
3. Taking action to prevent or solve problems through iteration, implementation, and recommendations.

Iteration involves defining a problem and soliciting the attention of other quality circles. Depending upon the situation, the quality circle may choose to implement the ideas developed or make recommendations to management for consideration. Even if ideas are adopted by the team, management should be informed before there is iteration with other circles or inclusion of team-generated ideas into company policies. However, the quality circle should have the authority to act when a process is out of control in order to return that process to pre-approved specifications.

8.6.4 HACCP implementation in a TQM company

The five phases of TQM implementation described by Jablonski (1991) may serve as a guide for establishing a company HACCP system. Corlett (1992) indicated that HACCP must be the cornerstone of a food processor's safety system and an integrated part of the company's quality assurance program.

In the preparation of a HACCP system, the company must be willing to set goals, commit resources, and offer management support. A HACCP team should be assembled and contain individuals with backgrounds appropriate to the food product or process. In the planning phase, the team will describe the food process, identify the intended use of the food product and develop a flow diagram that characterizes the food process. The flow diagram must be verified for the food process when assessing the HACCP plan. In addition, a hazard analysis will be conducted to identify where significant hazards may occur in the food process, and what preventive measures will be needed to control these hazards.

When the HACCP team is confident that they have thoroughly characterized the food process, the HACCP system is ready for implementation. Modifications of the HACCP plan may occur during implementation to further enhance the safety of the food process. Diversification of the HACCP system will require that the company seek cooperation from ingredient suppliers to further ensure food safety. Letters of guarantee from each supplier should indicate that the ingredients provided to the company meet the specifications of hazard levels outlined by the HACCP plan.

Some elements of TQM should be considered important in the

implementation of an effective HACCP program (NFPA, 1992). These include:

1. Management and employee training and education.
2. Operator control.
3. Teamwork.
4. Effective communication between management and workers.
5. Constancy of purpose by management.

8.6.5 Application of a HACCP system in a TQM meat processing company

Although HACCP focuses on food safety, incorporating HACCP principles within the TQM plan allows monitoring of both food safety and food quality. In addition to the critical control points (CCPs) defined by a HACCP system, essential quality control points (QCPs) can be specified and implemented by employing the same seven-principle system used for HACCP. Thus, the same procedures that are employed to define CCPs in a HACCP system can be effectively used to define QCPs in a TQM program. Identification and monitoring of both CCPs and QCPs are necessary in an effective TQM program.

At this point, it is critical to note that HACCP should deal almost exclusively with food safety issues. Therefore, CCPs should remain the priority of the HACCP system, with the QCPs being a separate but important part of the TQM program.

A ground beef patty process is used as an example to demonstrate the implementation of a HACCP system within a TQM program. Figure 8.1 is a flow diagram illustrating the steps of the ground beef patty process (USDA, 1991), indicating ingredient and product handling from receiving to distribution. The flow diagram should reveal all the potential points where food safety could be a concern. Once the process points are agreed upon, the HACCP team should perform an on-site verification of the flow diagram.

Hazard analysis and risk assessment are conducted under the first principle of HACCP to provide a basis for determining CCPs. All potential microbiological, chemical and physical hazards associated with the process must be addressed by the team during hazard analysis. A list of steps are then prepared for the process indicating where significant hazards occur along with the appropriate preventive measures (NACMCF, 1992).

Figure 8.2 shows a microbiological hazard analysis for the ground beef patty. Chemical and physical analyses also should be conducted. Product and ingredient examples (meat and non-meat) were evaluated using established hazard analysis and risk categories (NACMCF, 1992).

The second principle of HACCP specifies that CCPs should be

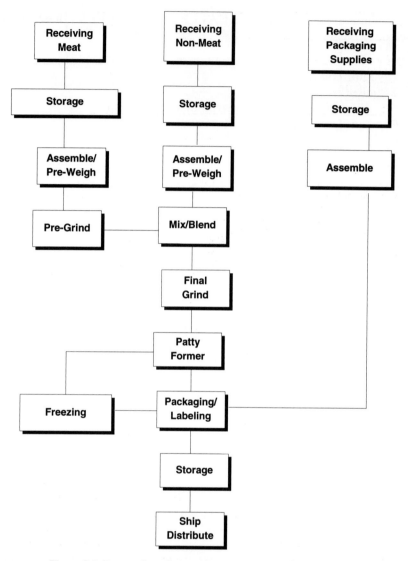

Figure 8.1 Process flow diagram for ground beef patty process.

determined for a food process. Using the flow diagram (Figure 8.1), the information from the hazard analysis (Figure 8.2), and the CCP decision tree (Figure 8.3), one can systematically assign CCPs to process steps. The CCP decision tree allows one to determine if a CCP exists at a certain step by asking and answering questions about the occurrence and elimination of certain hazards.

	A	B	C	D	E	F	RISK CATEGORY
PRODUCT Ground Beef	0	+	+	0	+	0	III
INGREDIENTS (Examples)							
Meat Fresh Chuck	0	+	+	+	+	+	V
Non-Meat Salt	0	0	0	0	0	0	0

Figure 8.2 Microbiological hazard analysis and assignment of risk categories for ground beef patty product. *Hazard analysis – Hazard A*: A special class that applies to nonsterile products designated and intended for consumption by at-risk populations, e.g., infants, the aged, the infirm, or immunocompromised individuals. *Hazard B*: The product contains 'sensitive ingredients' in terms of microbiological hazards. *Hazard C*: The process does not contain a controlled processing step that effectively destroys harmful microorganisms. *Hazard D*: The product is subject to recontamination after processing before packaging. *Hazard E*: There is substantial potential for abusive handling in distribution or in consumer handling that could render the product harmful when consumed. *Hazard F*: There is no terminal heat process after packaging or when cooked in the home. *Analysis note*: Hazards can also be stated for chemical or physical hazards, particularly if a food is subject to them. *Risk categories – Category VI*. A special category that applies to nonsterile products designated and intended for consumption by at-risk populations, e.g., infants, the aged, the infirm, or immunocompromised individuals. All six hazard characteristics must be considered. *Category V*. Food products subject to all five general hazard characteristics. Hazard Class B, C, D, E, F. *Category IV*. Food products subject to four general hazard characteristics. *Category III*. Food products subject to three of the general hazard characteristics. *Category II*. Food products subject to two of the general hazard characteristics. *Category I*. Food products subject to one of the general hazard characteristics. *Category 0*. No hazard. *Categories note*: Ingredients are treated in the same manner in respect to how they are received at the plant, *before* processing. This permits determination of how to reduce risk in the food system. *Source*: NACMCF (1992).

Within the context of TQM, a QCP decision tree (similar to the CCP decision tree) can be used to assign QCPs to the flow diagram to indicate where a loss of control could lead to a reduction in product quality.

In many cases, the assignment of a CCP to a given step will be debatable. For example, storing or handling meat at elevated temperatures could permit better competition of some pathogenic microorganisms with inherent spoilage microorganisms, allowing such pathogens to grow to levels that may cause foodborne illness. This situation presents a potential microbiological food hazard (especially if the end-user inadequately cooks the product), and thus, warrants the assignment of a CCP(s) at the appropriate step(s). Conversely, holding meat for extended periods of time even at proper temperatures could compromise product quality due to the outgrowth of psychrotrophic spoilage organisms. Under these conditions, one may elect to assign a QCP to the step in question.

Some may feel that the two situations mentioned above should be

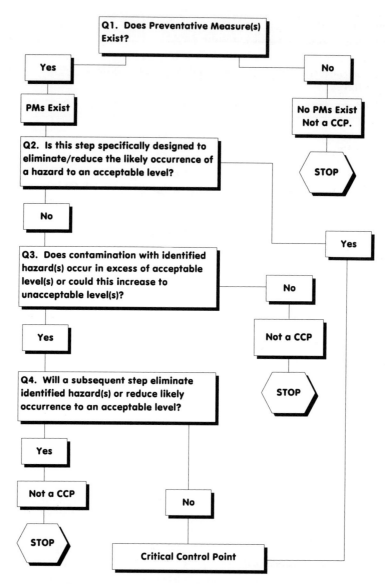

Figure 8.3 Critical control point (CCP) decision tree.

characterized as safety hazards, because of the possible outgrowth of pathogens even at proper holding temperatures (second situation). However, the assignment of CCPs and QCPs must rely on sound scientific evidence and probability (e.g. in most situations at a given step, a question evolves – is a foodborne illness likely to occur or will spoilage microorganisms out-compete pathogens?).

Humber (1992) suggested that a CCP should be characterized as any point where a loss of control may result in a high probability of a health risk. Using this as a guideline, CCPs (Figure 8.4) and QCPs (Figure 8.5) were assigned to the ground beef patty process flow diagram depicted in Figure 8.1.

Principle three of HACCP dictates that critical limits should be

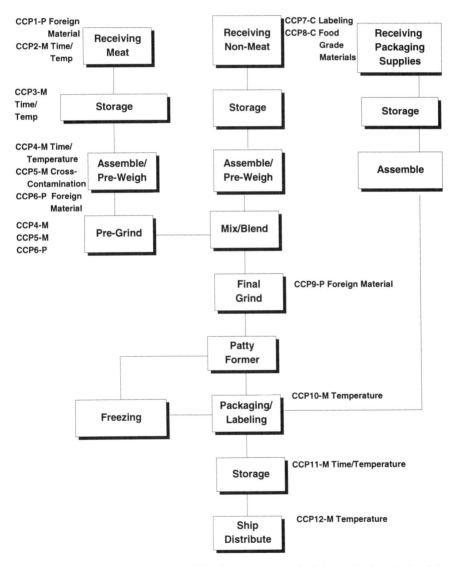

Figure 8.4 Flow diagram for ground beef patty process depicting critical control points (CCPs). M = microbiological; P = physical; C = chemical.

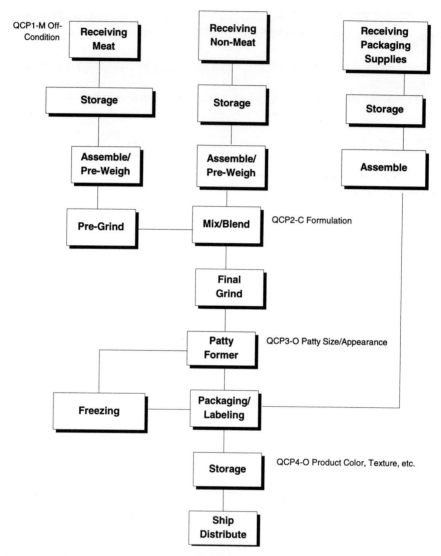

Figure 8.5 Flow diagram for ground beef patty process depicting quality control points (QCPs). M = microbiological; C = chemical; O = organoleptic.

ascertained for each CCP. Figure 8.6 illustrates critical limits for CCPs and a QCP in the meat receiving step of the ground beef patty process. Critical limited created for some CCPs may also be adequate to control quality losses at the same steps. However, some steps in the process will require assignment of separate critical limits where only QCPs and no CCPs exist.

Effective monitoring (specified in principle 4) allows an operator to

PROCESS STEP	CCP/QCP NUMBER	CCP/QCP DESCRIPTION	CRITICAL LIMITS
Receiving Meat	CCP 1-P	Foreign Material	**None detected.**
	CCP 2-M	Time/Temperature	**Time/Temperature To meet buyer specification.**
	QCP 1-M	Off Condition	**Odor and appearance acceptable to plant specifications.**

Figure 8.6 Critical limits for meat receiving step of ground beef patty process. CCP = critical control point; M = microbiological; P = physical.

PROCESS STEP	CCP/QCP NUMBER	CCP/QCP DESCRIPTION	CRITICAL LIMITS	MONITORING
Receiving Meat	CCP 1-P	Foreign Material	None detected.	**Visual inspection.**
	CCP 2-M	Time/Temperature	Time/Temperature To meet buyer specification.	**Take internal temperature of product; check pack date, calculate age.**
	QCP 1-M	Off Condition	Odor and appearance acceptable to plant specifications.	**Organoleptic inspection.**

Figure 8.7 Monitoring actions for critical control points of meat receiving step in ground beef patty process. CCP = critical control point; M = microbiological; P = physical.

maintain control of a process at each CCP (Figure 8.7). Monitoring techniques (e.g. temperature measurement and visual inspection) must also be applied at designated QCPs to effectively control quality. Appropriate corrective actions (principle 5) need to be in place in the event that CCPs or QCPs become out-of-control (exceed critical limits) to maintain product safety and quality.

Record keeping (e.g. Figure 8.8) and verification (HACCP principles 6 and 7, respectively) are critical to proving, maintaining and ensuring food safety. These principles should also be effectively applied within TQM to document product quality and assure customers that measures are being taken to continuously improve product quality in addition to food safety. Records for temperature, time, condition, etc., should be maintained in special HACCP files. Random sample analysis (e.g. microbiological testing), reevaluation of critical limits, and review of the HACCP plan will be included in the verification phase.

Form: Meat Receiving		Evaluator:	Date:
TIME OF RECEIPT	CCP 1-P FOREIGN MATERIAL	CCP 2-M TIME/ TEMPERATURE	QCP 1-M OFF CONDITION
7:30 AM	None	12 Hr/30°F	None
10:15 AM	None	14 Hr/31°F	None
Additional Comments:			

Figure 8.8 Example of a record keeping form that may be used for the meat receiving step of the ground beef patty process. CCP = critical control point.

8.7 ISO 9000

In 1987, the ISO 9000 standards were published by the International Organization for Standardization in Geneva Switzerland (Surak, 1993). The European Community adopted the ISO 9000 series to facilitate trade, increase confidence in outside quality systems and establish procedures for product certification. The series of standards are relevant to all types of industries including chemicals, electronics, steel, transportation, banking, insurance and food processing.

Until recently, only a few US companies have attempted ISO 9000 registration. However, several factors are now increasing US interest in these standards, namely:

1. The nearly unanimous acceptance of ISO 9000 series as quality system standards.
2. The perception that ISO 9000 will be required in order to conduct business in European markets in the future.
3. The potential for regulatory agencies to require ISO 9000 registration as a prerequisite to product certification (Kallnosky, 1990).

The ISO 9000 series is comprised of five individual standards. Three standards provide models for a quality management system. The remaining two standards are guidelines for selection and employment of the appropriate quality system. The five standards are:

ISO 9000: Quality management and quality assurance standards – guidelines for selection and use.

ISO 9001: Quality systems – model for quality assurance in design/ development, production, installation, and servicing.

ISO 9002: Quality systems – model for quality assurance in production and installation.

ISO 9003: Quality systems – model for quality assurance in final inspection and test.

ISO 9004: Quality management and quality system elements – guidelines

The ISO 9001 standard is designed for companies that want to assure conformance to requirements as dictated by the customer for design, development, production, installation and service (Rothery, 1993). ISO 9002 is the standard most often employed by manufacturers. Conformance to this standard indicates that the company is continuing to meet the established designs or specifications for a product. ISO 9003 applies only to companies that demonstrate the ability to competently perform inspection and testing of their own products. Certain elements of ISO 9004 apply to establishing quality systems in service organizations.

ISO 9000 standards should be viewed as a set of minimum quality system requirements for TQM programs to build upon. To put it another way, the standards can be considered the lowest common denominator of quality system requirements for all industry and service groups. Therefore, TQM should go beyond ISO 9000 in respect to incorporating specific technological and competitive elements. This provides a company with the tools needed for continued success.

8.8 The National Quality Award

American companies that successfully implement TQM and incorporate its principles at the highest level can be recognized for their efforts. The National Quality Award resulted from legislation that created a program to honor American companies achieving exceptionally high levels of quality. The award was eventually named in honor of the late Malcolm Baldrige, an avid quality promoter and former Secretary of Commerce, who died in a rodeo accident in 1987 (Marchese, 1991). As a result, the award today is commonly known as the Malcolm Baldrige National Quality Award, or simply as the Baldrige Award.

The Baldrige Award was established to encourage the following goals (Hart and Bogan, 1992):

1. To stimulate American companies to improve quality and productivity for the pride of recognition while obtaining a competitive edge through increased profits.
2. To recognize the achievement of those companies that enhance the quality of their products and services and provide an example to others.
3. To establish guidelines and criteria that can be used by businesses, industrial, and other organizations in evaluating their own quality improvement efforts.
4. To provide specific guidance for other American organizations that wish to learn how to manage for high quality by making available detailed information on how winning organizations were able to change their cultures and achieve eminence.

There are three business divisions that are acknowledged by the Baldrige Award: manufacturing, small business and service. Only two awards can be conferred in any division per year. Judges have the right to withhold awards in a division for a given year.

The Baldrige Award is based on seven categories: (i) leadership, (ii) information and analysis, (iii) quality planning, (iv) human resource utilization, (v) quality assurance, (vi) quality and operational results, and (vii) customer focus and satisfaction (Marchese, 1991; Haavind, 1992; Hart and Bogan, 1992). These categories are further subdivided into 32 subcategories. To be considered worthy of the Baldrige Award, a company obviously must excel in more than one area.

The application and review process for the Baldrige Award is rigorous. However, companies that are interested in revamping their procedures in the pursuit of quality improvement may use the application guidelines for a company 'self' examination. Companies that actually apply receive feedback from Baldrige judging panels and may use the comments to enhance their quality programs.

In addition to the Baldrige Award, there are other national, regional and state quality awards available to companies involved in the quality improvement process. The national newspaper *USA Today* presents a quality award annually. The Erie Quality Award, established in Erie, Pennsylvania and based upon the Baldrige Award guidelines, encourages all Erie County organizations, including non-profit, to continuously improve in quality performance. The North Carolina and Florida Quality Leadership Awards, which have also adopted the Baldrige Award categories, recognize manufacturing and service companies for quality excellence.

8.9 Summary

In the modern industrial world, quality stipulates rigid standards in company operations, products and services. Consumers are becoming more demanding and will generally seek products and services from companies with sound quality reputations. Consequently, satisfying consumer expectations relative to specific product quality attributes such as food safety, aesthetics, convenience and nutrition must be a major priority of the meat, poultry and seafood industries in the future.

For a modern company to compete on a quality basis, a 'culture' change or a new quality mind-set must spread throughout the corporate framework. To establish this new 'culture', many corporations, governmental agencies and other groups have instituted Total Quality Management (TQM) programs. Successfully implemented TQM programs can positively alter management and employee mind-sets concerning quality.

Under TQM, a strategy is developed involving all company levels and functions with the primary goal of satisfying customer needs. This type of program is the most consistent and best technique to ensure that meat, poultry and seafood products are at a level of quality and safety that consumers expect.

Implementation of a HACCP system utilizes many of the same concepts required to incorporate TQM successfully into a company's framework. Effective HACCP systems will advance the TQM principles of team-oriented problem solving and problem prevention, employee motivation and contribution, management support and education. Therefore, a company considering HACCP system implementation should establish a TQM program, if such a program already does not exist.

Those meat, poultry and seafood processing companies wishing to establish international markets will need to create TQM and HACCP programs revolving around the ISO 9000 standards. However, ISO 9000 standards should serve as only basic guidelines for establishing effective TQM and HACCP programs.

Acknowledgements

The authors wish to express their appreciation to Dr. W. Payton Pruett, Jr. for his assistance in the preparation and review of the manuscript and to Mr. James R. Ball and Mrs. Pamela S. Stachelek for their assistance in the research and review of the manuscript.

References

ASQC (1987) Quality systems terminology, in *American National Standard*. American Society for Quality Control, Milwaukee, Wisconsin. p. 2.

Amsden, D.M. and Amsden, R.T. (1976) QC circles = participative problem solving, in *QC Circles: Applications, Tools, and Theory*. American Society for Quality Control, Milwaukee, Wisconsin. pp. 2–4.

Archer, D.L. (1990) The need for flexibility in HACCP. *Food Technol.* **44**(5), 174.

Axland, S. (1993) Forecasting the future of quality. *Qual. Prog.* **26**(2), 21.

Bauman, H.E. (1990) HACCP: Concept, development, and application. *Food Technol.* **44**(5), 156.

Corlett, D.A., Jr. (1992) Putting the pieces together: Developing an action plan for implementing HACCP, in *HACCP: Principles and Applications* (M.D. Pierson and D.A. Corlett eds). Van Nostrand Reinhold, New York. pp. 105–114.

Crosby, P.B. (1979) *Quality Is Free.* McGraw-Hill, New York.

Crosby, P.B. (1984) *Quality Without Tears: The Art of Hassle-Free Management.* McGraw-Hill, New York.

Crosby, P.B. (1985) *Quality Improvement Through Defect Prevention.* Phillip Crosby Assoc., Inc., Winter Park, Florida.

Crosby, P.B. (1986) *Running Things, The Art of Making Things Happen.* McGraw-Hill, New York.

Crosby, P.B. (1989) *Let's Talk Quality, 96 Questions You Always Wanted to Ask Phil Crosby.* McGraw-Hill, New York. pp. 177–185.

Deming, W.E. (1986) Principles for transformation, in *Out of the Crisis.* Massachusetts Institute of Technology, Center for Advanced Engineering Study, Cambridge, Massachusetts. pp. 23–25.

Doty, L.A. (1991) The nature of SPC, in *Statistical Process Control.* Industrial Press, New York. pp. 1–23.

Gibson, T.C. (1987) The total quality management resource. *Qual. Prog.* **20**(11), 62.

Haavind, R. (1992) A new view of quality, in *The Road to the Baldrige Award: Quest for Total Quality.* Butterworth-Heinemann, Stoneham, Massachusetts. p. 6.

Hart, C.W.L. and Bogan, C.E. (1992) *The Baldrige: What it is, How it's Won, How to Use it to Improve Quality in Your Company.* McGraw-Hill, New York. pp. 3–29.

Humber, J. (1992) Control points and critical control points, in *HACCP: Principles and Applications* (M.D. Pierson and D.A. Corlett eds). Van Nostrand Reinhold, New York. pp. 97–104.

Jablonski, J.R. (1991) TQM implementation, in *Implementing Total Quality Management: An Overview.* Pfeiffer & Co., San Diego, California. pp. 25–41.

Juran, J.M. (1967) The QC circle phenomenon. *Indust. Qual. Control* **23**(7), 15.

Juran, J.M. (1979) *Quality Control Handbook.* 3rd edn. McGraw-Hill, New York.

Juran, J.M. (1993) Basic concepts, in *Quality Planning and Analysis.* 3rd edn. McGraw-Hill, New York. pp. 1–13.

Kallnosky, I.S. (1990) The total quality system: Going beyond ISO 9000. *Qual. Prog.* **23**(6), 50.

King, B. (1989) Hoshin planning and total quality management, in *Hoshin Planning: The Developmental Approach.* GOAL/QCP, Methven, Massachusetts. pp. 1–18.

Marchese, T. (1991) TQM reaches the academy. *Amer. Assoc. Higher Ed.* **14**(3), 1.

NACMCF (1992) *Hazard Analysis and Critical Control Point System.* National Advisory Committee on Microbiological Criteria for Foods, Washington, D.C.

NFPA (1992) HACCP and total quality management – Winning concepts for the 90s: A review. *J. Food Prot.* **55**(6): 459.

Peters, T.J. and Waterman, R.H., Jr. (1982) *In Search of Excellence.* Harper and Row, New York.

Price, F. (1990) The long-neglected tools of quality, in *Right Every Time.* Gower Publishing Company Ltd., Aldershot, UK. pp. 1–18.

Rothery, B. (1993) The standards in detail, in *ISO 9000.* 2nd edn. Gower Press, Brookfield, Vermont. pp. 29–37.

Sarvandan, S. (1992) The quality revolution, in *Total Quality Control Essentials: Key Elements, Methodologies, and Managing for Success.* McGraw-Hill, New York. pp. 1–11.

Sashkin, M. and Kiser, K.H. (1993) *Putting Total Quality Management to Work.* Berrett-Koehler, San Francisco.

Sperber, W. (1991) The modern HACCP system. *Food Technol.* **45**(6), 116.

Surak, J.G. (1993) Understanding the ISO 9000 quality standards. Paper no. 2. Presented at Session 13 of *IFT Ann. Mtg. Symposium: ISO 9000: A Cornerstone of Total Quality Management.* Chicago.

Taylor, J.K. (1987) Quality circles, in *Quality Assurance of Chemical Measurements*. Lewis Publishers, Inc., Chelsea, Michigan. pp. 187–191.

USDA (1987) *Chemistry Quality Assurance Handbook*. Vol. 1, Food Safety and Quality Service, United States Department of Agriculture, Washington, D.C.

USDA (1991) *HACCP Workshop – Fresh Ground Beef*. Food Safety and Inspection Service, United States Department of Agriculture, Dec. 3–5, Phoenix.

Webb, N.B. (1979) The dollars and sense of quality control. *Meat Ind.*, March, 50.

Webb, N.B. and Price, J.F. (1987) Quality control concepts and systems, in *The Science of Meat and Meat Products*. 3rd edn (J.F. Price and B.S. Schweigert eds). Food & Nutrition Press, Westport, Connecticut. pp. 587–621.

Webster's Ninth New Collegiate Dictionary (1989) F.C. Mish (ed), Merriam-Webster Inc., Springfield, Massachusetts.

9 HACCP for delicatessens and meat, poultry and seafood retailers
R.J. PRICE

9.1 Introduction

The application of Hazard Analysis Critical Control Point (HACCP) systems in delicatessens and meat, poultry and seafood retail food stores is the best available means to ensure food safety. An effective HACCP system assures that retail food store customers will not become ill or injured after eating foods handled, processed or prepared in the store. The complexity of HACCP plans for retail deli, meat, poultry and seafood products varies with the raw materials, the amount of handling, processing and preparation involved, and the amount of training workers receive. HACCP plans for fresh raw meat, poultry and seafood that will be fully cooked before consumption may be relatively simple. Plans for ready-to-eat deli products prepared from several potentially hazardous ingredients generally are more complex.

9.2 Potential hazards

Identifying potential hazards for retail deli, meat, poultry and seafood products, and devising means to control them, is the basis for developing a HACCP plan. All predictable biological, chemical and physical hazards that can affect the safety of a food must be identified. Potential food safety problems with retail deli, meat, poultry and seafood products include possible hazards associated with the raw materials received, potentially hazardous handling, preparation, storage and display practices in the retail store, and potential mishandling by the consumer.

9.2.1 Raw materials and ingredients

9.2.1.1 Meat. Animals are often infected by *Salmonella, Campylobacter jejuni, Yersinia enterocolitica, Clostridium perfringens, Escherichia coli* and *Staphylococcus aureus.* The surfaces of meat may become contaminated with these bacteria during slaughter and cutting operations (Bryan, 1988).

Grinding of meat distributes the surface contaminants throughout the product.

Most meats, including beef, pork, lamb, poultry and goat, also contain the parasite *Toxoplasma gondii* which is usually transmitted to humans through consumption of raw or undercooked meat. In healthy individuals, toxoplasmosis is generally asymptomatic. During pregnancy, toxoplasmosis can cause birth defects or fetal death. In immunocompromised individuals, toxoplasmosis can be life threatening (Smith, 1992).

Raw meat can support rapid growth of pathogenic bacteria, but is not a health hazard if thoroughly cooked and handled properly before consumption. Improperly handled and temperature-abused meat is potentially hazardous.

9.2.1.1.1 Beef. Beef is a major vehicle of foodborne illness. It has been associated with outbreaks of *C. perfringens* enteritis, *E. coli* hemorrhagic diarrhea, salmonellosis and staphylococcal food poisoning. Roast beef may be difficult to cook rapidly and mishandling after cooking is common. Spores of *C. perfringens* survive most cooking processes and can germinate and multiply rapidly when products are improperly cooled or stored. Adequately cooked products may be recontaminated with *Salmonella* after cooking through cross-contamination. Staphylococci may contaminate the product during handling after cooking (Bryan, 1988). Improperly cooked ground beef has been implicated in foodborne illness outbreaks of *E. coli* 0157:H7 (Reed, 1994).

9.2.1.1.2 Pork. Bacterial contaminants on pork are similar to those on beef. In addition, raw pork can contain the parasite *Trichinella spiralis* that can cause trichinosis in humans. Risks of pork serving as vehicles in foodborne illness are low when it is adequately cooked and eaten promptly after cooking. Cooked pork spare ribs have been implicated as a vehicle in foodborne illness (Bryan, 1988).

Illness outbreaks from ham are usually due to staphylococcal food poisoning. The elevated salt content of hams selectively favors the growth of staphylococci over other bacteria that normally out compete them on raw, unsalted meats. Contamination occurs during handling. Whole hams or sliced hams are often left at room temperature, or stored in large containers in refrigerators. These conditions provide an opportunity for staphylococci growth and enterotoxin formation. Sliced ham is sometimes made into sandwiches where the bread insulates the ham from rapid cooling, and stacked at room temperature or in display cases (Bryan, 1988).

The handling and mixing associated with the preparation of sausages usually incorporates bacterial contaminants into the sausages. Raw or inadequately cooked pork sausages are common vehicles of *Trichinella spiralis*. Smoked sausages may be a potential problem unless adequately cooked and product temperatures are monitored (Bryan, 1988).

9.2.1.1.3 Other meats and meat products.   Cold cuts have been identified as the vehicle in hepatitis A. Temperature abused meat-loaf, pot pies and stew have caused botulism. Products containing ground or shredded meat are often vehicles in outbreaks involving Mexican foods. Barbecued meat is subject to contamination during slicing, chopping or shredding by hand. Holding barbecued ribs warm, but not hot, and cooling large amounts of ribs in one container promote bacterial growth. Risks of food poisoning vary with the methods of preparation, the amount of post-cooking handling, and storage and cooling practices (Bryan, 1988).

9.2.1.2 Poultry.   Poultry are frequently infected by, or contaminated with, *Salmonella, C. jejuni, Y. enterocolitica, C. perfringens, E. coli*, and *S. aureus*. As with meat, poultry can support rapid bacterial growth. Turkey and chicken are major vehicles of foodborne illness (Bryan, 1988).

9.2.1.2.1 Turkey.   Turkeys are frequently implicated as vehicles of *C. perfringens* enteritis, salmonellosis, and staphyloccal food poisoning. Turkeys usually carry these contaminants into the retail food store. After cooking, turkeys can be recontaminated during slicing and boning. Storage or cooling of whole-cooked turkeys, or boned meat in deep containers, can lead to bacterial growth (Bryan, 1988).

9.2.1.2.2 Chicken.   Bacterial contaminants on chickens are similar to those on turkeys. Risks of properly cooked chicken serving as vehicles in foodborne illness are low when it is eaten promptly after cooking, but increase with subsequent handling and holding time after cooking (Bryan, 1988).

9.2.1.3 Seafood.   Seafood can be contaminated by naturally occurring pathogenic marine bacteria, toxins produced by certain marine plankton, heavy metals that accumulate through the food chain, and bacteria from mishandling. Pathogens may also be derived from sewage pollution of the waters in which fish and shellfish live. As with meat and poultry, seafoods support the rapid growth of bacteria.

Marine biotoxins are produced by species of naturally occurring marine phytoplankton. Biotoxins produced by some of these phytoplankton collect and are carried through intermediate levels in the food chain to the fish and shellfish that are ultimately eaten by humans. There are five recognized biotoxin syndromes in the USA: paralytic (PSP), neurotoxic (NSP), diarrhetic (DSP), and amnesic (ASP) shellfish poisonings, and ciguatera fish poisoning (CFP) (FDA, 1994).

9.2.1.3.1   Fish.   Fish have been implicated in outbreaks of scombroid poisoning, ciguatoxin food poisoning, illnesses from other natural marine toxins, and illnesses from other pathogens (Bryan, 1988).

Scombroid poisoning or histamine toxicity is caused by eating fish that have undergone some spoilage due to certain bacteria, including *Morganella morganii, Hafnia alvei, C. perfringens, Aeromonas aerogenes, Klebsiella pneumonia* and *Vibrio alginolyticus.* These bacteria produce the enzyme histidine decarboxylase, which reacts with the free amino acid histidine, present in some species of fish, to produce histamine. Histamine may form without the usual odors of decomposition. Fish that have been implicated in scombroid poisonings include tunas, mahi mahi, bluefish, sardines, amberjack and mackerel. The toxic nature of such products is not reduced by cooking or canning.

The histamine-forming bacteria usually grow rapidly only at high temperatures. At 32.2°C (90°F), high levels of histamine may appear within 6 hours while 24 hours may be required at 21°C (70°F). Periodic increases in product temperature during storage can result in more histamine being formed. If spoilage occurs at high temperatures, there may be increased levels of histamine without the usual formation of putrid odors, associated with decomposed fish.

Ciguatera food poisoning is caused by the dinoflagellate *Gambierciscus toxicus*, and is carried to humans by contaminated fish from the extreme southeastern USA, Hawaii and tropical waters throughout the world. In south Florida, Bahamian and Caribbean regions, barracuda, amberjack, horseye jack, black jack, other species of jack, king mackerel, large groupers and snappers have, at times, contained ciguatoxin. In Hawaii and throughout the central Pacific, barracuda, amberjack and snapper are at times ciguatoxic. From mid to northeastern Australia, mackerel and barracuda are frequently ciguatoxic. Other naturally occurring biotoxins include tetrodotoxin in puffer fish or fugu, chondrichthytoxin in some sharks, and gempylotoxin, a strongly purgative oil in escolar.

Methyl mercury is a potential hazard in some fish species. Mercury is a naturally occurring metallic substance. Minute quantities of mercury are found in all living matter. Some bacteria convert metallic mercury to organic methyl mercury and the methyl mercury is carried through the food chain. High levels of methyl mercury in fish are a potential health hazard. Nearly all human exposure to methyl mercury is from fresh water and marine seafood. Some marine fish, especially those at the top of the food chain such as swordfish and shark, concentrate methyl mercury from their diet and may contain levels near or above the current FDA action level of one part per million (ppm).

Parasites consumed in raw or undercooked, unfrozen seafood can present a human health hazard. Some seafood species, due to their feeding habits or natural resistance, are less likely to have parasites than other species. Translucent, white-fleshed fish are responsible for over 95% of the parasite related complaints received by the FDA. Some seafood that have been implicated in human infection include ceviche, lomi lomi salmon, salmon roe, sushi, sashimi, green herring, drunken crab, cold smoked fish and undercooked grilled fish (FDA, 1994).

9.2.1.3.2 Molluscan shellfish.   The water quality in molluscan shellfish (clams, mussels, oysters, and scallops) growing areas has a direct impact on the potential health hazard to consumers. This is because:

1. Environments in which shellfish grow are commonly subject to some domestic, industrial or naturally occurring pollution.
2. Shellfish filter and concentrate illness-causing microorganisms and toxic substances present in surrounding waters.
3. Shellfish are often consumed in their entirety, either raw or partially cooked.

Properly cooked scallops are not a hazard when the product is the shucked adductor muscle only.

Most illnesses from molluscan shellfish follow consumption of raw or insufficiently cooked shellfish. Generally, these illnesses are caused by enteric viruses such as hepatitis A and Norwalk virus from sewage pollution or cross contamination, or from *Vibrio* species such as *V. parahaemolyticus*, *V. cholerae* 01, *V. cholerae* non-01 and *V. vulnificus* that naturally occur in warm coastal waters.

The shellfish biotoxin syndromes PSP, DSP and ASP are caused by contaminated shellfish primarily from the northeast and northwest coastal regions of the USA, and from imports from similar climates around the world. ASP has also been found in the viscera of dungeness crab and anchovies along the US west coast. PSP has also been found in the liver of Atlantic mackerel. NSP is caused by contaminated shellfish from the southeastern USA (FDA, 1994).

9.2.1.3.3 Crustaceans.   Shrimp and crab, particularly those from warm coastal waters, are likely to be contaminated with *V. parahaemolyticus*. This bacteria is easily killed by adequate cooking, but recontamination after cooking sometimes occurs (Bryan, 1988).

9.2.1.4 Deli products and ingredients.   Dairy products, raw fruits and vegetables, pasta and eggs may contain pathogenic bacteria. Spices may also contain bacterial spores that may survive cooking processes. Most of these bacteria occur naturally in the foods. Retail food store workers may also add pathogens during the handling and preparation of deli products (Price *et al.*, 1993).

9.2.1.4.1 Dairy products. Raw milk and cheeses made from raw milk are common causes of foodborne illness from *Salmonella, Campylobacter jejuni, Yersinia enterocolitica, E. coli, Brucella* spp., *Listeria* and *S. aureus* (Bryan, 1988). Pasteurized milk and cheeses made from pasteurized milk are pathogen free, but can serve as an excellent medium for rapid bacterial growth when incorporated into deli products. A 1985 outbreak of food poisoning from *Salmonella* included about 20 000 cases, and was probably due to post-pasteurization contamination of pasteurized milk (Mermelstein, 1986).

9.2.1.4.2 Eggs. Egg yolks provide an excellent medium for bacterial growth. Egg whites, however, do not support rapid pathogen growth because they contain inhibitory substances such as lysozyme and conalbumin and have a pH value greater than pH 9. Egg shell mucin and membranes serve as protective barriers, but bacteria such as *Salmonella* can penetrate the shell and survive within the egg. Cracked eggs may also contain pathogens (Bryan, 1988). Eggs from infected flocks may contain *Salmonella* (Bradshaw *et al.*, 1990). Incorporating eggs into deli products enhances the chances of bacterial growth.

9.2.1.4.3 Fruits. Most fruits have a relatively low pH that inhibits growth of pathogenic bacteria. Outbreaks of foodborne illness have been caused by fruit juices contaminated with hepatitis A virus during squeezing and after handling by hepatitis carriers (Bryan, 1988). A 1991 outbreak of *Salmonella* food poisoning in 23 states and Canada was traced to contaminated cantaloupe, watermelon and honeydew melons (CDC, 1991).

9.2.1.4.4 Vegetables. Vegetables are either grown in the ground or close to it and are usually contaminated by soil and by bacteria in the soil. *C. botulinum, C. perfringens* and *Bacillus cereus* are likely contaminants. Baked potatoes held at room temperature for several days and then made into potato salad, and onions held warm in butter all day, were both identified as vehicles of botulism. Tofu has been implicated as a vehicle of *Y. entercolitica.* Coleslaw made from contaminated cabbage was identified as a vehicle in listeriosis. Pinto beans readily support the growth of *B. cereus* and *C. perfringens*, and are a common cause of outbreaks involving Mexican foods.

Fried rice is a common vehicle of foodborne illness outbreaks from Chinese foods. Rice is frequently contaminated with *B. cereus* spores that survive cooking. Holding rice at room temperature, cooling rice in large containers, or time–temperature abuse during storage and display allow the bacteria to multiply and produce an emetic toxin. Egg rolls have also been implicated in foodborne illness outbreaks (Bryan, 1988).

9.2.1.4.5 Pasta. On occasion, pasta dishes have been implicated in outbreaks of foodborne illness. *Salmonella* and other vegetative forms of pathogens survive during the manufacture of spaghetti, macaroni and noodles, but the temperature attained during heating in boiling water kill them. Moist pasta products are a good medium for microbial growth and may allow bacteria such as *B. cereus* to multiply (Bryan, 1988).

9.2.1.4.6 Salads. Salads are commonly-reported vehicles of staphylococcal food poisoning, shigellosis, hepatitis A and Norwalk viral infection. Salads often become contaminated through cross-contamination during peeling, slicing, chopping or mixing operations. Temperature abuse during storage and display can result in bacterial growth (Bryan, 1988).

9.2.1.5 Chemical and physical hazards. All raw ingredients may contain chemical hazards such as improperly used: pesticides, cleaning compounds, petrochemicals and food additives. Raw foods and ingredients may also contain foreign objects such as metal, glass, plastic, bone, stones, and wood (Rhodehamel, 1992).

9.2.2 Handling and storage practices

The following potentially hazardous practices have been observed during routine food preparation and display in deli, meat, poultry and seafood retail food operations (FMI, 1989a; Stier, 1994). These practices increase the risk of food safety hazards.

1. Receiving:
   - Potentially hazardous foods left at room temperature for extended periods of time.
2. Storage:
   a. Dry storage
      - Foods unprotected from contamination.
      - Chemicals and personal items stored improperly.
   b. Refrigerated storage
      - Refrigerator temperatures higher than 5° (41°F)
      - Refrigerators without thermometers.
      - Insufficient refrigerator racks to store shallow pans of food adequately.
      - Foods stored in unmarked or improperly labeled containers.
      - Raw foods stored above or near cooked foods.
   c. Live storage
      - Live tanks containing dead animals.
      - Tanks with cloudy, dirty water.
   d. Hot storage
      - Foods held warm, but not hot, for 8 hours or longer.

- Foods held at 21.1–48.9°C (70–120°F), temperatures that support rapid bacterial growth.
- Hot holding units not used as designed. For example, foods displayed in tilted baking pans or baskets, foods displayed in bowls or plates while in steam tables, packaged foods on edges of heating elements and framing, and products stacked on top of others.
- Hot holding units not operated as intended. For example, thermostats turned lower than 60°C (140°F), fans in units not working, and glass walls removed from units.
- Whole roast beef, turkey and other large cooked products held at room temperature or in warmers.
- Hot holding units without thermometers.
- Poorly maintained hot-holding units.

3. Food preparation:
   - Salad ingredients handled with bare hands during preparation.
   - Cooked products handled with bare hands.
   - Vegetables soaked in a sink previously used for thawing or rinsing raw poultry.
   - Slicing, chopping and grating equipment and utensils not properly cleaned and sanitized.
   - Ingredients not prechilled before preparing cold salads.
   - Kitchen personnel handling raw foods or egg shells with their hands or gloves and then handling cooked foods.
   - Table surfaces and cutting boards used for raw meat, poultry or seafood and then, without washing and sanitizing, used for cooked foods.
   - Workers using cloths/sponges to wipe surfaces used for raw foods, and then, without washing and sanitizing, using the same cloths/sponges to clean surfaces used for cooked foods.
   - Utensils or food contact surfaces made from improper materials.

4. Thawing frozen foods:
   - Potentially hazardous foods thawed at room temperature.
   - Foods insufficiently thawed before being cooked, possibly contributing to undercooking.

5. Cooking:
   - Inadequately cooked poultry, beef, pork and seafood.
   - Inadequately heated soups.
   - Internal temperatures of meat, poultry and seafood, products containing ground meat and stuffed products not monitored after cooking.
   - Cooked foods left in kitchen area for long periods of time after cooking.
   - Cooking equipment not maintained properly.

6. Cooling:
  - Foods cooled in large containers such as 23 l (5 gallon) buckets, stock pots, soup-kettle inserts, rice cookers and plastic or metal pans greater than 10 cm (4 inches) deep.
  - Hot foods put in tightly covered containers while cooling.
  - Containers of foods stacked on top of each other during cooling.
7. Reheating:
  - Inadequately reheated leftover soups, refried beans, fried rice, sauces and other cooked products.
8. Refrigerated display:
  - Raw and cooked products handled with bare hands, the same pair of gloves or the same utensil.
  - Reuse of vegetable garnish.
  - Cooked meat, poultry or seafood products displayed in the same case as raw or live products without dividers separating the groups of foods.
  - Cooked foods displayed in physical contact with raw or live foods.
  - Cooked foods displayed below raw or live foods so that raw or live food drippings reach the cooked foods below.
  - Display cases not kept at or below 5°C (41°F).
  - Display cases without thermometers or with inoperable thermo-meters.
  - Ready-to-eat items displayed on top of display cases, or outside of refrigerated areas.
9. Personal hygiene:
  - Infrequent hand washing that leads to cross-contamination from raw to cooked products.
  - Foods handled by pathogen carriers.
  - Workers with dirty clothes handling and preparing foods.
  - Workers with open sores on their hands handling foods.
10. Sanitation:
  - Unclean equipment and utensils.
  - Improperly stored refuse in food-preparation areas.
  - Improperly cleaned and sanitized utensils and equipment.

9.3 Hazard controls

Identifying critical control points, setting critical limits and determining appropriate corrective actions requires a thorough knowledge of proper retail food handling, preparation, storage and display practices. Critical control points and critical limits must prevent, eliminate or control all identified hazards. Appropriate corrective actions ensure that unsafe products will not reach customers (Stevenson, 1993). Hazard control for deli, meat, poultry and seafood retail store operations include the following.

9.3.1 Food sources

The following restrictions apply to foods and ingredients purchased for sale or service in retail deli, meat, poultry and seafood operations (DHHS, 1994).

1. Food shall be obtained from sources that comply with law.
2. Food prepared in a private home may not be used or offered for human consumption in a food establishment.
3. Packaged foods shall be labeled as specified in law.
4. To destroy parasites, raw, marinated or partially cooked fish, other than molluscan shellfish, that are intended for consumption in their raw form shall be:
   a. Frozen throughout to a temperature of:
      (1) −20° (−4°F) or below for 168 hours (7 days) in a freezer; or
      (2) −35°C (−31°F) or below for 15 hours in a blast freezer.
   b. Obtained from a supplier that freezes the fish and provides a written agreement or statement that the fish have been frozen to the proper temperature and for the proper time, or
   c. Processed on the premises, providing that the internal frozen temperature of the fish and the length of time the fish was held at that temperature is recorded, and the record is retained for 90 calendar days beyond the time of service or sale of the fish.
5. Food in a hermetically sealed container shall be obtained from a food processing plant that is regulated by the food regulatory agency that has jurisdiction over the plant.
6. Fluid milk and milk products shall be obtained from sources that comply with Grade A standards as specified in law.
7. Fish may not be received for sale or service unless they are:
   a. Commercially and legally caught or harvested; or
   b. Caught recreationally, and:
      (1) approved for sale or service by the regulatory authority, and
      (2) if the fish are scombrotoxin-prone or are reef fish subject to ciguatera toxin, their source, preparation and distribution are controlled under conditions of a variance granted by the regulatory authority based on a HACCP plan.
8. Molluscan shellfish:
   a. That are recreationally caught may not be received for sale or service.
   b. Shall be obtained from sources according to law and the requirements specified in the US Department of Health and Human

Services, Public Health Service, FDA, National Shellfish Sanitation Program Manual of Operations.

    c. Received in interstate commerce shall be from sources that are listed in the interstate Certified Shellfish Shippers List.

9. Wild mushrooms may be received for sale or service if they are:

    a. Mushroom species picked in the wild and obtained from sources where each individual mushroom is individually inspected and found to be safe by a mushroom identification expert approved by the regulatory authority; or

    b. Cultivated wild mushrooms species that are grown, harvested, and processed in an operation that is regulated by the food regulatory agency that has jurisdiction over the operation; or

    c. Wild mushroom species if they are in packaged form and are the product of a food processing plant that is regulated by the food regulatory agency that has jurisdiction over the plant.

10. Game animals may not be received for sale or service unless they are:

    a. Game animals commercially raised for food that:

        (1) are raised, slaughtered, and processed under a voluntary inspection program that is conducted by the agency that has animal health jurisdiction, or

        (2) are under a routine inspection program conducted by a regulatory agency other than the agency that has animal health jurisdiction and are raised, slaughtered and processed according to laws governing meat and poultry as determined by the agency that has animal health jurisdiction and the agency that conducts the inspection program.

    b. As allowed by law, field-dressed wild game animals that are under a routine inspection program under which the animals:

        (1) receive a postmortem examination by a veterinarian or a veterinarian's designee, approved by the regulatory authority,

        (2) are field-dressed and transported according to requirements specified by the agency that has animal health jurisdiction and the agency that conducts the inspection program, and

        (3) are processed according to laws governing meat and poultry as determined by the agency that has animal health jurisdiction and the agency that conducts the inspection programme; or

    c. Exotic species of animals raised for exhibition purposes in a zoo or circus that:

        (1) are raised, slaughtered, and processed under a voluntary inspection program that is conducted by the agency that has animal health jurisdiction, or

        (2) receive antemortem and postmortem examination by a veterin-

arian or a veterinarian's designee, approved by the regulatory authority, and

(3) are slaughtered and processed according to laws governing meat and poultry as determined by the agency that has animal health jurisdiction and the agency that conducts the inspection program.

9.3.2 Specifications for receiving

Written purchasing specifications for all foods and supplies should be an important part of every HACCP system. The following examples of purchasing specifications are designed to prevent some potential hazards in foods received in retail deli, meat, poultry and seafood operations (DHHS, 1994; FDA, 1994).

1. Refrigerated, potentially hazardous food shall be at a temperature of 5°C (41°F) or below when received. Except that fluid milk and milk products, molluscan shellfish, and shell eggs may be received at their respective temperatures according to law governing their distribution.
2. Potentially hazardous food that is adequately cooked and received hot shall be at a temperature of 60°C (140°F) or above.
3. Upon receipt, potentially hazardous food shall be free of evidence of previous temperature abuse.
4. Food may not contain unapproved food additives or additives that exceed amounts allowed, or pesticide residues that exceed specified tolerances.
5. Shell eggs shall be clean and received whole and without cracks or checks.
6. Liquid, frozen and dry eggs and egg products shall be obtained pasteurized.
7. Fluid, frozen and dry milk and milk products shall be obtained pasteurized unless alternative procedures to pasteurization are provided for in the Code of Federal Regulations.
8. Food packages shall be in good condition and protect the integrity of the contents so that the food is not exposed to adulteration or potential contaminants.
9. Ice for use as a food or a cooling medium shall be made from drinking water.
10. Raw and frozen shucked molluscan shellfish shall be obtained in nonreturnable packages legibly bearing:
    a. the name of the person who shucks and packs the shellfish, and
    b. the person's authorized certification number, and
    c. the 'sell by' date for packages with a capacity of less than 1.87 l (one-half gallon) or the date shucked for packages with a capacity of 1.87 l (one-half gallon) or more.

11. Molluscan shellfish shall be obtained in containers bearing legible source identification tags or labels that are affixed by the harvester and each dealer that depurates, ships, or reships the shellstock.
   a. If a place is provided on the harvester's tag or label for a dealer's name, address and certification number, the dealer's information shall be listed first. Otherwise, the harvester's tag or label shall include in the following order:
      (1) the harvester's identification number that is assigned by the shellfish control authority,
      (2) the date of harvesting,
      (3) the most precise identification of the harvest location or aquaculture site that is practicable based on the system of harvest area designations that is in use by the shellfish control authority and including the abbreviation of the name of the state or country in which the shellfish are harvested,
      (4) the type and quantity of shellfish,
      (5) the following statement in bold, capitalized type:

      'THIS TAG IS REQUIRED TO BE ATTACHED UNTIL CONTAINER IS EMPTY OR RETAGGED AND THEREAFTER KEPT ON FILE FOR 90 DAYS.'

   b. If the harvester's tag or label is designed to accommodate each dealer's identification as specified in 1 and 2 below, individual dealer tags or labels need not be provided. Otherwise, the dealer's tag or label shall include in the following order:
      (1) the dealer's name and address, and the certification number assigned by the shellfish control authority,
      (2) the original shipper's certification number including the abbreviation of the name of the state or country in which the shellfish are harvested,
      (3) the date of harvesting,
      (4) the most precise identification of the harvest location or aquaculture site that is practicable based on the system of harvest area designations that is in use by the shellfish control authority and including the abbreviation of the name of the state or country in which the shellfish are harvested,
      (5) the type and quantity of shellfish,
      (6) the following statement in bold, capitalized type:

      'THIS TAG IS REQUIRED TO BE ATTACHED UNTIL CONTAINER IS EMPTY OR RETAGGED AND THEREAFTER KEPT ON FILE FOR 90 DAYS.'

12. Fish shall contain less than:
   a. 1 ppm methyl mercury in the edible portion of the fish, and

b. 5 mg histamine/100 g flesh (20 mg histamine/100 g flesh for canned product).
13. Fish shall contain less than the following action levels for parasites:
    a. Tullibies, ciscoes, inconnus, chubs, and whitefish – 50 cysts per 45.45 kg (100 lbs);
    b. Blue fin and other freshwater herring averaging one pound or less – 60 cysts per 100 fish, if 20% of the fish examined are infested;
    c. Blue fin and other freshwater herring averaging more than one pound – 60 cysts per 45.45 kg (100 lbs), if 20% of the fish examined are infested;
    d. Rose fish (red fish and ocean perch) 3% of fillets examined contain one or more copepods accompanied by pus pockets;
    e. Other fish should have visible parasites removed.
14. Shellfish shall contain less than:
    a. 0.8 ppm saxitoxin;
    b. 0.8 ppm brevetoxin-2;
    c. 0.2 ppm okadaic acid plus 35-methyl okadaic acid (DXT-1); and
    d. 30 ppm domoic acid in the viscera of dungeness crab and 20 ppm in other tissues and species.
15. Puffer fish shall not be imported without specific FDA authorization.

9.3.3   Controls at receiving

The following controls should be used to minimize or prevent hazards at receiving, and during storage, preparation and display of deli, meat, poultry and seafood products in retail stores (DHHS, 1994; FMI, 1989b):

1. Inspect all inbound foods, food packaging supplies, single service items, laundry, pallets and slip sheets, etc. Also check the recording thermometers inside of delivery trucks. Evaluate and reject or discard:
    a. Products that do not meet purchasing specifications.
    b. Out-of-condition, outdated, damaged, leaking, contaminated or soiled items.
    c. Items that may have been contaminated by water, condensation or by pests.
    d. Canned foods that are leaking, badly dented, pitted with rust or have swollen ends.
    e. Molluscan shellfish that are not reasonably free of mud, are dead or have badly broken shells.
    f. Foods containing foreign materials such as metal, glass, plastic and wood.
2. Inspect potentially hazardous foods first and move them into proper storage as soon as possible.
3. Record rejected items on the invoice or on a Receiving Reject Form,

and make sure rejected items do not enter the store. Clearly label all rejected product.

9.3.4   Controls for storage (DHHS, 1994; FMI, 1989b; Price, 1990a; Price 1990b)

9.3.4.1   Storage of all foods.

a. Store food in clean, dry storage areas where it is not exposed to splash, dust, pests or other contamination.
b. Do not store food:
   (1) in locker rooms;
   (2) in toilet rooms;
   (3) in dressing rooms;
   (4) in garbage rooms;
   (5) in mechanical rooms;
   (6) under sewer lines that are not shielded to intercept potential drips;
   (7) under leaking water lines, including leaking automatic fire sprinkler heads, or under lines on which water has condensed;
   (8) under open stairwells; or
   (9) under other sources of contamination.
c. Store all products in an orderly manner, at least six inches off the floor, and on clean shelves, dollies, racks or pallets.
d. Arrange items in the proper order for FIFO (First-In-First-Out) rotation. Place the newest items at the bottom or in back of older items.
e. Store products that might leak or drip below other items to prevent cross-contamination. Store uncooked foods below cooked foods.
f. Store foods in clean, covered, labeled containers if they have been removed from their original containers.
g. Standardize and maintain thermometers and temperature recorders for hot and cold storage/holding/display on a regular basis.

9.3.4.2   Dry storage.

a. Close securely or transfer contents of opened bags or boxes of foods to clean, sanitized, covered, labeled, approved plastic or metal containers.
b. Frequently check grain products, rice, raw nuts, seeds, spices and similar products for signs of pest infestation.
c. Store spices in sealed containers in a cool, dry location.
d. Store clean utensils, packaging and single service supplies under the same sanitary conditions as for foods.
e. Do not store cleaners and sanitizers above or close to food, packaging supplies, single service items or food contact items.
f. Store insecticides and other toxic compounds separately from cleaners

and sanitizers. Do not store them above or close to food, packaging supplies, single service items or food contact items.

g. Clearly identify storage rooms.

9.3.4.3 Frozen storage.

a. Check freezer temperature at least twice daily. Ideally, freezers should be equipped with recording thermometers and high temperature alarms.

b. Store potentially hazardous frozen products at −18°C (0°F) or lower.

9.3.4.4 Refrigerated storage/display.

a. Check refrigerator/display temperatures at least twice daily. Ideally, monitor cold storage rooms every 4 hours and equip them with recording thermometers and high temperature alarms.

b. Store/display refrigerated products at 5°C (41°F) or below. If necessary, lower the thermostat to keep the temperature of food at 5°C (41°F) or below.

c. Store/display raw animal foods separately from:
   (1) raw ready-to-eat food including other raw animal food such as fish for sushi or molluscan shellfish, or other raw ready-to-eat food such as vegetables, and
   (2) cooked ready-to-eat food.

d. Except when combined as ingredients, store/display raw animal foods such as beef, seafood, lamb, pork and poultry separately from each other so that cross-contamination is prevented by:
   (1) using separate equipment for each type, or
   (2) arranging each type of food in equipment so that cross-contamination is prevented.

e. Do not mix lots of molluscan shellfish in storage rooms or display cases.

f. Do not store/display raw animal foods and ready-to-eat foods in contact with water or undrained ice.

g. Store molluscan shellfish in the container in which they were received.

h. Store primal cuts, quarters, or sides of raw meat or slab bacon on clean, sanitized racks or on clean, sanitized hooks.

i. Store whole, uncut, processed meats such as country hams, and smoked or cured sausages on clean, sanitized racks.

j. Check fresh produce for pest infestation, slime, mold or decay.

k. Lots of raw meat, poultry and seafood should not be held in refrigerated storage for more than three days before being used or sold.

9.3.4.5 Live storage.

a. Follow manufacturer's instructions for temperature control, operation, sanitation and maintenance of live display tanks.

b. Do not combine different lots of molluscan shellfish in the same display tank.
c. Do not combine different species in the same display tank.
d. Do not use the same water circulation system for more than one display tank.

9.3.4.6 Hot storage.

a. Hold hot foods so that all parts of the food are maintained at a temperature of 60°C (140°F) or above. Hold roast beef at a minimum center temperature of 54.4°C (130°F).
b. Measure and record the center temperature of the hot food item every 2 hours. If the temperature is below 60°C (140°F), reheat or cool the product.
c. Batches of hot food products should be held no longer than about 5 hours.

9.3.5 Controls for food preparation (DHHS, 1994; FMI, 1989b; Price, 1990a; Price 1990b)

9.3.5.1 All foods.

a. Use food-contact surfaces made from easily cleanable materials.
b. Always clean and sanitize all food contact surfaces, equipment and utensils:
  (1) when switching from one kind of raw animal product to another;
  (2) when switching from raw to ready-to-eat foods;
  (3) after four hours interruption in use; and
  (4) after final use each work day.
c. Keep wiping cloths clean and stored in a sanitizer solution, and replace sanitizer solution and cloths at least every four hours. Monitor sanitizer strength and change more frequently if needed.
d. Keep wiping cloths used with raw animal foods separate from cloths used for other purposes.
e. Store paper towels in a dispenser.
f. Except when washing fruits and vegetables, food employees may not contact exposed ready-to-eat food with their bare hands and shall use suitable utensils such as deli tissue, spatulas, tongs, or single-use gloves.
g. Single-use gloves shall be used for only one task such as working with ready-to-eat food or with raw animal food, used for no other purpose, and discarded when damaged or soiled, or when interruptions occur in the operation.
h. Keep food preparation area free of clutter. Clean, sanitize and put

away equipment not being used. Store equipment so that it will stay clean and sanitary.

i. Wash hands frequently using the restroom sink or the handwashing sink in the work area.

j. Clean and sanitize utensils and other food contact items that fall to the floor, before reuse.

k. Pick up and handle utensils only by the handles.

l. Use a suitable clean utensil to remove any utensil that falls to the floor.

m. During pauses in food preparation, store utensils:
   (1) in the food with their handles above the top of the food and the container;
   (2) on a clean portion of the food preparation table or cooking equipment;
   (3) in running water of sufficient velocity to flush particulates to the drain, if used with moist food; and
   (4) in a clean, protected location if the utensils are used for a food that is not potentially hazardous.

n. Use an approved scoop to transfer ice. Do not use hands, cups, glasses or cans to scoop ice. Keep scoops protected when not in use.

o. Discard single service items after one use.

p. Hold packaging and single service supplies, stocked at work stations, on shelves or racks located above the level of food preparation surfaces. Limit the amount to a one-day supply.

q. Break out from storage only the amount of ingredients needed.

r. Do not keep potentially hazardous food products in the temperature danger zone (5–60°C, 41–140°F) any longer than necessary to prepare them. Potentially hazardous ready-to-eat food products should be kept at 5°C (41°F) or below. Potentially hazardous raw foods should not exceed 5°C (41°F) for more than 4 hours.

s. Do not taste foods with any utensil used to prepare foods. Use a clean spoon. Do not use fingers to sample food.

t. Do not store food items on ice intended for drinks or food preparation.

9.3.5.2 Eggs.

a. Do not use cracked eggs.
b. Break only as many eggs as needed.
c. Wash hands thoroughly and often, when handling eggs.

9.3.5.3 Sandwiches, salads and unbaked pizzas.

a. Wrap finished items in plastic.
b. Discard items if not used within two days.

9.3.5.4   Canned foods.

a. Clean can lids before opening.
b. Use a clean and sanitized can opener. Remove can lids completely.
c. Transfer leftovers to clean, sanitized, covered and labeled containers for refrigerated storage.

9.3.5.5   Frozen foods.

a. Do not refreeze thawed frozen foods.

9.3.5.6   Cold leftovers.

a. Store leftovers in clean, sanitized, covered and labeled containers in the refrigerator.
b. Discard leftovers if not consumed in two days.

9.3.5.7   Fruits and vegetables.

a. Wash thoroughly in potable running water to remove soil and other contaminants before they are cut, combined with other ingredients, cooked, served or offered for human consumption in ready-to-eat form.

9.3.5.8   Condiments.

a. Store condiments in refrigerator after opening.

9.3.5.9   Raw animal foods.

a. Cut and package meat and poultry in a room at a temperature of 7°C (45°F) or below.
b. Prepare raw animal foods separately from:
   (1) raw ready-to-eat food including other raw animal food such as fish for sushi or molluscan shellfish, or other raw ready-to-eat food such as vegetables; and
   (2) cooked ready-to-eat food.
c. Except when combined as ingredients, prepare raw animal foods such as beef, fish, lamb, pork and poultry separately from each other by:
   (1) using separate equipment for each type; or
   (2) arranging each type of food in equipment so that cross-contamination is prevented; and
   (3) preparing each type of food at different times or in separate areas.

9.3.6   Controls for thawing frozen foods (DHSS, 1994)

1. Thaw frozen potentially hazardous foods:
   a. under refrigeration at 5°C (41°F) or lower; or

   b. completely submerged under running water at a water temperature of 21°C (70°F) or below and with sufficient water velocity to agitate and float off loose particles in an overflow:

     (1) for a period of time that does not allow thawed portions of ready-to-eat foods to rise above 5°C (41°F);

     (2) for a period of time that does not allow thawed portions of raw animal foods requiring cooking to be above 5°C (41°F) for more than 4 hours, including the time the food is exposed to the running water and the time needed for preparation for cooking or the time it takes under refrigeration to lower the food temperature to 5°C (41°F).

   c. By continuously cooking from the frozen state until thoroughly cooked.

9.3.7 Controls for cooking (DHHS, 1994)

1. Ovens or other cooking devices must be heated to cooking temperature before placing foods in them.
2. All raw animal foods such as shell eggs that are broken and prepared in response to a customer's order and for immediate service, fish, poultry, meat and foods containing these raw animal foods, shall be cooked to heat all parts of the food to 63°C (145°F) for at least 15 seconds.
3. Pork and game animals, comminuted fish and meats, injected meats and eggs that are not prepared as specified in 2. above, shall be cooked to heat all parts of the food to:

   a. 68°C (155°F) for at least 15 seconds; or

   b. 66°C (150°F) for at least 1 minute; or

   c. 63°C (145°F) for at least 3 minutes.

4. Field-dressed wild game animals, poultry, stuffed fish, stuffed meat, stuffed pasta, stuffed poultry or stuffing containing fish, meat or poultry shall be cooked to heat all parts of the food to 74°C (165°F) for at least 15 seconds.
5. Beef roasts and corned beef:

   a. Shall be cooked in a:

     (1) still dry oven that is preheated to, and maintained at or above:

       (a) 121°C (250°F) for roasts greater than 4.5 kg (10 lbs); or

       (b) 177°C (350°F) for roasts less than or equal to 4.5 kg (10 lbs);

     (2) convection oven that is preheated to, and maintained at or above 163°C (325°F);

     (3) high humidity oven where the relative humidity is greater than 90% for at least 1 hour as measured in the cooking chamber or exit of the oven, or in a moisture-impermeable bag that provides 100% humidity, and that is preheated to, and maintained at less than 121°C (250°F).

  b. Shall be cooked to heat all parts of the food to:
    (1) 54°C (130°F) for at least 121 minutes; or
    (2) 56°C (132°F) for at least 77 minutes; or
    (3) 57°C (134°F) for at least 47 minutes; or
    (4) 58°C (136°F) for at least 32 minutes; or
    (5) 59°C (138°F) for at least 19 minutes; or
    (6) 60°C (140°F) for at least 12 minutes; or
    (7) 61°C (142°F) for at least 8 minutes; or
    (8) 62°C (144°F) for at least 5 minutes; or
    (9) 63°C (145°F) for at least 3 minutes.
6. Raw animal foods cooked in a microwave oven shall be:
  a. Rotated or stirred throughout or midway during cooking to compensate for uneven distribution or heat;
  b. Covered to retain surface moisture;
  c. Heated an additional 14°C (25°F) above the temperatures specified in sections 2, 3 and 4 above for non-microwave cooking to compensate for shorter cooking times.
  d. Allowed to stand covered for 2 minutes after cooking to obtain temperature equilibrium.
7. Measure temperatures with a thermometer.

9.3.8   Controls for cooling (DHHS, 1994)

1. Cooked potentially hazardous foods shall be cooled:
  a. from 60°C (140°F) to 21°C (70°F) within 2 hours; and
  b. from 21°C (70°F) to 5°C (41°F), or below, within 4 hours.
2. Potentially hazardous food shall be cooled to 5°C (41°F) or below within 4 hours if prepared from ingredients at ambient temperature, such as reconstituted foods and canned tuna.
3. Fluid milk and milk products, shell eggs and molluscan shellstock received in compliance with laws regulating the respective food during shipment from the supplier shall be cooled to 5°C (41°F) or below within 4 hours.
4. Cooling shall be accomplished by using one or more of the following methods based on the type of food being cooled:
  a. Placing the food in shallow pans.
  b. Separating the food into smaller or thinner portions.
  c. Using rapid cooling equipment.
  d. Stirring the food in a container placed in an ice water bath.
  e. Using containers that facilitate heat transfer.
  f. Adding ice as an ingredient.
  g. Other effective means.
5. When placed in cooling or cold holding equipment, food containers in which food is being cooled shall be:

a. Arranged in the equipment to provide maximum heat transfer through the container wall.
b. Loosely covered, or uncovered if protected from overhead contamination, during the cooling period to facilitate heat transfer from the surface of the food.

9.3.9 Controls for reheating (DHHS, 1994)

1. Ready-to-eat food taken from a commercially processed hermetically sealed container, such as canned soup or chili, or from an intact package from a food processing plant that is inspected by the food regulatory authority that has jurisdiction over the plant, shall be heated to a temperature of at least 60°C (140°F) for hot holding.
2. Food reheated in a microwave oven shall be:
    a. Covered.
    b. Rotated or stirred throughout or midway during cooking or according to label instructions during heating.
    c. Heated to a temperature of at least 88°C (190°F).
    d. Allowed to stand covered 2 minutes after reheating.
3. All other potentially hazardous food that is cooked, cooled, and reheated for hot holding shall be reheated so that all parts of the food reach a temperature of at least 74°C (165°F) for 15 seconds.
4. Reheating of food shall be done rapidly and the minimum temperature shall be reached within 2 hours.

9.3.10 Controls for display (DHHS, 1994)

1. All foods and beverages must be displayed off the floor.
2. Except for nuts in the shell and whole, raw fruits and vegetables that are intended for hulling, peeling or washing by the consumer before consumption, food on display must be protected from contamination by the use of packaging; counter, service line or salad bar food guards; display cases; or other effective means.
3. Use only clean utensils that have been washed, rinsed and sanitized.
4. Use separate utensils for raw and cooked food products.
5. Store utensils as described under 'Controls for Food Preparation/All Foods/#m.'
6. Food may not contact:
    a. Probe-type price or identification tags.
    b. Surfaces of utensils and equipment that are not clean.
7. Food employees may not contact exposed ready-to-eat food with their bare hands and shall use suitable utensils such as deli tissue, spatulas, tongs, or single-use gloves.
8. Single-use gloves shall be used for only one task such as working with

ready-to-eat food or with raw animal food, used for no other purpose, and discarded when damaged or soiled, or when interruptions occur in the operation.

9. Fresh garnish must not contact ready-to-eat foods.
10. Display food in clean containers that have been washed, rinsed and sanitized.

9.3.11   Controls for sanitation

HACCP food safety systems are based on effective sanitation programs. Sanitation is not limited to cleaning of equipment. It includes all aspects that are needed to ensure that foods are handled, stored, and prepared in a clean and safe environment. Sanitation Standard Operating Procedures (SOPs) should include procedures for:

1. Personnel.
2. Buildings and grounds.
3. Sanitary operations, including storage of toxic materials, pest control, sanitation of food-contact surfaces, and storage and handling of cleaned equipment.
4. Sanitary facilities and controls, including water supply, sewage disposal, toilet facilities and hand-washing facilities.
5. Design and construction of equipment and utensils.
6. Processes and controls.
7. Warehousing and distribution practices.

Requirements and guidelines for developing effective sanitation SOPs for deli, meat, poultry and seafood retail operations are contained in the Current Good Manufacturing Practice in Manufacturing, Packing, or Holding Human Food, *Code of Federal Regulations* (21 CFR 110) (DHHS, 1993), and the *Food Code 1993* (DHHS, 1994).

9.4   Monitoring

Monitoring critical control points in deli, meat, poultry and seafood retail operations can involve visual observations, sensory evaluations, chemical measurements and physical measurements. Visual observations (watching worker practices, inspecting raw materials) and sensory evaluations (smelling for off-odors, looking for off-colors or feeling for texture) require a knowledge of proper food handling, storage and preparation practices and experience in evaluating product quality (Price *et al.*, 1993).

Chemical measurements (pH or acidity, viscosity, salt content or water activity) are normally not required in retail deli, meat, poultry and seafood stores. Following recipes exactly and making sure exact measurements are used will generally ensure that critical control points involving chemical criteria are in control.

Physical measurements (time and temperature) are critical monitoring procedures for receiving, heating and cooling processes, and storage and display. Temperature recording devices make some of these measurements less time consuming.

9.5   Corrective actions

Corrective actions taken when criteria for critical control points are not met can include:

1. Rejecting products that do not meet purchasing specifications.
2. Adjusting a refrigerator's thermostat to get the proper temperature.
3. Extending a cooking time.
4. Recooking or reheating a product to the proper temperature.
5. Chilling a hot item that has cooled below the minimum required temperature.
6. Modifying food handling practices.
7. Modifying food preparation procedures.
8. Discarding products.
9. Labeling suspect products to ensure they are not used until they have been evaluated for safety.

9.6   Records

Ideally, monitoring results from all critical control points should be recorded or logged as the monitoring is being done. With temperature recording devices, recording is automatic and a permanent record is produced. For other monitoring procedures, sensory evaluation and chemical and physical measurements may be necessary and should be recorded. Combining existing records with HACCP records can save time and expense. For example, inspection results at receiving can be entered on the receiving invoice. Records should be reviewed daily to ensure that controls are working and that workers handled food properly. If daily records indicate potential problems, investigate immediately.

Records should also be maintained for scale and thermometer calibrations, and equipment maintenance. Examples of recording forms are shown in Figure 9.1 (Receiving Reject Form), Figure 9.2 (Receiving Temperature Form), Figure 9.3 (Cooler Temperature Form) and Figure 9.4 (Display Temperature Form).

RECEIVING REJECT FORM

Date_____

Product	Rejected for:	Initials/Comments

Reviewed By:_____   Date_____

Figure 9.1 Receiving reject form.

9.7 Verification

Management should also conduct an in-depth audit of the entire HACCP system at least once a year. Additional audits should be conducted whenever raw materials, ingredients, recipes, preparation procedures or processes change. Each of these requires a new HACCP plan.

9.8 A deli HACCP plan

9.8.1 Recipe review

The first step in developing a HACCP plan for a deli is a recipe review for every item prepared and sold. This review should list each ingredient and

RECEIVING TEMPERATURE FORM

Date_____

Product	Temperature	Initials/Comments

Reviewed By:_____   Date_____

Figure 9.2 Receiving temperature form.

step preparation and storage step from raw materials to sale. For example, a recipe for seafood salad might include the following ingredients and preparation steps:

9.8.1.1   Ingredients.

- Chilled cooked seafood
- Salad dressing
- Celery
- Onions
- Lemon juice
- Spices

COOLER TEMPERATURE FORM

Date_____

Time	Temperature #1	#2	#3	Initials/Comments
7:00 a.m.				
11:00 a.m.				
3:00 p.m.				
7:00 p.m.				
11:00 p.m.				
3:00 a.m.				

Reviewed By:_____   Date_____

Figure 9.3 Cooler temperature form.

DISPLAY TEMPERATURE FORM

Date_____

Product:	Product Temperature					Initials
Time						
7:00 a.m.						
11:00 a.m.						
1:00 p.m.						
3:00 p.m.						
5:00 p.m.						
7:00 p.m.						
9:00 p.m.						
11:00 p.m.						
1:00 a.m.						
3:00 a.m.						
5:00 a.m.						

Reviewed By:_____   Date_____

Figure 9.4 Display temperature form.

9.8.1.2   Preparation steps.

- Receiving
- Peeling and chopping of onion
- Washing and chopping of celery
- Pre-chilling of ingredients
- Mixing of ingredients
- Transfer to display and storage containers
- Storage in refrigerator
- Display in case
- Restocking

9.8.2   Flowcharts

Flow diagrams are essential to define processing and storage steps and to identify potential handling and storage hazards. The flow chart for the seafood salad (Figure 9.5) shows the process from raw materials to finished product. The chart shows all of the handling procedures involved and indicates where contamination, mishandling and temperature abuse may occur.

9.8.3   Hazard analysis

Potential hazards are described for each step of the operation. The cooked seafood and raw celery contain spoilage bacteria. They may also contain pathogens. The spices also contain many bacteria, including bacterial spores that will survive cooking. The lemon juice and salad dressing are acidic and will aid in controlling bacterial growth if enough is added and thoroughly mixed with the other ingredients.

   People who handle food, utensils, equipment and raw foods are sources of contamination. People frequently carry pathogens on their skin, in sores and lesions, in their noses, in their intestinal tract and in their mouths (FMI, 1989a). Improperly cleaned and sanitized utensils, equipment, and food-contact surfaces are additional sources of bacteria. Bacteria multiply rapidly at room temperature and in large containers of food in refrigerators. During the processing of seafood salad, contamination can occur at receiving, during the peeling of the onions, during the chopping of the onions and celery, during the mixing step, when transferring the salad to a dish or storage container, and when restocking. Temperature abuse can occur during prechilling, and during storage in the display case or refrigerator. Once all hazards are identified, when and how to prevent, eliminate, or control the hazards can be determined.

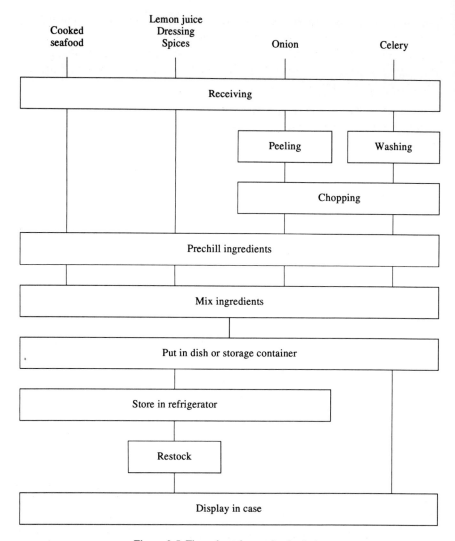

Figure 9.5 Flow chart for seafood salad.

9.8.4 Receiving

Receiving is a critical control point for controlling potential problems from rapid bacterial growth, contamination and foreign objects. Trying to correct these hazards later in the preparation and storage process may be uneconomical and impossible.

Set critical limits for accepting or rejecting each ingredient based on potential risk for each hazard. Include these limits in purchasing specifications. For example, set limits on accepting damaged, outdated, and contaminated products. Set maximum acceptable temperature limits for potentially hazardous foods such as cooked seafood. Critical limits for the salad ingredients might include:

- Chilled cooked seafood below 5°C (41°F)
- No contamination, damage or spoilage
- No foreign materials

Monitor the limits to control potential hazards by:

- Checking for proper temperature
- A sensory examination for damage, contamination, spoilage and foreign material

When incoming products do not meet the critical limits, immediate action is needed. Reject or discard products that do not meet the critical limits. For example, reject:

- Damaged, spoiled, or contaminated food
- Chilled potentially hazardous food above 5°C (41°F)
- Ingredients that do not meet purchasing specifications

Record rejected or discarded items, and chilled food temperatures, on the invoice or similar form. Sign or initial the form after the inspection to indicate that the products are acceptable. Ensure that rejected food does not get into the store.

9.8.5 Preparation, storage and display

Contamination is a potential problem at several steps during the preparation, storage and display of seafood salad (Figure 9.6). Potential contamination from workers during handling, mixing and transfer are not considered critical control points because later stages in the process (storage and display below 5°C (41°F)) will control any potential hazard from bacterial contamination. Controls for potential contamination include following good manufacturing practices and complying with sanitation and personal hygiene standard operating procedures. Monitoring is usually done through observation. Corrective actions can involve employee training, changing employee practices or changing preparation procedures.

Steps in the salad preparation process involving chilling, and cold storage and display are critical control points. Control at these steps is essential to ensure that the final product is safe. Chilling and refrigerated storage steps must be monitored, and the temperatures recorded, to demonstrate complete safety control. Monitoring can be done by hand or

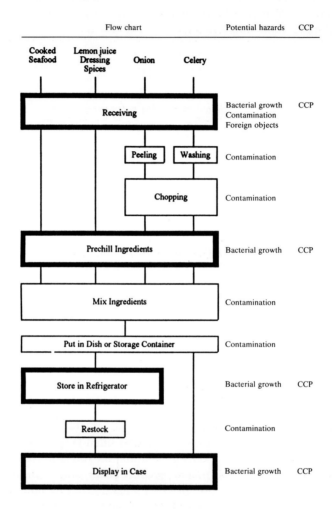

Critical limits	Monitoring procedures	Corrective actions	Records
Chilled items below 41°F (5°C) No contamination, spoilage or foreign objects	Measure/record temperature Visual inspection	Reject if above 41°F (5°C) Reject items with spoilage, contamination or foreign objects	Receiving invoice
Use clean utensils	Observe practices	Modify practices	
Minimize hand contact Use clean utensils	Observe practices	Modify practices	
Chill to 41°F (5°C) or below	Measure/record air temperature every 4 hours	Adjust thermostat	Recording thermometer
Minimize hand contact Use clean container	Observe practices	Modify practices	
Use clean container	Observe practices	Modify practices	
Product below 41°F (5°C)	Measure/record air temperature every 4 hours	Adjust thermostat	Recording thermometer
Minimize hand contact	Observe practices	Modify practices	
Product below 41°F (5°C)	Measure/record air temperature every 4 hours	Adjust thermostat	Recording thermometer

Figure 9.6 Seafood salad.

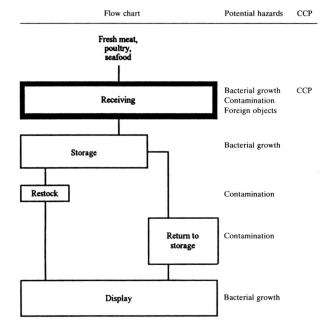

Flow chart	Potential hazards	CCP
Fresh meat, poultry, seafood		
Receiving	Bacterial growth Contamination Foreign objects	CCP
Storage	Bacterial growth	
Restock	Contamination	
Return to storage	Contamination	
Display	Bacterial growth	

Critical limits	Monitoring procedures	Corrective actions	Records
Chilled items below 41°F (5°C) No contamination, spoilage No foreign objects	Measure/record temperature Visual inspection	Reject if above 41°F (5°C) Reject items with spoilage, contamination or foreign objects	Receiving invoice
Product below 41°F (5°C)	Measure/record air temperature every 4 hours	Adjust thermostat	Recording thermometer
Use disposable gloves or utensils	Observe practices	Modify practices	
Use disposable gloves or clean containers and utensils	Observe practices	Modify practices	
Product below 41°F (5°C)	Measure/record air temperature every 4 hours	Adjust thermostat	Recording thermometer

Figure 9.7 Fresh raw meat, poultry and seafood.

Flow chart	Potential hazards	CCP

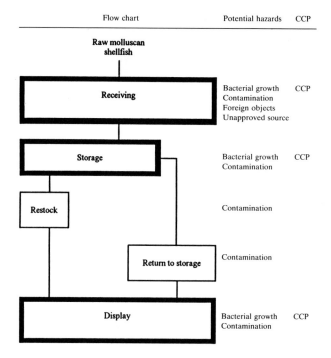

Raw molluscan
shellfish

Receiving — Bacterial growth CCP
Contamination
Foreign objects
Unapproved source

Storage — Bacterial growth CCP
Contamination

Restock — Contamination

Return to storage — Contamination

Display — Bacterial growth CCP
Contamination

Critical limits	Monitoring procedures	Corrective actions	Records
Chilled items below 41°F (5°C) No contamination, spoilage No foreign objects From approved source	Visual inspection Measure/record temperature Check tags	Reject if above 41°F (5°C) Reject items with spoilage, contamination or foreign objects Reject if no tags	Receiving invoice Shellfish tags
Product below 41°F (5°C) Separate from live, raw animal products	Measure/record air temperature every 4 hours Visual inspection	Adjust thermostat Discard if contaminated	Recording thermometer
Use disposable gloves or clean utensils	Observe practices	Modify practices	
Use disposable gloves or clean utensils	Observe practices	Modify practices	
Product below 41°F (5°C) Separate from live, raw animal products	Measure/record air temperature every 4 hours	Adjust thermostat Discard if contaminated	Recording thermometer

Figure 9.8 Raw molluscan shellfish.

Flow chart	Potential hazards	CCP

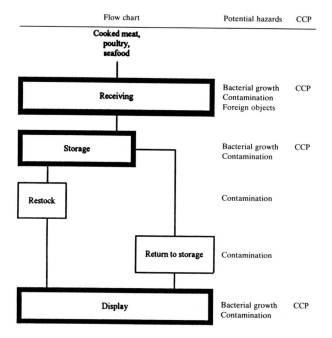

Cooked meat, poultry, seafood

Receiving — Bacterial growth / Contamination / Foreign objects — CCP

Storage — Bacterial growth / Contamination — CCP

Restock — Contamination

Return to storage — Contamination

Display — Bacterial growth / Contamination — CCP

Critical limits	Monitoring procedures	Corrective actions	Records
Chilled items below 41°F (5°C) No contamination, spoilage No foreign objects	Measure/record temperature Visual inspection	Reject if above 41°F (5°C) Reject items with spoilage, contamination or foreign objects	Receiving invoice
Product below 41°F (5°C) Separate from live, raw animal products	Measure/record air temperature every 4 hours Visual inspection	Adjust thermostat Discard if contaminated	Recording thermometer
Use disposable gloves or clean utensils	Observe practices	Modify practices	
Use disposable gloves or clean utensils	Observe practices	Modify practices	
Product below 41°F (5°C) Separate from live, raw animal products	Measure/record air temperature every 4 hours	Adjust thermostat Discard if contaminated	Recording thermometer

Figure 9.9 Fresh cooked meat, poultry and seafood.

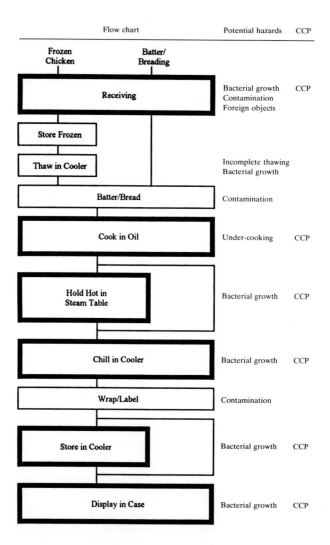

Critical limits	Monitoring procedures	Corrective actions	Records
Chilled items below 41°F (5°C) No contamination, spoilage No foreign objects	Visual inspection Measure/record temperature	Reject chilled if above 41°F (5°C) Reject items with spoilage, contamination or foreign objects	Receiving invoice
Thaw completely Temperature below 41°F (5°C)	Observe thawing	Modify thawing practice	
Do not recycle used batter/ breading	Observe practices	Modify practices	
Internal temperature of 145°F (63°C) for 15 seconds	Follow time/temperature instructions Measure/record center temperature	Continue cooking until center temperature reaches 145°F (63°C) for 15 seconds	Cooking log
Product above 140°F (60°C)	Measure/record center temperature every 2 hours	Reheat or chill	Display log
Product below 41°F (5°C)	Measure/record air temperature every 4 hours	Adjust thermostat	Recording thermometer
Avoid hand contact	Observe practices	Modify practices	
Product below 41°F (5°C)	Measure/record air temperature every 4 hours	Adjust thermostat	Recording thermometer
Product below 41°F (5°C)	Measure/record air temperature every 4 hours	Adjust thermostat	Recording thermometer

Figure 9.10 Fried chicken.

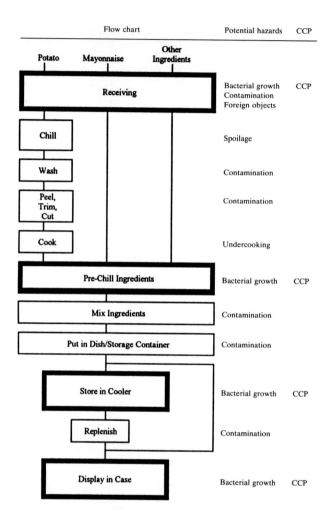

Flow chart	Potential hazards	CCP
Potato Mayonnaise Other Ingredients		
Receiving	Bacterial growth Contamination Foreign objects	CCP
Chill	Spoilage	
Wash	Contamination	
Peel, Trim, Cut	Contamination	
Cook	Undercooking	
Pre-Chill Ingredients	Bacterial growth	CCP
Mix Ingredients	Contamination	
Put in Dish/Storage Container	Contamination	
Store in Cooler	Bacterial growth	CCP
Replenish	Contamination	
Display in Case	Bacterial growth	CCP

Critical limits	Monitoring procedures	Corrective actions	Records
No contamination, spoilage No foreign objects	Visual inspection	Reject items with spoilage, contamination or foreign objects	Receiving invoice
Chill to below 41°F (5°C)	Measure/record cooler air temperature	Adjust thermostat	
Use clean sink Rinse sink between items	Observe practices	Modify practices	
Spoilage removed	Observe practices	Modify practices	
Cook until done	Follow time/temperature instructions	Adjust cooking time	
Chill in shallow containers to below 41°F (5°C)	Measure/record cooler air temperature every 4 hours	Adjust cooler thermostat	Recording thermometer
Minimize hand contact Use clean utensils	Observe practices	Modify practices	
Use clean dish/container	Observe practices	Modify practices	
Product below 41°F (5°C)	Measure/record air temperature every 4 hours	Adjust cooler thermostat	Recording thermometer
Avoid hand contact	Observe practices	Modify practices	
Product below 41°F (5°C)	Measure/record air temperature every 4 hours	Adjust case thermostat	Recording thermometer

Figure 9.11 Potato salad.

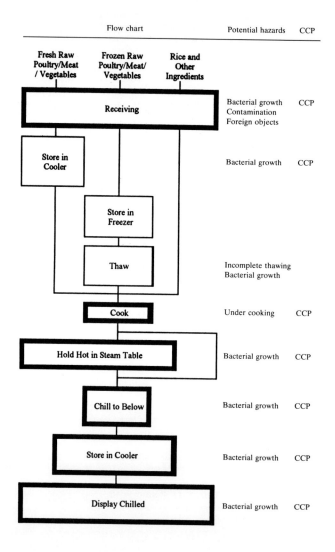

Flow chart	Potential hazards	CCP
Fresh Raw Poultry/Meat / Vegetables **Frozen Raw Poultry/Meat/ Vegetables** **Rice and Other Ingredients**		
Receiving	Bacterial growth Contamination Foreign objects	CCP
Store in Cooler	Bacterial growth	CCP
Store in Freezer		
Thaw	Incomplete thawing Bacterial growth	
Cook	Under cooking	CCP
Hold Hot in Steam Table	Bacterial growth	CCP
Chill to Below	Bacterial growth	CCP
Store in Cooler	Bacterial growth	CCP
Display Chilled	Bacterial growth	CCP

Critical limits	Monitoring procedures	Corrective actions	Records
Chilled items below 41°F (5°C) No contamination, spoilage No foreign objects	Measure/record temperature Visual inspection	Reject chilled items above 41°F (5°C) Reject items with spoilage, contamination or foreign objects	Receiving invoice
Chill to below 41°F (5°C)	Measure/record air temperature every 4 hours	Adjust thermostat	
Thaw completely Keep below 41°F (5°C)	Observe thawing	Modify thawing practice	
Cook to 145°F (63°C) for 15 seconds	Measure/record temperature	Increase cooking time	Cooking log
Product above 140°F (60°C)	Measure/record center every 2 hours	Reheat or chill	Display log
Chill in shallow container to below 41°F (5°C)	Measure/record air temperature every 4 hours	Adjust thermostat	Recording thermometer
Product below 41°F (5°C)	Measure/record air temperature every 4 hours	Adjust thermostat	Recording thermometer
Product below 41°F (5°C)	Measure/record air temperature every 4 hours	Adjust thermostat	Recording thermometer

Figure 9.12 Hot entrees.

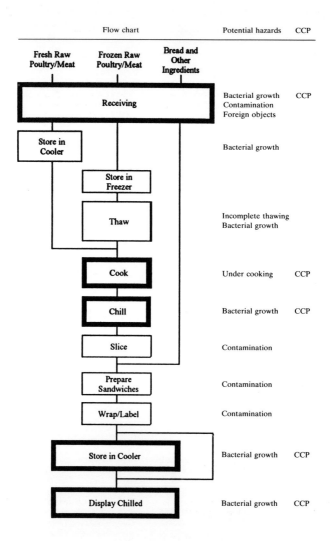

Flow chart	Potential hazards	CCP
Fresh Raw Poultry/Meat **Frozen Raw Poultry/Meat** **Bread and Other Ingredients**		
Receiving	Bacterial growth Contamination Foreign objects	CCP
Store in Cooler	Bacterial growth	
Store in Freezer		
Thaw	Incomplete thawing Bacterial growth	
Cook	Under cooking	CCP
Chill	Bacterial growth	CCP
Slice	Contamination	
Prepare Sandwiches	Contamination	
Wrap/Label	Contamination	
Store in Cooler	Bacterial growth	CCP
Display Chilled	Bacterial growth	CCP

Critical limits	Monitoring procedures	Corrective actions	Records
Chilled items below 41°F (5°C) No spoilage, contamination No foreign objects	Measure/record temperature Visual inspection	Reject if above 41°F (5°C) Reject items with spoilage, contamination or foreign objects	Receiving invoice
Chill to below 41°F (5°C)	Measure/record cooler air temperature every 4 hours	Adjust cooler thermostat	
Thaw completely Keep below 41°F (5°C)	Observe thawing	Modify thawing practice	
Cook to specified temperature	Measure/record temperature	Increase cooking time	Cooking log
Chill in shallow container to below 41°F (5°C)	Measure/record cooler air temperature every 4 hours	Adjust cooler thermostat	Recording thermometer
Avoid hand contact Use disposable gloves	Observe practices	Modify practices	
Avoid hand contact Use disposable gloves	Observe practices	Modify practices	
Avoid hand contact Use disposable gloves	Observe practices	Modify practices	
Product below 41°F (5°C)	Measure/record cooler air temperature every 4 hours	Adjust cooler thermostat	Recording thermometer
Product below 41°F (5°C)	Measure/record cooler air temperature every 4 hours	Adjust display thermostat	Recording thermometer

Figure 9.13 Sliced poultry/meat sandwich.

with a recording thermometer. Corrective actions may involve resetting the thermostat on the refrigerated unit, evaluating product, or changing cooling or storage practices.

9.9 Example HACCP plans

The charts in Figure 9.7 through 9.13 outline examples of HACCP plans for selected retail deli, meat, poultry and seafood products. The information in these examples should be modified for each store and process to ensure that all potential hazards are addressed. Additional seafood and deli examples can be found in *A Program to Ensure Food Safety in the Supermarket – The Hazard Analysis Critical Control Point System* (FMI, 1989a). This notebook is available from the Food Marketing Institute, 1750 K Street NW, Washington, D.C. Snyder (1991, 1994) provides further information on HACCP systems for retail food operations.

9.10 Summary

HACCP is a preventive system for assuring the safe processing and preparation of food products. Outbreaks of foodborne illness from retail food operations are preventable. The proper application of HACCP principles to deli and meat, poultry and seafood retail operations will assure the safety of foods handled, processed or prepared in the store. Designing, implementing and verifying a HACCP plan for retail food operations requires a thorough knowledge of potential hazards and handling, processing, preparation and display practices to control these hazards. Several publications and training materials are available from FDA, trade associations and universities to assist the retail food industry in identifying potential hazards, developing effective HACCP systems and training employees.

The retail food industry has primary responsibility for the safety of the foods that it sells to consumers. Implementing a HACCP system is an important first step toward assuring the safety of foods offered for consumption.

References

Bradshaw, J.G., Shah, D.B., Forney, E. and Madden, J.M. (1990) Growth of *Salmonella enteritidis* in yolk of shell eggs from normal and seropositive hens. *J. Food Protect.* **53**, 1033.

Bryan, F.L. (1988) Risks associated with vehicles of foodborne pathogens and toxins. *J. Food Protect.* **51**, 498.

CDC (1991) Multistate outbreak of *Salmonella poona* infections – United States and Canada. *Centers for Disease Control, Morbidity and Mortality Weekly Report* **40**(32), 549.

DHHS (1993) *Code of Federal Regulations*, Title 21, Chapter 1, Subchapter B, Part 110 – Current Good Manufacturing Practice in Manufacturing, Packing, or Holding Human Food. US Department of Health and Human Services, Public Health Service, Food and Drug Administration, US Government Printing Office, Washington, D.C.

DHHS (1994) *Food Code 1993*. US Department of Health and Human Services, Public Health Service, Food and Drug Administration, Washington, D.C.

FDA (1994) *Fish and Fishery Products Hazards and Controls Guide*. US Food and Drug Administration, Washington, D.C.

FMI (1989a) *A Program to Ensure Food Safety in the Supermarket – The Hazard Analysis Critical Control Point System*. Food Marketing Institute, Washington, D.C.

FMI (1989b) *Food Handler's Pocket Guide for Food Safety & Quality*. Food Marketing Institute, Washington, D.C.

Mermelstein, N.H. (1986) New bacteria in the news. *Food Technol.* **40**(8), 16.

Price, R.J. (1990a) Retail seafood cross-contamination. *UCSGEP 90–6*. University of California, Food Science & Technology Department. Davis, California 95616.

Price, R.J. (1990b) Retail seafood temperature control. *UCSGEP 90–5*. University of California, Food Science & Technology Department. Davis, California 95616.

Price, R.J., Tom, P.D. and Stevenson, K.E. (1993) *Ensuring Food Safety . . . The HACCP Way*. Publication T-CSGCP-030. Sea Grant Extension Program, Food Science and Technology, University of California, Davis, California.

Reed, G.H. (1994) Foodborne illness (Part 8): *Escherichia coli. Dairy, Food Environ. Sanitat.* **14**(6), 329.

Rhodehamel, E.J. (1992) Overview of biological, chemical, and physical hazards, Ch. 3, in HACCP Principles and Applications (M.D. Pierson and D.M. Corlett eds). Van Nostrand Reinhold, New York. pp. 8–28.

Smith, J.L. (1992) *Toxoplasma gondii* in meats – A matter of concern? *Dairy, Food Environ. Sanitat.* **12**(6), 341.

Snyder, O.P. (1991) HACCP in the retail food industry. *Dairy, Food Environ. Sanitat.* **11**(2), 73.

Snyder, O.P. (1994) Retail food operation food hazard control checklist. *Dairy, Food Environ. Sanitat.* **14**(3), 168.

Stevenson, K.E. (ed) (1993) *HACCP – Establishing Hazard Analysis Critical Control Point Programs: A Workshop Manual*. The Food Processors Institute, Washington, D.C.

Stier, R.F. (1994) Personal communication. Libra Laboratories, Inc., Emeryville, California.

10 HACCP-TQM for retail and food service operations

O.P. SNYDER, Jr.

10.1 Introduction

The Hazard Analysis and Critical Control Point method for process safety assurance is not new. It has been used by the chemical process industry for over 40 years and the nuclear reactor and human safety engineering industries for more than 30 years, as cited by Battelle Columbus Division for The Center for Chemical Process Safety of the American Institute of Chemical Engineers (1992) and Center for Chemical Process Safety (1989, 1992). NASA was using it in the construction of space vehicles in 1968, when it was adopted by the US Army Natick Laboratories to assure the safety of the astronauts' food (Heidelbaugh et al., 1973; Bourland et al., 1974). Pillsbury applied it in the formulation of the first rations and documented it in the first HACCP publications (The Pillsbury Company, 1973; Bauman, 1974).

People have known for thousands of years that food contained harmful substances and that food preparation processes must be controlled if the food is to be safe to eat. This has been applied historically as 'cook the food well done', which means 'no blood', relating to temperatures above 165°F (73.9°C). At this temperature, there is virtually instant vegetative pathogen death. It has also been applied in many food fermentation processes whereby the fermentative microorganisms exclude the pathogens, as in aged cheese.

The logic for HACCP-based process design is simple. Assuming that there are 50 million foodborne illnesses per year in the USA, and that 250 million people have eaten about 273.75 billion meals (250 billion $\times$ 3 $\times$ 365) annually, this means that approximately 1 meal in 5475 makes people ill. The probability of sampling the final product, finding the defective food and removing it to assure safety, is virtually zero. There must be at least a 5% defective product rate before sampling the final product has any value. Since raw chicken has at least a 30% product pathogen defect rate, sampling a lot of raw chicken to determine its safety has meaning (CAST, 1994). After cooking, the contamination rate depends on the person cooking the food, but characteristically will be less than 1 in 1000 meals of chicken, according to CDC outbreak data (Bean et al., 1990). Sampling cooked pasteurized food for pathogens, therefore, is totally impractical.

The problem has been that the regulatory agencies, especially in the USA, and the food service industry have not used correct scientific facts from foodborne illness cases to pinpoint the hazards and establish effective hazard controls. Historically, the government has focused on filth, facilities, equipment construction and fraud, and has said that GMPs (Good Manufacturing Practices), which are fundamentally cleanliness controls, assure safety. GMPs do not assure safety because they are not process controls. When there is a foodborne illness incident, the epidemiologists focus on the number of people who become ill and the pathogen. If operators are to improve prevention, illness investigations must identify the failures in the operator's prevention program that allowed the illness to occur. In HACCP terms, this is called, 'doing a Root Cause Analysis'.

Today it is known, through a simple Failure Mode Effect Analysis (FMEA), that environment and facilities in retail food operations have little to do with microbiological hazard control. Occasionally, environment and facilities do contribute to chemical hazard contamination from piping and equipment, and to physical object contamination. Because regulatory agencies have not totally focused on process control in retail food operations, the result is that the number of illness cases worldwide is increasing (CAST, 1994). Since the liability cost from customer illness and injury has increased dramatically in the past ten years, it is essential to return to a scientifically proven hazard-based zero-defect process control to assure production of safe food.

10.2 What is quality?

In actual implementation, it is extremely difficult to isolate process hazard control from process quality control and productivity. The safer a product is, the more processed it is. For example, commercially canned sterilized food, whereby all pathogens including the spores are inactivated, has much less risk of causing illness than a rare hamburger or a fresh green salad. However, people want fresh, minimally processed food. Since both government and the food industry are customer driven, it means that the food industry must strive to provide what the customers want. Just as canned food has been made virtually hazard free with scientifically sound process design, fresh pasteurized food processes can also be as safe with correct process design, as will be outlined below.

There are three food system quality attributes that must be provided in order to have an acceptable retail food process.

1. *Safety*: The government and the food establishment's insurance company must be satisfied because no one is made ill or injured by the food.

2. *Customer satisfaction*: The food operation must develop repeat customer sales because the food, service and ambiance meet the customers' needs, wants and value expectations.
3. *Productivity/profit*: Productivity and the cost of quality must be optimum, resulting in a competitively low-cost operation and a profit that meets the owner's expectations and assures continuing quality and safety improvement.

10.2.1 The safety assurance component of quality

Safety assurance begins with the identification of the *biological, chemical* and *physical* threats in the establishment that can become hazards and result in customer (and employee) illness and injury if not controlled. Then there must be the establishment of critical limits for process-product safety at hazard control points. This chapter will describe this procedure. The standards presented below are not necessarily based on current government regulations because in some cases they are incomplete and not up to date. Actually, there are scientific reasons for every safety standard. Once correct, scientifically referenced safety standards are defined, they can be accepted worldwide because the same biological, chemical and physical threats are worldwide.

An example of an incorrect government standard is the cold holding temperature for food at 41°F (5.0°C). *Listeria monocytogenes* and *Yersinia enterocolitica* begin to multiply slightly below 32°F (0°C) (Hanna *et al.*, 1977; Grau and Vanderline, 1990). This is the lowest growth temperature known for pathogens, and it applies to food anywhere in the world. Research by Hudson *et al.* (1994) indicates that *L. monocytogenes, Y. enterocolitica* and *Aeromonas hydrophila* can multiply at temperatures of 29°F (−1.7°C) in vacuum packaged sliced roast beef. This means that 32°F (0°C), not 40°F (4.4°C) or 41°F (5°C), becomes a critical safety limit when food that is not to be reheated is to be stored chilled for a long time. The author's standard is 5 days, which at 40°F (4.4°C) is approximately 5 generations of *L. monocytogenes* in meat and vegetable foods. In the same way, the highest temperature at which a pathogen (*Clostridium perfringens*) has been shown to multiply is 127.5°F (53.1°C) (Shoemaker and Pierson, 1976). Above this temperature, food is safe. The regulatory standard that states that most food will be held at 140°F (60.0°C) is excessively high and leads to food waste and nutrient destruction. In both cases these temperature requirements are the same anywhere in the world because the microorganisms are the same. In the case of applying these facts to process specifications, if the refrigerator cycles ±2°F (±1.1°C), the refrigerator would have to be specified as 30°F ± 2°F (−1.1°C ± 1.1°C) for hazard control. Likewise, if the hot holding device's thermostat is specified as ±5° at 130°F (±2.8° at 54.4°C), the minimum food holding thermostat hazard control setting for that piece of equipment would be 132.5°F (55.9°C). As can be seen, measuring food hazard control process variables, such as food temperature and calibrating operating equipment, become very important hazard control procedures in a safety-assured (safety pre-control) system.

10.3 HACCP principles for food production

The National Advisory Committee on Microbiological Criteria for Foods (NACMCF, 1992), Hazard Analysis and Critical Control Point System listed the following seven principles for applying HACCP.

1. Conduct a hazard analysis. Prepare a list of steps in the process (from growing, harvesting raw materials and ingredients, processing manu-facturing, distribution, marketing, preparation and consumption of the food) where significant hazards occur. Describe the preventive measures.
2. Identify the CCPs in the process.
3. Establish the critical limits for preventive measures associated with each identified CCP.
4. Establish CCP monitoring requirements. Establish procedures for using the results of monitoring to adjust the process and maintain control.
5. Establish corrective action to be taken when monitoring indicates that there is a deviation from a critical limit.
6. Establish effective record keeping procedures that document the HACCP system.
7. Establish procedures for verification that the HACCP system is working correctly.

Actually, these seven principles of HACCP are incomplete. They only describe the process for problem analysis and prevention covered in many quality control books. First of all, building a team and collecting correct knowledge are not included as principles. The NACMCF (1992) principles assume that one knows the correct hazard information. However, this is not so. Nowhere are the safe and unsafe levels for pathogenic micro-organisms, chemicals and physical objects in food specified. For example, what size of stone and metal fragment is safe? In the same way, *Clostridium botulinum*, *Bacillus cereus*, *Staphylococcus aureus* and *C. perfringens* cannot be kept out of food. But, at low levels of 100/g, even the vegetative cells are not a hazard to people's health. Truly, one cannot do HACCP today because safe/unsafe levels are not defined by the government.

10.4   Food science HACCP principles

The author has established the necessary principles and levels as presented in this chapter based on food science and food process development. These HACCP principles are focused on management as the critical control points, and continuous quality improvement as the most important critical controls. HACCP programs are totally ineffective if the HACCP operations and training manual are left on the shelf and the employees are not trained to mastery and empowered to control hazards at critical points. Employee training and empowerment are management actions and responsibilities. There is a critical point of correct food hazard and control knowledge. However, it must be used and improved, which is a management function. The following is the author's integrated HACCP-TQM program.

1. Describe the food system. Specify the person responsible for the program. The president of the company must be the leader of the HACCP program. Identify all regulations that must be met. Establish the HACCP team(s).
2. Describe the food and its intended use/product description/specifications. Prepare product specifications and consumer warning labels that ensure safety after the food is purchased by the consumer and until it is consumed.
3. Ensure adequate environment, facilities and equipment for the manufacture of food.
4. Make a list of raw materials and all supplies to be used. Write purchase specifications (GMPs). When possible, use suppliers who have HACCP programs or do enough microbiological testing to know the levels of spoilage and pathogenic microorganisms in the raw food.
5. Do a flow diagram, including food temperature in and out and time for each process step for the food products. Identify proposed safety assurance policies, procedures and standards for each step from growing/harvesting to consumption.
6. Do a root cause hazard and process failure mode assessment at each step in the flow diagram for the eight components of the system.

Management	Equipment
Personnel	Materials and supplies
Environment	Food production and service
Facility	Customer

7. Where the failure mode assessment has shown that controls are inadequate, revise and test improved policies, procedures and standards until they are capable of controlling the hazards. Set target operating limits, quality limits and hazardous condition limits for each hazard variable at each step.

8. Establish employee monitoring requirements: temperature, sanitation, barriers, package integrity, shelf life, finished product specifications and distribution (biological, chemical and physical hazards).
9. Establish corrective action to be taken by the employee when there is a target, quality or hazardous deviation in a policy, procedure or standard of any of the eight system components at a control point.
10. Establish an effective information system that documents the performance of process controls and the HACCP-based TQM program. The data will be used by the quality improvement (QI) process to increase the reliability of quality control (QC) and quality assurance (QA).
11. Establish a verification program to ensure that the HACCP program is being followed.
12. Establish a process for using all system performance information for improved process quality and customer satisfaction in the next operating cycle.

10.4.1   The unit as a food process system

Figure 10.1 provides process control nomenclature and a systematic way to look at the processes in order to make flow diagrams of them. At the top of the system is management, providing resources, leadership and a good environment in which people can function. The HACCP-based design begins with consideration of consumer wants and the threshold levels for consumer safety. This information is then fed into the input of the process in order to design the food process environment, facilities, equipment, employees and supplies that will give a safe output. Then, the process takes the input supplies and makes them safe for the consumer.

10.5   The HACCP-based TQM process

Figure 10.2 shows how the system is divided into processes for analysis. Every task and action that takes place in the facility, from cleaning the floor to cooking the meat, to changing light bulbs, is a process with hazards that require controls to assure that safety standards (and quality standards) are met and not exceeded. In other words, as with the overall system, each process can always be described in terms of input, processes (procedures) and output. A *process* can be divided into three levels, as shown in Figure 10.2. Four examples of processes are given: training employees; washing fruits and vegetables; cooking thick foods; removing feces from fingertips.

The process, then, is further divided into *tasks*. For example, for Process N (removing feces from fingertips), firstly, the water must be turned on. Secondly, the employee must wet the hands and get the fingernail brush. Thirdly, soap is put on the brush and on fingertips.

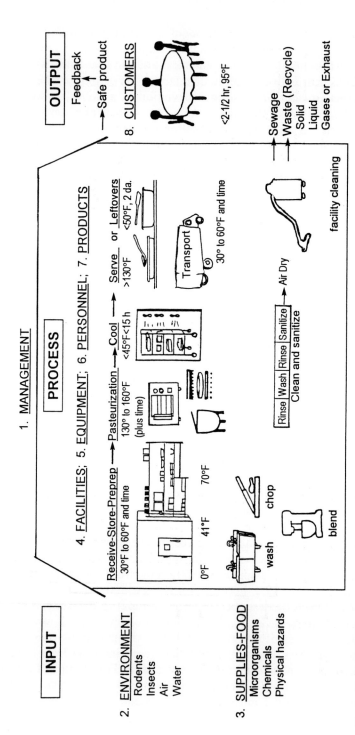

Figure 10.1 The unit as a food process system. *Hazards:* Microorganisms [bacteria (vegetative cells and spores), viruses, parasites]; chemicals; hard foreign objects. *Controls:* Management involvement, hazard analysis and control; written procedures; employee training and empowerment, process measurement, control, and improvement; discipline and consequences.

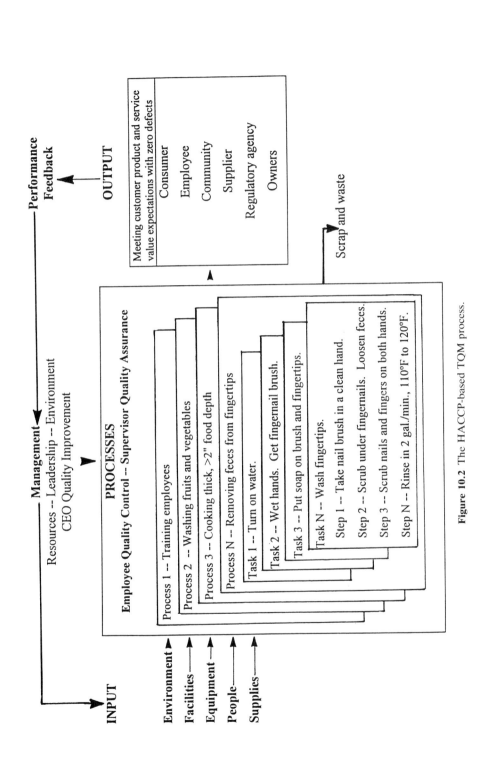

Figure 10.2 The HACCP-based TQM process.

Performance
→ **Feedback** ←

Management
Resources -- Leadership -- Environment
CEO Quality Improvement

OUTPUT

Meeting customer product and service value expectations with zero defects
Consumer
Employee
Community
Supplier
Regulatory agency
Owners

PROCESSES

Employee Quality Control -- Supervisor Quality Assurance

Process 1 -- Training employees

Process 2 -- Washing fruits and vegetables

Process 3 -- Cooking thick, >2" food depth

Process N -- Removing feces from fingertips

Task 1 -- Turn on water.

Task 2 -- Wet hands. Get fingernail brush.

Task 3 -- Put soap on brush and fingertips.

Task N -- Wash fingertips.

   Step 1 -- Take nail brush in a clean hand.

   Step 2 -- Scrub under fingernails. Loosen feces.

   Step 3 -- Scrub nails and fingers on both hands.

   Step N -- Rinse in 2 gal./min., 110°F to 120°F.

INPUT

Environment →
Facilities →
Equipment →
People →
Supplies →

Scrap and waste

Tasks are finally divided into *steps*, which are the individual actions that control the process. In the case of the task of washing fingertips, the employee first takes the nail brush in the clean hand. The second step is to scrub under the fingernails to loosen feces. The third step is to scrub the nails and fingers on both hands. Step N is to rinse the hands in 110–120°F (43.3–48.9°C) water flowing at 2 gallons per minute (9 l min^{-1}). Until every process in the food system is safety certified to the step level, the system is not assured to produce a safe output of products. When a process authority or government official certifies a process as safe, he/she must review the hazards, standards, and controls at each step in order to certify that the process is safe.

The box-type flow diagram is a very useful engineering analysis method for systematically discovering all of the variables in a process. However, it is difficult for employees to understand. The effective food safety policies, procedures, and standards manual is the process flow analysis in a written form.

10.5.1   The system for HACCP-based food safety TQM

Once management makes the long-term commitment to food safety assurance and a HACCP development team is formed, the operation's food system must be described in order to identify all of the threats that can become hazards.

Figure 10.3 shows the system for HACCP-based food safety TQM. The system has three components: *input*, *process* and *output*. The *output* for the system is the consumer who wants a proper balance between pleasurable and safe food, while at the same time has an immune threshold which may be immune compromised or immune complete. Consumers also will have a variety of sensitivities to toxic and allergic compounds in the food. If customers do not eat the food at the establishment (e.g. carry-out or take-home food after dining out), they are also likely to time–temperature abuse the food if they are not properly informed about correct handling. Depending on the intended use of the food, the food operator should introduce various hurdles such as temperature, time, water activity, oxidation reduction, chemical additives and packaging into the process design in order to assure safe food after it is given to the customer. The spores survive the retail food processing and, given about 10 hours of 90–100°F (32.2–37.8°C) temperature abuse, are almost sure to cause illness.

After examining the output and setting microbiological, chemical and physical (hard foreign object) safety levels, the *input* of supplies and material is considered. The fewer the pathogens, chemicals and hard foreign objects in the input material, the less the food will need to be processed in order to be safe. All food will be contaminated with various environmental organisms such as *C. botulinum* and *L. monocytogenes*.

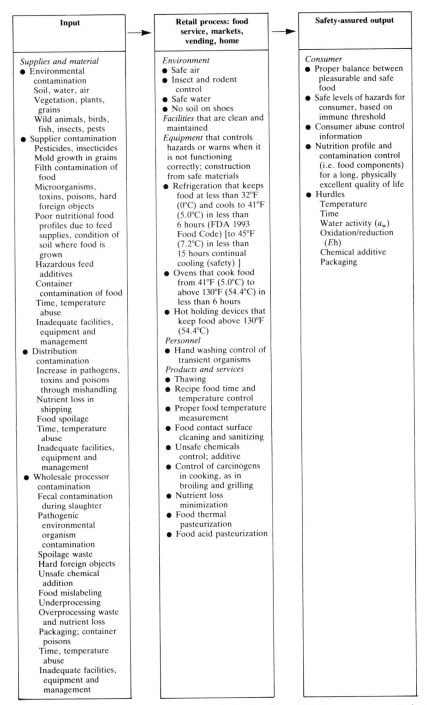

Input	Retail process: food service, markets, vending, home	Safety-assured output

Supplies and material
● Environmental contamination
  Soil, water, air
  Vegetation, plants, grains
  Wild animals, birds, fish, insects, pests
● Supplier contamination
  Pesticides, insecticides
  Mold growth in grains
  Filth contamination of food
  Microorganisms, toxins, poisons, hard foreign objects
  Poor nutritional food profiles due to feed supplies, condition of soil where food is grown
  Hazardous feed additives
  Container contamination of food
  Time, temperature abuse
  Inadequate facilities, equipment and management
● Distribution contamination
  Increase in pathogens, toxins and poisons through mishandling
  Nutrient loss in shipping
  Food spoilage
  Time, temperature abuse
  Inadequate facilities, equipment and management
● Wholesale processor contamination
  Fecal contamination during slaughter
  Pathogenic environmental organism contamination
  Spoilage waste
  Hard foreign objects
  Unsafe chemical addition
  Food mislabeling
  Underprocessing
  Overprocessing waste and nutrient loss
  Packaging; container poisons
  Time, temperature abuse
  Inadequate facilities, equipment and management
	Environment
	● Safe air
	● Insect and rodent control
	● Safe water
	● No soil on shoes
	Facilities that are clean and maintained
	Equipment that controls hazards or warns when it is not functioning correctly; construction from safe materials
	● Refrigeration that keeps food at less than 32°F (0°C) and cools to 41°F (5.0°C) in less than 6 hours (FDA 1993 Food Code) [to 45°F (7.2°C) in less than 15 hours continual cooling (safety)]
	● Ovens that cook food from 41°F (5.0°C) to above 130°F (54.4°C) in less than 6 hours
	● Hot holding devices that keep food above 130°F (54.4°C)
	Personnel
	● Hand washing control of transient organisms
	Products and services
	● Thawing
	● Recipe food time and temperature control
	● Proper food temperature measurement
	● Food contact surface cleaning and sanitizing
	● Unsafe chemicals control; additive
	● Control of carcinogens in cooking, as in broiling and grilling
	● Nutrient loss minimization
	● Food thermal pasteurization
	● Food acid pasteurization
		Consumer
		● Proper balance between pleasurable and safe food
		● Safe levels of hazards for consumer, based on immune threshold
		● Consumer abuse control information
		● Nutrition profile and contamination control (i.e. food components) for a long, physically excellent quality of life
		● Hurdles
		  Temperature
		  Time
		  Water activity (a_w)
		  Oxidation/reduction (Eh)
		  Chemical additive
		  Packaging

Figure 10.3 The system for HACCP-based food safety TQM in management (and government).

However, the cleaner the growing conditions of food animals, poultry, fish, etc. or fruits and vegetables, the less the chance of fecal organisms such as *Salmonella* spp. and *Campylobacter jejuni* being on the food. If people wish to eat raw foods such as oysters, beef tartar or raw cured products, then it is essential that the ingredients have a pathogen level below the illness threshold level of the consumer.

Based on the output hazards and the hazards in the input supplies and material, the *process* standards for the environment, facilities, equipment, personnel and food processing must be developed. The food process will take the raw ingredients and produce finished products which, when eaten by the consumer, will nourish the consumer and not make him/her ill.

10.5.2 Hazards in the food system

What are the hazards to be controlled? Figure 10.4 provides an overview of the hazards that can harm people. Initially, in the 1970s, HACCP was only applied to microorganisms (biological). Then, chemicals, followed by hard foreign objects (physical), were also incorporated. Actually, many other hazards are found in the food environment. How are hazards selected? Simply, hazards are identified from insurance liability claims and medical records showing what hurts people in a specific environment. The goal of HACCP in economic terms is *zero liability costs*.

First of all, there are the microorganisms and toxins, as listed in Figure 10.4. Next are listed several toxic substances that either exist within the food, or are added accidentally or intentionally during processing. Consumer adverse food reactions, caused by either natural ingredients or additives, are also a serious problem.

Even though not currently included, nutrition, or lack of it, is also a public health problem and a hazard if not properly provided to people, especially those in an institution such as a prison, for the rest of their lives. If an elderly person who requires additional levels of calcium or other nutrients in his/her diet is denied proper nutrition, then that person's quality of life and life span are seriously diminished. Many micro-nutrients are required for a life with minimum medical problems.

Hard foreign objects are a major problem, but are not considered in most retail food safety programs because only one person per incident is harmed (i.e. breaks a tooth or chokes on the substance). Nonetheless, hard foreign objects are legitimate and serious food hazards, and are a very common problem. Finally, there are functional hazards. These include particle size deviations, packaging defects and sabotage of the food by the consumer or employee.

Note that while some government documents include fraud as a hazard, it is not. It is in fact a regulatory issue. Fraud is a major problem. There are many recalls of products each year in the USA due to careless or

Biological	**Chemical**	**Physical**
Organisms and their toxins	*Poisonous substances*	*Hard foreign objects*
Bacteria: vegetative cells and spores	Toxic plant material	Glass
	Intentional (GRAS) food additives	Wood
Molds [mycotoxins (e.g. aflatoxin)]	Chemicals created by the process	Stones, sand and dirt
		Metal
Yeasts (*Candida albicans*)	Agricultural chemicals	Packaging materials
Viruses and Rickettsia	Antibiotic and other drug residues in meat, poultry and dairy products	Bones
Parasites		Building materials
Marine animals as sources of toxic compounds	Unintentional additives	Filth from insects, rodents and any other unwanted animal parts or excreta
Fish	Sabotage	Personal effects
Shellfish	Equipment material leaching	*Functional hazards*
	Packaging material leaching	Particle size deviation
	Industrial pollutants	Packaging defects
	Heavy metals	Sabotage
	Radioactive isotopes	
	Adverse food reactions (food sensitivity)	
	Food allergies	
	Food intolerances	
	Metabolic disorder-based reactions	
	Pharmacological food reactions	
	Idiosyncratic reactions to food	
	Anaphylactoid reactions	
	Nutrition	
	Excessive addition of nutrients	
	Nutritional deficiencies and/or inaccurate formulation of synthesized formulas	
	Anti-nutritional factors	
	Destruction and unnecessary loss of nutrients during processing and storage	
	Inaccurate nutritional labeling	

Figure 10.4 Hazards in the food system. Goal: zero defects.

purposeful manipulations of food. There are many dishonest food suppliers whose business practices are unethical. However, HACCP is meant to address public health issues and fraud, labeling, net weights, etc. should be covered in separate government regulations, so that the effectiveness of controlling hazards is not diluted.

10.5.3 Risk clientele

The following are those persons who are considered to have reduced resistance to illness.

1. Infants
2. Hospital patients
3. People with allergies
4. Pregnant women
5. Frail, elderly people
6. Malnourished individuals
7. People with controlled physical or metabolic disorders (e.g. diabetes or high blood pressure)

These individuals are sensitive to lower levels of microbiological contaminants and are at greater risk of death from foodborne disease. In hospitals or health care facilities, it is easy to assure that these people receive more thoroughly pasteurized food. In the public feeding arena, operators have no idea of the immune status of their customers. As a basic rule, though, if young children (i.e. less than 5 years old) or frail senior citizens (i.e. over 65 years old) wish to eat raw or rare product, it is probably prudent for the operator to refuse to serve them.

Other people who are at risk must be in charge of their own protection or protected by companions (e.g. parents). If they have allergies, they must ask the wait staff about the ingredients in the food. If they are on immune-suppressant drugs, they must ask for food that is well cooked or otherwise made safe for their consumption, because the operator has no obvious way to identify these people.

10.5.4 What constitutes a hazard?

The World Health Organization (WHO) Division of Food and Nutrition, in the 1993 document FOS/93.3 (WHO, 1993), identifies a *hazard* as a 'biological, chemical, or physical agent or condition with the potential to cause harm'. It states that *hazard analysis* is the process of 'collecting and interpreting information to assess the risk and severity of potential hazards'.

Actually, food is never risk free. The EPA has developed many risk criteria for water and chemicals of all forms. Unfortunately, the government goal for retail food operations is still zero risk, which is unattainable. There will never be totally pathogen-free cows, fruits and vegetables, nor will there ever be human populations who excrete totally pathogen-free fecal material. Therefore, we must deal with hazards and risks, and reduce them as much as possible.

It is appropriate to classify hazards as *high concern, low concern* and *no concern* because government regulations deal mostly with items of no concern. The following are definitions.

1. *High concern*: without control, there is life-threatening risk
2. *Low concern*: a threat that must be controlled but is not life threatening
3. *No concern*: no threat to the consumer

For example, spoilage bacteria, even at 50 000 000 per gram, are of no concern. Coliforms at 1000s per gram are of no concern. Properly controlled levels of salt, sugar and MSG are of no concern. Floors, walls and ceilings are really zero risk, compared with feces on workers' fingertips.

Of low concern would be the presence of 1000 *S. aureus* cells, *B. cereus* spores or *C. perfringens* spores per gram. These organisms are not hazardous until they reach 1 000 000 per gram.

A high concern hazard, on the other hand, would be 100 *E. coli* 0157:H7 per gram, or 100 000 *Salmonella* or *C. jejuni* per gram of raw hamburger. Even healthy people will undoubtedly be made sick at these levels of contamination if the levels are not reduced through effective pasteurization.

In order to develop a process or operation capable of zero liability costs, it is essential that a logical process for hazard identification be followed. This includes the analysis of:

1. Evidence of a hazard to health based on epidemiological data or a hazard analysis
2. The nature of the natural and commonly acquired microflora of the ingredient or food and the ability of the food to support microbial growth
3. The effect of processing on the microflora of the food
4. The potential for microbial contamination (or re-contamination) and/ or growth during processing, handling, storage and distribution
5. The category of consumers at risk
6. The state in which food is distributed (e.g. frozen, refrigerated, heat processed, etc.)
7. Potential for abuse at the consumer level
8. Spoilage potential, utility (suitability depending on how the food will be used) and (the existence of) GMPs
9. The manner in which the food is prepared for ultimate consumption (i.e. heated or not)
10. Reliability of methods available to detect and/or quantify the microorganism(s) and toxin(s) of concern
11. The costs/benefits associated with the application of the criterion

Coupling hazard analysis with correct hazard control standards and operating procedures enables the operator to show a high degree of 'due diligence' in the prevention of problems and to minimize liability costs if there is a problem.

10.5.5 Government microbiological standards for raw and pasteurized food

The government has only one standard for both raw and pasteurized food: that *Salmonella* will be undetectable in a 25 g sample from a lot. In the last few years, there has been an informal standard for the amount of *L. monocytogenes* in a 10 or 25 sample, but this applies only to processing plants.

10.5.6 Foodborne illness: annual estimated cases and deaths in the USA

While the USA has the capability of producing the 'safest' food in the world, there is still an enormous number of illnesses and deaths which occur each year because of foodborne illness. Table 10.1 presents data on annual estimated cases and deaths due to foodborne illness in the USA. Between 6 and 30 million Americans become ill each year from microorganisms in their food. An estimated 9000 die. It has also been estimated that the cost of foodborne illness in the USA represents $4 to $14 billion a year in terms of medical expenses, lost wages, insurance costs and liability (Bennett *et al.*, 1987; Todd, 1989; Roberts and Van Ravenswaay, 1989; Roberts, 1990). Statistics clearly show that microorganisms consumed in food and water are a significant cause of illness. In most instances the illnesses and deaths that result from these sources can be prevented.

Most American consumers assume that if the food looks fresh, the food must be safe. They do not realize that the visual appearance, smell and taste of food are not indications of safety. Pathogens and toxic compounds can be present in food products despite the food's appearance, smell and taste.

The sources of the foodborne illness pathogens are ubiquitous. Because of environmental and animal contamination, food and food products will always be contaminated with low levels of pathogens. At low levels, pathogenic microorganisms cause no problems. People build up immunity, depending on their environment. At illness thresholds, however, pathogens can make people ill and cause death. Pathogens in food can only be controlled when food producers, food retailers and consumers know the potential hazards and handle food according to safe methods.

How do pathogens in food get to high levels? A major reason is that no one who raises, processes, distributes and sells food is required to have any knowledge of foodborne illness causes or to establish a food safety program before being allowed to produce and sell food. Therefore, they implement incomplete hazard control processes.

Another problem is that in many areas of the country, regulatory food

Table 10.1 Foodborne illness: annual estimated cases and deaths in the USA

Cause	Cases	Deaths
Bacteria		
Spore-forming Bacteria		
Bacillus cereus	84 000	0
Clostridium perfringens	650 000	6–7
Clostridium botulinum (adults)	100	2–3
Infant botulism	60	?
Vegetative Bacteria		
Streptococcus (grp. A)	500 000	175
Yersinia enterocolitica (32°F/0°C)	20 000	2–3
Staphylococcus aureus (toxin)	8 900 000	7120
Salmonella (non-typhi)	3 000 000	2000
Campylobacter spp. (cutting boards)	2 100 000	2100
Shigella spp.	300 000	600
Escherichia coli (enteric)	200 000	400
Brucella spp.	50 000	0.1
Vibrio cholerae/vulnificus	13 000	1–2
Vibrio (non-cholera)	30 000	300–900
Salmonella typhi	600	36
Listeria monocytogenes (32°F/0°C)	25 000	1000
Miscellaneous microorganisms	107 000	11
Viruses (fingertips)		
Hepatitis A	48 000	150
Norwalk virus	181 000	0
Other viruses	6 000 000	6
Parasites		
Trichinella spiralis	100 000	1000
Giardia lamblia (water)	7000	0
Toxoplasma gondii	2 300 000	450
Taena spp.	1000	10
Fish parasites	1000	0
Chemicals/toxins		
Ciguatera toxin	27 000	2.1
Chemical poisons	96 000	5.4
Plant poisons	7000	5.9
Scrombroid toxin	31 000	0
Paralytic shellfish poison	260	0.3
Hard foreign objects	?	?
Total	Cases 24 779 020	Deaths 15 990

Source: Adapted from Snyder and Poland (1990, 1991).

safety inspectors are not accredited to detect and control pathogens in food operations or to safety-certify food processing procedures. Most health inspectors look only for visual indications of cleanliness and defects. The raw food must be subjected to laboratory analysis to measure its risk potential.

10.5.6.1 Potential pathogens in food. Since there are many different pathogens of concern, relating to pasteurized retail food, what is a simple approach to microbiological hazard control?

Table 10.2 separates the most important pathogens in various food groups into *infective* organisms (vegetative cells), which can be controlled by pasteurization, acid, washing, fermentation, ionizing radiation, etc., to safe levels of 10 CFU per g to 1 CFU per 25 g and then, *toxin producers* and *spore producers*, which cannot be eliminated but must be controlled at a non-hazardous level of 1000–100 CFU per g.

Table 10.2 Potential pathogens in food

Food	Pathogens		
	Infective (inactivated by pasteurization)		Toxin and/or spore producers (not inactivated by pasteurization)
Meat, poultry and eggs	*Salmonella* spp. *Campylobacter jejuni* *Escherichia coli* *Y. enterocolitica*	*L. monocytogenes* Foot and mouth virus Hepatitis A virus *Trichinella spiralis* Tapeworms	*S. aureus* (toxin) *C. perfringens* *C. botulinum* *Bacillus cereus*
Fin fish	*Salmonella* spp. *Vibrio* spp. *Y. enterocolitica*	Hepatitis A virus Anisakis Tapeworms	*S. aureus* (toxin) *C. botulinum* Microbial by-products (Histamine poisoning)
Shellfish	*Salmonella* spp. *Vibrio* spp. *Shigella* spp. *Y. enterocolitica*	Hepatitis A virus Norwalk virus	*S. aureus* (toxin) *C. botulinum* Microbial by-products (Paralytic shellfish poisoning)
Vegetables	*Salmonella* spp. *L. monocytogenes* *Shigella* spp.	Hepatitis A virus Norwalk virus *Giardia lamblia*	*S. aureus* (toxin) *C. botulinum* *Bacillus cereus*
Cereals, grains, legumes and nuts	*Salmonella* spp. Aflatoxins (mold) Hepatitis A virus Norwalk virus		*S. aureus* (toxin) *C. botulinum* *Bacillus cereus*
Spices	*Salmonella* spp.		*S. aureus* (toxin) *C. botulinum* *Bacillus cereus* *C. perfringens*
Milk and dairy products	*Salmonella* spp. *Y. enterocolitica* *L. monocytogenes* *Escherichia coli*	*C. jejuni* *Shigella* spp. Hepatitis A virus Norwalk virus	*S. aureus* (toxin) *C. perfringens* *Bacillus cereus*

Source: Snyder (1992a).

10.5.6.2 Food product pathogen contamination. In order to focus on the microbiological hazards, which are the primary problem in retail food operations, it will be assumed that all hazards caused by toxic substances, adverse food reactions, incorrect nutrition, hard foreign objects, fraud and functional hazards are controlled through warning labels on the food, ethical practices, purchasing, etc. This leaves only one hazard, the *microbiological* (biological) hazard.

Is the raw food from the wholesale system contaminated? Absolutely! It is wrong on the part of the government to state that food is wholesome when in fact it is only wholesome when properly prepared by the chef or consumer to eliminate the pathogens which have been allowed to contaminate the food through careless growing, harvesting and processing. In the USA, raw food is grossly contaminated with pathogenic bacteria. Table 10.3 shows a sample of some contamination levels. Even water from commercial sources is now recognized as being risky, especially when ground water is used in municipal water supplies.

10.5.6.3 Pathogen contamination from human sources. In addition to contamination of raw food supplies, there is the problem caused by contaminated people who come to work each day. While most codes

Table 10.3 Food product pathogen contamination

Bacteria	Food	Percentage contaminated
Salmonella spp.	Raw poultry	40–100
	Raw pork	3–20
	Raw shellfish	16
Staphylococcus aureus	Raw chicken	73
	Raw pork	13–33
	Raw beef	16
Clostridium perfringens	Raw pork and chicken	39–45
Campylobacter jejuni	Raw chicken and turkey	45–64
Escherichia coli 0157:H7	Raw beef/pork/poultry	1.5–3.7
Bacillus cereus	Raw ground beef	43–63
	Raw rice	100
Listeria monocytogenes	Fresh potatoes	26
	Fresh radishes	30
Yersinia enterocolitica	Raw pork	49
	Raw milk	48
	Raw vegetables	46
Vibrio spp.	Raw seafood	33–46
Giardia lamblia, Norwalk virus	Water	30

Source: Adapted from Snyder and Poland (1990, 1991).

Table 10.4 Pathogen contamination from human sources

Microorganism	Source	Percentage contaminated
Shigella spp., Hepatitis A, Norwalk virus, *E. coli*, *Salmonella* spp., *Giardia lamblia*	Feces	1 in 50 (2%) of the employees who come to work each day are highly infective.
Norwalk virus	Vomit	
Staphylococcus aureus	Skin, nose, boils and skin infections.	
Streptococcus Group A	Throat and skin	

Source: Snyder (1993).

require that when an employee is sick, he/she should stay home, people actually shed pathogenic bacteria normally a few hours to many days before they have major symptoms of illness. Food workers can become permanent carriers, as for example, with *Salmonella*. Therefore, as shown in Table 10.4, the only safe assumption is that all employees who work with food every day have skin, feces and urine that are contaminated with pathogens, which must be kept out of the food.

10.5.6.4 Foodborne illness hazards: threshold and quality levels. The next step in the systematic approach to hazard control is to recognize that certain pathogens can be selected as the basis for process control standards. Table 10.5 shows the levels of microorganisms that can cause illness based on volunteer feeding tests of healthy people.

For example, the three spore formers, *B. cereus*, *C. botulinum* and *C. perfringens*, all must outgrow after the food is cooked, and multiply to a level of at least 10^4 to 10^6 in order to become a hazard to consumers. Low levels of these spore-forming organisms (10^2 to 10^3) are not a hazard, with the exception of *C. botulinum* found in honey fed to infants at an age of less than one year. In this case, the infant has no competitive microflora, and the *C. botulinum* in the honey is able to outgrow in the infant's intestines at a level sufficient to cause illness. The hazard is controlled very simply by educating people not to feed honey to babies.

C. jejuni is the organism that is the principal cross-contamination problem. It seems to be the one microorganism that is in a wide variety of food at a 'natural' level after slaughter that will cause illness without having to multiply. Chicken and other poultry are grossly contaminated at high levels (i.e. 1000 to 10 000 organisms). The threshold for illness in healthy people is approximately 500 organisms in 180 ml of milk, which means approximately 2 organisms per ml. Comparing this infective level with those for *Salmonella*, *E. coli*, *Vibrio*, etc., it is obvious that *C. jejuni*, as long as food is grossly contaminated, will be a major cause of foodborne

Table 10.5 Foodborne illness hazards: threshold and quality levels

Agent	Healthy person (estimated illness dose)*	HITM suggested purchaser raw food quality standards
Bacteria	(Number of microorganisms)	(Number of microorganisms)
Spore-forming bacteria		
Bacillus cereus	3.4×10^4 to $9.5 \times 10^8/g$[5]	$<10^2/g$
Clostridium botulinum	$3 \times 10^{3[11]a}$	$<1/g$[b]
Clostridium perfringens	10^6 to $10^7/g$[6]	$<10^2/g$
Vegetative bacteria		
Escherichia coli	10^6 to $>10^7$ (dose)[2]	$<10/g$
Escherichia coli 0157:H7	10 organisms[4]	$<1/g$
Campylobacter jejuni	5×10^2 in 180 ml milk[18]	$<1/g$
Salmonella spp.		
S. anatum	10^5 to $>10^8$ (dose)[12]c	$<10/g$
S. bareilly	10^5 to $>10^6$ (dose)[13]c	$<10/g$
S. derby	10^7 (dose)[13]c	$<10/g$
S. meleagridus	10^7 (dose)[12]c	$<10/g$
S. newport	10^5 (dose)[13]c	$<10/g$
S. pullorum	10^9 to $>10^{10}$ (dose)[14]c	$<10/g$
S. typhi	10^4 to $>10^8$ (dose)[8]c	$<10/g$
Shigella spp.		
S. flexneri	10^2 to $>10^9$ (dose)[1,3,19]	$<1/g$
S. dysenteriae	10 to $>10^4$ (dose)[10]	$<1/g$
Staphylococcus aureus	10^5 to $>10^6/g$[4,7,17]d	$<10^2/g$
Vibrio cholerae	10^3 (dose)[9]	$<1/g$
Vibrio parahaemolyticus	10^6 to 10^9 (dose)[21]	$<10/g$
Yersinia enterocolitica	3.9×10^7 (dose)[16]e	$<10^2/g$
Listeria monocytogenes	probably >1000[4]	$<10/g$
Viruses	(Number of microorganisms)	(Number of microorganisms)
Hepatitis A virus	<10	$<1/g$
Norwalk virus	<10	$<1/g$
Chemicals	(Amount in food)	(Amount in food)
Monosodium glutamate	3.0% (dose)[20]	$<0.5\%$
Sodium nitrate, residuals in smoked fish	8–15 grams[15]	<500 ppm
Sodium nitrite, residuals in smoked fish	?	<200 ppm
Sulfites	>0.7 mg/kg body weight/day[22]	<10 ppm
Hard foreign objects	?	?

*Numbers in parentheses indicate references following on from main reference list.
Source: HITM (Hospitality Institute of Technology and Management), St. Paul, Minnesota.
[a]Indicates the number of bacteria necessary to produce sufficient toxin for mouse LD50. [b]If a product is to be considered shelf-stable above 50°F (10°C), then it should be heat processed to reduce a spore population of *Clostridium botulinum* types A and B by 10^{12}, or have a water activity (a_w) <0.86, or the pH of the product should be 4.1 or less, or a combination of processes should be used to control the growth of *Clostridium botulinum* types A and B and *Salmonella* spp. [c]Results from feeding studies. Data from outbreaks indicate lower values. [d]Indicates number of pathogenic bacteria necessary to produce sufficient amount of illness producing toxin. [e]Probably lower.

illness. When washing cutting boards, other food contact surfaces and hands, it is essential that the surface be thoroughly pre-rinsed, washed, rinsed and sanitized in order to reduce the level of pathogens to a level at which *C. jejuni* will not cause illness and will not be a cross-contamination hazard for a low-pathogen product, such as cooked chicken and lettuce which has been double washed.

The human fecal organism of concern is *Shigella dysenteriae*, which can have a threshold dose of 10 organisms for healthy people. Therefore, in hand washing, where there can be approximately 10^9 organisms per g of fecal material, the organisms must be reduced to approximately 10 on the fingertips in order to prevent foodborne illness. Note that probably the safe level for Hepatitis A virus and Norwalk virus is in the range of 10 as well, but currently, there are very few data to indicate their threshold levels. If *Shigella* is controlled, then Hepatitis and Norwalk will also be controlled. Assuming toilet paper is 99% effective, 10^7 of the 10^9 pathogens in the feces of an ill employee will get on the employee's fingertips and underneath his/her fingernails. The fingertips washing process must reduce these organisms to below 10 if the employee is not to make customers ill. Since antimicrobial chemicals used on hands only reduce pathogens from about 100 to 1, the key safety strategy involves good detergent, physical agitation of the fingertips with a fingernail brush to loosen the feces, a lot of hot water, and then a second hand wash without the brush.

Some chemical additives are also listed in Table 10.5. Clearly, it is essential that all chemical additives must be measured before being placed in food. For instance, in foodservice there are no standards for monosodium glutamate, and MSG is commonly overused. Hard foreign objects are not listed because currently, there are no established hazardous size thresholds for choking or tooth breakage.

10.5.6.5 Assumed microbiological standards for food in chilled food processes. Based on threshold levels that make healthy people ill and normal contaminations as listed in the literature, the author has developed a series of beginning contamination levels for raw food coming into typical foodservice systems. These are shown in Table 10.6. They pertain to food in the USA. Other nations would need to develop numbers for their own specific raw foods. When designing a safe food process, these are the levels that must be controlled.

Often there is the question, 'What is a microbiological standard for good food quality?' Table 10.7 gives a working value, which can be used when communicating with suppliers as to whether or not the raw food is spoiled. There are no government guidelines for these. Of course, the purpose of foodservice is to provide pleasurable food. Therefore, the ultimate quality goal is control of spoilage microorganisms.

Table 10.6 Expected pathogen contamination[a] on raw food

Microorganism(s)	Meat and poultry	Fish and shellfish	Fruits and vegetables	Starches
Salmonella spp., Vibrio, Hepatitis A, Shigella spp., E. coli, L. monocytogenes	10	10	10	10
Campylobacter jejuni	1000	–	–	–
Clostridium botulinum	0.01	0.01	0.01	0.01
Clostridium perfringens	100	10	–	–
Bacillus cereus	100	–	100	100
Mold toxins[b]	–	–	–	–
Chemicals and poisons[b]	–	–	–	–

[a]Number of pathogens per gram of food. [b]Below government tolerances.

Table 10.7 Microbial standards for food quality

Number of spoilage microorganisms[a]	Rating
<10 000	Good
10 000–5 000 000	Average
5 000 000–50 000 000	Poor
>50 000 000	Spoiled

[a]Aerobic plate count at 70°F (21.1°C); numbers per gram.

Note that safe food for immune-compromised people in the USA has been basically defined by the government as no detectable *Salmonella* spp. or *L. monocytogenes* in one or two 25 g samples from a lot. It can be expected that in the near future, the government will accept the fact that *L. monocytogenes* is a natural contaminant of food throughout the world, and can no more be kept out of food than *C. botulinum* or *B. cereus*. A level of 100 to 1000 *L. monocytogenes* bacteria per g in raw food, such as radishes and potatoes, is probably realistic. Immune-compromised people need to take the responsibility themselves for staying healthy. For example, they must know that typical foodservice salads are high-risk items for *L. monocytogenes* and should avoid them. They should insist on well-cooked food.

10.5.6.6 Assumed microbiological standards for food handlers and food contact surfaces in chilled food processes. In addition to the food, it is also necessary to define contamination levels for food handlers and facilities and equipment. It is assumed that 1 in 50 people in the USA are shedding 1 billion pathogens per g in their feces. It is assumed that 0.01 of a gram of fecal material leaks through toilet paper or gets around toilet paper, thus contaminating fingertips and underneath fingernails when using toilet paper, or when changing diapers, cleaning up vomit or cleaning up after animals at home. It is known, as pointed out earlier with *Shigella*, that the hand washing method must reduce fecal organisms to less than 10 on the fingertips and under the fingernails.

The facilities and equipment will also be contaminated. If the food contact surfaces are washed and rinsed every 4 hours, and if the facilities are cleaned and sanitized well at the end of production, then the pathogenic build-up on the equipment and facilities can be kept to a safe level. Note that *L. monocytogenes* is an environmental pathogen that arrives on food or on the people who enter the facility. It is quite different from most pathogens which are either on raw food or on food handlers. Since *L. monocytogenes* is an environmental hazard, it is essential that the facility be as well maintained as possible so that there are no cracks in the floors, walls or ceilings, where *L. monocytogenes* can accumulate. Then, when cleaning is done regularly, *L. monocytogenes* can be reduced to an undetectable level. It is also essential that the food processing area be kept at a humidity of less than 50% to minimize mold and microbiological multiplication in the facility.

In a pasteurized food area where cooked, cooled food is being assembled and packaged for refrigerated meals, there must be no pathogens on food contact surfaces. This is defined as no pathogens in a 50 cm^2 swabbed area of a surface.

The standards for number of spoilage microorganisms on food contact surfaces are shown in Table 10.8. If these standards are maintained, foods with long shelf lives can be produced.

10.5.6.7 Food pathogen control data summary. The next step is to develop the microbiological basis for the time and temperature and pH process standards. Table 10.9 provides the data base for process standards development.

Table 10.8 Standards for number of spoilage microorganisms on food contact surfaces

Number of spoilage microorganisms[a]	Rating
$<1/\text{cm}^2$ or $<1/\text{ml}$ of rinse solution	Excellent
$2–10/\text{cm}^2$	Good
$11–100/\text{cm}^2$	Clean-up time
$101–>1000/\text{cm}^2$	Out of control, shut down and find the problem

Source: Snyder (1992b).

Since *Y. enterocolitica* and *L. monocytogenes* both begin to multiply at 32°F (0°C), food must be kept below a temperature of 32°F (0°C) if it is to be considered safe from pathogenic multiplication. Since *Salmonella* spp. will multiply at a pH as low as 4.1, it is essential that if food, such as mayonnaise made with raw eggs (notorious for being contaminated with *Salmonella*), the pH must be below 4.1 in order to assure that there is no *Salmonella* growth and in fact, to assure its destruction. After about 5 days of room temperature at a pH of less than 4.1, *Salmonella* literally dissolves, as do the other vegetative pathogens remaining in the product, and the dressing is safe.

The data on *C. jejuni* point out that it grows very poorly and is quite easily destroyed. Therefore, the major problem with *C. jejuni* is cross-contamination, as mentioned earlier. It can be assumed that 10 000 *Campylobacter* spp. per cm^2 will be deposited on the food contact surface by raw food and it must be reduced to less than 2 per cm^2 to be safe.

C. botulinum type E is a spore former that dies easily at 180°F (82.2°C). However, many chilled foods are not cooked to this high a temperature. It must be assumed, then, that *C. botulinum* type E and other non-proteolytic *C. botulinum* organisms will survive the cooking process. For absolute control, food must be stored below 38°F (3.3°C) in order to assure safety from the spores.

S. aureus begins to multiply at 43°F (6.1°C), but does not produce a toxin until it reaches a temperature of 50°F (10.0°C). Since there is some likelihood of recontamination of food with *S. aureus* when people make salads with their hands, if salad ingredients are pre-chilled to less than 50°F (10.0°C) and are kept below this temperature when mixed, there will be no chance of *S. aureus* toxin production. Even 1000 *S. aureus* organisms per g are not hazardous. If the toxin is produced, the D value (decimal reduction time) of 2 hours means that it is virtually impossible to destroy the toxin with heat. Therefore, reheating to 165°F (73.9°C), for example, should never be used as a critical control procedure. After food is cooked, the only zero defect control is to prevent the production of toxin, cross-contamination, and growth of pathogens to a hazardous level.

B. cereus begins to multiply just below 40°F (4.4°C). It is a very common contaminant of many cereal products, and most likely will survive cooking. If cooked food is maintained at less than 38°F (3.3°C) in order to control type E *C. botulinum*, then *B. cereus* will be controlled as well.

Proteolytic strains of *C. botulinum*, types A and B, do not begin to multiply and produce a toxin until they reach a temperature of 50°F (10.0°C). Again, if produce such as fruits and vegetables, which are today frequently vacuum packaged and contaminated with low levels of *C. botulinum*, are kept at a temperature of less than 50°F (10.0°C), then types A and B *C. botulinum* will not cause illness.

Finally, *C. perfringens* becomes another control organism. First, it will

Table 10.9 Food pathogen control data summary*

Microorganisms	Temperature range for growth	pH range and minimal (a_w) water activity for growth	Data
Infective microorganisms (inactivated by pasteurization)			
1. *Yersinia enterocolitica*	32–111°F (0–44°C)[1]	4.6–9.0 pH[2]	G [32°F (0°C)] = 2 days[3] G [41°F (5°C)] = 17 hours[3] D [145°F (62.8°C)] = 0.24–0.96 min.[1] Z = 9.2–10.4°F (5.1–5.8°C)[1]
2. *Listeria monocytogenes*	32–112°F (0–44°C)[4,5]	4.5–9.5 pH[5] 0.93 a_w	G [32°F (0°C)] = 7.5 days[4] G [40°F (4.4°C)] = 1 day[7] D [140°F (60°C)] = 2.85 min.[8] Z = 10.4–11.3°F (5.8–6.3°C)[9]
3. *Vibrio parahaemolyticus*	41–109.4°F (5–43°C)[10]	4.5–11.0 pH[10] 0.937 a_w[11]	D [116°F (47°C)] = 0.8–48 min.[12,13]
4. *Salmonella* spp.	41.5–114°F (5.5–45.6°C)[14,15]	4.1–9.0 pH[16] 0.95 a_w[11]	D [140°F (60°C)] = 1.7 min.[17] Z = 10°F (5.6°C)[18]
5. *Campylobacter jejuni*	90–113°F (32.2–45°C)[19]	4.9–8.0 pH[19]	D [137°F (58.3°C)] = 12–21 sec.[20] Z = 10.6–11.4°F (6.0–6.4°C)[21]
Toxin producers and/or spore-formers (not inactivated by pasteurization)			
6. *Clostridium botulinum*, (Type E and other non-proteolytic strains)	38–113°F (3.3–45°C)[22]	5.0–9.0 pH[22] 0.97 a_w[22]	Spores D [180°F (82.2°C)] = 0.49–0.74 min.[23] Z = 9.9–19.3°F (5.6–10.7°C)[24] Toxin destruction (any botulinal toxin) D [185°F (85°C)] = 5 min.[25] Z = 7.2–11.2°F (4.0–6.2°C)[25]

Organism	Temperature	pH / a_w	Destruction data
7. *Staphylococcus aureus*	43.8–122°F (6.5–50°C)[26] Toxin production 50–114.8°F (10–46°C)[29]	4.5–9.3 pH[27] 0.83 a_w[11]	Vegetative cells D [140°F (60°C)] = 5.2–7.8 min.[28] Z = 9.7–10.4°F (5.8–5.4°C)[28] Toxin destruction D [210°F (98.9°C)] = >2 hours[31] Z = about 50°F (27.8°C)[32]
8. *Bacillus cereus*	39.2–122°F (4.0–50°C)[33,34]	4.3–9.0 pH[35] 0.912 a_w[35]	Vegetative cells D [140°F (60°C)] = 1 min.[36] Z = 12.4°F (6.9°C)[36] Spores D [212°F (100°C)] = 2.7–3.1 min.[35] Z = 11°F (6.1°C)[35] Toxin destruction Diarrheal: D [133°F (56.1°C)] = 5 min.[34] Emetic: Stable at [249.8°F (121°C)][34]
9. *Clostridium botulinum*, (Type A and Proteolytic B strains)	50–118°F (10–47.8°C)[22]	4.6–9.0 pH[22] 0.94 a_w[22]	Spores D [250°F (121.1°C)] = 0.2 min.[22] Z = 18°F (10°C)[22] Toxin destruction (see above)
10. *Clostridium perfringens*	59–127.5°F (15–52.3°C)[37,38]	5.0–9.0 pH[39] 0.95 a_w	Vegetative cells G [105.8°F (41°C)] = 7.2 min.[40] D [138°F (59°C)] = 7.2 min.[41] Z = 6.8°F (3.8°C)[41] Spores D [210°F (98.9°C)] = 26–31 min.[42] Z = 13°F (7.2°C)[42]

*Numbers in parenthesis indicate references following on from main reference list. G = Growth or doubling time. D = Death rate for 10:1 reduction time. Z = Temperature increase for 10 × faster kill.

multiply up to 127.5°F (53.1°C). Therefore, the upper temperature limit for pathogenic microorganism control is 127.5°F (53.1°C) [rounded to 130°F (54.4°C)]. Because of its rapid growth, as frequent as once every 7.2 minutes at 105.8°F (41.0°C), it dictates the heating and cooling rates for food. Food must be heated from 40 to 130°F (4.4 to 54.4°C) in less than 6 hours in order to assure no multiplication. Food must be cooled from 130 to 40°F (54.4 to 4.4°C) within 15 hours in order to prevent the outgrowth of *C. perfringens* spores during cooling (Juneja *et al.*, 1994). Note that the 2-hour and 4-hour cooling rates specified in many nations are *not* based on correct scientific data.

10.5.6.8   Personal hygiene and hand washing for food production and foodservice personnel.   One out of 50 persons coming to work each day feels fine but could be shedding 10^9 pathogens per g in his/her feces; more than 10^8 *S. aureus* per drop of pus from an infected cut on a finger; and 10^5 or more *Streptococcus pyogenes* from a cough. The main threat is in salad/cold food preparation, because these menu items are composed of many ingredients that are not cooked or heated sufficiently to inactivate pathogenic microorganisms and are not held at temperatures that prevent the multiplication of pathogens.

Employees should be banned from carrying all forms of nose wipes. If employees must blow their noses, they must be trained to go to the sink, get a nose tissue and use it to wipe or blow their nose. After discarding the nose tissue, they should then thoroughly wash and dry their hands. If employees need to sneeze or cough, they should step away from the food preparation area, or sneeze into their shoulder. When employees have cuts or infections on their hands, the cut or infection must be cleaned, bandaged and covered with a glove. The glove is used to keep the bandage on the hand and prevent it from falling into food. The glove must be washed or changed as often as hand washing is necessary for safe food preparation.

People should stay home when they are sick, especially with diarrhea, but they do not. It is the responsibility of the supervisor to watch for people who are using the toilet frequently. If these individuals seem ill, they should be asked if they are sick and if so, sent home.

The only real control for safe food preparation is fingertip and hand washing because the hazard of pathogen (viruses, bacteria and parasites) transfer exists days before infected persons feel ill.

10.5.6.8.1   Hand washing.   There are about 10^9 pathogens per g in the feces of ill people. If the toilet paper slips just a little, and infected individuals get only 0.01 gram or 10^7 pathogens on their fingertips, as few as 5–10 microorganisms can get into a salad and make a consumer ill.

There is only one procedure to reduce pathogens by 10^6, and that is the double hand/fingertip wash that is described below:

1. Turn on the water at a temperature of 110–120°F (43.3–48.9°C) at 2 gallons per minute (7.85 litres per minute). A lot of water must be used to wash the detergent with microorganisms from the fingertips and hands. Wet the hands and brush.
2. Put 2–3 ml of plain, not medicated, hand soap or detergent on a fingernail brush.
3. Produce a lather by using the fingernail brush on the fingertips. Use the fingernail brush to scrub the fingernails. Special attention must be made to the fingertips that held the toilet paper. The purpose of using the fingernail brush is to ensure safe removal of any fecal material and any other material that harbors pathogens from the fingertips and under the fingernails.
4. Rinsing is also a critical step. The microorganisms in the lather are not dead, they are just loosened from the skin and fingertips and are suspended in the lather. Rinsing in flowing water removes the lather and produces a 10^{-3} microbial reduction. Rinse the fingernail brush and put it down, placing the bristles up to dry.
5. Again apply 2–3 ml of detergent to the hands.
6. Lather the hands and skin of arms up to the tips of sleeves.
7. Thoroughly rinse the lather from the hands and arms in warm, flowing water.
8. Dry hands thoroughly with clean paper towels. The second hand washing produces another 10^{-3} microbial reduction, and the paper towel about 10^{-2} reduction.

10.5.6.8.2 Clean. 'Clean' means free of dirt and soil such as grease. Detergents, hot water, acid cleaners and wetting agents are used to dissolve grease and soil and remove it from a surface. Cleaning must be done with warm to hot water to be effective. Cleaning prior to sanitizing is a critical step. If a surface is not clean, the organic matter neutralizes the sanitizer, and the sanitizer becomes ineffective and does not inactivate any microorganisms.

10.5.6.8.3 Sanitized. 'Sanitized' means the reduction of disease-producing organisms by a factor of 10^{-5} or by 99.999%. Unfortunately, this standard only applies to a laboratory test of a few types of pathogens, with fresh sanitizer solutions on a scrupulously clean stainless steel disk. The Public Health Service suggests that a sanitized surface must have less than 100 non-specific aerobic organisms per 8 square inches (52 cm^2) of surface (e.g cutting board, dish, table top, etc.) or 100 organisms per utensil (e.g. spoon). There is no standard for hands at this time. Visual cleanliness is not a reliable indicator that a surface is sanitized. Dirty looking surfaces that have been hot and are dry, such as a stove or grill surface or can opener blade, may have few organisms. Clean looking plastic, Formica, or stainless steel surfaces that have been wiped with a contaminated towel will have high levels of microorganisms adhering to them.

10.5.6.8.4 The critical controls for the five-step surface sanitizing process. Use a clean, hot [110°–120°F (43.3–48.9°C)] detergent solution and a scrub brush to wash and clean surfaces. Rinse surfaces with a lot of hot [110–120°F (43.3–48.9°C)] water. The temperature of the sanitizing solution must be 75–100°F (23.9–37.8°C) or above. Common household bleach may be used to prepare a 50 ppm chlorine sanitizing solution (1 teaspoon of bleach per gallon of water, pH 4–7).

Effective sanitizing involves the following five basic steps:

1. Scrap and rinse the surface with 110–120°F (43.3–48.9°C) water. This gives about a 1000:1 reduction per cm^2.
2. Wash, scrub with a brush and detergent, and loosen and dissolve debris on the surface.
3. Rinse and float off the debris. At this point, the surface must be clean and free of soil and grease. Steps #2 and #3 reduce counts by another 1000:1 per cm^2.
4. Sanitize. Use a 50 ppm free chlorine solution. Dispense this solution from a squirt bottle and wipe it across the surface to be sanitized with a clean paper towel. The chlorine sanitizing solution should be made fresh each morning. A bucket of chlorine solution and a rag should not be used. The dirt from the rag neutralizes the free chlorine after about 3 or 4 rinses in the chlorine water. Paper test strips for determining the effectiveness of chlorine sanitizing solutions do not accurately indicate the amount of free chlorine. Oxidation-reduction potential should be measured and a level of more than +800 mv maintained.
5. Air dry. This is a critical step. The microorganism level is not zero on the surface. Some microorganisms and organic material will still adhere to the surface. If the surface remains wet, bacteria can multiply 1:1000 overnight at 75°F (23.9°C). Surfaces must be allowed to air dry thoroughly. Dry surfaces will not support the multiplication of bacteria.

10.5.6.9 Controlling bacteria: recipe process engineering. Favorable environmental conditions of temperature, nutrient, pH, a_w and oxidation-reduction conditions over a period of time promote the multiplication of microorganisms. By altering these conditions, the multiplication of microorganisms can be controlled and/or their destruction can be achieved.

10.5.6.9.1   Water activity.   Microorganisms require moisture to multiply. Multiplication is restricted in an environment where water is not available or bound by other food components such as salt, sugar and glycerol. Foods high in moisture, such as fresh fruits and vegetables, meat, fish, poultry, etc., permit rapid multiplication of microorganisms. The water in the structural system of these foods is available for the metabolic functions of microorganisms. When water is removed to a sufficiently low level (e.g. cereals, dried fruits and vegetables), the multiplication of microorganisms is suppressed.

It is much more difficult to inactivate these surviving microorganisms in lower water activity foods, starch-thickened sauces and desserts containing substantial amounts of sugar. Higher temperatures for longer periods of time are required to ensure destruction. A practical application of this knowledge is to add sugar and salt to a food product only when it has reached the pasteurization temperature of 165°F (73.9°C).

10.5.6.9.2   Nutrients and acids (pH).   When the supply of nutrients is low or not optimum, the multiplication of microorganisms is slow and a decline in numbers occurs.

Incorporation of food components such as lemon juice, vinegar or wine, which lower the pH of food products, also contributes to the destruction of microorganisms. If the pH is less than 4.6, the food will be safe from *C. botulinum* multiplication. But *Salmonella* will multiply down to pH 4.1. It is assumed that all salad dressing and cold sauces are contaminated with *Salmonella*; therefore, they are normally manufactured with a pH of 3.8 or less. At this pH, the salmonellae not only do not multiply, they actually dissolve in a brief period of 5 minutes to a few hours at room temperature. Tomatoes, raw or cut up at a pH of 4.2–4.4, may be contaminated with *Salmonella* and must be maintained at a temperature of less than 50°F (10.0°C).

10.5.6.9.3   Preservatives.   Common preservatives include nitrite used in sausage making, and benzoates and sorbates for mold control in salad dressings. Used correctly, they are safe. Overuse leads to illness. If used, the correct usage must be taught to all food preparers.

10.5.6.9.4   Oxidation-reduction.   The main application of this control is for proteolytic *C. botulinum* types A and B in vegetables. If many vegetables and some fruits are packaged anaerobically and left at room temperature for 1–2 days, there is the likelihood of *C. botulinum* toxin production. The control is to raise the oxygen level to more than 4% in the package, or keep the food at less than 50°F (10.0°C). This assures that *C. botulinum* will not multiply.

10.5.6.10 Safe food holding times at specified temperatures

10.5.6.10.1 Pathogen growth during processing and food handling.
Since the hazardous temperatures are 32–127.5°F (0–53.1°C), and there is
very little refrigerated food in the retail sector stored below 41°F (5.0°C),
time must be introduced to control the acceptable limits of growth during
storage and processing in retail operations.

A review of all of the infective bacterial pathogen growth leads to the
conclusion that one can select *L. monocytogenes* as the low temperature
process design organism. It begins to multiply at 32°F (0°C), as does *Y.
enterocolitica* (Hanna *et al.*, 1977; Grau and Vanderline, 1990). However,
L. monocytogenes is the 'organism of choice' for control up to approximately
70°F (21.1°C) because of the severity of its illness, vs. *A. hydrophila* and *Y.
enterocolitica* illness. Illness from *L. monocytogenes* is fatal about 40% of
the time. *L. monocytogenes* multiplies in food approximately once per day
at 41°F (5.0°C). Since the 1993 FDA Food Code allows 10 day holding at
41°F (5.0°C), this means that the FDA is willing to allow approximately
10 multiplications of *L. monocytogenes* (1:1024 multiplication). From
approximately 70–105°F (21.1–40.6°C), *Salmonella* is the control choice
pathogen because it multiplies faster than *L. monocytogenes*, causes
serious illness, and is second only to *C. jejuni* in causing illness. It
multiplies about once every 25 minutes at 104°F (40.0°C) in barbecued
chicken (Pivnick *et al.*, 1968). If the FDA's 4 hour food holding standard is
applied at 102°F (38.9°C), this indicates, again, that the FDA is indicating
that 10 multiplications of a pathogen at 102°F (38.9°C) is safe if the food is
eaten or discarded at the end of 4 hours. From 105–127.5°F (40.6–53.1°C),
the control microorganisms of choice is *C. perfringens*. It multiplies every
8–15 minutes at about 105°F (40.6°C) and is the pathogen that grows at the
highest temperature, 127.5°F (53.1°C). This sets the upper temperature
growth limit at about 130°F (54.4°C).

The author has accumulated extensive pathogen growth data over the
range 32–127.5°F (0–53.1°C) from scientific literature. The growth rate can
be predicted by using the formula of Ratkowsky *et al.* (1982) as explained
by Skinner *et al.* (1994):

$$r = b(T - T_0)$$

where r is the generation time (1/hour); b is the intercept of the line with
the y-axis; T_0 is 0°C; and T is the growth temperature (°C) for the
microorganisms. For example, at 5°C:

$1/h$ = 0.0405 (5 − 0) + 0.0016
$1/h$ = 0.2041
and h = 24 hours

Using the FDA time-temperature standards of 41°F (5°C) for 10 days

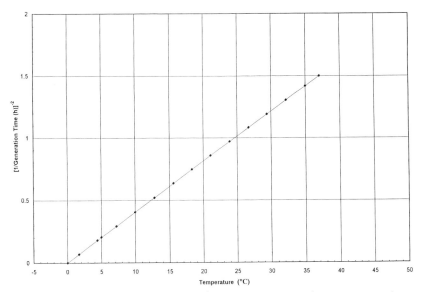

Figure 10.5 Generation time. *Source*: FDA 1993 Food Code. ◆, $\sqrt{(1/h)}$; — linear $\sqrt{(1/h)}$.
$y = 0.0405x + 0.0016$.

and assigning 4 hours to the most rapid growing point of about 102°F (38.9°C), the graph shown in Figure 10.5 can be developed.

The formula for the regression line is:

$$y = 0.0405x + 0.0016$$

Applying this for the times at temperatures between 32 and 127.5°F (0 and 53.1°C), the results are shown in Table 10.10. Using this set of standards allows one to tolerate the poor performing refrigeration that exists today, which holds most food between 40 and 55°F (4.4 and 12.8°C) during normal operations because the doors are opened so often. Typically, iced food, such as on salad bars, are at 55°F (12.8°C). If a retail food operation has a policy which states that freshly prepared food will be put on a salad bar at 10:00 am, held at 55°F (12.8°C) or less, and is discarded at 10:00 pm, this is more than safe.

Similarly, within the fast growth range of 90 to 115°F (32.2 to 46.1°C), for which the generation time is once approximately every 24 minutes, there is about 4 hours of safe time. This is more than adequate for gourmet displays of foods at buffet dinners, provided leftovers are thrown out.

10.5.6.10.2 Times at specified temperatures for 3D and 7D Salmonella *inactivation (kill)*

1. Food pasteurization standard. In some countries, *Streptococcus faecalis* is used as the pasteurization standard. Since it is doubtful that *S. faecalis* is

Table 10.10 Safe food holding times at specified temperatures

	Temp. (°F)	Safety[a]	Quality[b]	Temp. (°C)
↑	130			54.4
↑		4 hr	2 hr	↑
	100			37.8
	95	5 hr	2.5 hr	35.0
Heat	90	6 hr	3 hr	32.2
<6 hrs	85	7 hr	3.5 hr	29.4
	80	8.5 hr	4 hr	26.7
	75	11 hr	5.5 hr	23.9
Cool	70	14 hr	7 hr	21.1
<15 hrs	65	18 hr	9 hr	18.3
	60	1 day	12 hr	15.6
	55	1.5 days	18 hr	12.8
	50	2.5 days	30 hr	10.0
↓	45	5 days	2.5 days	7.2
	41	10 days	5 days	5.0
	40	13 days	6.5 days	4.4
	35	30 days	15 days	1.7
	32	60 days	30 days	0.0
	30	Safe chilled food holding		−1.1
	28	Meat, poultry, fish thaw		−2.2
	23	Spoilage bacteria begin to multiply		−5.0
	14	Yeasts and molds begin to multiply		−10.0

[a]10 multiplications of pathogens. [b]5 multiplications of pathogens.

actually a pathogen, it is more appropriate to use *Salmonella* for a standard because it causes 30% of the illnesses and deaths. In fact, *Salmonella* is a rather difficult organism to inactivate. Its resistance varies with water activity, and if one tries to destroy *Salmonella* in a high sugar, salt or dry environment, its D value can increase by more than 200%. This fact helps to further assure that if *Salmonella* is used as the pasteurization control organism, there will be adequate safety.

2. 3D and 7D inactivation. The 3D and 7D inactivation times shown in Figure 10.6 will reduce the population of *Salmonella* on meat by a factor of 1000:1 or 10 000 000:1, respectively.

The D value (time to reduce a pathogen by a factor of 10) times are derived from US Department of Agriculture (USDA) chunked and formed roast beef data (USDA, 1991). Literally billions of pounds of pasteurized deli roast beef have been produced over the last 30 years in the USA using the 7D pasteurization standard. There have been no cases of *Salmonella* or other pathogenic organisms surviving 7D pasteurization. The standard has proven to be quite robust because much of the product is distributed

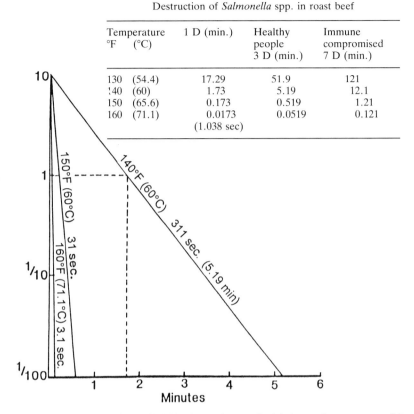

Destruction of *Salmonella* spp. in roast beef

Temperature °F (°C)	1 D (min.)	Healthy people 3 D (min.)	Immune compromised 7 D (min.)
130 (54.4)	17.29	51.9	121
:40 (60)	1.73	5.19	12.1
150 (65.6)	0.173	0.519	1.21
160 (71.1)	0.0173	0.0519	0.121
	(1.038 sec)		

Figure 10.6 Destruction of *Salmonella* in food. *Death controls*: (a) time and temperature; (b) nutrients and acids; (c) water activity; and (d) vegetative *vs*. spore state.

through food markets, which typically hold food at 40–45°F (4.4–7.2°C) for up to 60 days from manufacture.

A 3D inactivation time is also shown because in gourmet restaurants, food is cooked as little as possible. These restaurants, most likely, are serving immune-complete customers and buying better quality food with very low vegetative pathogen levels, less than 100 per g. Hence, probably there is an acceptable risk for retail foodservice establishments with effective HACCP programs to use a 3D pasteurization standard for a 1000:1 destruction. Note that at 140°F (60.0°C), which is the rare temperature for beef, if one were to cook a hamburger rare, it would take 5.19 minutes in order to reduce the pathogen population by a minimum factor of 1000:1. (It would take 12.1 minutes for a 10 000 000:1 reduction.) There is no reasonable way that a hamburger can be kept on a grill or griddle for 5 minutes, and not have the temperature continue to rise to above 140°F (60.0°C). This points out that rare food cooked on a grill is probably as unsafe as raw food and should never be eaten by an immune-compromised person, unless the food is certified as having less than 1 pathogen per 25 g.

At the same time, note that when 150°F (65.6°C) is used as the pasteurization temperature, it only takes 31 seconds. This is very practical because this is the approximate time it takes for a hamburger to 'coast' before it begins to cool after removal from a grill or broiler.

Finally, note that *Salmonella* in this USDA standard has a Z value (temperature difference for a 10-fold increase in rate of kill) of 10°F (5.6°C). For every 10°F (5.6°C) increase, *Salmonella* bacteria are destroyed 10 times faster. This means that one must use a very precise temperature measuring device for pasteurization ±1°F (0.56°C), or there can be serious errors in kill. The time for inactivation of a load of pathogens changes by 100% (doubles) if the food temperature is 3°F (1.7°C) lower than believed.

3. Thermometers. Currently throughout the world, the bimetallic stem thermometer is commonly used to measure food temperature. Figure 10.7 shows the construction of the typical bimetallic thermometer.

Since the bimetallic spring thermal element stretches up the stem of the thermometer approximately 2½ inches (65 mm) and averages the temperature over this distance, there is no way that this instrument can be used to find the coldest spot in hamburgers, pork chops, or any other thin food [less than 2 inches (50 mm)], and validate that the food has been adequately pasteurized. It is essential for correct pasteurization of the

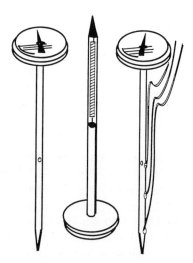

Figure 10.7 Bimetallic stem thermometer.

contaminated food that comes from the wholesale system, that all cooks use point-sensitive thermocouples with a point diameter of 0.062 inch (1.5 mm) or less and an accuracy of $\pm 1°F$ ($\pm 0.56°C$) over the range of 0–400°F (-17.8–204.4°C), that will verify food pasteurization.

10.5.6.10.3 Food cooling calculations. Every foodservice operator has the responsibility to make sure that refrigerators have the capacity to cool foods safely. Cooling is the major cause of foodborne illness (Bryan, 1988). While the 1993 FDA Food Code calls for cooling food to 41°F (5.0°C) in 6 hours, the requirement covered is based on incorrect research data. Juneja *et al.* (1994) have shown that the critical cooling time to control the multiplication of surviving *C. perfringens* spores is 15 hours from 140–45°F (60.0–7.2°C) in a 38°F (3.3°C) cooling environment. This is the normal time needed to cool 2 inches of hot food in a 2½-inch steam table pan, from 140–45°F (60.0–7.2°C) in a 50 fpm (feet per minute) (0.25 ms^{-1}) air flow, which is characteristic of commercial walk-in and reach-in refrigerators. This means that normal storage refrigerators can cool food overnight if there is not too big a mass [less thasn 25 lb (11.3 kg)] and heat load.

Since foodservice refrigerators are designed only to hold (store) food at cool temperatures and not designed to cool food, additional horsepower (Btu/min) of refrigeration capacity and a lower chilling temperature of 35 to 25°F (1.7 to $-3.9°C$) must be requested when blast cooling units are purchased. A temperature below 25°F ($-3.9°C$) should not be used because food begins to freeze, and cooling is slowed. Typically, the operator can purchase a freezer with a thermostat so that it can operate at 25 to 35°F (-3.9 to 1.7°C), and the problem is solved. Specifying a freezer means that there will be an electric or hot gas defrost evaporator coil in the refrigerator, which prevents normal refrigerator coil freeze-up at 35°F (1.7°C). Blast chilling units that are used to cool foods to 41°F (5.0°C) in 6 hours or less must have a rapid flow of air at 1000–1500 fpm (5.08–7.62 ms^{-1}) blowing across the food. An important part of the cooling rate is turbulence of the air around the food. Air at 1000 fpm (5.08 ms^{-1}) cools 3 times faster than typical refrigeration air flows of 50 fpm (0.25 ms^{-1}). If cooling is done in turbulent water, then the heat transfer at the surface of the food is improved above high-velocity air to a factor of about 5. The graph shown in Figure 10.8 depicts a typical food cooling process. Note, the process follows a semilog relationship. When plotted with the ΔT food center vs. air temperature on the y-axis, the cooling curve is a straight line (Pflug and Blaisdell, 1963; Pflug *et al.*, 1965).

Since 75% of the heat is removed through the bottom of the pan of food, containers of food must rest on an open or wire rack where there is no blockage of air to the bottom of the pan. Research has shown that the maximum food thickness which can be cooled to 41°F (5.0°C) in 6 hours in

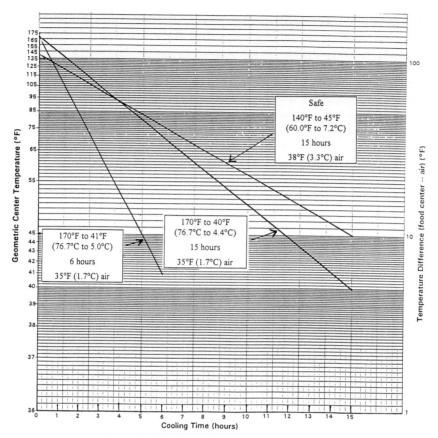

Figure 10.8 Typical chilled food system cooling.

a 30°F (−1.1°C) high-velocity air stream is about 2 inches (5 cm). It does not matter if stainless steel pans or plastic containers are used.

The food must be covered to prevent mold contamination from the air circulating through the evaporator coil, which is not designed to be clean. If the food is acidic, and the pan is covered with aluminum foil in contact with the acid food, the acid will attack the aluminum foil and eventually make holes. On the other hand, if plastic wrap is used, it may blow off. The best solution is to put a layer of silicone paper or plastic over the food first and then cover with aluminum foil.

The ability of refrigerators and cold holding units in food operations to cool food can be tested in a simple manner. Make a pan of 'soupy' instant mashed potatoes in a food pan by adding 7% by weight potato flakes to the water, so that the water in the pan is 'gelled'. The temperature of the cooling potato-water mixture should be 140–150°F (60–65.5°C). The temperature in the middle of the mixture is measured at the time it is placed in the refrigeration unit and then at 30 minute intervals. The exact center of the food needs to be repeatedly measured. The data can then be plotted on semilog graph paper as shown in Figure 10.8. Start with the bottom line marked 1°F above the refrigerator air temperature. When the data are plotted, there will be a straight line.

Holding temperatures in salad bars can be checked in the same manner, except that the potato–water mixture is prepared with cold water and the mixture should be 39–40°F (3.9–4.4°C). The mixture should hold a temperature of less than 41°F (5.0°C) throughout the container.

10.5.6.10.4   Effective methods for cooling food to 41°F (5°C) in 6 hours – effective blast chilling.   Figure 10.9 shows the simple ways to cool food. The simplest way to cool food to 41°F (5.0°C) in less than 6 hours is to use a blast chill refrigeration system. Experiments have shown that the key factors in chilling are (i) the velocity of the air across the bottom of the pan; (ii) the thickness of the food; and (iii) the temperature of the cooling air system. Whether the pan is stainless steel, aluminum or plastic makes little difference in cooling rates. The air velocity across the pan of food must be 1000–1500 fpm (5.08–7.62 ms^{-1}). Most industrial fans, if placed 4 inches (10 cm) from the side of the pan, provide adequate air velocity, either sucking or blowing the air.

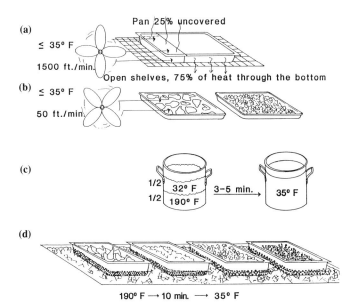

Figure 10.9 Methods of cooling for 6 hrs. to 41°F (5°C). (a) Blast chilling; 2″ (51 mm) thick. (b) Thin layers; ¾″ (19 mm) and less. (c) Ice sauces; CO_2. (d) Cubes and pieces of food.

10.5.6.10.5 Small piece cooling.   If foods are in small pieces in thin layers on sheet pans and many sides are exposed (e.g. cubed beef, vegetables for stew), the foods cool very rapidly. These types of food will cool to 41°F (5.0°C) in approximately 90 minutes in a 35°F (1.7°C) refrigeration unit with air blowing across the pan even at 50 fpm (0.25 ms^{-1}). This is an effective way to cool ingredients before they are combined into a salad, sauce or casserole-type dish. Combining ingredients previously chilled to below 41°F (5.0°C) eliminates the problem of outgrowth of pathogens from the hands used to mix the salad. Note that if the food is uncovered, it cools about twice as fast. However, it will become contaminated with mold and yeast and other spoilage microorganisms which will grow in the food and cause it to spoil in about 5 days. If the food is to be used within 2–3 days, there is no problem.

10.5.6.10.6 Cooling gravies and sauces.   Gravies can be quickly cooled if half of the liquid is not added during preparation. When the gravy/sauce has the correct flavor, thicken it to a double thick consistency with a roux or starch. Then add the other half of the liquid as ice (or frozen milk) to chill the liquid to 35°C (1.7°C). This chilling will take only 3–6 minutes. At the same time, the product is diluted to the correct strength and viscosity. When individual item pan cooling is combined with this procedure, sauces, gravies and stocks may be stored at 33–35°F (0–1.7°C). To make a stew or casserole, one simply gets the correct amount of refrigerated cubed beef and vegetables and the correct amount of sauce or gravy and then reheats the combined product in a convection oven or microwave oven in 20 minutes or less. This system eliminates the hazardous procedure of inadequate hot holding.

Solid or liquid carbon dioxide can also be used to cool sauces. CO_2 is particularly effective because it does not dilute the liquid. It also has an excellent inhibiting effect on pathogens and can extend refrigerated shelf life by 3 times (e.g. 15 days becomes 45 days). Carbon dioxide may give a sauce or gravy a slightly acid, carbonated flavor. When products containing carbon dioxide are reheated, the CO_2 vaporizes and the flavor of this addition is no longer evident.

10.5.6.10.7 Ice bath cooling.   When refrigeration is limited, chunk solid foods such as chicken, beef cubes, pot roast, turkey, potato cubes, macaroni or rice in perforated pans can be placed hot into an ice bed. The items should then be covered with a layer of ice. Most cubed products can be removed from the ice bath in about 30 minutes when the temperature has dropped to below 35°F (1.7°C). Large items such as a whole, cooked turkey and roast beef may require 4 hours to cool in an ice bath. Cold food should be stored covered in any size container in the refrigerator at 32–35°F (0–1.7°C). Products prepared in this manner have a much longer shelf life because the cooling process keeps spoilage microorganisms to a very low level.

Note, it is very important that the sink or large container containing the slush ice be sanitized prior to using this method in order to prevent any cross-contamination of products.

10.5.6.10.8 Salad preparation.   All ingredients used to prepare salads should be cooled to less than 41°F (5.0°C) before ingredients are combined. An easy way to cool freshly cooked salad ingredients, such as macaroni or potatoes, is to use the ice bath method. If all ingredients (including salad dressing) are less than 41°F (5.0°C), it is possible to mix a salad and return it to refrigerator storage before the salad temperature reaches 50°F (10°C). This prevents the multiplication of *S. aureus* from hand contamination and proteolytic *C. botulinum*.

10.6   Food operations hazard analysis

Figure 10.10 presents a summary of the common critical control points in a foodservice operation. Note, consumer nutrition, consumer allergies, and consumer abuse of the food are included, since they are problems that have been identified in lawsuits.

10.6.1   Pasteurized–chilled food process hazard and control flow diagram

The flow diagram presented in Figure 10.11 summarizes the standards for the control of chilled food processes.

First, employees must wash their hands using the double hand wash with a fingernail brush. Water is controlled by the water supplier. Insects and rodents are kept out, and all food contact surfaces are cleaned and sanitized between contact with different products to a standard of less than 2 colony forming units (CFU) per cm^2. Assuming that raw food is contaminated as shown, there is just-in-time delivery of fresh product to assure minimal pathogen multiplication in the wholesale supply system. Food is then stored before the temperature rises more than 5°F (2.8°C). Damaged packages are returned and moldy food is destroyed. Food is stored for less than 4 days so that *L. monocytogenes*, which will be multiplying once per day at 41°F (5.0°C), will not multiply more than 4 generations. The FDA 10 day limit allows too much spoilage.

Pre-preparation of the food begins within 24 hours of the time it will be consumed. The food temperature is kept to less than 50°F (10.0°C) during pre-preparation. This way, total multiplication of *L. monocytogenes* will be less than 5 generations from the time the food is received until it is cooked or consumed. Heating the food to above 130°F (54.4°C) in less than 6 hours

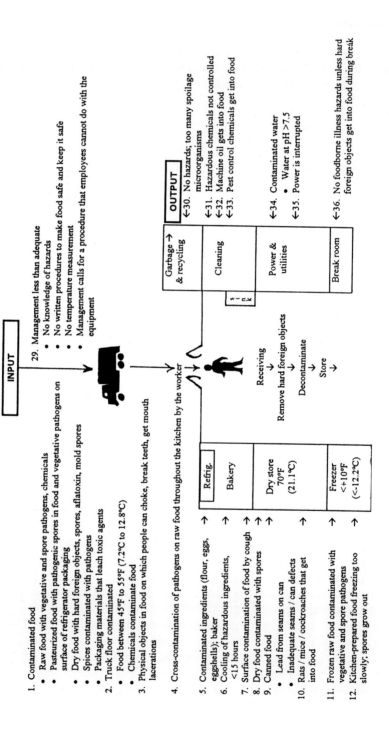

INPUT

1. Contaminated food
   • Raw food with vegetative and spore pathogens, chemicals
   • Pasteurized food with pathogenic spores in food and vegetative pathogens on surface of refrigerator packaging
   • Dry food with hard foreign objects, spores, aflatoxin, mold spores
   • Spices contaminated with pathogens
   • Packaging materials that leach toxic agents
2. Truck floor contaminated
   • Food between 45°F to 55°F (7.2°C to 12.8°C)
   • Chemicals contaminate food
3. Physical objects in food on which people can choke, break teeth, get mouth lacerations
4. Cross-contamination of pathogens on raw food throughout the kitchen by the worker
5. Contaminated ingredients (flour, eggs, eggshells); baker
6. Cooling of hazardous ingredients, <15 hours
7. Surface contamination of food by cough
8. Dry food contaminated with spores
9. Canned food
   • Lead from seams on can
   • Inadequate seams / can defects
10. Rats / mice / cockroaches that get into food
11. Frozen raw food contaminated with vegetative and spore pathogens
12. Kitchen-prepared food freezing too slowly, spores grow out

29. Management less than adequate
   • No knowledge of hazards
   • No written procedures to make food safe and keep it safe
   • No temperature measurement
   • Management calls for a procedure that employees cannot do with the equipment

Refrig.

Bakery

Dry store
70°F
(21.1°C)

Freezer
<+10°F
(<-12.2°C)

Receiving →
Remove hard foreign objects →
Decontaminate →
Store →

Garbage & recycling →

Cleaning

Power & utilities

Break room

OUTPUT

←30. No hazards; too many spoilage microorganisms
←31. Hazardous chemicals not controlled
←32. Machine oil gets into food
←33. Pest control chemicals get into food
←34. Contaminated water
   • Water at pH >7.5
←35. Power is interrupted
←36. No foodborne illness hazards unless hard foreign objects get into food during break

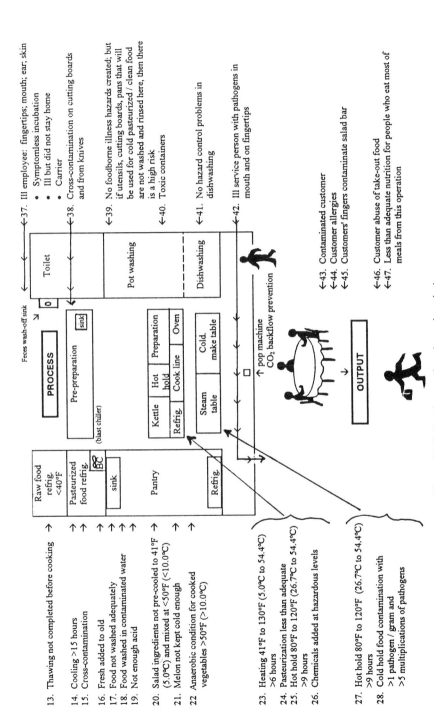

37. Ill employee: fingertips; mouth; ear; skin
    • Symptomless incubation
    • Ill but did not stay home
    • Carrier

38. Cross-contamination on cutting boards and from knives

39. No foodborne illness hazards created; but if utensils, cutting boards, pans that will be used for cold pasteurized / clean food are not washed and rinsed here, then there is a high risk

40. Toxic containers

41. No hazard control problems in dishwashing

42. Ill service person with pathogens in mouth and on fingertips

43. Contaminated customer
44. Customer allergies
45. Customers' fingers contaminate salad bar

46. Customer abuse of take-out food
47. Less than adequate nutrition for people who eat most of meals from this operation

Feces wash-off sink

PROCESS

Toilet

Pre-preparation

(blast chiller)

sink

| Kettle | Hot hold | Preparation |
| Refrig. | Cook line | Oven |

Steam table

Cold make table

Pot washing

Dishwashing

pop machine
CO₂ backflow prevention

OUTPUT

Raw food refrig. <40°F

Pasteurized food refrig.

BC

sink

Pantry

Refrig.

13. Thawing not completed before cooking

14. Cooling >15 hours
15. Cross-contamination

16. Fresh added to old
17. Food not washed adequately
18. Food washed in contaminated water
19. Not enough acid

20. Salad ingredients not pre-cooled to 41°F (5.0°C) and mixed at <50°F (<10.0°C)

21. Melon not kept cold enough

22. Anaerobic condition for cooked vegetables >50°F (>10.0°C)

23. Heating 41°F to 130°F (5.0°C to 54.4°C) >6 hours
24. Pasteurization less than adequate
25. Hot hold 80°F to 120°F (26.7°C to 54.4°C) >9 hours
26. Chemicals added at hazardous levels

27. Hot hold 80°F to 120°F (26.7°C to 54.4°C) >9 hours
28. Cold hold food contamination with >1 pathogen / gram and >5 multiplications of pathogens

Figure 10.10 Food operations hazard analysis.

- Employee hand washing . . . . *Shigella* spp. and Hepatitis A control by use of fingernail brush and double hand wash.
- Water . . . . Pathogen control by water supplier.
- Insects and rodents . . . . Exclusion through cleanliness and construction.
- Food contact surfaces . . . . Only use surfaces cleaned and sanitized to <2 CFU/cm².

Expected threat level in raw food to be controlled:

Salmonella spp	<10/g
Listeria monocytogenes	<1/g
Staphylococcus aureus	<100/g
Clostridium perfringens	<100/g
Clostridium botulinum	<.01/g
Bacillus cereus	<100/g

- Control of hard foreign objects.
- If meat, fish, or poultry is to be eaten rare or raw, the supplier assures and certifies safe pathogen levels.
- The producers/suppliers provide standard plate count data that proves they have a stable, HACCP controlled process.
- Just-in-time delivery at <0°F (<−18°C) or 41°F (<5.0°C) maximizes freshness and minimizes pathogen multiplication. If food is maintained at <32°F (<0°C), there will be no *Listeria monocytogenes* multiplication.

↓

Receiving: Some food and beverages will be contaminated and must be checked, sorted, trimmed

- Food must be stored before temperature reaches 45°F (7.2°C) or 5°F (−15°C).
- Damaged packages and cans of food are returned.
- Infested packages and defective products (moldy or spoiled foods) are returned.

↓

Storage: <41°F (<5.0°C) <4 days

- At 41°F (<5.0°C) and <4 days, *Listeria monocytogenes* will be controlled to an acceptable increase of <1:16 (4 generations).

↓

Pre-preparation and staging for production <24 hours before use. Cut, chop, wash fruits and vegetables. Weigh and measure. Keep temperatures <50°F (<10°C).

- Clean-as-you-go prevents pathogen cross-contamination.
- Control multiplication of *Listeria monocytogenes* to <1 additional generation. [Total *Listeria monocytogenes* multiplication is <1:32 (5 generations).]
- Fruits and vegetables are double washed to remove surface filth and reduce pathogens >100:1.

↓

Cook <41° to 130°F (<5.0°C to >54.4°C) <6 hr.

Pasteurize.
Reduce *Salmonella* spp. 10^{-7}.

Cool >130°F to 45°F (>54.4°C to 7.2°C) < 15 hours

Mix salads to maintain <50°F (<10°C)

- Heat from <41° to >130°F (5.0°C to >54.4°C) <6 hours to prevent multiplication of *Clostridium perfringens*
- Food pasteurization for 10 000 000:1 *Salmonella* spp. reduction by temperature [130°F (54.4°C) – 121 min.; 140°F (60°C) – 12.1 min.; 150°F (65.6°C) – 1.21 min.; 160°F (71.1°C) – 0.121 min.] or by addition of sufficient organic acid to decrease the pH below 4.1 with a 2-day hold at 75°F (23.9°C).
- Cool food from <130°F to 45°F (>54.4°C to 7.2°C) in <15 hours to control multiplication of *Clostridium perfringens*
- Prevent toxin production of *Staphylococcus aureus* in salads by pre-cooling ingredients to 40°F (4.4°C) before mixing and then keeping the ingredients <50°F (<10°C) during mixing and use.

Finish Production.
Serve at 140°F (60°C) in <30 minutes, or
Package, chill, and distribute at <41°F (<5.0°C).

- Retain nutrients at 140°F (60°C) by serving in <30 minutes.
- Prevent cross-contamination.
- Prevent customer abuse. Label consume within 2 hours, or begin cooling within 2 hours and cool to 41°F (5.0°C) in less than 2 hours.

Food holding and leftovers.

- If stored at 32°F to 41°F (0°C to 5.0°C), use within 5 days of production to control possible post-processing *Listeria monocytogenes* contamination to < 5 generations.
- If stored at <32°F (<0°C), food can be held until spoiled.
- Since post-cooking contamination is controlled, reheating is not required as a critical control.

Figure 10.11 Pasteurized–chilled food process hazard control flow diagram.

will control the multiplication of *C. perfringens*. The food will then be pasteurized to reduce *Salmonella* by 10 000 000 to 1, according to the standards shown. If a cold temperature process is used, the food must be acidified to 4.1 pH and held for 2 days at room temperature to destroy *Salmonella* and other vegetative pathogens. Leftovers of cooked/pasteurized food will be cooled to 45°F (7.2°C) in less than 15 hours in order to control the multiplication of *C. perfringens*. If salads are being made, they will be mixed at a temperature of less than 50°F (10.0°C) in order to control the toxin production of *S. aureus* and *C. botulinum*.

Food held hot on a steam table will be served in less than 30 minutes in order to retain the thermally sensitive nutrients, vitamin C, niacin and thiamin. Cross-contamination will be controlled. If the food is given to the consumer hot, then the consumer will be told to eat it within 2 hours or to cool it immediately to 41°F (5.0°C). If the consumer wants to keep the food longer than this, then he/she should buy and take home cold food, at 41°F (5.0°C).

Food should be held either below 32°F (0°C) or used within 5 days after production to control possible post-processing *L. monocytogenes* contamination to less than 5 generations. Reheating is not used as a critical hazard control process. If toxins have been produced, they cannot be inactivated by reheating. The process standards listed assure that toxins will not be produced after food is cooked. Keeping food at less than 38°F (3.3°C) would assure the control of non-proteolytic *C. botulinum*. It would not control *L. monocytogenes* if it leaked into plastic-wrapped food after processing.

10.6.2   The seven recipe processes

All recipes can be clustered into seven process styles in terms of vegetative cell destruction and toxin-spore control. These are:

1. *Thick foods*, greater than 2 inches;
2. *Thin foods*, less than 2 inches;
3. *Sauces and brews*, hot or cold;
4. *Fruits, vegetables and starches*;
5. *Bread and batters*;
6. *Cold combinations*;
7. *Hot combinations*.

Figure 10.12 summarizes the seven recipe processes.

Thick foods such as large pieces of meat are characterized by surface contamination and slow cooking, which destroys all vegetative pathogens on the surface. The hazard control point for a large piece of meat occurs after it has been cooked, when it is left for some period of time for carving and serving. Often during serving, the meat will be at 100–110°F (37.8–43.3°C). Therefore, if it is not served and consumed in a period of

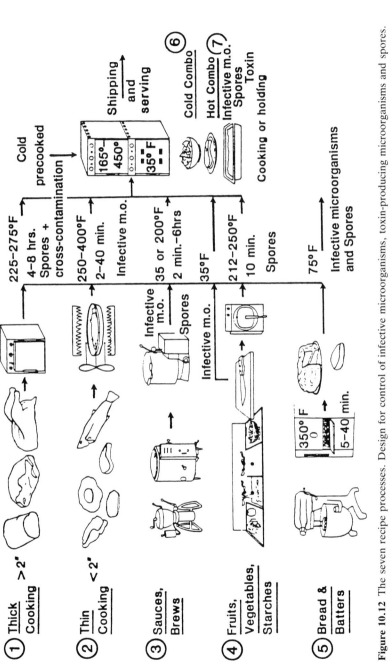

Figure 10.12 The seven recipe processes. Design for control of infective microorganisms, toxin-producing microorganisms and spores.

approximately 2–5 hours, there is a serious risk that the *C. perfringens* in the meat will have enough time to multiply to an illness-causing level. The critical control point for any thick food is after it has been cooked.

The problem with *thin foods* is that the center most likely will be contaminated (e.g. *Salmonella* in eggs, *Trichinella spiralis* in pork, Hepatitis A in hamburger, etc.). The cooking process is likely to be so fast that the infective microorganisms may not be inactivated with heat. There is also the problem, as with microwave ovens, that the heat may be non-uniform, allowing vegetative cells to survive. After the food is cooked, since thin foods are usually individual portions, they should be eaten almost immediately, and spores will have no chance to outgrow, nor will *S. aureus* produce a toxin. The critical control point is correct uniform cooking of the food for proper pasteurization.

Hot *sauces and brews* such as soups and gravies get sufficiently hot during production to easily destroy vegetative cells. However, spores survive. Therefore, if the soups and sauces are not kept hot, above 130°F (54.4°C) after cooking, spores of *C. perfringens* and other microorganisms can grow out and multiply, and make people ill. For a low temperature sauce, such as mayonnaise made with raw egg, pasteurization is accomplished by the acid formulation. If the pH is less than 4.1, and if the product is held for 2 days at room temperature before use, the *Salmonella* bacteria are destroyed.

Fruits, vegetables and starches will be contaminated with both fecal vegetative organisms as well as spores, and perhaps chemicals. All fruits and vegetables must be double washed in a clean, sanitized vegetable prep sink. Each washing will reduce the organisms by approximately 100 to 1. Therefore, overall, there will be a pathogen reduction of about 10^3 to 10^4 on the surface of the fruits and vegetables. This is the only control for contamination of fruits and vegetables that are to be consumed raw. Hence, washing in a clean, sanitized sink is an extremely important critical procedure. If the fruits or vegetables are cooked and have a pH above 4.6, *C. botulinum* and *B. cereus* will become a serious hazard. Hot fruits and vegetables and starches must be kept above 130°F (54.4°C) to remain safe or cooled to 45°F (7.2°C) within 15 hours, and held at 41°F (5.0°C) or less.

Breads and batters are inherently safe because first, breads are fermented with yeast or sourdough bacteria that provide competitive exclusion. Then, they are cooked to a high temperature, over 180°F (82.2°C) for a long enough period of time, which destroys infective organisms that may multiply in the product. On the other hand, many dessert products are iced, filled and manipulated by the baker after cooking. Hence, the baker's hands must be extremely clean. Otherwise, fecal organisms and other pathogens can be introduced, which will make the baked products hazardous. Hand washing becomes an important critical control point as well as correctly pasteurizing and cooling hazardous fillings, such as egg custards.

Finally, *hot and cold combinations* are simply mixtures of the other ingredients that have been prepared. Cold combinations are typically a protein mixed with a sauce, such as mayonnaise, and a starch, such as macaroni. The critical control procedures involve making sure that no microorganisms grow during the ingredient cooling step, and then preventing cross-contamination during mixing. If all ingredients are cooled to 41°F (5.0°C) and kept below 50°F (10.0°C) during mixing, there is no hazard from *S. aureus* or proteolytic *C. botulinum*.

Hot combinations are safer in that if there is some infective microorganism contamination during the mixing step, the organisms can be inactivated during reheating. However, there will be spore and *S. aureus* contamination when the ingredients are mixed. Casseroles, then, must be kept below 50°F (10.0°C) until heating, and then heated to above 130°F (54.4°C) in less than 6 hours to prevent multiplication of *C. perfringens* during cooking.

Remember, if *S. aureus* or *B. cereus* are allowed to multiply due to careless food handling after cooking, the toxins they produce will not be inactivated in the reheating step.

10.6.3   Recipe flow charting

The first step in doing a HACCP recipe is to do a flow chart. Figure 10.13 shows a simple illustration of a recipe flow chart. There are three columns identified as *a*, *b*, and *c* columns. Each step is numbered sequentially from *1* to the end.

One problem with most recipes is that the sequence is illogical and inefficient. By flow diagramming the recipe, the proper order in which steps should be accomplished to minimize labor and maximize safety, becomes obvious. Fundamentally, all raw food is prepared, chopped, cubed and made ready, as in ingredient preparation.

For preparation, sauces are made first because they can be put into a *bain marie* and held hot. Next, the meat is cooked to the point at which the pre-prepared vegetables, which take less cooking time, can be added. Then, the sauce is combined at the correct point, and the product is finished, panned or bagged, and served. An important point is *not* to begin the meat cooking first and let it sit in the kitchen at a lukewarm temperature while sauces and vegetables are prepared. Clearly, this can lead to food safety problems.

At each step in the flow, the step is identified by one of the five industrial engineering symbols, *operate*, *transport*, *delay*, *inspect* and *store*. The use of these five terms is very important to recipe analysis because it allows one to compare one recipe with another. The optimum recipe has a minimum of *operate* steps to achieve the desired sensory properties for the finished

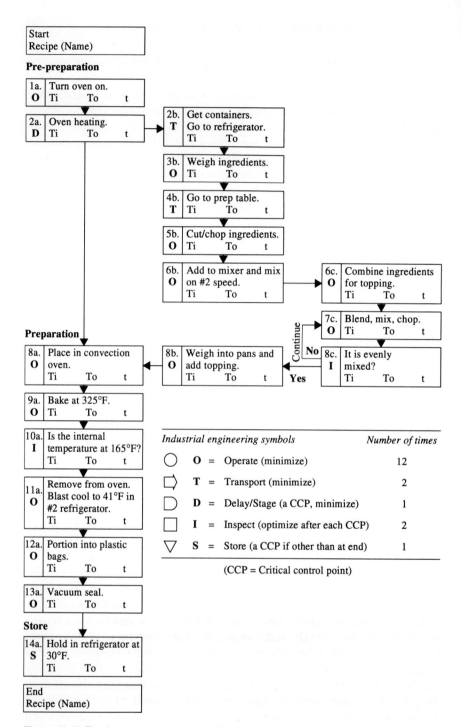

Start
Recipe (Name)

Pre-preparation

1a. Turn oven on.
O | Ti   To   t

2a. Oven heating.
D | Ti   To   t

2b. Get containers.
T | Go to refrigerator.
Ti   To   t

3b. Weigh ingredients.
O | Ti   To   t

4b. Go to prep table.
T | Ti   To   t

5b. Cut/chop ingredients.
O | Ti   To   t

6b. Add to mixer and mix
O | on #2 speed.
Ti   To   t

6c. Combine ingredients
O | for topping.
Ti   To   t

7c. Blend, mix, chop.
O | Ti   To   t

Preparation

8a. Place in convection
O | oven.
Ti   To   t

8b. Weigh into pans and
O | add topping.
Ti   To   t

Continue

No | 8c. It is evenly
I | mixed?
Ti   To   t

Yes

9a. Bake at 325°F.
O | Ti   To   t

10a. Is the internal
I | temperature at 165°F?
Ti   To   t

11a. Remove from oven.
O | Blast cool to 41°F in
#2 refrigerator.
Ti   To   t

12a. Portion into plastic
O | bags.
Ti   To   t

13a. Vacuum seal.
O | Ti   To   t

Store

14a. Hold in refrigerator at
S | 30°F.
Ti   To   t

End
Recipe (Name)

Industrial engineering symbols   *Number of times*

○ O = Operate (minimize)   12

▷ T = Transport (minimize)   2

▷ D = Delay/Stage (a CCP, minimize)   1

□ I = Inspect (optimize after each CCP)   2

▽ S = Store (a CCP if other than at end)   1

(CCP = Critical control point)

Figure 10.13 Food process flow charting. Cooking and branching of a recipe process flow.

product. It has a minimum of *transport* steps. Ideally, it should have no *delay* steps. It has an optimum number of *inspect* steps whereby the employee is given specific instructions to verify the quality and safety of the product. Finally, there is only one *store* step at the end. Any unnecessary delay in *store* steps represent hazard control points.

Each step has provisions for 'temperature in' (Ti) of the food, the 'temperature out' (To) of the food, and the time (t) it will take to complete the step. When this information is used in combination with the growth and death temperatures and times previously listed, one is instantly able to validate the control of vegetative and spore pathogens in a process.

10.6.3.1 Barley soup QA recipe flow. As mentioned earlier, all tasks that are done in the food facility are parts of processes and can be flow diagrammed. Only the seven recipe processes need to be flow diagrammed, one for each style of product (thick foods; thin foods; sauces; brews; fruits, vegetables, starches; bread, batters; cold combinations; hot combinations). The processes of each recipe style can be applied to all of the recipes categorized under that style. The only variable is flavor, which has no relation to HACCP.

An example of a quality-assured recipe flow process is shown in Figure 10.14.

All processes can be divided into pre-preparation (getting ready), preparation (doing), chill-store/transport-holding, serving, and leftovers. Each process step is numbered so that it can be referenced. Each step is identified as: *O* for *operation*; *I* for *inspect*; *T* for *transport*; *D* for *delay*; or *S* for *store*. The object is to have a minimum number of delay steps, only one store step at the end, a minimum number of transport steps, and just enough operating steps, controlled by inspecting steps, to safely produce the product.

Each block has a brief description of the step. Since the critical controls in pasteurized food processes are temperature and time, temperature and time are indicated in the block so that by using the microbiological rules which have been previously described, one can verify that the process is safe. Very conventional computer logic is used in material flow diagramming. The symbols come from industrial engineering and are used to optimize processes. When comparing two process methods, the one with the fewest operations that give the desired product, the least amount of transport and delay, only one store step at the end, and adequate inspect steps, is the best process. Note the inclusion of the inspect step. This is one of the most important elements of hazard control. It emphasizes that the process designer and management must also prescribe precisely how the employee is to check that he/she has performed a step correctly and what standard must be met.

Pre-preparation (begin barley soup)

1a. **O**	Get firm, dry onions. Peel. Dice to ¼ inch. Weigh. Ti 40°F To 50°F t 20 min.	

2a. **I**	Inspect. Remove any non-uniform pieces. Package. Label. Ti 50°F To 51°F t 1 min.	

| 3a.
T | Place in cart and move to refrigerator
(40°F).
Ti 51°F   To 52°F   t 2 min. | → | 3b.
D | Hold at 40°F.

Ti 52°F   To <50°F   t <24 hr. |

| 4a.
O | Get barley. Inspect and remove any
HFO. Weigh, package, label. Put in
refrigerator (40°F) with onions.
Ti 75°F   To 75°F   t 10 min. | → | 4b.
D | Hold at 40°F.

Ti 75°F   To <75°F   t <24 hr. |

| 5a.
O | Get beef base. Weigh, package, label.
Put in refrigerator (40°F) with onions.
Ti 40°F   To 42°F   t 10 min. | → | 5b.
D | Hold at 40°F.

Ti 42°F   To <42°F   t <24 hr. |

| 6a.
O | Get worcestershire sauce. Weight,
packeage, label. Put in refrigerator
(40°F) with onions.
Ti 75°F   To 75°F   t 10 min. | → | 6b.
D | Hold at 40°F.

Ti 75°F   To <75°F   t <24 hr. |

Preparation

| 7a.
I | Inspect kettle and equipment. Be sure
it is 'ready'. |

| 8a.
T | Bring cart from refrigerator to the
kettle. Note numbers and kinds of
containers.
Ti 40°F   To 41°F   t 3 min. |

| 9a.
O | Turn on kettle (150°F). Add water
(150°F) to the kettle. Mixer is off.
Ti 150°F   To 150°F   t 5 min. |

| 10a.
O | Set mixer speed to 2–3. |

| 11a.
O | Add beef base to kettle.
Ti 40°F   To 150°F   t 1 min. |

| 12a.
O | Add barley, onions, worcestershire
sauce to kettle. Check and account for
all containers and closures.
Ti 40°F   To 150°F   t 2 min. |

| 13a.
O | Set temperature to 212°F. Bring to a
boil.
Ti 150°F   To 212°F   t 15 min. | → | 13b.
T | Return dirty containers to pot and pan
washing. |

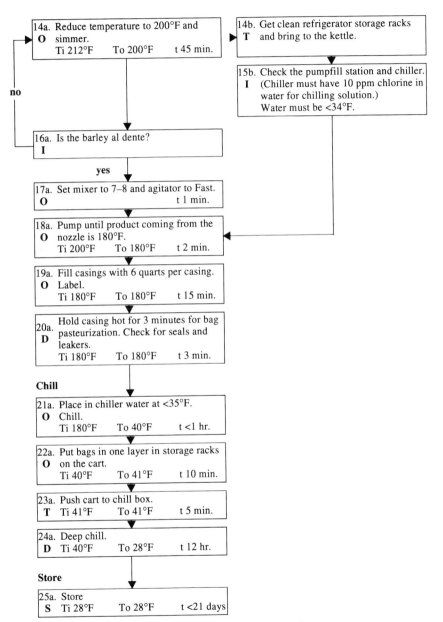

Figure 10.14 Barley soup QA recipe flow.

10.6.4 Quality-assured HACCP recipe procedures, the critical hazard control document

Since a flow diagram is extremely useful for analysis but very difficult for a foodservice worker to read, the information is transferred to a conventional recipe format for use by the cook. Figure 10.15 shows such a format for the first page of the barley soup recipe.

The recipe is the conventional process control document which has been used for centuries in order to control the quality and uniformity of the food production. The problem is that food time–temperature rules have not

Recipe Name: **Barley Soup**
Recipe #: **100**
Production style: **Soup/Sauce**

Written by: D.M. Poland   Date: 3/93

Portion size (vol./wt.): **7 oz**
Number of portions: **477**
Final yield (AS): **25 gal.(208.35 lb)**
Yield: **90%**
SA/QA by: J. Campbell   Date: 4/93

Preparation time: **4 hours**
To be prepared by: **P. Snyder**
Supervisor:

Gp. #	Ingred. #	Ingredients and Specifications	EP Weight %	Edible Portion (EP) (weight or volume)		User Rec. (wt./vol.)	Nutrition Ref. #
I	1	Barley	11.65	27.0 lbs	(12,258.0 g)		
	2	Onions, chopped 1/4 inch dice	3.46	8.0 lbs	(3,632.0 g)		
	3	Worcestershire sauce	0.22	.50 lbs	(227.0 g)		
II	4	Beef base	5.62	13.0 lbs	(5,902.0 g)		
III	5	Water (22 gal)	79.05	183.0 lbs	(83,082.0 g)		
		Total	100.00	231.5 lbs	(105,101.0 g)		
		Approx. gallons		27.8 gal			

Pre-preparation   1/13/93 Begin

Time/ Initials
1600 CM4

1. Get clean dry onions (40°F). Dice to 1/4 inch and weigh. Inspect for uniformity. Package and label. Place on a cart and move to the refrigerator . (50°F, 23 min)   1630 CM4
2. Get barley (75°F). Weigh, package, and label. Put in refrigerator with onions. (75°F, 10 min)   1640 CM4
3. Get beef base (40°F). Weigh, package, and label. Put into refrigerator with onions. (42°F, 10 min)   1655 CM4
4. Get worcestershire sauce (75°F). Weigh, package, and label. Put in the refrigerator with onions. (75°F, 10 min)   1700 CM4
5. Take cart to kettle preparation area or hold < 40°F until time for preparation (< 3 day).

Preparation   1/14/93 Begin

6. Inspect kettle and equipment to be sure it is ready.
7. Bring the cart with food supplies (40°F) from refrigerator to the kettle. (41°F, 3 min)   0630 CM
8. With the mixer off, turn on the kettle to 150°F and add tap water. (150°F, 5 min)   0635 CM4
9. Add beef base (40°F) to the kettle. (150°F, 1 min)   0640 CM4
10. Add barley, onions, worcestershire sauce (40°F) to the kettle. (150°F, 2 min)   0645 CM4
11. Set temperature to 212° and bring to a boil. (212°F, 15 min)   0646 CM4
12. Return dirty containers to pot and pan washing area. Get clean refrigerator storage racks and bring back to the kettle.   0648 CM4
13. Reduce kettle temperature to 200°F and simmer (200°F) until barley is *al dente* (45 min).   0659 CM4
    0740 CM4

Pumping

14. Check the pumpfill station. Check that the water chiller station has 5 ppm chlorine for chilling.
15. When barley is *al dente*, set mixer to # 7 and agitator to Fast.   0742 CM4
16. Pump enough product into a bag to get the product temperature coming from the pump to 180°F. (2 min)   0743 CM4
17. Fill casings with 6 quarts of soup (180°F) per casing. Label. Hold each bag for 3 minutes to allow for inside bag surface pasteurization. Check seal before adding the bag to the chiller. Put a special label on the last bag so this bag can be found in the chiller. The product temperature of this bag is measured to assess cooling of contents of all bags before they are removed from the chiller. (15 min)   Ⓐ Ⓑ   0801 CM4

Process step #	Start food ctr. temp., °F	Thickest food dimension (in.)	Container size H x W x L (in.)	Cover Yes/No	Temp. on/ around food	End food ctr. temp., °F	Process step time, hr./min.

Figure 10.15 Quality-assured HACCP recipe procedures. (Page 1).

Recipe Name: Barley Soup

Time / Initials

Chilling
18. Place in chiller water (<35°). Chill < 1 hour. When temperature of control bag is < 40°F, all bags can
    be removed.
19. Put bags (<40°F) one layer deep in storage racks on the cart. (<40°F,10 min)
20. Push cart to chill box. (40°F, 5 min)
21. Allow food to deep chill to 29°F (± 1°F) in < 12 hours.

0905   (A)
0910   (B)
0912   (B)
       (C)

Store
22. Hold at 29°F (± 1°F) and use within < 21 days.

Reheating, Plating and Serving
16. When needed, heat chowder to 165°F (no higher for quality) by an appropriate method.
17. Hold covered at 165°F and serve within 30 minutes so that food is >150°F when consumed.

Leftovers
18. Dispose of leftovers, or cool to 40°F in < 4 hours and serve within 24 hours.

Comments:
(A) QC took a sample of the soup from the first bag pumped for micro.
(B) Got 15½ ea 6 qt bags rather than 16 ½   · OK J.C.
(C) Checked bags at 1745. Temperature was 30°F   (B)

1/16/93 The APC was 55/ml Donna Poland.

Figure 10.15 (Page 2).

been provided for pathogen control. Using the simple rules presented in this paper, a food safety process authority can read the recipe steps and verify the safety of the recipe. For example, with Step 10 [Add barley, onions, Worcestershire sauce (40°F) to the kettle (150°F, $t = 1$ minute).] there is no problem because the time of 1 minute is too brief. Step 11 [Set temperature to 212°F and bring to a boil (212°F, $t = 15$ minutes).] is, again, too short a time for any microbiological multiplication. Additionally, when the ingredients reach 212°F (100.0°C), all of the infective vegetative microorganisms have been destroyed. Step 12 [Return dirty containers to pot and pan washing area. Get clean refrigerator storage racks and bring back to the kettle.] assures that the containers will be properly washed, rinsed, and sanitized before the food dries on them. Step 13 [Reduce kettle temperature to 200°F and simmer (200°F) for 45 minutes or until barley is done *al dente*.] assures the destruction of all infective microorganisms and non-proteolytic *C. botulinum* is this product. The spores of proteolytic *C. botulinum*, *B. cereus* and *C. perfringens*, of course, survive.

At the end of each line, a clock time and initials can be written in by the employee. This is the time that the employee completed this step. In a typical restaurant, this information would not be entered because the work is repetitive. However, in a hospital chilled food foodservice system where there is a requirement for documented process control for liability reasons, the written information provides the documentation which can be given to

Servings (Yield)	24 (1 pan)	96 (4 pans)	Process steps: Policies, procedures and standards	Threats	Threat control analysis (effectiveness of the policies, procedures and standards)
Beef cube base	3½ qt	3½ gal			
Vegetables, cooked	6½ lb	26 lb			
Total	6 qt	6 gal			
Ingredients:					
Beef cube base:			*Pre-preparation:*	Vegetative pathogens. Spores.	Cooking at 190°F kills vegetative pathogens. Spores survive but temperature is too high for growth.
Beef cubes, 1 inch	4½ lb	18 lb	• Take beef cubes from the refrigerator (40°F) (15 min.) and brown in kettle or heavy skillet (190°F) (15 min.).		
Tomatoes, ground	2 C	2 qt	*Preparation:*	Bay leaf: HFO. Black pepper has high pathogen counts. Tomatoes reduce pH. Beef base only has spores.	Cheese cloth bag controls HFO. 1 hour kills vegetative pathogens. Spores that survive will not multiply because temperature is >130°F.
(No. 10 can)	–	(⅔ can)	• Add tomatoes, bay leaf in cheese-cloth bag, black pepper, soy sauce, beef base, and water (70°F) (15 min.).		
Bay leaf	1 ea	4 ea	• Bring to boil (212°F). Cover and simmer (190°F) for approximately 1 hour or until meat is tender (212°F).		
Pepper, black	¼ t	1 t			
Soy sauce	3 T	¾ C			
Beef base	1½ oz	6 oz			
Water	1½ qt	1½ gal			
Beef stew:					
Flour	4 oz	1 lb	• Combine flour and room temperature water, add while stirring, to boiling beef base.	Flour and water have pathogens.	Simmering inactivates vegetative cells. Vegetables must be washed and rinsed. Heating in the next step will kill vegetative pathogens.
Water, cold	¾ can	3 C	• Simmer (195°F) for 5 minutes to thicken while vegetables are prepared, <50°F.	Vegetables have pathogens.	

Ingredient			Procedure	Microbiology	Control
Carrots, ¼ inch slice	1½ lb	6 lb	• Boil prepared carrots, celery, onions, and potatoes 8 to 10 minutes in a minimum amount of water or steam for 5 to 8 minutes (vegetables >212°F). Drain vegetables if necessary.	Vegetative and spore microorganisms.	Vegetative cells are killed. Spores are controlled by temperature >130°F.
Celery, ¼ inch slice	1½ lb	6 lb			
Onions, ¾ inch dice	1½ lb	6 lb			
Potatoes, ¾ inch dice	2 lb	8 lb	• Add vegetables to thickened meat mixture.		
			• Bring combination to >185°F.	Spores survive.	Vegetative cells are dead.
			• Pour 6 qt of beef stew into each steam table pan and cover with film. Do this in 10 minutes and maintain food temperature of >165°F.	Spores survive.	Temperature >165°F, vegetative cells killed. No time for spore outgrowth.
			• Transfer immediately to a 165°F hot holding box. Use in 1 hour.	Spores survive.	Temperature >165°F, all pathogens controlled. Use in <1 hour controls nutrient loss.
			• Unserved stew should be cooled covered 2 inches deep in a 2½-inch pan in a 35°F refrigerator at an air flow of >1000 fpm to 41°F in <6 hours.	Spore outgrowth.	No vegetative cells introduced. Spores controlled by cooling to 45°F in <15 hours.

Figure 10.16 Beef stew. Portion: 6 oz ladle (8 oz weight).

the government to show that this process was done according to government-approved standards.

At the bottom of Figure 10.15 (Page 1) is the format for each line entry in the most stringent hazard-controlled process. The line should be identified by a (i) process step number, (ii) the starting food center temperature, (iii) the thickest food dimension, (iv) container size, (v) whether or not the food is covered, (vi) the temperature on or around the food, (vii) the ending food center temperature, and (viii) the time (in hours and minutes) it takes to complete the process step. If these variables are indicated for each process step, then any process control authority can read this recipe and certify whether or not it is safe, and determine the competency of the person who wrote the HACCP recipe.

Figure 10.15 (Page 2) is the reverse side of the *barley soup* recipe procedure. The end of the form contains additional spaces for reconstitution instructions, items with which it might be served, and plating instructions.

As another critical control, ingredients that could produce allergic reactions are included. About 1% of the US population have serious, life-threatening allergies to certain foods. If the server is unaware of the ingredients used in a food product, the consumer can become extremely ill or be killed. This provides the necessary information so that the employee can be informed about this problem.

There is also space for leftovers. Leftovers are grossly abused in most foodservice operations. There is either a tremendous waste, and they are discarded, or they are reheated multiple times in an attempt to get rid of them. In a good food operation, there is an accurate head count, and there are virtually no leftovers. The few leftovers remaining often can be fed to the employees. In HACCP, food is not safe until consumed because the spores survive until consumption. Therefore, the HACCP analysis must include controls up to consumption.

Finally, there is a comment section, which complements the first side of the recipe sheet, where special comments can be made regarding the specific preparation procedure. This is a place to note irregularities, so that if there are customer comments that the recipe is worse or better than normal, one can refer to the comments to find out what was done differently, and then execute a quality control change in the recipe procedure if appropriate.

10.6.4.1 Beef stew.   There are many forms that the recipe can take. Figure 10.16 using beef stew is specifically written for regulatory analysis.

The ingredients are listed in standard form, along with process steps. There is a column for *threats*, in which the various hazards associated with a given step are identified. The last column provides a *threat control analysis*, which includes, when appropriate, the effectiveness of the policies, procedures and standards manual to control these threats. In writing normal recipes, these two columns are usually omitted because they can be completed by a trained food safety process certifier when he/she reads the recipe.

10.6.4.1.1 Beef stew: quality-assured HACCP recipe procedures. Figure 10.17 gives another version of the beef stew recipe done in the more traditional format, like the barley soup, where the ingredients are listed on the top of the page. They are listed in weight form, because this is the

Recipe Name: **Beef Stew**
Recipe #:
Production style: **Hot combination**
Written by: Cleveland Range   Date: 3/93

Portion size (vol./wt.):
Number of portions:
Final yield (AS): **90 gal.**
Yield: **88%:**
SA/QA by: P. Snyder   Date: 4/93

Preparation time:
To be prepared by: **P. Snyder**
Supervisor:

Gp. #	Ingred. #	Ingredients and Specifications	EP Weight %	Edible Portion (EP) (weight or volume)		User Rec. (wt./vol.)	Nutrition Ref. #
I	1	Cooking oil	0.12	1.06 lbs	(480.0g)		
II	2	Beef, boneless, raw, cut in 1" cubes	33.45	288.00 lbs	(130,752.0 g)		
	3	Onions, chopped	7.78	67.00 lbs	(30,418.0 g)		
III	4	Beef stock (20 gallons)	19.40	167.0 lbs	(75,818.0 g)		
IV	5	Carrots diced 1/2 inch	7.78	67.00 lbs	(30,418.0 g)		
	6	Celery	7.78	67.00 lbs	(30,418.0 g)		
	7	Potatoes	20.91	180.00 lbs	(81,720.0 g)		
V	8	Flour	1.16	10.00 lbs	(4,540.0 g)		
	9	Water, cold (5 quarts)	1.21	10.44 lbs	(4,739.8 g)		
VI	10	Salt	.35	3.00 lbs	(1,362.0 g)		
	11	Pepper	.02	0.19 lbs	(86.3 g)		
	12	Garlic powder	.02	0.19 lbs	(86.3 g)		
		Total	99.98	860.88 lbs	(390,838.4 g)		
		Approx. gallons		103 gal.			

Pre-preparation   Time/ Initials
1. Inspect the weight and condition of all ingredients.
Preparation
2. Pour oil (72°F) into kettle, or use a lecithin spray and omit the oil.
3. Set mixer on #3 setting. Add 24% of the cubed beef (40°F). Turn heat **On**. Add remaining meat. Brown the meat. (225°F, 10 min.)
4. Add beef stock and onions (40°F). Heat to 200°F.
5. Simmer at 190°F until meat is tender (approx. 1.5 hours).
6. Add carrots, celery and potatoes (40°F). Heat to 190°F. Simmer 10 min.
7. While kettle is heating, mix flour (72°F, room temperature) and water (70°F). (10 min.).
8. Add flour/water mixture to kettle mixture. Add salt, pepper, and garlic powder. Cook until thickened. (200°F, 10 min.)
Pumping
9. Set mixer speed at #4 and agitator speed on **slow to medium**.
10. Fill casings with 6 quarts of soup (180°F) per casing. Label. Hold each bag for 3 minutes to allow for inside bag surface pasteurization. Check seal before adding the bag to the chiller. Put a special label on the last bag so this bag can be found in the chiller. The product temperature of this bag is measured to assess cooling of contents of all bags before they are removed from the chiller. (15 min)
Chilling
11. Place casings in chiller water (<35°). (Make sure the tumble chiller water has 5 ppm chlorine or equivalent chemical.) Chill to <40°F in < 1 hour. When temperature of control bag is < 40°F, all bags can be removed.
12. Put bags (<40°F) one layer deep in storage racks on the cart. Push cart to chill box (<40°F, 15 min)
13. Cool food to 29°F (± 1°F) in < 12 hours.
Store
14. Hold at 29°F (± 1°F) and use within < 21 days.
Reheating, Plating and Serving
15. When needed, heat beef stew to 165°F (no higher for quality) by an appropriate method.
16. Hold covered at 165°F and serve within 30 minutes so that food is >150°F when consumed.
Leftovers
17. Dispose of leftovers, or cool to 40°F in < 4 hours and serve within 24 hours.
Ingredients that could produce possible allergic reactions: Flour

Process step #	Start food ctr. temp., °F	Thickest food dimension (in.)	Container size H x W x L (in.)	Cover Yes/No	Temp. on/ around food	End food ctr. temp., °F	Process step time, hr/min.

Figure 10.17 Quality-assured HACCP recipe procedures.

easiest way to accurately control food preparation. They are listed in both pounds/ounces and grams, depending on which system the kitchen is utilizing.

Particularly important is that the weights are then converted to an edible portion weight percent. When this is done, one can look at an ingredient, such as black pepper at approximately 0.004%, to determine whether or not the customer will be able to taste it. If monosodium glutamate or nitrite/nitrate are added to a recipe, the edible portion weight percent becomes extremely important because it warns about overuse of the ingredient.

The second part of the quality-assured HACCP recipe procedure is the written instructions. What makes a HACCP recipe different from a typical recipe is that each step must include food time and temperature. Because of these times and temperatures in each step, one can read the recipe and almost instantly verify that the times and temperatures are adequate to prevent food safety problems. Any unusual/incomplete steps can be discussed and modified to become correct.

It should be obvious from this type of procedure that if the food process safety authority does not have cooking experience, he/she will have a lot of trouble certifying recipe procedures as safe.

10.6.5 Components of an effective HACCP program

The most important elements of an effective (zero-defect) HACCP-based food safety program is the management process, which pre-controls the system to be safe. A major reason that most food safety regulations are ineffective is that they do not require unit *management* to demonstrate control. Rather, they are based on the false premise that government inspection is control. This is totally incorrect. The employee on the line is the one who assures zero defects because management makes it possible through correct knowledge, training and adequate resources for employees to do so. Government's only responsibility in assuring zero defects is to make sure that the owner has a complete, effective HACCP-based Total Quality Management program.

The following are the six components of an effective HACCP program. These must be in place in order to assure virtual zero-defect control of the hazards.

10.6.5.1 Management, supervisor and employee responsibility for food safety

a. Demonstrate *management commitment* through food safety promotion actions (e.g. safety committees, incentives, awards, etc.).
   (1) Set challenging, measurable and attainable improvement safety goals.

    (2) Set the safety example in all activities.

    (3) Interview employees during walkaround, to hear and respond to their suggestions for process improvement.

b. Allocate *sufficient resources* to accomplish food safety goals.

c. Establish an *organizational chart* showing assigned line and staff responsibility for specific workplace food hazard controls.

d. Establish the system to measure the *cost saving* from doing the right tasks right the first time.

e. Develop *food safety committees*.

f. Establish *accountability measurers* for meeting food safety responsibilities.

g. Hold regular *staff meetings* to reinforce the safety principles and to listen to employee suggestions for improvement.

h. Implement *ongoing inspection and monitoring* programs to identify and improve controls of changing workplace hazards.

10.6.5.2 *Hazard analysis and control*

a. Identify and analyze *workplace food hazards* through food safety audits, environmental monitoring and self-inspections to identify jobs that have hazards which could lead to foodborne illness.

b. Examine *each job hazard* and list the following:

    (1) Sequence of job process steps identifying ingredients, time, temperature and equipment essential to hazard control

    (2) How hazards can lead to illness

    (3) Procedures and standards, which, when used, will control the hazards.

c. Make arrangements for a *hazard control quality-assured manager* to be available on all work shifts.

d. Evaluate the *safety performance* of new equipment, supplies and materials before purchase, and processes before implementation to assure zero-defect control.

10.6.5.3 *Written program with clearly stated goals and objectives for food safety assurance, that promotes safe and sanitary working conditions, and has a clearly stated plan for meeting the goals and objectives*

a. Write an executive food safety *policy statement* to control hazards specific to the workplace.

b. Write a *food safety action plan and program* clearly describing how food safety assurance (pre-control), safety control and safety improvement goals will be met.

c. Develop and implement *written zero defect-based food safety procedures and standards*.

d. Write plans for conducting and documenting at least an *annual review* of the program effectiveness, and then for improving the program based on the findings.

e. Institute appropriate *equipment programs* to cover the calibration, use, cleaning, maintenance and eventual replacement of equipment.

10.6.5.4 Communication and training

a. Communicate the *food safety program* to all employees.
b. Allow for *employee input* in bringing hazardous food operating conditions to management's attention.
c. Provide *training prior to all new job assignments* including training on specific hazard controls.
d. Update *training* at least annually or as work processes and ingredients change.
e. Maintain *records of training* (date/topic/content/attendance).
f. Train *supervisors* in pertinent food safety matters, food safety leadership, coaching and employee empowerment to take action at any time to prevent a problem.
g. Evaluate *training needs* to determine specialized training and retraining. Use supervisors and employees to give feedback as to how to improve training.

10.6.5.5 Process control problem investigation and corrective action

a. Develop *procedures* for process control problem reporting, problem investigation, corrective action and follow-up.
b. Conduct *workplace prevention* inspection of facilities and equipment (e.g. refrigeration, cooking and hot holding devices, pot and dish washing and sanitizing, insect and rodent control).
c. Write reports following process control problems showing what *preventive/corrective action* is being taken to prevent similar problems; for example:
   (1) Equipment modified
   (2) Work method modified
   (3) Equipment changed or added
   (4) Employee retrained or special needs accommodated.
d. Maintain, summarize and analyze *foodborne illness data* (e.g. first reports of illness) to determine tasks and operations where incidents have occurred. Take action to prevent recurrence.

10.6.5.6 Program enforcement

a. Write an *enforcement statement* on safe food operation practices, food safety rules and standard operating procedures.
b. Maintain *records of disciplinary actions and warnings*.

c. Develop policies that hold *managers and supervisors accountable* for fulfillment of food safety responsibilities. Safety is behavioral control. Hold everyone responsible for his/her safety behavior.

10.6.6   *Food safety through Quality Assurance: policies, procedures and standards manual*

All of this information is assembled in the foodservice HACCP-based QA policies, procedures and standards manual. The following outlines the chapters in the HACCP-based QA manual.

Food safety through Quality Assurance: policies, procedures and standards manual
(A plan and program leading to zero liability costs)

Table of contents

1. Planning
  Food Safety Policy
  Organization for Assured Food Safety
  Food System Input – Process – Output Description
  Food Safety Policies, Procedures, and Standards for All Personnel
  Supplier HACCP/QA Qualification List
  Supplier Quality Assurance Qualification Report
  Menu Item HACCP Process Summary
  Quality-Assured Recipe Procedures
  Cleaning and Sanitizing Schedule and Instructions
  Detailed Sanitation Procedures and Standards
  Maintenance Schedule and Instructions
  Pest Control Schedule and Instructions
  Strategy to Implement Change
  Weekly Action Schedule
  Yearly Action Schedule

2. Organization and Training
  New Employee Training Record
   Continuing Education Training Record
  Quality Improvement Training Outline
  Monthly Food Safety News Letter

3. Operating and Controlling
  Employee–Customer Quality and Hazard Problem Report
  Action to Correct

Quality and Hazard Problem Action Log
Foodborne Illness Information Form
Emergency Procedures

4. Measuring and Enforcing

Quality Management Team: Problem–Opportunity Identification
Worksheet
  Cause–Effect Analysis Diagram
  Cause–Effect Analysis Worksheet
  Problem–Opportunity Action Plan and Program
  Group Action Log
  Individual Action Log
  Retail Food Operation Abbreviated Food Hazard Control Checklist
  Retail Food Operation Food Hazard Control Checklist
  Employee Improvement Worksheet
  Food Safety Program Certification

The manual is key to the zero-defect goal. Since all process – tasks – steps are described in the manual, it is the basis for training employees. Next, the manual becomes the basis for process evaluation and improvement. After the processes are completed each day, each employee is given a chance to suggest ways to improve the system. All suggestions are references to what is written so that the training/operations manual can be improved immediately and then, the new way of doing a process can be integrated immediately into operations.

5. Food Operation Evaluation

There is a fundamental management principle that says, if a standard is not measured it will not be enforced. This food operation evaluation form shown in Figure 10.18 gives the operator the tool to validate the operation to assure that standards are followed and that the processes are stable.

Stability is the basis for continuous quality improvement and continuously safe products. The results of this evaluation should never be used to punish employees but only to coach them and to assure improved performance.

10.7 Summary

In summary the actual rules for food safety HACCP-based self-control are simple.

1. Assume that the raw food and the people who are producing the food are contaminated.
2. Use the raw food as soon as possible.
3. Employees wash their fingertips and clean cutting boards correctly.

Operation _____ Date _____

Director of SA / QA _____

Criteria	Capabl. (0 - 5)[1]	Perfor.[2]	Haz. Cn. Y / N[3]	Comments
1. Management Safety commitment & resources Safety leadership Safety enforcement Action Log				
2. Quality Control, Assure, Improve Improvement audits Continuous improvement program Hazard analysis Hazard control policies, procedures, and standards Quality costs Schedules for maintenance, cleaning, training Operational safety self-evaluation System changes are controlled Safety controlled by the line employee(s) Recipes are HACCP'd				
3. Personnel Everyone knows their responsibilities Selection and qualification Training and performance certification Coaching and improvement by supervisors Personal hygiene and dress, hand washing Knowledge of hazards and controls				
4. Facilities Sufficient capacity Maintenance Cleanliness and sanitation Insect and rodent control Waste and trash control				
5. Equipment Adequate capacity Maintenance Cleaning and sanitizing Backflow CO_2 prevention Calibration of control and temperature measuring thermometers				

---

[1] **Capability**
   0 - No measurable activity in the performance area.
   1 - Partial but inadequate activity in the performance area
   2 - An informal program that meets minimal criteria of the performance area.
   3 - A formal program that has not been fully developed and implemented in the performance area.
   4 - A formal program that meets all basic criteria of the performance area and is backed by management.
   5 - A formal written program that meets or exceeds all performance criteria and is fully implemented, communicated and reviewed
      annually.
[2] **Performance:** Quality defects per 1,000 items.
[3] **Hazard Control:** Explain No's.

Figure 10.18 Food operation evaluation. (Page 1).

4. Pasteurize the food by heating it, washing it or acidifying it to reduce the infective pathogens to a safe level. *Do not* wash meat and poultry because washing these foods has very little benefit and will dangerously contaminate the sink used for washing. Heat it in less than 6 hours to over 130°F (54.4°C).

5. Serve as soon as possible, or cool to 45°F (7.2°C) in less than 15 hours,

Criteria	Capabl. (0 - 5)	Perfor.	Haz. Cn. Y / N	Comments
6. Supplies Specifications Supplier food safety certification Chemical MSDS and control				

7. Receiving and storage
Package and container damage control
Spoilage culling, cleaning of fruits and
  vegetables
Rapid and correct storage; food covered,
  off floor
Product dated; FIFO; <41°F (5.0°C), use in
  < 5 days.				

8. Production
Pre-prep temperatures <50°F (10°C)
Cross-contamination control; clean-as-you-go
Salad ingredients cooled to 41°F (5.0°C)
  before mixing; kept at <50°F (10°C) during
  mixing
Heat food to >130°F (54.4°C) in <6 hours
7D *Salmonella* pasteurization:
  130°F (54.4°C) - 121 min.
  140°F (60°C) - 12.1 min.
  150°F (65.6°C) - 1.21 min.
  160°F (71.1°C) - 0.121 min.				

9. Finished product and service
Hot hold >150°F (65.6°C); serve in <30 min.
  for maximum nutrition.
Cool unpasteurized food to <45°F (7.2°C)
  in <15 h.
Cool pasteurized food to <45°F (7.2°C)
  in <15 h.
Cold holding <41°F (5.0°C) <5 days.
Service persons know possible allergenic
  ingredients in recipes and can communicate
  to customers.
Leftovers not mixed with fresh.
Leftovers kept <41°F (5.0°C). (Reheating to
  165°F (73.9°C), not used for critical control).
Consumer abuse is controlled.				

Figure 10.18 (Page 2).

store at 41°F (5.0°C), and consume it as soon as possible. If the food temperature is not below 32°F (0°C), above 127.5°F (70.8°C), or pathogen controlled in some other way, then make sure it is used in a time that controls *L. monocytogenes* to less than 5 generations.

Of course, chemicals and hard foreign objects must be controlled.

There is the very real problem of allergic reactions. Therefore, consumers who ask questions regarding the ingredient contents of any food product must be given accurate answers in order to protect themselves.

The key to performing these simple food safety tasks is for the line employee to do them the same way 100% of the time until the rules are officially changed. With documentation of all recipe procedures and policies on hand washing, cutting board cleaning, etc., the only remaining factor is behavioral control. This is why management and leadership are crucial. With effective management and then, training and certifying all employees in correct procedures before they are allowed to perform their tasks, followed by providing positive reinforcement so that the procedures are performed with zero defects, a zero defect hazard controlled process is possible.

References

Battelle Columbus Division for The Center for Chemical Process Safety of the American Institute of Chemical Engineers (1992) *Guidelines for Hazard Evaluation Procedures*, 2nd edn. American Institute of Chemical Engineers, New York.

Bauman, H.E. (1974) The HACCP concept and microbiological hazard categories. *Food Technol.* **28**, 30.

Bean, N.H., Griffin, P.M., Goulding, J.S. and Ivey, C.B. (1990) Foodborne disease outbreaks, 5 year summary, 1983–1987. *MMWR* **39**(SS-1), 15.

Bennett, J.V., Scott, D.H., Roger, M.F. and Solomon, S.L. (1987) Infectious and parasitic diseases, in *The Burden of Unnecessary Illness* (R.W Amler and H.B. Dull eds) Oxford University Press, New York, p. 104.

Bourland, C.T., Heidelbaugh, N.D., Huber, C.S., Kiser, P.R. and Rowley, D.B. (1974) Hazard analysis of *Clostridium perfringens* in the skylab food systems. *J. Food Protect.* **37**, 624.

Bryan, F.L. (1988) Risks associated with practices, procedures and processes that lead to outbreaks of foodborne disease. *J. Food Protect.* **51**, 663.

CAST (1994) *Foodborne Pathogens: Risks and Consequences*. Task Force Report #122. Council for Agricultural Science and Technology, Ames, Iowa.

Center for Chemical Process Safety (1989) *Guidelines for Technical Management of Chemical Process Safety*. American Institute of Chemical Engineers, New York.

Center for Chemical Process Safety (1992) *Plant Guidelines for Technical Management of Chemical Process Safety*. American Institute of Chemical Engineers, New York.

Grau, F.H. and Vanderline, P.B. (1990) Growth of *Listeria monocytogenes* on vacuum packaged beef. *J. Food Protect.* **53**, 739.

Hanna, M.O., Stewart, J.C., Zink, D.L., Carpenter, Z.L. and Vanderzant, C. (1977) Development of *Yersinia enterocolitica* on raw and cooked beef or pork at different temperatures. *J. Food Sci.* **42**, 1180.

Heidelbaugh, N.D., Smith, H.C., Jr. and Rambout, P.C. (1973) Food safety in NASA nutrition programs. *Am. Vet. Med. Assoc. J.* **163**, 1065.

Hudson, J.A., Mott, S.J. and Penney, N. (1994) Growth of *Listeria monocytogenes*, *Aeromonas hydrophila* and *Yersinia enterocolitica* on vacuum and saturated carbon dioxide controlled atmosphere packaged sliced roast beef. *J. Food Protect.* **57**, 204.

Juneja, V.K., Snyder, O.P. and Cygnarowicz-Provost, M. (1994) Influence of cooling rate on outgrowth of *Clostridium perfringens* spores in cooked ground beef. *J. Food Protect.* **57**, 1063.

NACMCF (The National Advisory Committee on Microbiological Criteria for Foods) (1992) Hazard Analysis and Critical Control Point System. *Interl. J. Food Microbiol.* **16**, 1.

Pflug, I.J. and Blaisdell, J.L. (1963) Methods of analysis of pre-cooling data. *ASHRAE J.* **5**, 133.

Pflug, I.J., Blaisdell, J.L. and Kopelman, I.J. (1965) Developing temperature–time curves for objects that can be approximated by sphere, infinate plate, or infinate cylinder. *ASHRAE Transactions. Part i* **71**, 238.

Pillsbury Company (1973) *Food Safety Through the Hazard Analysis and Critical Control Point System*. The Pillsbury Co., Minneapolis, Minnesota.

Pivnick, H., Erdman, I.E., Manzatiuk, S. and Pommier, E. (1968) Growth of food poisoning bacteria on barbecued chicken. *J. Milk Food Technol.* **31**, 198.

Ratkowsky, D.A., Olley, J., McMeekin, T.A and Ball, A. (1982) Relationship between temperature and growth rate of bacterial starter cultures. *J. Bacteriol.* **149**, 1.

Roberts, T. (1990) 1987 Bacterial foodborne illness costs in the USA. *Food Laboratory News* **19** (Mar) 53.

Roberts, T. and van Ravenswaay, E. (1989) The economics of safe guarding the U.S. Food Supply. *USDA Agr. Info. Bulletin No.* **566**, 1.

Shoemaker, S.P. and Pierson, M.D. (1976) 'Phoenix Phenomenon' in the growth of *Clostridium perfringens. Appl. Microbiol.* **32**, 803.

Skinner, G.E., Larkin, J.W. and Rhodehamel, E.J. (1994) Mathematical modeling of microbial growth: A review. *J. Food Safety* **14**, 175.

Snyder, O.P. (1992a) Developing A Total Quality Management-Based Food Safety Program for a Chilled Food System. p. 6–1. Hospitality Institute of Technology and Management. St. Paul, Minnesota.

Snyder, O.P. (1992b) Developing A Total Quality Management-Based Food Safety Program for a Chilled Food System. p. 8–1. Hospitality Institute of Technology and Management. St. Paul, Minnesota.

Snyder, O.P. (1993) The Hazard Control Base for Zero-Liability Food Operation Total Quality Management. p. 7. Hospitality Institute of Technology and Management. St. Paul, Minnesota.

Snyder, O.P. and Poland, D.P. (1990) America's 'safe' food, Part I. *Dairy, Food and Environ. Sanit.* **10**, 719.

Snyder, O.P. and Poland, D.P. (1991) America's 'safe' food. Part II. *Dairy, Food and Environ. Sanit.* **11**, 14.

Todd, E.C.D. (1989) Preliminary estimates of costs of foodborne illness in the United States. *J. Food Protect.* **52**, 595.

USDA (1991) 9 CFR (Code of Federal Regulations) Part 200 to end. Office of the Federal Register. National Archives and Records Adm. Washington, D.C.

WHO (1993) Training Considerations for the Application of the Hazard Analysis Critical Control Point System to Food Processing and Manufacturing. FOS/93.3. World Health Organization Division of Food and Nutrition. Geneva, Switzerland.

References for Table 10.5

1. DuPont, H.L., Hornick, R.B., Dawkins, A.T., Snyder, M.J. and Formal, S.B. (1969) The response of man to virulent *Shigella flexneri* 2a. *J. Infect. Dis.* **119**, 296.

2. DuPont, H.L., Formal, S.B., Hornick, R.B., Snyder, M.J., Libonati, J.P., Sheahan, D.G., LaBrec, E.H. and Kalas, J.P. (1971) Pathogenesis of *Escherichia coli* diarrhea. *N. Engl. J. Med.* **285**, 1.

3. DuPont, H.L, Hornick, R.B., Snyder, M.J., Libonati, J.P., Formal, S.B. and Ganarosa, E.J. (1972) Immunity in shigellosis. II. Protection induced by oral live vaccine or primary infection. *J. Infect. Dis.* **125**, 12.

4. FDA (1993) *HACCP. Regulatory Food Applications in Retail Food Establishments.* Dept. of Health and Human Services. Division of Human Resource Development, HFC-60. Rockville, Maryland.

5. Goepfert, J.M., Spira, W.M. and Kim, H.U. (1972) *Bacillus cereus*: Food poisoning organism. A review. *J. Milk Food Technol.* **35**, 213.

6. Hauschild, A.H.W. (1973) Food poisoning by *Clostridium perfringens. Can. Inst. Food Sci. Technol. J.* **6**, 106.

7. Hobbs, B.C. (1960) Staphylococcal and *Clostridium welchi* food poisoning. Roy. Soc. Health J. **80**, 267.

8. Hornick, R.B., Greisman, S.E., Woodward, T.E., DuPont, H.L., Dawkins, A.T. and Snyder, M.J. (1970) Typhoid fever: Pathogenesis and immunologic control. *New Engl. J., Med.* **283**, 686.

9. Hornick, R.B., Music, S.I., Wenzel, R., Cash, R., Libonati, J.P., Snyder, M.J. and Woodward, T.E. (1971) The Broad Street pump revisited: Response of volunteer to ingested cholera vibrios. *Bull. N.Y. Acad. Med.* [2]**47**, 1181.

10. Levine, M.J., DuPont, H.L., Formal, S.B., Hornick, R.B., Takeuchi, A., Gangarosa,

E.J., Snyder, M.J. and Libonati, J.P. (1973) Pathogenesis of *Shigella dysenteriae* I (Shiga) dysentery. *J. Infect. Dis.* **127**, 261.

11. Lubin, L.B., Morton, R.D. and Bernard, D.T. (1985) Toxin production in hard-cooked eggs experimentally inoculated with *Clostridium botulinum*. *J. Food Sci.* **50**, 969.

12. McCullough, M.G. and Eisele, C.W. (1951a) Experimental human salmonellosis. I. Pathogenicity of strains of *Salmonella meleagridis* and *Salmonella anatum* obtained from spray-dried whole egg. *J. Infect. Dis.* **88**, 278.

13. McCullough, M.B. and Eisele, C.W. (1951b) Experimental human salmonellosis. III. Pathogenicity of strains of *Salmonella newport*, *Salmonella derby* and *Salmonella bareilly* obtained from spray-dried whole egg. *J. Infect. Dis.* **89**, 209.

14. McCullough, M.B. and Eisele, C.W. (1951c) Experimental human salmonellosis. IV. Pathogenicity of strains of *Salmonella pullorum* obtained from spray-dried whole egg. *J. Infect. Dis.* **89**, 259.

15. Magee, P.N. (1983) Nitrate, in *Environmental Aspects of Cancer. The Role of Macro and Micro Components of Foods* (E.L. Wynder, G.A. Leveille, J.H. Weisburger and G.E. Livingstone, eds) Food and Nutrition Press. Westport, Connecticut. p. 198.

16. Moustafa, M.K., Ahmed, A.A.-H. and Marth, E.H. (1983) Behavior of virulent *Yersinia enterocolitica* during manufacture and storage of colby-like cheese. *J. Food Protect.* **46**, 318.

17. Newsome, R.L. (1988) *Staphylococcus aureus*. *Food Technol.* **42**, 194.

18. Robinson, D.A. (1981) Infective dose of *Campylobacter jejuni* in milk. *Brit. Med. J.* **282**, 1584.

19. Shaughnessy, H.J., Olsson, R.C., Bass, K., Friewer, F. and Levinson, S.O. (1946) Experimental human bacillary dysentery. *J. Am. Med. Assoc.* **132**, 362.

20. Snyder, O.P. (1985) Personal Communication.

21. Stern, N.J. (1982) Foodborne pathogens of lesser notoriety: Viruses, *Vibrio*, *Yersinia* and *Campylobacter*, in *ABMPS Report No. 125*. National Academy of Science Press. Washington, D.C. p. 57.

22. Taylor, S.L. and Bush, R.K. (1986) Sulfites as food ingredients. *Food Technol.* **40**, 47.

References for Table 10.9

1. Lovett, J., Bradshaw, J.G. and Peeler, J.T. (1982) Thermal inactivation of *Yersinia enterocolitica* in milk. *Appl. Environ. Microbiol.* **44**, 517.

2. Stern, N.J., Pierson, M.D. and Kotula, A.W. (1980) Effects of pH and sodium chloride on *Yersinia enterocolitica* growth at room temperature and refrigeration temperatures. *J. Food Sci.* 4564.

3. Hanna, M.O., Stewart, J.C., Carpenter, Z.I. and Vanderzant, C. (1977a) Effect of heating, freezing and pH on *Yersinia enterolcolitica*-like organisms from meat. *J. Food Protect.* **40**, 689.

4. Grau, F.H. and Vanderline, P.B. (1990) Growth of *Listeria monocytogenes* on vacuum packaged beef. *J. Food Protect.* **53**, 452.

5. Lovett, J. (1989) *Listeria monocytogenes*, in *Foodborne Bacterial Pathogens* (M.P. Doyle, ed), Marcel Dekker, Inc. New York.

6. Faber, J.M., Coates, F. and Daley, E. (1992) Minimum water activity requirements for the growth of *Listeria monocytogenes*. *Letters in App. Microbiol.* **15**, 103.

7. Rosenow, E.M. and Marth, E.H. (1987) Growth of *Listeria monocytogenes* in skim, whole and chocolate milk, and in whipping cream during incubation at 4°C, 8°C, 13°C, 21°C and 35°C. *J. Food Protect.* **50**, 452.

8. USDA, FSIS (1990) Recommendations of the National Advisory Committee on Microbiological Criteria for Foods for Refrigeration of foods containing cooked, uncured meat or poultry products that are packaged for extended refrigerated shelf life and that are ready-to-eat or prepared with little or no additional heat treatment. USDA-FSIS. Washington, D.C.

9. Bradshaw, J.G., Peeler, J.T., Coorwing, J.J., Hunt, J.M., Tierney, J.T., Larken, E.P.

and Twedt, R.M. (1985) Thermal resistance of *Listeria monocytogenes* in milk. *J. Food Protect.* **48**, 743.

10. Twedt, R.M. (1989) *Vibrio parahaemolyticus*, in *Foodborne Bacterial Pathogens* (M.P. Doyle, ed) Marcel Dekker, Inc. New York.
11. Sperber, W.H. (1983) Influence of water activity on foodborne bacteria – A review. *J. Food Protect.* **46**, 142.
12. Beuchat, L.R. and Worthington, R.E. (1976) Relationship between heat resistance and phospholipid fatty acid composition of *Vibrio parahaemolyticus*. *Appl. Environ. Microbiol.* **31**, 80.
13. Beuchat, L.R. (1982) *Vibrio parahaemolyticus*: Public health significance. *Food Technol.* **36**, 80.
14. Matches, J.R. and Liston, J. (1968) Low temperature growth of *Salmonella*. *J. Food Sci.* **33**, 641.
15. Angelotti, R., Foter, M.J. and Lewis, K.H. (1961a) Time–temperature effects on Salmonellae and Staphylococci in Foods. I. Behavior in refrigerated foods. II. Behavior at warm holding temperatures. *Am. J. Pub. Health.* **51**, 83.
16. Silliker, J.H. (1982) *Salmonella* foodborne illness, in *Microbiological Safety of Foods in Feeding Systems*. A.B.M.P.S. Report **125**, 22.
17. Code of Federal Regulations (CFR)9 (1987) 318.17. *Requirements for the Production of Cooked Beef, Roast Beef, Roast Beef and Cooked Corned Beef*. Office of Federal Register National Archives and Records and Administration. Washington, D.C.
18. Goodfellow, S.J. and Brown, W.L. (1978) Fate of *Salmonella* inoculated into beef for cooking. *J. Food Protect.* **41**, 598.
19. Doyle, M.P. and Roman, D.J. (1981) Growth and survival of *Campylobacter fetus* subsp. *jejuni* as a function of temperature and pH. *J. Food Protect.* **44**, 596.
20. Koidis, P. and Doyle, M.P. (1983) Survival of *Campylobacter jejuni* in fresh and heated red meat. *J. Food Protect.* **46**, 771.
21. Blankenship, L.C. and Craven, S.E. (1982) Survival of *Campylobacter jejuni* in chicken meats as a function of temperature. *Appl. Microbiol.* **44**, 88.
22. Hauschild, A.H.W. (1989) *Clostridium botulinum*, in *Foodborne Bacterial Pathogens* (M.P. Doyle, ed), Marcel Dekker, Inc. New York.
23. Lynt, R.K., Kautter, D.A. and Solomon, H.M. (1982) Differences and similarities among proteolytic and nonproteolytic strains of *Clostridium botulinum* Types A, B, E and F: A review. *J. Food Protect.* **45**, 466.
24. Riemann, H. and Bryan, F.L. (1979) *Foodborne Infections and Intoxications*. 2nd edn. Academic Press. New York. p. 625.
25. Woodburn, M.J., Somers, E., Rodriguez, J. and Shantz, E.J. (1979) Heat inactivation rates of botulism toxins A, B, E and F in some foods and buffers. *J. Food Sci.* **44**, 1658.
26. Halpin-Dohnalek, M.I. and Marth, E.H. (1989b) *Staphylococcus aureus*: Production of extracellular compounds and behavior in foods – A review. *J. Food Protect.* **52**, 267.
27. Bergdoll, M.D. (1989) *Staphylococcus aureus*, in *Foodborne Bacterial Pathogens* (M.P. Doyle, ed) Marcel Dekker. New York, p. 463.
28. Angelotti, R., Foster, M.J. and Lewis, K.H. (1961b) Time–temperature effects on Salmonellae and Staphylococci in Foods. III. Thermal death time studies. *Appl. Microbiol.* **9**, 308.
29. Tatini, S.R. (1973) Influence of food environments of growth of *Staphylococcus aureus* and production of various enterotoxins. *J. Milk Food Technol.* **36**, 474.
30. Schneusner, D.L., Hood, L.L. and Harmon, L.G. (1973) Effect of temperature and pH on growth and enterotoxin production by *Staphylococcus aureus*. *J. Milk Food Technol.* **36**, 249.
31. Read, R.B. and Bradshaw, J.G. (1966) Staphylococcal enterotoxin B thermal inactivation in milk. *J. Dairy Science.* **49**, 202.
32. Denny, C.B. (1971) Effect of toxin concentration on the inactivation of Staphylococcal enterotoxin A in beef bouillion and in phosphate buffer. *Appl. Microbiol.* **21**, 1064.
33. van Netten, P., van de Moosdijk, A., van Hoensel, P., Mossel, D.A.A. and Perales, I. (1990) Psychrotrophic strains of *Bacillus cereus* producing enterotoxin. *J. Appl. Microbiol.* **69**, 73.
34. Johnson, K.M., Nelson, C.L. and Busta, F.F. (1983) Influence of temperature on

germination and growth of spores of emetic and diarrheal strains of *Bacillus cereus* in a growth medium and in rice. *J. Food Sci.* **48**, 286.
35. Kramer, J.M. and Gilbert, R.J. (1989) *Bacillus cereus* and other bacillus species, in *Foodborne Bacterial Pathogens* (M.P. Doyle, ed), Marcel Dekker, Inc. New York.
36. Johnson, K.M. (1986) Personal communication.
37. Labbe, R. (1989) *Clostridium perfringens*, in *Foodborne Bacterial Pathogens* (M.P. Doyle, ed) Marcel Dekker, Inc. New York.
38. Shoemaker, S.P. and Pierson, M.D. (1976) 'Phoenix Phenomenon' in the growth of *Clostridium perfringens. Appl. Microbiol.* **32**, 803.
39. Fuchs, A. and Bonde, G.J. (1957) The nutritional requirements of *Clostridium perfringens. J. Gen. Microbiol.* **34**, 280.
40. Willardsen, R.R., Busta, F.F., Allen, C.E. and Smith, L.B. (1977) Growth and survival of *Clostridium perfringens* during constantly rising temperatures. *J. Food Sci.* **43**, 470.
41. Roy, R.J., Busta, F.F. and Thompson, D.R. (1981) Thermal inactivation of *Clostridium perfringens* after growth at several constant and linearly rising temperatures. *J. Food Sci.* **46**, 1586.
42. Bradshaw, J.G., Peeler, J.T. and Twedt, R.M. (1977) Thermal inactivation of ileal loop-reactive *Clostridium perfringens* type A strains in phosphate buffer and beef gravy. *Appl. Environ. Microbiol.* **34**, 280.

11 The HACCP program and the consumer
M.R. ROBERTS

11.1 Introduction

Prevention and control of food safety risks at the consumer level represents the weakest link in our chain of food protection systems. In this day of ever changing lifestyles and ever increasing demands on the consumer's time and energies, consumers are demanding convenience, freshness, long shelf lives and little preparation time before consumption. Food technology has responded by applying the knowledge of science to produce an increasing array of new foods, some partially processed, minimally preserved, of high quality and with extended shelf life. Consumers knowledge and practices in food handling have not kept pace with cultural and scientific changes.

Constant media reports of foodborne illnesses and even deaths, frequent exposés of poor industry practices, and diminishing credibility of government officials in the eyes of the public all add to increasing consumer concerns and the perception that our food may not be safe. A part of that perception includes a sense of powerlessness in the face of a complex food production and distribution system and what some people may view as uncontrollable obstacles in food safety.

In addition, our modern food supply is a truly global food supply with possible production in one country, processing in another and consumption in a third after extended shipment and storage. The traditional family structure where food handling practices were passed down to other generations and the traditional practice of local food production no longer exist.

Although our food supply is safe according to the majority of food safety experts, disease from food mishandling and other causes affects up to 14% of our population each year. From 6.5 to 81 million individuals have cases of microbial foodborne illnesses each year (Archer and Kvenberg, 1985; Archer and Young, 1988). Epidemiological investigations of foodborne disease by the Centers for Disease Control and Prevention still reveal basically half of all known cases to be of unknown etiology.

In 1990, the Centers for Disease Control and Prevention reported that approximately 79% of foodborne outbreaks of known etiology could be attributed to restaurants or food service establishments, 21% to abuse in homes and 3% to food processing plants (Bean and Griffin, 1990). Kayser and Mossel (1984) stated that too frequently we place reliance on control by monitoring – an ingrained habit that has repeatedly been demonstrated to be ineffective. They further reiterated that we must intervene, we must prevent. This is the only valid approach to microbiological safety of food.

Regrettably, the public's trust in government monitoring and regulation of the food supply has declined according to Sachs *et al.* (1987) and Warren *et al.* (1990). The earlier survey by Sachs *et al.* (1987) illustrates that there was a dramatic decline in trust in the safety of foods from 1965 to 1984. Dittmus and Hillers (1993) examined the interrelationship between trust and concerns for personal health. In relation to food risks, individuals with little trust actually practiced more preventive behaviors but did not necessarily believe in the benefits of their behaviour.

The US Public Health Service organized a consortium of public health experts and organizations associated with public health to formulate a plan to improve the health of the USA by the year 2000 (USPHS, 1991, 1993). Foodborne disease reduction was identified as one of the major health promotion and disease prevention objectives. Foodborne disease reduction can best be achieved through (i) education and training of industry, the regulators, consumers and health professionals; and by (ii) implementation of HACCP principles from production to consumption.

Unless consumer education is aggressive and current, it will not reach or be integrated into the everyday practices of the public. Just as every HACCP plan in the food processing industry is unique to the plant and to the site, HACCP for the consumer must be unique to affect their particular environment.

We must change public choices if we are indeed to reduce foodborne disease. Our best opportunity to achieve disease reduction and behavioral change is through application of the preventive system of Hazard Analysis Critical Control Points (HACCP) from production to consumption. HACCP, as a proactive, preventive and prospective approach to food safety, is also the best concept to allow for rational decision making at the consumer level.

11.2 The HACCP program

11.2.1 *The Hazard Analysis Critical Control Point (HACCP) system*

The initial research of The Pillsbury Company and other scientists into safe food production for the space program in the 1960s evolved into an effective and preventive system of quality control. The system provided for a systematic study of all aspects of food production and allowed for the identification of those areas where lack of control could result in an unacceptable food safety risk. The Hazard Analysis Critical Control Point

(HACCP) program as a broad concept was first introduced publicly by Howard Bauman at the first National Conference for Food Protection in 1971. See chapter 1 for details about the concept and its acceptance by leaders in the food industry.

The need for a better system of food safety control and prevention of hazards was recognized by many authorities. Advances in science and technology, our increased knowledge and understanding of food safety risks, and continuing epidemiologic reports on foodborne outbreaks have merely emphasized the need for an enhanced preventive system. Evolution and refinement of the HACCP system has been ongoing for over 30 years. The HACCP system as a goal was recommended by the National Academy of Sciences in 1985. Later, the National Advisory Committee on Microbiological Criteria for Foods recommended that implementation of HACCP was essential for control of microbiological hazards.

Howard Bauman detailed to the Advisory Committee in a letter on October 13, 1988 that:

'The Hazard Analysis Critical Control Point (HACCP) system is being accepted and implemented by food processors and regulators in many countries as a proactive and efficient means of assuring food safety.'

Further:

'since the establishment and maintenance of HACCP systems is a lengthy process, it will be some time before the industry can be regulated on this basis.'

He further indicated the need for application of interim microbiological guidelines to assist in the achievement of this goal.

The HACCP system was refined in 1992 by the National Advisory Committee on Microbiological Criteria for Foods (NACMCF, 1992) after reviewing international modifications.

The seven basic principles of the HACCP system are listed as follows:

1. Conduct a hazard analysis – prepare a list of steps where hazards occur and describe preventive measures
2. Identify critical control points (CCP)
3. Establish critical limits for preventive measures for each CCP
4. Establish CCP monitoring requirements
5. Establish corrective actions when monitoring finds a deviation
6. Establish effective record keeping
7. Establish procedures for verification that the HACCP system is working effectively.

Various industry entities and regulatory agencies have clearly endorsed and moved to implement HACCP. The Pillsbury Company has incorporated the system in all plants since 1971. The National Marine Fisheries Service has actively provided support to the industry through the development of generic HACCP plans for specific seafoods. The Food and Drug Administration has announced that HACCP must be utilized on a mandatory basis in the seafood industry. FDA has also expressed the desire to ultimately require the HACCP system for all food production.

In 1989 the Food Safety and Inspection Service of USDA issued a concept paper on the HACCP systems approach for food safety and process control and announced their intention to implement HACCP in the meat and poultry inspection activities. USDA had been evaluating their inspection procedures for meat and poultry for many years, but had met opposition to any changes viewed as a lessening of inspectional scrutiny. USDA announced in 1994 the intent to draft a plan to make HACCP mandatory in all meat and poultry establishments.

The evolution and application of HACCP has been focused in the food processing arena. While the initial concept only contemplated application and scrutiny of critical control points at the processor level, the fundamental concept has been judged sound and valid and can be applied to all other areas throughout the food chain.

The application of HACCP to fill this preventive role in all food areas has great support and potential. Although major application of HACCP has been in the processing arena, these statistics demonstrate the great need for expanded application to all food service establishments and homes. In January, 1993, a serious outbreak of E. coli 0157:H7 was traced to a restaurant chain's inadequate cooking of hamburger, which infected more than 500 people in four states and resulted in four deaths and a total reevaluation of the effectiveness of the current inspection system for meats (FSIS, 1993; Tarr, 1994). The reevaluation of food safety systems at USDA/FSIS has involved many facets including pilot studies, pathogen reduction programs and a HACCP Roundtable that served as a forum for broad input into a mandatory HACCP system for meat and poultry.

Effective implementation of HACCP at the processing level and development of HACCP controls in production only implement intervention strategies for part of the food safety equation. The application of HACCP to foods from the retail store to the consumer's mouth is currently unchartered territory. Thousands of decisions in food handling and critical control points occur each day in the grocery store and in homes. The consumer is the unknown component in the HACCP equation. For us to have any effect on foodborne illness, some control and adequate decision making must be made at the consumer public level.

11.2.2   The goal of HACCP

The ultimate goal of food safety programs and of HACCP must be the protection of the public from foodborne illnesses from harvest to consumption. The National Advisory Committee on Microbiological

Criteria for Foods has emphasized the need for control of food safety risks at all levels and has endorsed HACCP systems as the goal to control these risks. Few have applied HACCP to targets other than processing, while others are examining the application of HACCP for farm production. It is just as critical to apply HACCP principles to consumer practices in the home.

Food safety is of critical importance to everyone. Although HACCP may have been originally designed to be used by the food industry to ensure the safe production of food products, HACCP is for everyone, not just the food industry. All individuals want to be able to protect themselves and their families from illness and death. Any information which we can provide to the general public to enable them to achieve this goal will be of great value.

Regrettably, many well intended efforts by food scientists and the media have served to frighten the general public instead of instructing us on appropriate food safety measures. If consumers are properly instructed in HACCP principles, they will have a powerful tool in their possession to enable them to better control their lives.

The way we live, the way foods are produced and distributed, the way we view figures of authority in government and science – these have all changed in recent years. Michael Taylor, FDA's Deputy Commissioner for Policy stated:

> 'We don't have a food safety crisis in this country. FDA has no problem saying that the food supply is safe, but we do have a system under stress.'

Better measures of control must be introduced to alleviate that stress and to prevent foodborne illness. Sir Graham Wilson almost 40 years ago observed:

> 'We must keep asking ourselves whether any measure we should like to introduce would in fact appreciably diminish the incidence of . . . foodborne disease.'

It is doubtful that we could answer that rhetorical question as yes if based on belief in only our current system of inspections and analytical testing.

11.2.3 Application of HACCP principles by consumers

The Hazard Analysis Critical Control Point (HACCP) program can and does apply specifically for the general public as a fundamental program by which they can protect themselves and their families. After over 20 years of exposure and eight years of recommended adoption, HACCP has still not been incorporated completely into industry practices. Incorporation of HACCP principles may likewise take an even greater extended period of implementation for the consumer, but an intensive effort must be made to do so.

11.2.3.1   Redefining HACCP.   First, for the general public, the acronym itself, HACCP, is very unwieldy and sounds foreign and somewhat threatening. Our efforts for incorporation must not only educate as to the principles, but may also need to create the additional concept that HACCP is really about Helping All Consumers Cope with Problems. To formulate the best program to achieve and to incorporate HACCP principles by the general public, we must first know how to define the elusive consumer.

For the consumer, HACCP must be redefined and relabeled in terms of their own understanding. HACCP as a scientific concept, however, is valid and can be applied across all levels of the food chain. All seven principles of HACCP are also essential to include no matter whether HACCP is for a seafood processor, a poultry plant, a fast food franchise, the corner grocery store, or a home setting.

11.3   HACCP and consumers

11.3.1   Defining the elusive consumer

The major difficulty in consumer education and in affecting consumer practices lies in defining the elusive consumer. The collective term 'consumer' is often viewed by many as one homogeneous population capable of easy targeting, but no term was ever more heterogeneous. Especially in relation to food safety, there are vast differences in consumers from an age, condition and ethnic perspective.

Who is that elusive consumer? The balance of demographics will vary from state to state, municipality to municipality. Yet, the defined need of each consumer is the same – how to purchase, handle, store, cook and consume foods safely.

11.3.2   Target populations for HACCP application

Certain consumers are more susceptible to foodborne illness than others and should follow special adherence to CCPs. Dr. Morris Potter (1993) of CDC estimated that approximately 25% of our population fall into an at risk or more susceptible group for reasons of pregnancy, age (either very young or very old), immunosuppressed or diseased state or taking large quantities of stomach acid suppressors. These susceptible populations need to practice extra precautions in food handling for safety reasons.

For the infant in the home, the major critical control points may be in the heating steps of preparation and the sterilization of certain formula containers. Also, extra care may be stressed to consumers on the handling of raw animal products, such as raw beef, chicken, pork and seafoods on kitchen counter surfaces where other foods for the infant may be prepared.

The elderly in the home will also have particular special control areas and food safety needs. The usual critical control points of correct temperature of storage, adequate heating in cooking steps, and extra caution in the thawing and storage of raw animal products so as to not contaminate other foods with salmonellae should be noted. Also, older citizens when eating out frequently can not consume the large portions served and take a 'doggy bag' of leftovers for a later meal. Prompt and careful refrigeration of left-overs is of utmost importance. The reheating step to prevent *Clostridium perfringens* food poisoning is also of great importance to these consumers.

What about the consumer with specific medical needs such as the immunosuppressed from diseases like AIDS or those receiving cancer chemotherapy, or those malnourished, stressed or otherwise sensitive individuals? Hopefully, their health care provider has properly instructed them about the particular critical control points essential in handling, preparation and consumption of foods. The Food and Drug Administration has prepared an excellent video on food and AIDS that can provide assistance. Pamphlets on food safety and pregnancy have been prepared by both the Centers for Disease Control and Prevention and the Florida Department of Agriculture and Consumer Services. These individuals as well as those with liver and kidney disease and diabetes should not consume raw oysters because of the serious concern of illness or death from *Vibrio vulnificus* infection. Likewise, all consumption of raw animal proteins, including raw eggs, raw milk, raw or inadequately cooked meat, seafood or poultry must be avoided.

And what about the typical teenager? Epidemiological statistics from the Centers for Disease Control and Prevention found a particular spike of campylobacteriosis in college age males. Perhaps, this indicated the need for more mothers to teach young men how to adequately cook chicken before leaving home. Most young men, without proper emphasis on adequate time for heating, would merely cook chicken until browned on the outside.

To properly instruct the consumer, not only do we need to define the demographic profile of the consumers, but also define the number of individuals in the home. Consumers must be provided adequate information and critical control points for the special occasions of life when greatly increased quantities of food and special handling needs surface around holidays and reunions with large quantity food storage and preparation.

11.4 HACCP incorporation into everyday life

11.4.1 Education and training of consumers in HACCP

The National Advisory Committee on Microbiological Criteria for Foods (NACMCF) was formed in 1988 as an advisory body to the US

Departments of Agriculture, Health and Human Services, Commerce and Defense. The committee concluded that education and training are most critical to food safety. The committee stated its belief that effective education can continue to assure the safety of foods and can significantly improve public health by providing consumers with key information on prevention of foodborne diseases.

In 1988, the NACMCF discussed the need for a formal instructional curriculum in food safety including visuals and videos that should be developed for public and private schools. The suggestion was made that the National Advisory Committee recommend and develop a curriculum with a transfer of later responsibility for implementation to the Department of Education and the USDA Extension Service (NACMCF, 1988).

The first official action of the National Advisory Committee on Microbiological Criteria for Foods was in the critical area of education and training. The committee concluded that:

'Training of regulatory officials and industry personnel in the application of Hazard Analysis Critical Control Points (HACCP) is essential. Likewise, consumer education in basic food safety is imperative.'

The requirements identified for such a basic food safety program were:

1. A thorough understanding of risk management and the HACCP system and the differences between HACCP and traditional food inspection systems
2. Knowledge to differentiate critical control points (CCP) from non-critical control points in specific food systems

Education and training in food safety were recommended to be targeted to four groups: regulators, industry, consumers and health professionals. Each of these groups must be given specific information about the safety concerns and critical control points for each food. The committee felt that a basic curriculum on food safety must be developed and implemented both in public and private school systems and should include the development of specific lesson plans in food safety with accompanying audiovisual materials for training. Adequate teacher training is essential with initially targeting teachers in the 4th, 5th and 6th grades. The NACMCF subcommittee also recommended that public service announcements be utilized to foster awareness on food safety principles.

The Advisory Group concluded that for consumers, the goal of microbiological criteria for foods must be an increase in public health and food safety. Education of the consumer is an essential component in achieving this goal. The Committee strongly felt:

'that effective education significantly improves public health by providing consumers key information on the prevention of foodborne illness. A curriculum on basic food safety must be developed and implemented within the public and private school systems.'

Further recommendations centered around targeting of 4th, 5th and 6th graders to effectively change practices and the need for uniform labeling requirements to denote safety needs for temperature control and safe handling.

Other consumer aids recommended were mandatory and uniform labeling for perishable refrigerated items for which temperature is the key element of safety. A uniform format would foster consumer recognition of the importance of temperature requirements to food safety.

11.4.2 Effective modes of communication and training

Communication specialists stress that for effectiveness the form of communication must vary between written, auditory and visual or graphic images. Each of us learn and receive information in a different manner. These same communication experts also stress the need for bright visual images with possible animation for the young while the older citizens prefer information in written form that they may take and refer to at a later time. No matter what our communication goals are, we need some mechanism to measure effectiveness to allow us to monitor whether or not we have communicated the information in such a way that it will be integrated into daily practices by the recipient.

11.4.2.1 Control. Food safety is important from production to ultimate consumption. Consumers have control only over foods from the time they purchase them until they consume them. Consumers do not have control over food production, nor do they control the foods they are served in restaurants or other food service providers. However, consumers can promote safe foods through: (i) their choice of restaurants and stores with good sanitation; (ii) their refusal to accept foods that have not been properly cooked or handled; (iii) their complaints to retail food store and restaurant managers when spoiled foods or problems have been noted; and (iv) their reporting problems to local health departments and state food programs. HACCP for consumers requires us to stress to consumers the areas under their control. We need to distinguish the control points under consumer control from those areas outside the scope of any consumer control.

11.4.2.2 Education and media efforts. Food safety principles have been taught to the general public at varying degrees for many years through the efforts of the Extension Service, universities, FDA and USDA and other agencies. The USDA series entitled *Food Safety is No Mystery* concentrated on areas considered most critical in (i) sanitation and personal hygiene; (ii) safe food preparation; (iii) preventing contamination; and (iv) safe cooling and reheating of food. All components were properly identified, but as in previous food safety educational efforts, although the isolated program was excellent, the integration into everyday life as an ingrained practice was not achieved.

Public perception of the safety of foods is often driven by the media attention of the month. Public perceptions and practices are often influenced by socioeconomic, demographic and ethnic factors. In an attempt to influence or incorporate a food safety practice into control of a food critical control point, we often achieve the undesired effect of merely creating concern and diverting the consumer's purchase to another food for the interim until media and educational focus shift to other targets.

11.4.2.3 Adequate public exposure. In today's hurried world, we either communicate to the public in 30 second sound bites or try to provide more in depth principles within the educational system. If dollars were no object, a food program could demand, as does an opposing political party, equal time to expound upon needed food safety principles after the airing of every food scare story over the TV waves and on nightly news.

11.4.2.4 Top level commitment. We can provide the most detailed and objective plans utilizing multi-disciplinary approaches and innovational education materials. But without top level commitment of all regulatory agencies, industry and health professionals to the incorporation of HACCP principles from harvest to consumption, the road to achievement will be exceedingly slow.

11.4.3 Base line knowledge of consumers on food safety

In a recent 1994 survey of California consumers, Bruhn (personal communication) reports that many of the consumer's food handling practices may lead to bacterial foodborne illnesses. While many had made food handling mistakes, many also relied on certain misinformation and myths regarding foods. Some consumers were even avoiding certain types of foods because of their concerns on safety.

As would be suspected many of the mistakes in handling foods related to temperature abuse. Consumers frequently thawed foods on the counter top or in warm water (56%). On refrigeration, 36% of consumers refrigerated cooked foods in large containers, 15% refrigerated foods in the pot in which it was cooked, and 49% believed that cooked foods should be cooled to room temperature before refrigerating or freezing. Of as much concern was the finding that 65% of consumers tasted leftovers before heating to determine if they were safe to eat and 37% did not regularly clean food preparation surfaces after preparing food. All indicate critical control points for the home food handler.

Accurate evaluation of consumer food safety knowledge and comprehension are difficult without utilizing baseline measurements. Questionnaires and surveys such as those by the Food Marketing Institute, the US Department of Agriculture and the cited survey of Bruhn in California shed some light on individual populations questioned. A baseline must also be gained to allow us to measure whether any programs of education and training that we attempt add to consumer knowledge or change consumer food safety practices.

All food safety information programs need to first incorporate a preliminary questionnaire of knowledge as well as a final evaluation as to whether knowledge has increased. It is very difficult to assess whether providing food safety information significantly improves health status regarding foodborne illness. Very few published reports indicate success of information campaigns on food safety. McLaughlin *et al.* (1991) described the successful informational efforts in the UK to reduce *Listeria* illnesses. Listeriosis cases peaked in 1991 but declined significantly after a massive media campaign to educate consumers.

11.5 Application of HACCP principles for consumers

11.5.1 HACCP implementation

Everyone involved recognizes that HACCP is the best system available for control of the safety of foods, yet many problems remain. A major difficulty is the subject with which we deal in this chapter, the general public or consumer. How citizens perceive HACCP and whether the general public will accept the protective strategy HACCP provides will determine ultimately the success of HACCP implementation.

11.5.2 Pilot community

Perhaps, some visionary community may grasp at the opportunity to show how we can really affect food safety and the life quality concepts of their citizens. If such a community can be found, they could be challenged to teach and incorporate HACCP food concepts and then measure their foodborne illness incidence and knowledge both before and after. Through commitment of day care centers, primary and secondary schools, senior citizen centers and attention of general media, this community could command world attention. In the past whole communities were caught up in weight loss diet focus. To satisfy our epidemiologists we would need to have appropriate investigations of foodborne illnesses, to satisfy our educators we should have pre- and post-assessments as well as lesson plans, to satisfy our scientists and regulators we could require inspections and analysis of food samples in the community, but the ultimate goal to achieve is internalization of the food safety message and change in life practices.

11.5.3   Consumer practices

In general the hygienic and sanitation practices in the home greatly reflect the practices of the previous generation. Traditional practices of cleanliness when handling raw foods, of prevention of cross contamination, of the critical role of refrigeration of foods once purchased, once prepared and after serving are principles rarely taught by the busy parents of today. In our changing demographics, there is rarely a grandmother in the home as an older generation teacher of sound practices. Schools are not emphasizing hygienic practices and health as in the past. An appalling lack of knowledge of basic concepts of food handling is rampant.

Bryan (1988) evaluated factors that contributed to more than 1% of the 345 recognized outbreaks of foodborne illness in homes in the USA from 1973–1982. Factors contributing to foodborne disease in homes in those years included:

- Contaminated raw foods or ingredients
- Unsafe food sources
- Toxic contaminants
- Improper thawing
- Improper fermentation
- Inadequate cooking/canning/heat processing
- Cross contamination
- Colonized person handling food
- Improper hot holding
- Improper use of leftovers
- Inadequate reheating

A later evaluation of these same outbreaks by FSIS indicated that 31.3% of the cases involved undercooking, 22.3% involved improper cooling and 12.8% involved cooking foods ahead with probable undercooking allowing some bacteria to survive.

11.5.4   HACCP principles applied by the consumer

Perhaps the best application of HACCP principles to consumers can be found in a FSIS (1989) summary of a HACCP approach to food safety entitled *A Margin of Safety*. The study covered measurement of food handling knowledge as well as a survey of consumer behavior. Consumer experts, microbiologists and members of a national advisory committee were also surveyed. Six major surveys from 1973 through 1988 were evaluated to determine consumer beliefs and practices.

The surveys included:

1. 1973 Gallop Survey of 816 individuals on *Salmonella* and food poisoning
2. 1974 Economic Research Service on *Food Safety – Homemaker's Attitudes and Practices* with a survey of 2197 individuals
3. 1983 Survey of 100 by M. Woodburn of the Department of Foods and Nutrition at Oregon State University
4. 1983 Survey of 403 individuals entitled *Kansas Food Safety Survey* conducted by C. Kramer, Extension Home Economics, Kansas State University
5. 1987 Survey of 1007 persons by the Food Marketing Institute entitled *Trends – Consumer Attitudes and the Supermarket*, and
6. 1988 FSIS Survey of 3202 consumers on *Health and Diet Cycles*

These surveys, as well as those conducted by FSIS in 1989, revealed an excellent cross section of identified critical control points at every stage of consumer contact with foods. The report concluded that food handling practices almost always determine whether microbial contamination on raw products results in foodborne illness.

For the area of consumer acquisition, USDA identified critical control points in cross contamination, soundness of packaging, and temperature handling. FSIS reported these critical control points as essential practices.

11.5.4.1   Acquisition.

Keep packages of raw meat and poultry separate from other foods, particularly foods that will be eaten without further cooking. For example, use plastic bags on fresh fruits and vegetables. Avoid placing raw meat or poultry in the cart in a manner that will allow fluids to drip on other foods.

Buy packaged precooked foods only if packaging is sound.

Buy products labeled 'keep refrigerated' only if they are stored in a refrigerated case.

Buy unpackaged meat or poultry from deli refrigerated cases only if not in contact with other foods.

Shop for meat and poultry last. Within 2 hours, serve, reheat, refrigerate or freeze cooked foods – within 1 hour if the weather is very warm.

Report problems to store management and if still unsatisfied to local health authorities.

11.5.4.2   Home storage.

Keep raw meat and poultry separate from other foods, particularly those eaten without further cooking. This should also include raw seafood.

Refrigerate food with labels that state 'keep refrigerated'.

If freezer or refrigerator fails, keep door closed. Refreeze meat and poultry only if ice crystals are still present.

11.5.4.3 Preparation.

Wash hands both before and after handling food.

Wash hands with soap and water:

- before preparing food, or
- after handling raw meat, poultry, seafood, or
- after touching animals, or
- after using bathroom, or
- after changing diapers

Do not let juices from raw foods contaminate other foods that are cooked. Wash hands, utensils, counter immediately after use.

Thaw only in the refrigerator, under cold water or in the microwave.

Do not taste any raw food of animal origin.

11.5.4.4 Cooking.

Use thermometer to judge safe cooking temperature recommendations for cooking.

Look for signs of doneness – clear juices, lack of pink in center, etc.

Avoid interrupted cooking and use slow cookers carefully so as to maintain adequate temperatures.

Microwave carefully adhering to recommended stand time, rotation, and cooking instructions.

11.5.4.5 Serving.

Wash hands before serving or eating. Serve cooked products on clean containers with clean utensils.

Keep hot foods hot – above 140°F (60°C).

Leave foods out no longer than 1 hour if hot, over (90°F), and no longer than 2 hours if below 90°F (32°C).

11.5.4.6 Leftovers.

Wash hands before handling food.

Refrigerate in shallow covered containers.

Do not taste leftovers to determine safety.

Reheat properly and thoroughly.

When in doubt, throw it out.

11.5.5   Formation of a HACCP plan for households

To initiate the formation of a HACCP plan for each household will be very difficult. The development of a generic plan incorporating the HACCP principles to be applied to all homes will be of great assistance to initiate the application with the general consumer. Each home's HACCP plan would need additions based on their exact environment, location and the hazards identified.

The HACCP team that will need to draft a HACCP plan for the home might consist of the whole family in a fun but serious exercise. Using a generic HACCP plan for the home (which regrettably, has not been developed), the parents could sit down with the children or other members of the household, devise a flow diagram of the kitchen and the home and complete their specific plan.

After the areas of hazard and the foods that represent a hazard are identified, a check list such as the following example for the refrigerator (Figure 11.1) may be developed. A common sense approach to monitoring through visual senses, adherence to temperature requirements, and appropriate containers of storage can be developed.

11.5.5.1   Conduct a hazards analysis and identify steps to prevent or reduce food safety risk.   Consumers need assistance to assess hazards in food handling unless they have knowledge of food science and food microbiology. Food regulatory agencies both state and federal, and the food industry have a responsibility to properly identify and effectively communicate the hazards and possible steps for their prevention.

Elementary schools for years have effectively sensitized children and their parents to the dangers of fire in the home by sending home check lists for home fire prevention and safety. The fire check list included do's and don'ts, evacuation routes and corrective measures. Properly crafted check lists for HACCP in the home need to be formulated and then taught in the schools along with take home exercises to educate and include parents in the process.

11.5.5.2   Determination of critical control points (CCPs).   The USDA document entitled *A Margin of Safety: The HACCP Approach to Food Safety Education* (FSIS, 1989) carefully outlined some of the critical control points involved in consumer's lives including food acquisition, home storage, preparation, serving and handling of leftovers. This document, while dealing chiefly with meat and poultry, incorporated the

☐ All products in the refrigerator should not show any visible signs of spoilage

☐ Thermometer in refrigerator should read 40°F (4.4°C) or below

☐ Raw meats, poultry and seafood should be separated from other foods and placed on lower shelves or in drawer where no dripping on other foods can occur

☐ All raw foods should be separated from cooked foods

☐ Raw eggs should be stored in adequately cold part of refrigerator

☐ Leftovers should be properly covered

☐ Foods should be rotated so first in are first out, or first purchased are first used

☐ Luncheon meats and refrigerated foods should be used before the 'use by' code date expires

☐ Food label temperature instructions should be followed carefully

☐ Do not store foods in large deep containers that won't cool adequately. Store all cooked foods in shallow pans

☐ Clean up drips and spills immediately

☐ Keep refrigerator clean and sanitary

☐ Store foods so that there is adequate air space around foods to let air circulate and to keep the foods properly cold

Figure 11.1 Refrigerator check list.

major principles that apply to all food handling and could be used as a framework for the formulation of a generic '*HACCP for the HOME Plan*'.

11.5.5.3   Establish critical limits for preventive measures at each CCP. Critical limits in a consumer HACCP plan must be common sense and easily understood. The critical limits might include such simple directions as limiting leftover use to four days. Throwing out all foods after a picnic if they have not been adequately refrigerated in a cooler for the entire day, and other common sense limits.

11.5.5.4 Monitoring and incentives for consumers to implement HACCP.
The main consumer incentive is increased food safety through prevention,
but this is difficult to monitor and document.

As a preventive system, HACCP can greatly contribute to the health
care needs of an individual. But, documentation of HACCP programs in
the home cannot be accomplished under ordinary circumstances. Perhaps,
one incentive might be a monetary reduction in health insurance costs if
HACCP in the home could be documented. Other precedents have been
set that may be applied to facilitate HACCP implementation. Historically,
certain insurance firms have given discounted automobile insurance and
reduced premiums upon proof of a teenager's completion of Driver's
Education courses in high school. Additionally, some corporations and
states provide lower cost health insurance programs if an individual is a
part of a HMO or preventive health maintenance group. Some innovative
insurance company in the idealistic world of tomorrow may contemplate a
reduction in health care costs with documentation of a home HACCP
program.

The latter incentives are perhaps beyond the realm of realistic
expectations for the 1990s yet we should not refrain from brainstorming for
the future. Other incentives that might be proposed include:

1. Teach 4th through 6th graders how to monitor for food safety hazards
   and include some credit or award for achievement.
2. Include a generic HACCP plan and implementing strategy in such
   programs as Women, Infants and Children (WIC).
3. Structure programs or badges on food safety and HACCP to be earned
   by Girl Scouts, Boy Scouts, 4-H clubs and other such organizations.

11.5.5.5 Corrective actions.   Corrective actions are even more difficult
to contemplate at the consumer level. Corrective actions need to be
outlined for each possible deviation or poor handling practice. HACCP
implementation will control and prevent microbial growth and food safety
hazards. If this is effective, there will be no need for corrective action.
Deviations would be found only through either an on-site visit or
occurrence of foodborne illness of some type.

For effective consumer HACCP programs, we should contemplate
mandatory HACCP training for any family associated with salmonellosis in
day care centers or foodborne illness from an implicated home origin.

11.5.5.6 Record keeping.   No one likes to keep records, neither consumers nor the industry. This principle will be difficult to encourage for
consumers. If HACCP for consumers is ever fully implemented, records of
their efforts may only be for incentive awards or some type of home audit.
Nevertheless, the importance of all seven principles and the reason for
their need should be emphasized.

11.5.5.7 HACCP verification.   Again, verification of HACCP implementation is a very difficult principle to achieve for consumer applications.
Through interviews and discussions with key target groups, some verification
of their implementation of HACCP may be gained. The true measure of
HACCP will be prevention, control and acceptance of responsibilities for
conditions involving food safety in the home.

11.6 Conclusions

Our world is now attempting to feed 5.5 billion people around the globe.
How can we maintain the safety of this massive food supply? In the next
four decades, how will we be able to harvest twice as much food
worldwide, according to projected population needs, and still provide
adequate nutrients in a safe manner? Changes and new food safety systems
must be incorporated to achieve the goal of a continued safe food supply.
   In *Future Shock 2000*, Alvin Toffler (1970) observes that:

   'The illiterate of the year 2000 will not be the individual who cannot read or
   write, but the one who cannot learn, unlearn and relearn.'

The year 2000 is upon us now.
   We must convince consumers that as popular authors John Naisbett and
Patricia Aburdene (1985) remind us in *Re-inventing the Corporation*:

   'In the new information society where the only constant is change, we no longer
   expect to get an education and be done with it . . . society has turned all of us
   into lifelong learners.'

Protection of the safety of our food supply and the application of
HACCP principles to assure safety and provide preventive control are such
lifelong learning processes. Practical common sense, the learning process,
willing and accessible assistance must be our emphasis for the everyday
citizen – not complicated scientific jargon. Helping All Consumers Cope
with Problems is our goal for the future.
   We must not forget to convey a very simple basic message to all
consumers. The message is that we all can exercise a great deal of control
in our everyday lives. HACCP provides consumers an effective tool for the
prevention and control of food safety hazards in the home.

References

Archer, D.L. and Kvenberg, J.E. (1985) Incidence and cost of foodborne diarrheal disease in
   the United States. *J. Food Protect.* **53**, 887.
Archer, D.L. and Young, F.E. (1988) Contemporary issues: Diseases with a food vector.
   Clinical Microbiol. Rev. **1**, 377.

Bean, N.H. and Griffin, P.M. (1990) Foodborne disease outbreaks in the United States 1973–1987: Pathogens, vehicles and trends. *J. Food Prot.* **53**, 804.

Brewer, M.S. and Sprouls, G.K, and Russon, C. (1993) Consumer attitudes toward food safety issues. *J. Food Safety* **14**, 63.

Bryan (1988) Risk of practices, procedures and processes that lead to foodborne disease. *J. Food Prot.* **51**, 663.

Bruhn (1994) *California Consumers Food Handling Mistakes and Myths*. Personal communication.

Ditmus, K.L. and Hillers, V.N. (1993) Consumer trust and behavior related to pesticides. *Food Technol.* **47**(7), 87.

FSIS (1989) *A Margin of Safety: The HACCP Approach to Food Safety Education*. US Department of Agriculture, Washington, D.C.

FSIS (1993) *Report on the* Escherichia coli *0157:H7 Outbreaks in the Western States*. The Food Safety and Inspection Service, US Department of Agriculture, Washington, D.C.

Karr, K., Maretzki, J.N. and Knabel, S.J. (1994) Meat and poultry companies assess USDA's hazard analysis and critical control point system. *Food Technol,* **48**(2), 117.

Kayser, A. and Mossel, A.A. (1984) Wilson: The only valid approach to microbiological safety of food. *Internat. J. Food Microbiol. Intervention Census* **11**:1.

McLaughlin, J., Hall, S.M., Velani, S.K, and Gilbert, R.J. (1991) Human listeriosis and pate: A possible association. *Brit. Med. J.* **303**, 773.

McNutt, K.W., Powers, M.E. and Sloan, A.E. (1986) Food colors, flavors and safety: A consumer viewpoint. *Food Technol.* **40**(1), 72.

NACMCF (1992) Hazard analysis and critical control point system. The National Advisory Committee on Microbiological Criteria for Foods. *Internat. J. Food Microbiol.* **16**, 1.

NACMCF (1993) *Generic HACCP for Raw Beef*. The National Advisory Committee on Microbiological Criteria for Foods. Food Safety and Inspection Services, Washington, D.C.

Naisbett, J. and Aburdene, P. (1985) *Re-inventing the Corporation*. Warner Books, New York.

National Academy Press (1985) An Evaluation of the Role of Microbiological Criteria for Foods and Food Ingredients. **1**, 329.

Potter, M. (1993) Personal communication to the National Advisory Committee on Microbiological Criteria for Foods.

Rhodes, M.E. (1991) Educating professionals and consumers about extended shelf-life refrigerated foods. *Food Technol.* **45**(4), 162.

Roberts, T. and Van Ravenswaay, E. (1989) *The Economics of Safeguarding the U.S. Food Supply*. Agric. Inform. Bull. No. 566, US Department of Agriculture, Economic Research Services, Washington, D.C.

Sachs, C., Blair, D. and Richter, C. (1987) Consumer pesticide concerns: A 1965–1984 comparison. *J. Consumer Affairs* **21**, 96.

Slovic, P. (1986) Informing and educating the public about risk. *Risk Analysis* **6**(4), 403.

Tarr, P.I. (1994) *Escherichia coli* 0157:H7: Overview of clinical and epidemiological issues. *J. Food Protect.* **57**(7), 632.

Toffler, A. (1970) *Future Shock 2000*. Random House, New York.

US Food and Drug Administration (1991) *Preventing foodborne illnesses in nursing homes*. Videos and Teaching Guide. Department of Health and Human Services, Washington, D.C.

US Public Health Service (1991) *Healthy People 2000: National Healthy Promotion and Disease Prevention Objectives*. Department of Health and Human Services, Washington, D.C.

US Public Health Service (1993) *Healthy People 2000 Review 1993*. Department of Health and Human Services, Washington, D.C.

US Government Printing Office (1994) *Federal Register*. January 11, **59**, 1499.

Warren, V.A., Hillers, V.N. and Jennings, G.E. (1990) Beliefs about food supply safety: A study of cooperative extension clientele. *J. Amer. Diet. Assoc.* **90**, 713.

Woodburn, M. and Van DeRiet, S. (1985) Safe food: Care labeling for perishable foods. *Home Econ. Res. J.* **14**(1), 1.

12 Organization and management of HACCP programs

D.M. THENO

12.1 Introduction

The function of management in the HACCP process is to provide focus and support. These efforts are to be directed solely toward the successful operation of the facility's food safety programs.

Focus and support within the context of this discussion may assume several roles, such as active personal support, financial support, integration with compensation programs, or bringing HACCP to operational equivalency with other key programs. In fact, the required level of support from management is the issue that concerns many senior managers when they are first confronted with HACCP systems. Management support is essential in that it sends a strong message to all participants about the HACCP system's importance to the success of the overall company. The continuing focus helps reinforce the importance of the programs. Full integration of HACCP program operation with performance evaluation or incentive systems can also help to provide system support and focus.

The complexity and scope of HACCP systems is what concerns, and in many cases scares managers. To help alleviate some of the fears, it is best to address them at the outset. Philosophically, HACCP systems are *common sense based* programs designed to prevent hazards. The wisdom of preventive vs. later remedial treatment is well understood. Because many of the hazards to be controlled cannot be detected visually, it is essential to rely on monitoring systems to ensure that safety is preserved. Virtually all machine driven functions rely on remote monitoring systems to provide an indication of their operating conditions, e.g. temperature, RPMs, speed, etc. So it is with the monitoring systems of HACCP.

12.2 Documentation of HACCP systems

Although paperwork has seemingly become the scourge of our existence, HACCP systems do require documentation to be effective. While it is true that HACCP systems do require an organized reporting system, many people find that the HACCP based paperwork will replace most, if not all, of the existing food safety based reports. It is not uncommon for the HACCP system to also replace some ongoing operationally based reports. As with other essential programs within a facility, the paper trail (hopefully soon to become primarily an electronic trail) is a tool for management to gauge the overall operating condition of the food safety programs. Appropriate comparative programs with similar requirements include employee safety, inventory management and productivity systems. An old management adage which applies to documentation is: you can't manage what you can't measure.

All this can seem somewhat overwhelming, but there is good news at hand. Within almost all food systems today the critical control points (which are the heart of the HACCP system) are being effectively met and controlled. This is evidenced by the continuing safety record of the products and processes that the plants produce every day without benefit of a formal HACCP system. The simple fact is, that HACCP based systems are a better management tool to ensure that food safety programs are actively managed and that hazards are prevented or controlled. When properly organized, the HACCP system will have a tiered operations and management reporting system similar to other production control programs.

12.3 Phases of HACCP system implementation and management requirements

The time requirement to install a HACCP system can vary greatly and can be dependent upon numerous factors, but will tie closely to the complexity of the food systems to be covered. All HACCP systems do, however, go through three generic phases from introduction through to the full integration into operations. These phases are: (1) design and introduction, (2) integration, and (3) operation. The reason for discussing these phases separately is that they often require different time and resource commitments from the management team.

12.3.1 Design and introduction

The design and introduction phase should be best viewed as a time when change and transitional management techniques can be applied. At this stage many companies seek outside help to deal with the risk assessment aspects of the HACCP program. An expert, whether outside or inside, can also help keep the process moving. It is this phase that contains numerous areas where development of the system can get mired down in details. An essential element of this stage is the initiation of an education program for all people who will be part of the program. The people who will be responsible for operation of the system must be told what is expected, why it is important, and what each individual employee's role is in ensuring the safety of the food products under their care.

12.3.1.1 Designing the HACCP program.   This phase requires allowance of time for employees to design and plan the HACCP system. Usually the team members are key players within the organization so it is especially important to be sensitive to the overall time demands and constraints of the project. A useful technique to minimize the effect on the entire organization's time is to initiate a pilot HACCP project with a relatively uncomplicated process or product. This small pilot project can then be utilized as a learning tool and also as a demonstration project for the rest of the organization (Schaffer, 1988).

12.3.1.2 The individual employee's role in HACCP.   The individual employee's role in the HACCP programs must start to be addressed at this phase. Within a HACCP based structure the responsibility *and* account- ability for complying with Critical Control Points (CCPs) and taking corrective action is placed in the hands of the people actually performing the task. The shift from supervision driven control to operator driven control is usually welcomed by the operators and viewed with skepticism by much of the supervisory staff. Part of the educational process must include the transition of the supervisory people into a new role as facilitators and coaches. Many management texts are available that describe techniques to help make that transition (Peters, 1987).

During the design and introduction phase the existing food safety systems must be maintained. The existing systems should be run in parallel with the new HACCP program *until* the HACCP team and the management team are confident that the HACCP system is fully operational.

12.3.2 Integrating the HACCP system into total operation

The integration of the HACCP system into the total operation is the next phase of the process. The programs at this stage are designed and should have been successfully tested, the educational requirements have been met or are well underway, and the transition of responsibility has been accomplished. Typically the integration phase will require 90–180 days. This phase should be viewed as an installation exercise requiring facilitation management techniques.

The management team needs to closely monitor this phase of the process to provide support or guidance as soon as the need is identified. This particular part of the process will require high levels of communication across all levels of the organization. Where/when communication barriers exist, they must be immediately resolved.

12.3.2.1 Reporting and verification.   Another key element of this phase is structuring the reporting and verification systems and integration with the corrective action plan. The monitoring system for the actual CCPs is generally driven by the requirement of the CCP (location, measurement, criteria, etc.). The verification systems and HACCP management programs must provide assurance that the food safety programs are being successfully operated. However they should assume the shape or form best suited to the needs of the HACCP system, HACCP team or facility management style (Peters, 1987).

The majority of facilities with HACCP systems format the HACCP management verification systems to be consistent with the other management reporting systems within the facility. Tiered exception reporting systems are frequently utilized. These can provide the level of detail necessary for each management level within the overall structure to effectively monitor their programs. The records kept from the HACCP program need not be kept forever. In rare instances, legal requirements may mandate that records be maintained for a specified duration. However, most people keep the records for the probable duration of the life of the food product through consumption. Thus, products with short shelf life (less than 30 days) probably do not need to retain records past 45 or 60 days. Products with a long shelf life will need to retain HACCP records for a longer duration.

12.3.2.2 Corrective actions.   One of the most important pieces of a HACCP system is the definition and execution of corrective actions to be performed when or where CCPs are exceeded. It is inevitable that CCPs will not be met all the time and proper corrective actions must then be implemented. The corrective actions should be thoroughly described in written and verbal formats to the person charged with the responsibility to take the corrective action. Many companies find it useful to visibly post the corrective actions with the CCPs at the CCP surveillance points. All corrective actions should also be logged with the CCP report. Thus, upon examination, the HACCP tracking record should profile when a CCP was not met along with who and what was accomplished to bring the process back under control. Because CCPs are the essential step in assuring food safety, it is advisable to have the operator notify a supervisor or technical support person when a CCP is not met, as part of the 'normal' corrective action process. This will serve as both an alert to supervision and help with team problem solving.

The simpler and more complete the described corrective actions are, the better their execution during operation. Good record keeping of CCP exceptions and resultant corrective actions will enable a management review to gauge the overall effectiveness of the HACCP program. The record keeping is also essential to demonstrate that the process has been brought back into the desired parameters of the HACCP program, which has also been found useful in situations where a legal defense is necessary.

12.3.2.3 Overcoming obstacles to HACCP systems. During the integration phase, obstacles will be encountered. Some will be structure related and will require program modification. Remember, there is no absolutely right way to structure a HACCP system, it is a tool for the operation to manage food safety. The tool should be structured so that it is entirely user friendly. Reporting systems that are easy to use must be utilized; those that are difficult to use will have complaints and problems. The solution to obstacles can be as simple as moving a clipboard to a more convenient location – or placing a sanitizing station in proximity to those that need it. Some of the problems encountered will be people related. Personnel that lack confidence in the HACCP approach can view the normal problems associated with any large system introduction as a sign of the HACCP program's weakness. It is vital that the communication channels remain open and active to correct misperception.

12.3.3 Operations of the HACCP program

Once the systems are installed and the team is confident that the HACCP system is complete, the operational phase of the process begins. At this point the HACCP systems are the management tool for food safety. The HACCP program must be on at least an operational equivalency with other major management programs in the facility.

Traditional (non-HACCP based) quality systems tended to be static programs. HACCP systems are designed to help identify areas for improvement resulting in program evolution and enhancement. The information necessary to allow the system to evolve will be developed from within the program itself. An organized periodic review of the program by the management team is an effective means to keep the evolutionary process moving.

Through combination with other management tools, the HACCP program can be fully integrated into the everyday structure and operation of the facility. Linking HACCP systems with performance criteria provides a clear message about the importance of food safety.

12.3.3.1 Evaluation of the HACCP program. System support through this phase requires ongoing education (retraining in some cases and full training for new employees). The management team can also help provide focus by simply asking/demonstrating interest in how the HACCP system is being operated. While walking through the facility it is possible to broadly assess the program's status by asking a few simple questions:

1. Have all CCPs been monitored at the established frequency? If not, why?
2. Where CCPs have not been met, have proper corrective actions been accomplished?
3. Have the foundation programs been acceptably maintained (potable water, refrigeration, etc.)?
4. Have any extraordinary circumstances occurred which may have compromised the integrity of the HACCP system (sewer back ups, ill employees, etc.)?

If these few questions can be answered satisfactorily, then there is good reason to be confident that the food safety management system is functioning as designed. As a result, if the program is properly designed, then the answers will also provide the necessary assurance of the safety of the food products covered by the HACCP program.

12.4   Producing the framework/structure to ensure that the HACCP program is a success

Management systems must always be structured so as to provide the intended end-result. Since HACCP-based food safety systems require active, 'real-time' management to be effective, the structure of the management program should reflect the real-time requirement. Designing the management program to fit the facility and staff needs will entail a review of documentation requirements, training systems and physical layout, as well as any other factors that will typically be germane to other effective management programs (Drucker, 1973).

12.4.1   Role of personnel to success of HACCP programs

Since people are the key element in successful program management, we will address this need first. Education and training are essential for the program to be successful. Individuals will be required to understand what they are to monitor, how they are to monitor and document, what to do if the critical control points are not met, and, perhaps most importantly, why they are doing what they are doing and the true importance of the tasks in the protection of public health.

12.4.1.1   Training programs.   Training programs must be tailored to the target audience which is predominantly a non-scientific population. Thus, the training should be structured to make it relevant and easy to comprehend by non-technical people. Examples of good programs include the National Restaurant Association's Education Foundation sponsored ServSafe program and/or any number of technical seminars in the manufacturing segment targeted to the production employee.

When possible it is advantageous in the educational process to include specific examples that are applicable to the individual employee's job. In short, any teaching which facilitates the learning process will help expedite the integration of the HACCP system. By providing the rationale behind the program, individual employee understanding and 'buy-in' is increased.

Once the employee commitment to HACCP is secured, the participants can help to design and structure the monitoring, recording, and corrective action systems. Having the participants design the monitoring programs for which they will ultimately be responsible further develops the level of commitment to the program. An interesting side benefit of the self-design process is that 'other' suggestions start to surface regarding non-HACCP programs such as productivity, efficiency, etc. The self-design elements allow the program to tap into the knowledge reservoir of the individual employee and the collective wisdom of the labor team's experiences.

12.4.1.2 Dealing with problems. The classic management mistake of actions not matching stated philosophy looms at all times with HACCP systems. It is imperative that management 'walk the talk' in all matters concerning the operation of the HACCP system. Even a slight shift in management commitment that is communicated (even inadvertently) to the employees involved in HACCP program operation can have a profound negative effect on the overall program.

Where or when HACCP problems arise within the program they must be dealt with immediately. In well designed, mature programs, most difficulties arise from either failed monitoring systems and/or human error. Problems with these two underlying causes are relatively easy to remedy. Of greater concern are problems which may arise from other non-directly related underlying areas within the production system, which contain structural weaknesses. Faults of this variety have the potential to compromise the entire system without providing any direct early warning through the normal HACCP program operation.

Thus, all support systems must also 'fit' the HACCP system. These can include ingredients/supplies, equipment, facility maintenance and even the occasional corporate visitor. The HACCP system is designed to operate independently within a designed controlled set of conditions. Any outside influence which alters those conditions may compromise the integrity of the system. Ingredients must meet all HACCP related specifications before they are utilized. The facility and its maintenance must allow the HACCP system to be operated without compromising food safety criteria such as temperature requirements or freedom from extraneous material contamination. All personnel that visit a HACCP based facility must understand enough about the working of the HACCP program that their presence in the facility does not compromise the program.

12.4.1.3 Monitoring, reporting and tracking the HACCP program.

In summary regarding organization, structure and framework, all parts of the facility/company must operate together to successfully utilize HACCP systems. All ingredients and materials related to the food systems must be integrated and fit the intended end product. All physical systems within the plant must operate as designed and calibrated to ensure that the process is accomplished as designed in a manner that provides an environment of food safety for the intended end product. Management monitoring, reporting and tracking systems must be sufficient to actively manage the programs and to resolve problems as they occur. Employee support programs such as training, analytical service or re-supply, must enable those charged with operating the program to do so efficiently. Groups that provide delivery service to your facility and those that transport the end product to the consumer must all be brought into the HACCP food safety chain. And lastly, helping to keep the HACCP program top of mind for all employees requires unwavering support and focus by senior management.

12.4.2 A few painful lessons and helpful hints

A failure of the HACCP program can lead to catastrophic consequences. Thus, where early failures by others have demonstrated system weakness, they should be shared for the betterment of all. A few institutional lessons that do not need repeating follow, the names, locales and participants' identities being omitted to protect all concerned.

12.4.2.1 Importance of instructions on corrective actions.

In one case a worker was tasked as part of their HACCP role with monitoring a sifting screen for foreign objects and instructed what to do if objects were found. However, no instructions were provided as to what actions to take if the screen were to fail, which it did over a period of several weeks. The deterioration of the screen was dutifully chronicled day by day as required by the operator. The helpful hints here are: make sure the operator knows the why of what they are doing so that they can take appropriate corrective action; someone should periodically verify the record keeping system; and lastly, it is always a good idea to involve another level of decision making into the corrective action loop when a CCP is exceeded. A large, expensive recall ensued, but public exposure to the contamination was avoided.

12.4.2.2 Importance of clear guidelines.

In a second situation, strict guidelines were provided to food service workers about minimum effective levels of sanitizing solutions. In this case, no guidelines were provided about maximum levels or the effects of higher than maximum concentrations. The employees diligently monitored the minimum standard concentration. To ensure that they would never fall below the minimum standard, they started adding an extra cup of the concentrated sanitizer. Luckily, the odor was strong enough that the situation become apparent rather quickly and was subsequently brought into the desired range without exposing customers to high levels of sanitizer. The helpful hints here once again center around full training regarding the employees' role in ensuring proper CCP operation, and providing thorough guidelines about how and why (e.g. minimum *and* maximum) a procedure is to be controlled.

12.4.2.3 Importance of providing tools and time for employee to perform duties. In a third example, a receiving dock employee was tasked with monitoring receiving temperatures of refrigerated ingredients. The HACCP forms called for taking an air temperature of the trailer and a temperature of the product. The employee was provided with a hand held metal thermometer with an 8 inch (20 cm) stem. On the day in question two major problems arose. A number of deliveries occurred in a short time period requiring the employee to do more than one trailer at a time. Due to the added stress of the need to unload rapidly, the employee just took surface temperature of the pallets in each trailer rather than the customary, more thorough sampling called for in the HACCP program. In addition, to accomplish the multiple trailer monitoring, the employee had borrowed another thermometer from a fellow employee that could be inserted into product and left in one spot to equilibrate while other tasks were being accomplished.

In this case, two failures occurred. First, one of the trailers had suffered a refrigeration unit malfunction enroute to the plant and the unit had stayed on a defrost cycle for greater than 30 hours with product temperatures probably exceeding 50°F (10°C) for a prolonged time. When the unit finally straightened itself out, it recooled the tops of the pallets, but the center and bottoms remained warm and microbiologically spoiled. The spoiled product was discovered through organoleptic means (it smelled bad) during the blending process and subsequent investigation revealed the source of the problem before it was compounded by blending.

Second, in the employee's haste to take care of the multiple trailers, the second thermometer was forgotten and lost. The missing thermometer unfortunately did not show up until one of the final CCPs in the plant located fragments of the thermometer in the finished product as it was being screened through a metal detector. In both cases, public health was protected, but either situation could have resulted in foodborne illnesses and/or foreign object exposure had other systems not been in effect.

The hints to take away from this event are: (i) provide employees with sufficient tools and time to do their HACCP assignment correctly;

(ii) closely monitor tools involved with the food to make sure they do not become a contaminant of the food stream either through loss or damage; and (iii) provide an environment that encourages people to stop the process and correct a problem situation immediately if a mistake occurs.

12.4.2.4   Product safety is the primary goal of HACCP system.   The final example involves an employee and plant supervisor. The employee's HACCP task was to monitor and operate a metal detector. The unit alarm went off and the employee tagged all product up to the last recorded lot number and stopped the line. The product in question was held and the unit re-calibrated before re-running the suspect product which again tripped the alarm. The product was removed for physical examination and a metal ball-point pen insert was found, mostly intact. Along with the ink barrel, several plastic pieces of the pen body were identified in some of the product during the physical examination. The employees in question placed the entire lot on hold. Later that afternoon, a supervisor reviewed the product and the process under which the product had been detained and decided that enough of the pen had been found to warrant release of the product for distribution. The remainder of the pen was subsequently found by consumers and appropriate regulatory agencies were later involved. No serious injuries resulted, but several legal actions were initiated, regulatory censure ensued and several employees were disciplined or terminated, including the supervisor who released the product. The hint to take away from this situation is that all people within the facility must understand that the safety of the product is of primary importance. A useful tool for gauging an employee's comfort level with the safety of a product is to ask whether they would be comfortable serving it to their own family.

These examples are not meant to be all inclusive nor to answer all questions. In retrospect, it is easy to see how situations may develop which can compromise the HACCP system. In all cases, had the HACCP system been implemented and operated correctly, with no gray areas for incomplete or miscommunication, none of the situations should ever have occurred.

12.5   Summary

The use of HACCP based systems to manage food safety is currently the best available technology to control the most critical management element of the food business environment. HACCP based food safety systems must be viewed for design, implementation, integration and operation at an awareness/focus level at least on par with other key management tools.

Management's primary function in this endeavor once again, is to provide support and focus.

Techniques, which can help facilitate the process, are starting with a small pilot project to help with the learning curve. Education and communication skills will play key roles in the success of the programs. Participant 'buy in' and commitment are good indications of the success of the process. A set of simple system reinforcement questions can help to ensure that everyone understands management's position on the importance of the HACCP program, and every employee's role in ensuring the safety of the food products that they produce.

References

Drucker, P.F. (1973) *Management*. Chapter 42. Harper and Row, New York.

Peters, T. (1987) *Thriving On Chaos*. Chapters S-2 , S-3, P-4 and P-5, Alfred A. Knopf, Inc., New York.

Schaffer, R.H. (1988) *The Breakthrough Strategy*. Chapter 7. Ballinger Publishing Co., Cambridge, Massachusetts.

13 Predictive microbiology and HACCP

T. ROSS and T.A. McMEEKIN

'In place of time-consuming, cost-prohibitive, and ineffective microbiological testing, physical and chemical measurements can be used as indirect measures of microbiological control. In these instances, the correlation between the physical or chemical parameters with the microbiological parameters would first need to be determined'.

(Moberg, 1992)

13.1 Introduction

The HACCP approach in the food industry has most often been applied to the prevention of microbiological problems, particularly the prevention of foodborne infection or intoxication. The analysis of microbiological hazards[1] and definition of critical control points remains, however, an inexact process. General sources of information to assist in this process include the scientific literature, consumer complaints, prior documentation of health risks associated with the product, regulatory authority recommendations and bulletins and reports of disease surveillance authorities, (e.g. CDC,[2] PHLS[3]). Structured systems to guide HACCP teams through this process, in the form of a series of pro forma and questionnaires, (IAMFES, 1991; NACMCF, 1992; CACFH, 1993), decision trees (NACMCF, 1992) or of interactive computer programmes (CFDRA, 1992) are valuable aids. Generic HACCP models, applicable to particular product types, have also been prepared and published (Stier, 1992; MFSCNFPA, 1993). Nonetheless, many fundamental questions cannot be answered quantitatively from such sources, e.g.:

1. Is this process step a *critical* control point, e.g. how many, if any, doublings of *Salmonella* could the time–temperature conditions of this process step lead to?
2. How will the substitution of a pH constraint for a water activity constraint in this product affect the probability that *C. botulinum* spores will germinate and grow if temperature abuse subsequently occurs?

---

[1]HACCP is applicable to problems of food spoilage also (*see* §13.3.3). In this context, food spoilage may also be considered a microbiological 'hazard'.
[2]CDC: Centers for Disease Control, Atlanta, Georgia, USA.
[3]PHLS: Public Health Laboratory Service, London, UK.

3. Will the energy savings involved in altering the time–temperature conditions of the pasteurisation step be nullified because the proportion of the microbial load killed is now inadequate to guarantee safety?
4. Given that a loss of pH control has occurred, what is the *magnitude* of the increased health risk, and what consequences does this have for the fate of the product (e.g. continue process, redirect to a more stringent process, discard)?

The ability to generate quantitative answers to such questions is now being made possible through the development of 'predictive microbiology'.

13.2 Predictive microbiology

Predictive microbiology is an emerging area of food microbiology in which microbial responses to environmental factors are measured under defined and controlled conditions. The responses are quantified and summarised in the form of mathematical equations which, by interpolation, can predict responses to novel sets of conditions, i.e. those which were not actually tested. Proponents claim that such an approach will enable:

1. Prediction of the consequences, for product shelf life and safety, of changes to product formulation.
2. Objective evaluation of the consequences of lapses in process and storage control.
3. The rational design of new processes and products to meet required levels of safety and shelf life.

13.2.1 Relationship of predictive modelling to HACCP

The general relationship between the HACCP approach and predictive modelling is almost intuitive, and has been discussed by a number of authors. Genigeorgis (1981) noted that 'predictive microbiology' would provide a rational basis for the drafting of guidelines, criteria and standards pertaining to the microbiological status of food. Broughall *et al.* (1983) considered that the concept of HACCP had often been applied to food processes in the absence of information about factors which influence microbial growth. They derived models to predict the growth rate of *Staphylococcus aureus* and *Salmonella typhimurium* in response to temperature and water activity. It was concluded that an interaction between the effects of temperature and water activity, revealed by their modelling studies, was an important consideration in the valid application of HACCP analysis to food processing and distribution cycles. Broughall and Brown (1984) extended this work to include pH effects and again stressed the wider application of their models to risk analysis and HACCP. Roberts

(1989) also indicated the complementary nature of HACCP and predictive modelling, a theme expanded by McMeekin *et al.* (1992) who considered that predictive microbiology could be viewed as an extension of the HACCP concept.

13.2.1.1 Advantages of predictive modelling.   Buchanan and Deroever (1993) discussed in detail the thought processes and evaluation of information that characterise the hazard analysis phase of good HACCP programs. They identified, implicitly, the role of predictive modelling in microbiological profiling, one of four approaches which they considered needed to be integrated to enable objective assessment of food safety, and as a precursor to the rational establishment of priorities and resource allocation in the area of food safety. Humber (1992) more specifically identified several of the roles of predictive models within HACCP programs. He wrote:

> 'Predictive models can be useful in assessing the safety risks of new product formulations even before the formulations have been manufactured for the first time in a pilot plant, or sold in a test market. Models can be used to predict both the microbiological safety and quality of a formula, thus giving the manufacturer the opportunity to review the health risks and spoilage potential of a product long before it is eaten by the consumer. Control points relating to safety, quality and regulatory issues can often be more easily identified in advance through the use of predictive models'.

In this chapter we will develop and exemplify our belief that:

> 'predictive modelling enables the objective evaluation of the microbiological consequences of food processing and handling operations and, from this, empowers the HACCP strategy' (McMeekin and Ross, 1993).

13.2.2 History of predictive microbiology

Reviews of predictive modelling are numerous (Farber, 1986; McMeekin and Olley, 1986; Baird-Parker and Kilsby, 1987; Gibson and Roberts, 1989; Gould 1989; Roberts, 1989, 1990; Buchanan, 1992a; Ross and McMeekin, 1994). A monograph on the subject has been prepared by McMeekin *et al.* (1993). A brief history, drawn from the latter two publications is given here.

The proposals of Roberts and Jarvis (1983) may be viewed as the foundation stone of the rapid development of predictive microbiology in the subsequent decade. They challenged traditional methods of food quality and assurance testing, which they described as 'an expensive and largely negative science', and advocated a more systematic and cooperative approach. Roberts (1990) recounts:

> 'we have proposed the concept of 'predictive microbiology' within which the growth responses of the microbes of concern would be modelled with respect to

the main controlling factors such as temperature, pH and a_w . . . Models relevant to broad categories of foods would greatly reduce the need for *ad hoc* microbiological examination and enable predictions of quality and safety to be made speedily with considerable financial benefit'.

The need for such an approach had been recognised earlier. Scott (1937) wrote:

'A knowledge of the rates of growth of certain microorganisms at different temperatures is essential to the studies of the spoilage of chilled beef. Having these data it should be possible to predict the relative influence on spoilage exerted by various microorganisms at each storage temperature. Further it would be feasible to predict the possible extent of changes in populations during the initial cooling of sides of beef in the meatworks when the meat surfaces are frequently at temperatures very favourable to microbial proliferation'.

It should be noted, however, that it is equally important to know which of the microorganisms present are the most important in terms of deterioration of product safety or quality. Dalgaard (1993) showed that, on vacuum- or modified atmosphere packed cod, the most abundant organism at spoilage was *Shewanella putrefaciens* but that the spoilage process was mainly due to *Photobacterium phosphoreum*, which represented only one-tenth of the total microbial population at spoilage. Dalgaard emphasised the importance of identifying 'specific spoilage organisms', and basing models to predict spoilage on the activity of these organisms. Similarly, modelling of food safety should be based on species and strains of relevance. This issue will be discussed further in §13.3.1.1.

McMeekin *et al.* (1993) suggested that two related trends contributed to increased willingness to consider predictive modelling in the 1980s. The first was the marked increase in the incidence of major food poisoning outbreaks during the 1980s, which led to an acutely increased public awareness of the requirement for a safe and wholesome food supply. The second was the realisation by many food microbiologists, and clearly identified by Roberts and Jarvis (1983), that traditional, and many 'rapid', microbiological methods to determine quality and safety were limited by the time needed to obtain results and had little *predictive* value. Buchanan (1991) pointed to another factor in the realisation of the concept: that of increased access to computing power.

The use of mathematical models in food microbiology is not new. Baird-Parker and Kilsby (1987) point out that models for the thermal destruction of microorganisms by heat are well established in the literature and industry, e.g. the 'botulinum cook' (Stumbo *et al.*, 1983). Mathematical modelling is also well established in the fermentation industry (Crueger and Crueger, 1990). The application of mathematical modelling techniques to the *growth* and *survival* of microorganisms in foods, however, did not receive wide attention until the 1980s.

13.2.3 Modelling approaches

'Predictive microbiology' has been considered to encompass two main sub-disciplines, namely *kinetic* modelling and *probability* modelling.

13.2.3.1 Kinetic models. The hypothesis underlying the kinetic modelling approach is that many perishable foods represent a 'pristine' environment open to exploitation by microorganisms, and that the growth of bacteria in this environment approximates a 'batch culture'. Typically, nutrients will not limit growth until spoilage has occurred or infectious dose levels are exceeded. Consequently, factors such as temperature, pH, water availability, gaseous atmosphere, preservatives, etc. dictate the rate and extent of microbial proliferation. Thus, a detailed knowledge of the growth responses of microorganisms to those environmental factors should enable prediction of the extent of microbial proliferation in foods during processing, distribution and storage by monitoring the *environment* presented to the organism by the food during those operations.

In the area of kinetic modelling, growth rates and lag times are modelled and predictions are made by evaluating the fitted function. Models are constructed by following the increase in numbers or biomass of the organism for a range of levels and combinations of environmental factors of interest to generate information about lag phase duration, rate of growth and maximum population density achieved.

13.2.3.2 Probability models. The hypothesis underlying the probability modelling approach is that the *probability* that a microbial cell will initiate growth in a specific environment is related to physico-chemical properties of the environment. Probability models seek to identify combinations of 'hurdles' which reduce to an acceptable level the chance that an organism of concern can grow in a particular food. Useful discussions of probability modelling may be found in Baker (1993), Dodds (1993), Lund (1993) and Maas (1993).

In the simplest case, when developing models to predict the probability that pathogens will germinate, grow or produce toxins in a given environment, replicate samples of known inocula are incubated under defined environmental conditions for a fixed period of time. The proportion of replicates which are positive for growth/toxin production is then assessed periodically. As this proportion is dependent upon the specific environmental conditions, an equation relating the probability to those conditions may be derived. Typically, the probability of detectable growth or toxin production increases with increasing incubation times.

13.2.3.3 Integration of models. The integration of models which describe the various possible responses of an organism in a particular environment is an ongoing objective. Models are being developed which integrate growth, survival and death responses (Casolari, 1981; Whiting and Cygnarowicz-Provost, 1992; Jones and Walker, 1993), and the integration of probability and kinetic approaches described above has also been suggested recently (Ross and McMeekin, 1994).

Ratkowsky *et al.* (1991) highlighted the increasing variability of microbial responses as the environments become less optimal. This theme was continued by McMeekin *et al.* (1993) in which an attempt was made to quantify the variability and show that under some conditions the confidence interval surrounding the predictions encompassed infinite lag times, or infinite generations times, i.e. no growth is predicted to occur. Under more favourable conditions, however, the probability of growth is almost unity.

Ross and McMeekin (1994) concluded that the division of predictive microbiology into probability and kinetic modelling is a somewhat artificial one. They considered the two types of models as the extremes of a spectrum of modelling needs, and suggested that research at both 'ends' is now converging. At near growth limiting conditions the kinetic modeller must consider the probability of a predicted growth rate, or no growth at all. Similarly, the probability modeller must include some kinetic considerations. For example, Baker *et al.* (1990) recognised that the rate of increase of the probability of growth is related to the growth rate, and developed models to predict the probability of growth which incorporated a kinetic model for the lag phase duration. In a situation where no growth of an organism of concern is tolerable, one would use a probability model to ensure that the chance of lag resolution or spore germination is insignificantly low. At the other extreme, in a product which must be handled under conditions for which the probability of growth of spoilage organisms is unity, one would need only a growth-rate estimate for shelf life prediction. The two approaches converge in situations where growth up to some threshold is acceptable, but for which the environmental conditions are such that the responses are highly variable. Under more stressful conditions it is necessary to model not only the average response but also the probability of that response occurring at all.

13.2.3.4 Predictive modelling and the hurdle concept. It is also desirable to define the boundaries of the conditions which prevent the growth of microorganisms of interest, i.e. the growth/no growth response surface, although from the preceding discussion it might be expected that the boundary is more likely to be a zone of rapidly diminishing probability of growth. Attempts to describe the interaction of environmental factors which combine to prevent growth have been undertaken in a qualitative manner by Leistner, in the approach he termed 'hurdle technology' (Leistner, 1985).

13.2.3.4.1   Conditional and unconditional models.   In most predictive microbiology studies, models are constructed under conditions that may be described as *unconditional*, i.e. a situation in which the effect of different constraints is measured over the whole, or a large part, of the biokinetic range. Indeed, this is one of the tenets of model construction enunciated by McMeekin *et al.* (1993) 'use as full a range of the explanatory (independent) variable as possible, to obtain as full a range of the response (dependent) variable as possible'. This is recommended to minimise problems in nonlinear regression modelling, such as failure to obtain convergence, and from a practical viewpoint to avoid the dangers of extrapolating model predictions beyond the range of the experimental observations.

In applying the hurdle concept the desired effect is often to select a combination of factors which, together, provide a desired level of stability for the product. Often each of the factors by themselves would be considered 'mild' treatments, not capable of preventing growth, but in combination they have 'an additive or even synergistic effect' (Leistner, 1992). We will return to this point.

Thus, the situation in applying hurdle technology may be regarded as *conditional*, i.e. one in which the full potential of an individual constraint is restricted and the level of that constraint is limited to a range in which it is acceptable for reasons other than preventing or delaying microbial growth. These reasons encompass energy savings by obviating the needs for refrigeration and considerations related to the aesthetic, organoleptic and nutritional properties of the products.

Under these conditions we have moved through the interface from kinetic modelling to considerations of the probability of a microbially significant event occurring and have reached the leading edge of a response surface. In such products

> 'even a small enhancement of different hurdles could bring about in summation a substantial improvement of the microbial stability of a food' (Leistner, 1992).

13.2.3.4.2   Modelling growth limits.   The hurdle technology approach remains semi-quantitative, however, and would greatly benefit by the systematic approach of the modeller, as was recognised by Leistner (1992). An approach to defining the growth/no growth boundary has been advanced by Ratkowsky and Ross (1995). In that approach the 'interface' between those variables combinations which permit growth (response designated as 1) and those which prohibit growth (response designated as 0) are modelled by logistic regression. Solving the resulting expression for the value 0.5 approximately defines the boundary between the growth and no-growth regions. Thus, by substituting values of all but one variable into the equation, the level of the remaining variable required to prevent growth can be calculated. Alternatively, the possible combinations of factors which are required to prevent growth can be summarised and presented, for ease of interpretation, as contour plots. The usefulness of this type of model in the safe design of new product formulations is clear. Unfortunately, because these data have not often been collected systematically, there are few such models currently published, and none to our knowledge have yet been tested in commercial practice.

13.2.3.4.3 Interactions. Returning to the question of the way in which the hurdles interact, the evidence suggests that, at least for temperature, water activity and pH, the effects are additive rather than synergistic (Chandler, 1988; Davey, 1989; McMeekin *et al.*, 1987; Adams *et al.*, 1991; Wijtzes *et al.*, 1993, Quintavalla and Parolari, 1993). Where synergism between growth-affecting factors may occur is in that most interesting region at the growth/no growth interface, where the limiting (i.e. minimum inhibitory/tolerable) level of one constraint is decreased as a result of an increase in the level of another constraint. McMeekin *et al.* (1993) postulated that the combined effects of temperature and water activity on *Staphylococcus xylosus* might be explained by the diversion of energy to the production of compatible solutes thereby reducing the energy available to overcome the activation energy barrier presented by temperature.

There is, as yet, no experimental evidence to support this hypothesis and indeed this may be difficult to obtain because of the high degree of variability at near growth limiting conditions (Ratkowsky, 1992).

13.2.4 Quantitative microbiology?

It is now possible to broaden the scope of what we mean by the term 'predictive microbiology' by considering models for growth, survival and death of microorganisms and the probability of the predicted response under various conditions. The integration of the existing data for all of these aspects of microbial responses to their environment into a single database appears desirable. In fact, such integration is already underway, and several 'expert systems' which combine these and other types of data to emulate and enhance the decision making process of expert food technologists are now being developed. These systems are briefly described in a subsequent section.

From the preceding discussion of types of models it is apparent that predictive microbiology is concerned with the quantification of microbial responses to the environment presented to them by foods, whether that be the specific growth rate, the rate of population decline or the probability of growth being possible within a given environment. Consequently, 'quantitative microbiology' may be a more general and informative description of the modelling approach to understand the microbial ecology of foods. In any case, the accumulation of such data in a consistent and comparable manner, its integration into common databases, and the expression of those vast data sets in the form of simple predictive equations, offers a potential means for assessing the microbiological safety of foods. The integration of microbial response data with existing process engineering models (e.g. heat transfer models) will further expand the potential applications of those models and data.

13.3 Predictive modelling and HACCP

NACMCF (1992) described the HACCP system, in terms of seven main stages in the development of HACCP programs. Quoting from that document, the following four stages may be identified as those in which predictive models can provide useful information and assist in decision making.

In the area of risk assessment . . . (Principle 1):

'Assess hazards and risks associated with growing, harvesting raw materials and ingredients, processing, manufacturing, distribution, marketing, preparation and consumption of the food.'

In the area of identification/definition of CCPs (Principle 2):

'Determine CCPs required to control the identified hzazards.'

To define limits (Principle 3):

'Establish the critical limits that must be met at each identified CCP.'

Specification of remedial action after loss of control (Principle 5):

'Establish corrective action to be taken when there is a deviation identified by monitoring a CCP'.

Before beginning a specific discussion of the use of predictive models in these HACCP steps it will be useful to consider the sources of models and the technology being developed to make those models accessible to industry and regulatory users.

13.3.1 Sources of models

Models for the effects of various combinations of variables on the growth responses of a wide range of pathogenic bacteria have been published. Some, though fewer, models have been prepared for the growth of spoilage bacteria and fungi. Apart from a few large research groups/ institutions model development has been somewhat *ad hoc*. Two large scale modelling programs are worthy of special mention.

13.3.1.1 'The Pathogen Modeling Program'. Applications software called 'The Pathogen Modeling Program' is the culmination of work

conducted by the USDA Food Safety group at the Eastern Regional Research Center in Philadelphia.[4] The Pathogen Modeling Program (PMP) is a spreadsheet-software-based system which includes models for the effect of temperature, pH, water activity, nitrite concentration and atmospheric composition on the growth and lag responses of *Listeria monocytogenes*, *Salmonella*, *Clostridium botulinum*, *Aeromonas hydrophila*, *Shigella flexneri*, *Escherichia coli* 0157 and *Yersinia enterocolitica*. The software generates the predicted growth curves for the selected organisms for nominated conditions of temperature, pH and NaCl and nitrite concentration under aerobic or anaerobic conditions. The software can also provide estimates of the time taken to reach a specific population density, and the lag and generation time (Buchanan, 1991, 1992b).

13.3.1.2 'Food Micromodel'. In the UK the results of a collaborative program coordinated by the Ministry of Agriculture, Fisheries and Food, have now been made available to industry in the form of a consultancy service called 'Food Micromodel',[5] and is based on a similar range of organisms and conditions as PMP (Walker and Jones, 1992). The possibility of making the database and models available as spreadsheet-based software for use on personal computers is also being considered (Sutherland *et al.*, 1994) and with the added ability of being able to use the software to interpret the effects of fluctuating environmental conditions.

13.3.1.3 Databases and expert systems. A yet more refined source of information to assist in the calculation of hazards within processes are so-called 'expert systems', i.e., software designed to function like a specialist consultant. Such software usually consists of a database of organised knowledge, which can be easily expanded subsequently, and a set of rules for reaching conclusions. Cole (1991) reviewed the use and potential of databases, including expert systems, in food microbiology and concluded that the most significant developments were in the area of predictive microbiology.

13.3.1.3.1 The 'Decision Support System'. Zwietering *et al.* (1992) described the basis of an expert system which models bacterial growth in food production and distribution chains. That example serves as a useful illustration of the basis of such systems, and of their potential as an aid to HACCP analyses.

---

[4]*For further details*: Dr. R.L. Buchanan, Microbial Food Safety Research Unit, Eastern Regional Research Center, Agricultural Research Service, United States Department of Agriculture, 600 East Mermaid Lane, Philadelphia, PA 19118.
[5]*For further details*: Food Micromodel, Campden Food and Drink Research Association, Chipping Campden, Gloucestershire, UK.

The objective of those authors was to develop a system which combined quantitative data with qualitative data to enable predictions of possible spoilage types and kinetics of deterioration. Two databases were established. The first included the physical parameters of foods considered most important in determining microbial growth (temperature, water activity, pH and oxygen availability). In a second database are listed a range of spoilage microorganisms and some of their physiological characteristics as well as temperature, water activity, and pH ranges and optima for growth, and the fastest growth rate. To make a prediction, the physical properties of the product are matched with the physiological properties of the microorganisms by simply determining if the physical variables of the product are within the growth limits of the microorganism, a process known as 'pattern matching'. For those organisms expected to be able to grow, an estimate of the growth rate is calculated on the basis of the physical variables, by reference to kinetic models contained in the second database. The organisms that could potentially grow in the product are sorted according to predicted growth rate.

A set of rules can be established, based upon the product, properties of the microorganism, or other more general knowledge or observations. These rules can be applied to reduce the list of organisms, so that a final list is obtained which is based upon the physical parameters of the product, growth parameters of the organism, kinetic models and qualitative reasoning. Qualitative knowledge, included in the system in the form of rules, was employed to predict the effects of other factors affecting the growth rate of microorganisms such as organic acids, nitrite etc. which are currently not well described by predictive models. The rules employed in the system are grouped into four categories:

1. Relationship between microorganism and product characteristics.
2. Interaction among microorganisms (e.g. lactic acid producers).
3. Interaction among microorganisms in combination with the product.
4. Other general rules (e.g. effect of pasteurisation on potential microbiota).

The system generates two lists of possible spoilage organisms. The first is the list of all organisms which could potentially grow in the product based on the product's physical characteristics. The second list contains the organisms predicted to spoil the product, taking into account the qualitative rules.

As more information becomes available the databases and qualitative rules can be readily altered and expanded. In principle, the system is limited only by the quality and quantity of the information included in the database. Several examples of the use of the decision support system are given in Zwietering *et al.* (1992).

The applications in decision making are obvious. Nonetheless, Zwietering *et al.* (1992) stressed that 'all the information, from the beginning to end, must be studied as it is always a result of a number of models, i.e., simplification'.

13.3.1.3.2 Other expert systems. 'Expert systems' are being developed in a number of institutions and programs including the Unilever company (Adair and Briggs, 1993) and Food Micromodel (Walker and Jones, 1992).

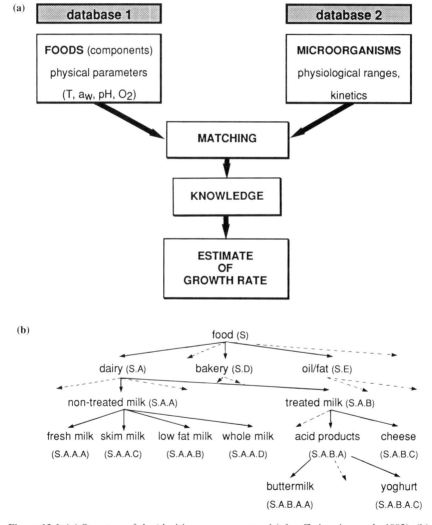

Figure 13.1 (a) Structure of the 'decision support system' (after Zwietering *et al.*, 1992). (b) Structure of database 1 of the decision support system in which foods are sorted by their physical characteristics (after Zwietering *et al.*, 1992). The letter codes in brackets indicate the hierarchy used to group the foods in the database.

Of particular interest is MKES (an acronym of Microbial Kinetics Expert System) Tools, being developed by Agriculture Canada to assess product safety and to define production system critical control points. MKES Tools simulates the growth and survival of pathogenic organisms when subjected to many different environmental conditions. The responses predicted are used to estimate the significance of the individual factors in that situation (Voyer and McKellar, 1993).

Though not strictly predictive microbiology, the expert systems are an extension of the general theme of predictive microbiology, i.e. that the growth responses of microorganisms to their environments are reproducible and quantifiable, and can be summarised, and that the important factors in the food environment which govern those responses can be characterised and quantified.

13.3.2   Principle 1. Risk and hazard assessment

Gould (1989) considered that predictive microbiology would:

> 'encourage a more integrated approach to food hygiene and safety which will impact on all stages of food production, from raw material acquisition and handling, through processing, storage, distribution, retailing and handling in the home'

an observation which reinforces the complementarity of the scope of predictive microbiology and HACCP.

Using the type of integrated approach advocated by Buchanan and Deroever (1993), or the sources indicated by Humber (1992), it should be possible to identify organisms which may be expected to contaminate a product. Models which delineate organism growth limits can be used to assess the probability of growth of a particular pathogen on the product, in essence a quantitative form of the pattern matching described above.

13.3.2.1   Role of kinetic models.   Using kinetic models it will be possible to estimate the potential for growth and survival of pathogens of concern within a given product/process combination and from those estimates to establish the level of significance, e.g. could *Salmonella* proliferate on the carcass within 3 hours if the temperature is 10°C. The growth rates estimated from product parameters for different pathogens can be compared to enable the identification of those most likely to grow to unsafe levels. As an example, and ignoring differences in infective doses, consider *Aeromonas hydrophila, Listeria monocytogenes* Scott A and *Staphylococcus aureus* 3b which are all able to grow at 13°C, pH 7 and water activity (NaCl): 0.96. Based on models developed in this laboratory, under the specified conditions the generation times are: *Listeria mono-cytogenes* Scott A: 4.8 h; *Aeromonas hydrophila* 3459: 69.3 h; and

Staphylococcus aureus 3b: 12.1 h. Thus, *Listeria monocytogenes* would be the most serious risk because it has the fastest growth rate, *A. hydrophila* being more inhibited by the water activity, and *S. aureus* 3b being more inhibited by the temperature than *L. monocytogenes* Scott A under those conditions.

Similarly the effect of processing conditions on the survival/destruction of those pathogens can be estimated without recourse to experiment, if the appropriate models are available, by monitoring of the environment presented to the microorganisms. The monitoring of the safety of processes by indirect measurements (i.e. temperature, pH, a_w, etc.), rather than enumeration of microorganisms, is a theme common to both HACCP and predictive modelling, and reinforces the concept that predictive microbiology provides the quantitative answers to HACCP's qualitative questions. The integration of the effects of these environmental factors over time, and their consequences for microbial growth, survival or death can be predicted using quantitative models. Furthermore, in relation to hazard analysis, the potential of expert systems which integrate various types of information is now apparent.

13.3.3   Principle 2. Determination of CCPs

13.3.3.1   Definitions of 'Critical Control Point'. NACMCF (1992) provides the following definitions:

(1) *Control points* (CPs) are any point, step or procedure at which biological, physical or chemical factors can be controlled.
(2) *Critical control points* (CCPs) are any point, step or procedure at which control can be applied and a food safety hazard can be prevented, eliminated or reduced to acceptable levels.

Several authors (Christian, 1994; MFSCNFPA, 1993, Moberg, 1992) have commented on the consequences of defining too many critical control points: the impact of, and attention paid to, each CCP is lessened. To avert this possibility, Humber (1992) suggested that critical control points be redefined as those points in a specific food system 'where loss of control would result in a *high* probability of a health risk'. Although NACMCF (1992) provides a decision tree (Figure 13.2) to assist in identifying critical control points, either definition still begs the question: 'How can one quantify the risk as 'high' or otherwise?'.

13.3.3.2   Role of models. Models can assist in answering this question. For example, if the temperature control of a 15 minute process designed to operate at 10°C were lost, what would be the consequence for the increase in numbers of *S. aureus*? Would it result in a significantly increased health

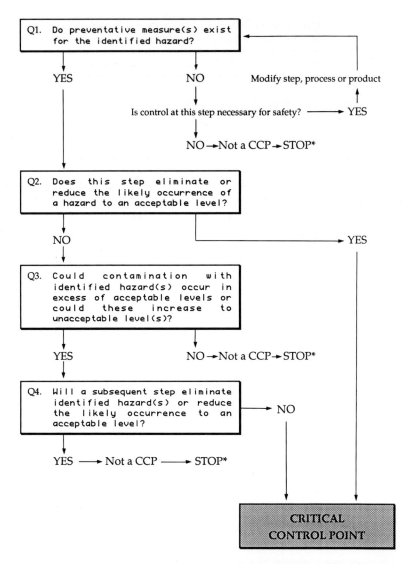

Figure 13.2 A 'decision tree' for the identification of critical control points within a process subject to HACCP analysis (NACMCF, 1992). *Proceed to next step in the described process.

risk? Table 13.1 lists the effect of different temperatures on the growth of a strain of *S. aureus* and also shows the predicted increase in numbers of *S. aureus* 3b if the duration of the process were 120 minutes. That table shows that the degree of risk increases as a function of time and temperature. In many situations it could be argued that the only significantly increased risk is after 120 min at 25°C or greater (n.b. a 100% increase represents a

Table 13.1 Predicted increase (%) in numbers of *S. aureus* 3b
for various time–temperature combinations

Temperature (°C)	In 15 min.	In 120 min.
10	0	0
15	3	30
20	10	108
25	20	321
30	35	978
35	56	3386

doubling of cell numbers). A doubling of population numbers may, however, represent the difference between compliance or non-compliance with a regulation, or an increase to a microbial dose which is infectious for a significant proportion of the consumer population. These considerations illustrate that questions relating to the assessment of hazards do not always have absolute answers. We will return to this issue in a subsequent section.

Similarly, interpretation of a particular process step by survival/death models may reveal that a particular process step results in significant decrease in the level of microbes of concern. Growth/no growth models can also help to gauge whether a particular product formulation is well away from the growth/no growth boundary, i.e. that it has a large safety margin to 'buffer' small variations in product formulation, and that the product formulation thus represents a control point only. Conversely, a product formulation poised just on the edge of that interface will be significantly affected if small formulation variations reduce the overall size of the 'hurdles'. Thus, in this situation, the product formulation will be a *critical* control point.

In general, the various classes of predictive models can be used to assess the microbiological consequences of individual handling/processing steps, i.e. to quantify the likely effect on microbial germination, growth/toxin production, or death in a given food environment. From this interpretation it will be possible to more objectively determine which steps are critical to product quality and safety.

13.3.4   Principle 3. Establishing critical limits

Following from the above discussion, critical limits can be defined by reversing the above analytical processes to calculate the limits of a process or a formulation beyond which a significant health risk would result. Using predictive models it is possible to specify the operating parameters which will prevent outgrowth; reduce the likelihood of germination or growth; which will limit proliferation to within acceptable limits; or which achieve the required reduction in bacterial load. Those limits could refer to minimum inhibitory levels and combinations of levels of controlling factors, to minimum time–temperature combinations which ensure the reduction of the microbial load to safe levels, or to maximum time–temperature combinations which limit microbial proliferation to safe levels.

Furthermore, using models it is possible to specify safety margins for the levels of specified hurdles or process parameters, so that there is a realistic degree of flexibility available to process operators and controllers.

13.3.5 Principle 5. Corrective action specification

Again, the preceding sections indicate that using predictive models it is possible to evaluate quantitatively the effect of losses of process control, and to make rational decisions regarding the fate of the product, e.g. reprocess, lower grade of product, use in product subject to a more stringent thermal treatment, etc. The information provided by predictive models also enables greater flexibility in the range of corrective actions which can be taken to achieve the same level of product safety, e.g. by slightly modifying subsequent processing steps.

Hudak-Roos and Garrett (1992) observed that the trend for measurement monitoring within HACCP programs is toward full automation. The possible corrective actions to be taken could, conceivably, also be automated. Davey (1992) foresaw a time when predictive models, coupled with indirect sensors and computers, would enable 'real-time' food process optimisation through automated in-line process control.

13.4 Examples of the application of predictive models in HACCP systems

In practice, most applications of predictive models within HACCP systems have been based on models in which temperature is the only fluctuating environmental variable. Part of the reason for this lies in the ease and relative non-invasiveness of temperature measurement compared to determination of other factors such as water activity or pH. Consequently, the applications have tended to focus on the interpretation of temperature histories of finished product during storage and distribution.

13.4.1 Use of the HACCP approach

Perhaps the most developed use of predictive models in the HACCP context stems from the work of C.O. Gill and colleagues in New Zealand during the 1980s and more recently in Alberta, Canada. These workers effectively used temperature function integration[6] to assess the hygienic

---

[6]*Temperature Function Integration* (Nixon, 1971): the summation of the temperature history of a product and its interpretation in terms of potential bacterial growth.

Table 13.2 Chronological development of models for process assurance

Reference	Significance
Gill (1984)	Development of anaerobic model for *E. coli* growth, validation in offal cooling procedures
Gill and Harrison (1985)	Validation of Gill (1984) model in offal cooling procedures
Smith (1985)	Model of coliforms growing aerobically on meat – implications for codes of practice (laboratory study)
Gill (1986)	As for Gill (1984)
Smith (1987)	Validation of Smith (1985) model in raw blended mutton (laboratory based study)
Mackey and Kerridge (1988)	Models for *Salmonella* in minced beef (growth rate and lag phase duration). Effect of inoculum size (laboratory study)
Gill *et al.* (1988a)	Development of computer programs to evaluate process hygiene. Models mentioned for aerobic and anaerobic conditions, lag phase duration and growth rate but no details given
Lowry *et al.* (1989)	Aerobic models for *E. coli* lag phase duration and growth rate. Validation for meat thawing procedures
Gill and Phillips (1990)	Gill (1984) model validated for offal cooling and Gill *et al.* (1988a) model for carcass cooling. Temperature function integration criteria for carcass cooling
Gill *et al.* (1991a)	Validation of Gill *et al.* (1988a) model (details now provided for conventional carcass cooling)
Gill *et al.* (1991b)	Validation as above for spray cooling of carcasses
Reichel *et al.* (1991)	Validation as above and anaerobic model of Gill (1984) in hot boning processes
Gill and Jones (1992a)	Validation of aerobic *E. coli* model in cooling of pig carcasses
Gill and Jones (1992b)	Validation of anaerobic model of Gill (1984) in beef offal

efficiency of various meat processing operations and to evaluate storage and distribution practices.

A series of papers in the decade from 1984, listed by McMeekin and Ross (1993) and shown in Table 13.2, shows chronologically the development of models for process assurance.

The publications prior to 1989 described the development and validation of models under laboratory conditions for commercial operations such as offal cooling, where the temperature profile of the process was the sole determinant of the extent of microbial proliferation.

13.4.1.1   Meat processing operations

13.4.1.1.1   E. coli models.   Considering processes such as meat thawing, however, other factors impinging on microbial development should also be taken into account. Thus, Lowry *et al.* (1989), in examining alternative meat thawing procedures had also to consider damage caused by freeze/

thawing cycles, variable rates of heat transfer at different locations in the carton and attainment of anaerobiosis because of the accumulation of drip from thawed areas.

This paper marked the transition of the research effort of Gill's group(s) to HACCP-type dissection of practical meat processing operations based on validity of models for *Escherichia coli* growth under aerobic and/or anaerobic conditions. In a direct comparison of calculated and directly determined growth of *E. coli* during a hot boning process, Reichel *et al.* (1991) found agreement within one generation in 76% of comparisons, with the model 'failing safe' (i.e. over-predicting the extent of proliferation) in 60% of cases.

A strong case is therefore in place for the application of predictive models as an integral part of the HACCP approach to controlling the hygienic adequacy of meat processing operations. In the work of Gill and colleagues, (Table 13.2), practical application occurred through the use of the Delphi Temperature Logging System[7] and associated software which interprets fluctuating temperature profiles in terms of the extent of *E. coli* proliferation. Figure 13.3 shows one application of the system: a report from a process assurance evaluation.

Importantly, Gill and Phillips (1990) added the caveat:

'Temperature function integration must assess the hygienic adequacy of a process, it cannot be used to assess the absolute hygienic status of individual units leaving the process'.

This statement cannot be challenged in absolute terms but, as a consequence of the accumulation of knowledge on the initial levels of contamination of products and the quantitative, comparative information of the effect of processing procedures on microbial development, one becomes increasingly confident in predictions of the number of individual units falling within specifications.

Beyond the processing works Gill and his colleagues also used the Delphi system to examine the hygienic adequacy of storage and distribution systems for meat including sea transport from New Zealand to Middle Eastern, European and US markets (Gill *et al.*, 1988b; Gill and Jones, 1992b). Further use of the system to compare shipments of meat across Canada by road or rail demonstrated the market advantage of the latter (Gill and Phillips, 1993).

The type of technology exemplified by the Delphi system is not limited to estimation of the growth of mesophilic indicator organisms such as *E. coli*. Systems of this type, on the basis of a single temperature history profile, could equally well be used to indicate the potential growth of spoilage bacteria. Temperature dependence models have been suggested

---

[7]*Delphi temperature logger*: A compact portable electronic temperature recording device.

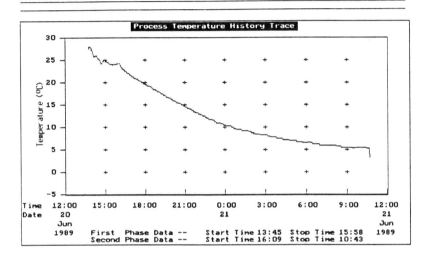

PROCESS ASSURANCE REPORT

Report prepared from data collected by logger Serial Number 10612

The data were collected between 13.45 on 20 Jun 1989

and 10.43 on 21 Jun 1989

Process Serial Number 10612030.919

Production of chilled or frozen Unpackaged Cuts (not in a barrier film).

The Plant name for that process is: _____

_____

Process Temperature History Trace

Process Hygiene Index (E.coli.) for the above trace
= 7.1

The section of the temperature history trace shown in a dotted line
is the temperature assumed during the product cutting operation
when the actual product temperature could not be monitored

Comments:

Figure 13.3 A 'Process Assurance Report', one component of an application of the Delphi Temperature Logging System and software, and an example of the use of predictive microbiology in HACCP-like systems. Reproduced with permission from Meat Research Institute of New Zealand (Inc.).

by Gill and coworkers for *Enterobacteriaceae* (Gill, 1984) and *Pseudomonas* (Gill and Jones, 1992b). A similar approach, based on spreadsheet software to interpret electronically logged temperature histories, has been developed at the University of Tasmania. Currently the prototype software includes a model for *Pseudomonas* growth, developed in laboratory media and validated in dairy and meat products, but other models can be incorporated easily. The software is currently being used in a trial in the

Australian dairy industry. An example of the output of the software is shown in Figure 13.4. Note that the reports of this and the Delphi system are based on an absolute, rather than relative, time scale which greatly assists in the identification and resolution of lapses of temperature control in production and distribution chains.

13.4.1.1.2   Models for B. thermosphacta.   Another PC-based system, which combines kinetic models with a heat transfer model to estimate the effect of fluctuating temperature histories, is described by Simpson *et al.* (1989) for the growth of *Brochothrix thermosphacta*. They concluded that the model could be used to predict the effect of management decisions on the shelf-life of a refrigerated product, such as whether it would be more beneficial to shelf life to reduce the frequency of temperature abuse in processing, or to lower the average storage temperature.

13.4.1.2   Listeria model.   Chen and Donnelly (1992) describe the development of a computer-aided HACCP program to control Listeria in dairy plants. They simulated a simplified dairy plant with potential Listeria contamination as a model system. Mathematical relationships to describe the thermal resistance and growth of *Listeria monocytogenes* were combined with process engineering models. In addition, a hypothetical probabilistic model was also used to represent contamination into production flow based upon the environmental presence of Listeria.

The preceding discussion suggests how it is possible, using predictive models, to design safer food products and processes. The ability to predict the consequences of different scenarios for product safety is a powerful tool for food technologists. It has also attracted the attention of regulatory authorities, e.g. The National Food Authority of Australia has tentatively endorsed within Australian Standards the use of predictive models to assess those foods able to support the growth of *L. monocytogenes*. For such foods, and those associated with listeriosis outbreaks, a nil tolerance was proposed (NFA, 1993).

With regard to biological hazards, Rhodehamel (1992) considered that when developing a HACCP program the food processor or grower should establish preventative measures with three basic aims in mind including:

1. Destruction.
2. Elimination or reduction of the hazard.
3. Inhibition of growth and toxin production.

Predictive microbiology enables the producer to more accurately hit those 'targets'.

It should also be stressed, however, that the use of predictive models to predict the consequences of changes to products and processes can not fully replace experiments. Models do not contain all the data that may be

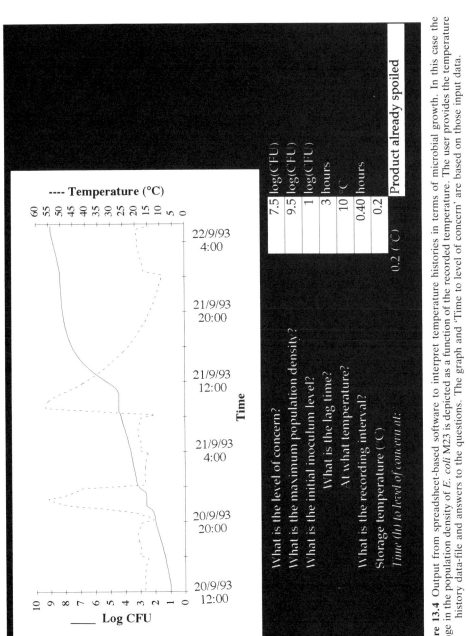

What is the level of concern?	7.5	log(CFU)
What is the maximum population density?	9.5	log(CFU)
What is the initial inoculum level?	1	log(CFU)
What is the lag time?	3	hours
At what temperature?	10	°C
What is the recording interval?	0.40	hours
Storage temperature (°C)	0.2	
Time (h) to level of concern at: 0.2 (°C)	Product already spoiled	

Figure 13.4 Output from spreadsheet-based software to interpret temperature histories in terms of microbial growth. In this case the change in the population density of *E. coli* M23 is depicted as a function of the recorded temperature. The user provides the temperature history data-file and answers to the questions. The graph and 'Time to level of concern' are based on those input data.

important in every situation. Existing models can, however, be used to greatly reduce the amount of experimental work required, and to identify those aspects of a problem which do require experimental resolution.

13.4.2 *Variability of responses*

We have presented a positive view of the practical usefulness of predictive models. There are, of course, limitations in relation to their use. These, and means to overcome or obviate those problems, are beyond the scope of this document but have been thoroughly discussed by McMeekin *et al.,* (1993), McMeekin and Ross (1993) and Ross and McMeekin (1994).

One aspect worthy of comment, however, is that of the variability of microbial responses and its commercial implications. In general, when confronted with a situation in which there is uncertainty concerning the absolute value of some factor necessary for making absolute predictions (e.g. duration of lag phase, initial bacterial load), modellers have adopted 'worst case scenarios'. One example is the use of data derived in liquid laboratory broth to generate models, in which responses are often faster than in food products. The use of worst-case scenarios result in the generation of 'fail-safe' i.e. conservative, predictions. In consequence, in some cases acceptable product may be discarded.

As stated in a preceding section, variability in microbial growth rates increase dramatically as environmental conditions become less favourable for growth. Ratkowsky (1992) demonstrated a means to describe and quantify the magnitude of the variability in microbial growth responses as a function of environmental constraints. With that information it is possible to select confidence intervals on the predictions of models which encompass as wide a range of possible response times as the model user requires.

Data presented by McMeekin *et al.* (1993) for *S. aureus* 3b, and shown in Table 13.3, illustrate this point. The table gives predicted generation times,

Table 13.3 Values of *GT* (minutes) at 12.5°C corresponding to certain selected probabilities[a]

$P[GT < GT_0]$	GT_0
0.000001	46
0.0001	69
0.01	136
0.05	203
0.95	2356

[a]$P[GT < GT_0]$. *Source*: Generation time data of Neumeyer (1992).

GT_0, for the case of *S. aureus* 3b, which should be used for predictive modelling to achieve a certain level of safety. For example, one in ten thousand *S. aureus* 3b have generation times, GT, at 12.5°C of less than 69 minutes so that predictions of response times based on this value should only *over*estimate the response time once in ten thousand events, i.e. the prediction will fail one time in 10 000. Conversely, one in twenty *S. aureus* 3b have a generation time greater (i.e slower growth) than 2356 minutes, so that predictions based on this generation time will fail, i.e. there will be more *S. aureus* 3b than predicted, in 95% of cases. In HACCP safety evaluations, in which a low level of failure is of paramount importance, a high level of confidence requires that more products are predicted to be unsafe than actually are, so that unnecessary wastage may result. Nonetheless, with this approach the critical limits can be adjusted to the level of risk the producer or regulatory authority is willing to accept.

13.5 Conclusions

One of the key themes of the HACCP approach is the recognition that safety cannot be inspected into a product, it must be designed in. This view was echoed by Roberts and Jarvis (1983), in which they formalised the concept of predictive microbiology.

The potential of the predictive modelling approach in food microbiology has not yet been fully realised and, in fact, relies heavily upon the accumulation of good quality data for inclusion in models and databases (Walker and Jones, 1993; McMeekin *et al.*, 1993). This can be an ongoing process to which many food microbiologists can contribute, often without additional effort. By implementing minor changes to the design and analysis of experiments not specifically intended for modelling purposes, data from diverse sources can often be made compatible with existing databases. Protocols for the generation of compatible data are described in Walker and Jones (1993). By describing foods in terms of environmental factors, predictive microbiology provides a rational approach in which the observations of diverse researchers can be combined and simplified to provide access to a vast pool of knowledge. This cooperative approach was advocated by Roberts and Jarvis (1983) also, and continues to be realised. At the time of writing, the governments of at least five nations are cooperating to create an international database of the measured growth responses of microorganisms in defined and semi-defined food and food-like environments.

Microbial responses to environmental factors of significance in foods, summarised as simple predictive equations, can be used to provide objective assessments of the risks of food borne microbial infection, intoxication or spoilage in specific circumstances. The potential applications of predictive models in HACCP systems are numerous but all derive from better understanding, and consequently the potential for control, of the microbial ecology of foods that predictive modelling offers.

Acknowledgements

The authors gratefully acknowledge the financial support of the Australian Rural Industries Research and Development Corporation and the Australian Meat Research Corporation throughout the preparation of this manuscript.

References

Adair, C. and Briggs, P.A. (1993) The concept and application of expert systems in the field of microbiological safety. *J. Indus. Microbiol.* **12**, 3.

Adams, M.R., Little, C.L. and Easter, M.C. (1991) Modelling the effect of pH, acidulant and temperature on the growth rate of *Yersinia enterocolitica. J. Appl. Bacteriol.* **71**, 65.

Baird-Parker, A.C. and Kilsby, D.C. (1987) Principles of predictive food microbiology. *J. Appl. Bacteriol. Sympos. Suppl.* **63**, 43S.

Baker, D. (1993) Probability models to assess the safety of foods with respect to *Clostridium botulinum. J. Indus. Microbiol.* **12**, 156.

Baker, D., Genigeorgis, C., Glover, J. and Razavilar, V. (1990) Growth and toxigenesis of *C. botulinum* type E in fishes packaged under modified atmospheres. *Internat. J. Food Microbiol.* **10**, 269.

Broughall, J.M. and Brown, C. (1984) Hazard analysis applied to microbial growth in foods: Development and application of three-dimensional models to predict bacterial growth. *Food Microbiol.* **1**, 13.

Broughall, J.M., Anslow, P. and Kilsby, D.C. (1983) Hazard analysis applied to microbial growth in foods: Development of mathematical models describing the effect of water activity. *J. Appl. Bacteriol.* **55**, 101.

Buchanan, R.L. (1991) Using spreadsheet software for predictive microbiology applications. *J. Food Safety* **11**, 123.

Buchanan, R.L. (1992a) Predictive microbiology: mathematical modeling of microbial growth. *ACS Sympos. Series* **484**, 250.

Buchanan, R.L. (1992b) Developing and distributing user-friendly application software. *J. Indus. Microbiol.* **12**, 251.

Buchanan, R.L. and Deroever, C.M. (1993) Limits in assessing microbiological food safety. *J. Food Prot.* **56**, 725.

CACFH (Codex Alimentarius Commission; Codex Committee on Food Hygiene) (1993) *Guidelines for the Application of Hazard Analysis Critical Control Point (HACCP) System* (Alinorm 93/13A. Appendix B), Food and Agriculture Organisation/World Health Organization, Rome.

Casolari, A. (1981) A model describing microbial inactivation and growth kinetics. *J. Theor. Biol.* **88**, 1.

CFDRA (Campden Food and Drink Research Association) (1992) *Hazard Analysis Critical Control Point software, Version 1.0*. Campden Food and Drink Research Association, Gloucestershire, UK.

Chandler, R.E. (1988) *The Effect of Temperature and Water Activity on Microbial Growth Rate and Food Spoilage*. Ph.D. Thesis, University of Tasmania, Hobart, Australia.

Chen, H. and Donnelly, C.W. (1992) Development of a computer-aided HACCP program to control *Listeria* in dairy plant environment. (Abstract only). *J. Indus. Microbiol.* **12**, 349.

Christian, J.H.B. (1994) Problems with HACCP. *Food Australia* **46**, 81.

Cole, M.B. (1991) Databases in modern food microbiology. *Trends Food Sci. Technol.* (**Nov.**), 293.

Crueger, W. and Crueger, A. (1990) *Biotechnology: A Textbook of Industrial Microbiology*, 2nd edn. (English translation editor: T.D. Brock). Sinauer Associates, Inc., Sunderland, Massachusetts, USA.

Dalgaard, P. (1993) *Evaluation and Prediction of Microbial Fish Spoilage*. Ph.D. Thesis, Royal Veterinary and Agricultural University, Copenhagen, Denmark.

Davey, K.R. (1989) A predictive model for combined temperature and water activity on microbial growth during the growth phase. *J. Appl. Bacteriol.* **67**, 483.

Davey, K.R. (1992) Opinion: Predictive modelling. *Letters Appl. Microbiol.* **14**, 217.

Dodds, K.L. (1993) An introduction to predictive microbiology and the development and use of probability models with *Clostridium botulinum*. *J. Indus. Microbiol.* **12**, 139.

Farber, J.M. (1986) Predictive modeling of food deterioration and safety. In *Foodborne Microorganisms and their Toxins*. (M.D. Pierson and N.J. Stern eds.), pp. 57–90, Marcel Dekker Inc, New York.

Genigeorgis, C.A. (1981) Factors affecting the probability of growth of pathogenic microorganisms in foods. *J. Am. Vet. Med. Assoc.* **179**, 1410.

Gibson, A.M. and Roberts, T.A. (1989) Predicting microbial growth: Development of a mathematical model to predict bacterial growth responses. *Food Australia* **41**, 1075.

Gill, C.O. (1984) Prevention of early spoilage of livers. *Proc. 30th Europ. Mtg. Meat Res. Workers*, Bristol, UK. pp. 240–241.

Gill, C.O. (1986) Temperature function integration for hygiene evaluation of food processing procedures. *Food Technol. Australia* **38**, 203.

Gill, C.O. and Harrison, J.C.L. (1985) Evaluation of the hygienic efficiency of offal cooling procedures. *Food Microbiol.* **2**, 63.

Gill, C.O. and Jones, T. (1992a) Assessment of the hygienic efficiencies of two commercial processes for cooling pig carcasses. *Food Microbiol.* **90**, 335.

Gill, C.O. and Jones, S.D.M. (1992b) Evaluation of a commercial process for collection and cooling of beef offals by a temperature function integration technique. *Internat. J. Food Microbiol.* **15**, 131.

Gill, C.O. and Phillips, D.M. (1990) Hygienically appropriate time/temperature parameters for raw meat processing. *Cong. Proc: 36th Internat. Cong. Meat Sci. Technol.*, Havana, Cuba. pp. 458–470.

Gill, C.O. and Phillips, D.M. (1993) The efficiency of storage during distant continental transportation of beef sides and quarters. *Food. Res. Internat.* **26**, 239.

Gill, C.O., Phillips, D.M., Loeffen, M.P.F. and Bishop, C. (1988a) A computer program for assessing the remaining storage life of chilled red meats from product temperature histories, in *Refrigeration for Food and People: Proc. Meetings Commissions C2, D1, D2/3, E1 (September 5–9, 1988)*, Institut Internat. du Froid – Internat. Institute of Refrigeration, Paris. pp. 73–77.

Gill, C.O., Phillips, D.M., Loeffen, M.P.F. and Bishop, C. (1988b) A computer program for evaluating the hygienic efficiency of meat processing procedures from product temperature history data. *Cong. Proc: 34th Internat. Cong. Meat Sci. Technol.*, Brisbane, Australia. pp. 531–532.

Gill, C.O., Harrison, J.C.L. and Phillips, D.M. (1991a) Use of a temperature function integration technique to assess the hygienic adequacy of a beef carcass cooling process. *Food Microbiol.* **8**, 83.

Gill, C.O., Jones, S.D.M. and Tong, A.K.W. (1991b) Application of a temperature function integration technique to assess the hygienic adequacy of a process for spray chilling beef carcasses. *J. Food Prot.* **54**, 731.

Gould, G. (1989) Predictive mathematical modelling of microbial growth and survival in foods. *Food Sci. Technol. Today* **3**, 89.

Hudak-Roos, M. and Garrett, E.S. (1992) Monitoring critical control point critical limits, in *HACCP: Principles and Application* (M.D. Pierson and D.A. Corlett, Jr. eds.), Van Nostrand Reinhold, New York. pp. 62–71.

Humber, J. (1992) Control points and critical control points, in *HACCP: Principles and Application* (M.D. Pierson and D.A. Corlett, Jr. eds.), Van Nostrand Reinhold, New York. pp. 97–194.

IAMFES (International Association of Milk, Food and Environmental Sanitarians, Inc.) (1991) *Procedures to Implement the Hazard Analysis Critical Control Point System.* IAMFES, Des Moines, Iowa, USA.

Jones, J.E. and Walker, S.J. (1993) Advances in modeling microbial growth. *J. Indus. Microbiol.* **12**, 200.

Leistner, L. (1985) Hurdle technology applied to meat products of the shelf stable and intermediate moisture food types, in *Properties of Water in Foods in Relation to Quality and Stability* (D. Simatos and J.L. Multon, eds.). Martinus Nijhoff Publishers, Dordrecht, Germany. p. 309.

Leistner, L. (1992) Food preservation by combined methods. *Food. Res. Internat.* **25**, 151.

Lowry, P.D., Gill, C.O. and Pham, Q.T. (1989) A quantitative method of determining the hygienic efficiency of meat thawing processes. *Food Australia* **41**, 1080.

Lund, B. (1993) Quantification of factors affecting the probability of development of pathogenic bacteria, in particular *Clostridium botulinum*, in foods. *J. Indus. Microbiol.* **12**, 256.

Maas, M.R. (1993) Development and use of probability models: The industry perspective. *J. Indus. Microbiol.* **12**, 256.

Mackey, B.A. and Kerridge, A.L. (1988) The effect of incubation temperature and inoculum size on growth of salmonellae in minced beef. *Int. J. Food Microbiol.* **6**, 57.

McMeekin, T.A. and Olley, J. (1986) Predictive microbiology. *Food Technol. Australia* **38**, 331.

McMeekin, T.A. and Ross, T. (1993) Use of predictive microbiology in relation to meat and meat products. *Rev. Papers and Abstr. 39th Internat. Cong. Meat Sci. Technol.* Calgary, Canada, Aug. 1–6, 1993. pp. 257–274.

McMeekin, T.A., Chandler, R.E., Doe, P.E., Garland, C.D., Olley, J., Putro, S. and Ratkowsky, D.A. (1987) Model for the combined effect of temperature and water activity on the growth rate of *Staphylococcus xylosus*. *J. Appl. Bacteriol.* **62**, 543.

McMeekin, T.A., Ross, T. and Olley, J. (1992) Application of predictive microbiology to assure the quality and safety of fish and fish products. *Internat. J. Food Microbiol.* **15**, 13.

McMeekin, T.A., Olley, J., Ross, T. and Ratkowsky, D.A. (1993) *Predictive Microbiology: Theory and Application.* Research Studies Press, Taunton, UK; J. Wiley & Sons Inc., New York.

MFSCNFPA (Microbiology and Food Safety Committee of the National Food Processors Association) (1993) HACCP implementation: A generic model for chilled foods. *J. Food Prot.* **56**, 1077.

Moberg, L.J. (1992) Establishing critical limits for control points, in *HACCP: Principles and Application* (M.D. Pierson and D.A. Corlett, Jr. eds.). Van Nostrand Rheinhold, New York. pp. 50–61.

NACMCF (National Advisory Committee on Microbiological Criteria for Foods) (1992) Hazard analysis and critical control point system. *Internat. J. Food Microbiol.* **16**, 1.

Neumeyer, K. (1992) Effect of temperature history on predicting the growth response of *Staphylococcus aureus*. *B.Sc. (Hons.) Thesis*, University of Tasmania, Hobart, Australia.

NFA (National Food Authority) (1993) Food standards: Food associated with Listeriosis outbreaks. *Draft Gazette Notice v.3.* National Food Authority, Canberra, Australia.

Nixon, P.A. (1971) Temperature integration as a means of assessing storage conditions, in *Report on Quality in Fish Products, Seminar No. 3.* Fishing Industry Board, Wellington, New Zealand. pp. 33–44.

Quintavalla, S. and Parolari, G. (1993) Effects of temperature, a_w and pH on the growth of *Bacillus* cells and spores – A response surface methodology study. *Internat. J. Food Microbiol.* **19**, 207.

Ratkowsky, D.A. (1992) Predicting response times in predictive food microbiology. *Occasional Paper No. 1992/1.* Department of Primary Industry, Fisheries and Energy, Tasmania, Research and Development Unit, Biometrics Section, Australia.

Ratkowsky, D.A. and Ross, T. (1995) Modelling the bacterial growth/no growth interface. *Lett. Appl. Microbiol.* **20**, 29.

Ratkowsky, D.A., Ross, T., McMeekin, T.A. and Olley, J. (1991) Comparison of Arrhenius-type and Bělehrádek-type models for prediction of bacterial growth in foods. *J. Appl. Bacteriol.* **71**, 452.

Reichel, M.P., Phillips, D.M., Jones, R. and Gill, C.O. (1991) Assessment of the hygienic adequacy of a commercial hot boning process for beef by a temperature function integration technique. *Internat. J. Food Microbiol.* **14**, 27.

Rhodehamel, E.J. (1992) Overview of biological, chemical and physical hazards, in *HACCP: Principles and Application* (M.D. Pierson and D.A. Corlett, Jr. eds.). Van Nostrand Reinhold, New York. pp. 8–28.

Roberts, T.A. (1989) Combinations of antimicrobials and processing methods. *Food Technol.* **Jan.**, 156.

Roberts, T.A. (1990) Predictive modelling of microbial growth. *Food Technol. Internat., Europe* **1990**, 231.

Roberts, T.A. and Jarvis, B. (1983) Predictive modelling of food safety with particular reference to *Clostridium botulinum* in model cured meat systems, in *Food Microbiology: Advances and Prospects* (T.A. Roberts and F.A. Skinner eds.). Academic Press, New York. pp. 85–95.

Ross, T. and McMeekin, T.A. (1994) Predictive microbiology: A review. *Internat. J. Food Microbiol.* **23**, 241.

Scott, W.J. (1937) The growth of micro-organisms on ox muscle. II. The influence of temperature. *J. Council Scient. Indus. Res., Australia* **10**, 338.

Simpson, R., Li, K.Y. and Torres, J.A. (1989) A management tool to improve the microbial quality of refrigerated foods, in *Proc. Internat. Conf. Technological Innovations in Freezing and Refrigeration of Fruit and Vegetables, University of California, Davis, CA.* Institut Internat. du Froid – Internat. Institute of Refrigeration, Paris. pp. 155–168.

Smith, M.G. (1985) The generation time, lag time and minimum temperature of growth of coliform organisms on meat, and the implications for codes of practice in abattoirs. *J. Hyg. Cambridge* **94**, 289.

Smith, M.G. (1987) Calculation of the expected increases of coliform organisms, *Escherichia coli* and *Salmonella typhimurium* in raw blended mutton tissue. *Epidemiolog. Infect.* **99**, 323.

Stier, R. (1992) Practical application of HACCP, in *HACCP: Principles and Application* (M.D. Pierson and D.A. Corlett, Jr. eds.). Van Nostrand Reinhold, New York. pp. 126–168.

Stumbo, C.R., Purokit, K.S., Ramakrishnan, T.V., Evans, D.A. and Francis, F.J. (1983) *CRC Handbook of Lethality Guides for Low-acid Canned Foods.* Vol. 1. CRC Press, Boca Raton.

Sutherland, J.P., Bayliss, A.J. and Roberts, T.A. (1994) Predictive modelling of growth of *Staphylococcus aureus*: the effects of temperature, pH and sodium chloride. *Internat. J. Food Microbiol.* **21**, 217.

Voyer, R. and McKellar, R.C. (1993) MKES Tools: A microbial kinetics expert system for developing and assessing food production systems. *J. Indus. Microbiol.* **12**, 256.

Walker, S.J. and Jones, J.E. (1992) Predictive microbiology: data and models bases. *Food Technol. Internat., Europe* **1992**, 209.

Walker, S.J. and Jones, J.E. (1993) Protocols for data generation for predictive modeling. *J. Indus. Microbiol.* **12**, 273.

Whiting, R.C. and Cygnarowicz-Provost, M. (1992) A quantitative model for bacterial growth and decline. *Food Microbiol.* **9**, 269.

Wijtzes, T., McClure, P.J., Zwietering, M.H. and Roberts, T.A. (1993) Modelling bacterial growth of *Listeria monocytogenes* as a function of water activity, pH and temperature. *Internat. J. Food. Microbiol.* **18**, 139.

Zwietering, M.H., Wijtzes, T., de Wit, J.C. and van't Reit, K. (1992) A decision support system for prediction of the microbial spoilage in foods. *J. Food Prot.* **55**, 973.

14 National and international cooperation on governmental regulations for meat, poultry and fish inspection

B.F. DENNIS

14.1 Overview

Several Federal agencies within the Executive Branch of government have direct or indirect roles in ensuring that the US food supply is not adulterated or misbranded. While the terms 'adulterated' and 'misbranded' have lengthy statutory and legal definitions, suffice it to say: adulterated generally means the food is unsafe, unhealthy or unwholesome; and/or contains ingredients which it should not contain, or contains such ingredients in quantities greater than is permitted. A product can be adulterated but still be safe. For example, a meat frankfurter containing fat in excess of the government standard could be considered adulterated, but it is not unsafe. If a product is adulterated, it most likely is also misbranded.

Misbranded generally means the food is misrepresented to the consumer in some manner, usually through labeling. For example, a butter or margarine substitute, generally referred to as 'spreads', that is labeled as margarine but does not meet the government standard for the fat content of margarine would be misbranded.

While terms such as unsafe, unhealthy, or unwholesome appear clear and understandable, one only needs to ponder very little to realize differently. For example, unsafe to whom; or under what circumstances? Raw milk containing pathogens may have no ill effects on a healthy person, but could cause serious illness or even death of a debilitated or immune compromised person, or of a small child.

The authority for the respective roles of the government agencies comes from federal legislation. That authority is interpreted and applied through regulations codified under the various Titles of the Code of Federal Regulations (CFR). The CFR is available in all law libraries as well as major community libraries.

While most agencies involved in some manner with food safety are identified herein, the chapter's main focus is on those agencies having major and direct responsibilities. The three agencies with major and direct responsibilities for food safety are: Food Safety and Inspection Service, and Agriculture Marketing Service, US Department of Agriculture (USDA); the Food and Drug Administration (FDA), US Department of Health and Human Services (USHHS); and the Environment Protection Agency (EPA).

Other agencies with less direct responsibility for ensuring food safety and wholesomeness, and agencies with responsibility relating to human diet and health include: Agriculture Marketing Service, USDA; Animal and Plant Health Inspection Service, USDA; National Marine Fisheries Services (NMFS), US Department of Commerce (USC); Food and Nutrition Service, USDA; Human and Nutrition Information Service, USDA; Agriculture Research Service, USDA; Centers for Disease Control and Prevention (CDC), USHHS; Foreign Agriculture Service, USDA; Office of General Counsel (one in each Department that services each of the agencies); and Office of Management and Budget.

In addition to their own cadre of professional employees who carry out the agencies' missions, the agencies also rely on highly specialized analytical laboratories, formal advisory committees and boards comprised mainly of experts from outside government, and contracts with state agencies, universities, or private organizations for specialized work, investigations, studies and recommendations.

During the last several decades senior managers of the three main agencies referred to earlier have recognized the increasing need for interagency cooperation and support, and have fostered it in many forms on many levels. Cooperation is essential and very dynamic. One major challenge facing the agencies, when elections bring personnel changes at the Cabinet and sub-cabinet levels, is that of quickly and effectively acquainting the new people with the myriad of ongoing cooperative activities, and of their importance.

While there are several other federal and state agencies, international bodies and other organizations that impact food safety policies and activities through their responsibilities for diet and health, their role in food safety in the classical sense is much less direct. This list would include such agencies as the National Institutes of Health, National Cancer Institute, and state inspection programs and public health departments.

Organizations that can influence certain issues include those representing the livestock (and poultry) producers, such as the American Cattlemen's Association, professional associations, such as the Institute of Food Technologists, trade associations, such as the National Broiler Council, consumer organizations, such as Consumers Union, and other special interest groups, such as Public Voice for Food and Health Policy. This chapter does not discuss their role or way they function. However, any serious study of the government process would need to include both the role and methods of operation of all such organizations.

14.2   Agencies and functions

14.2.1   Main agencies

14.2.1.1   Food Safety and Inspection Service (FSIS).   The major mission of FSIS is ensuring the safety of all meat and poultry, whether raw or processed, under the Federal Meat Inspection Act, 21 USC 601 *et seq.*, and the Poultry Products Inspection Act, 21 USC 451 *et seq.* FSIS's regulations are codified in Title 9 of the CFR.

There are a few exceptions, however. Because the policies for the exceptions are not totally consistent, having been heavily influenced by historical precedent, and because their complexity would require consider-able discussion, they are not further elaborated on in this chapter. Suffice it to say that in cases where a processed meat or poultry product contains such small quantities of meat or poultry that it is generally has not been considered a product of the meat or poultry industries, it is not covered by FSIS but by the Food and Drug Administration (FDA). Other meat and poultry operations that have been left to FDA's jurisdiction are those generally and historically considered usual for food service and/or retail outlets. The ambiguities and problems associated with the threshold between FSIS and FDA's jurisdiction have significantly increased in recent years due to changes in the food processing industry, the multiplicity of new products in the marketplace, and the emergence of such things as 'wholesale clubs' that prepare products for resale to food service establishments, grocery stores and delicatessens.

14.2.1.2   Food and Drug Administration (FDA).   The FDA is responsible for ensuring the safety of all food products, raw or processed, except meat, poultry and processed eggs. While FDA is not absolved of or does not relinquish its statutory responsibilities, some companies elect to have their fishery operations under the oversight of NMFS on a 'fee for service' basis. In such cases, there is a certain reliance by FDA on NMFS to ensure those fish and fishery products are safe and wholesome.

FDA derives its food regulatory authority from the following: Pure Food and Drugs Act of 1906; Federal Import Milk Act of 1928; Federal Food, Drug and Cosmetic Act of 1938; Public Health Service Act of 1944; Fair Packaging and Labeling Act of 1966; Infant Formula Act of 1980; and the Nutrition Labeling and Education Act of 1990. FDA's food regulations are codified in Title 21 of the CFR. In addition to food, FDA is also responsible for cosmetics, drugs, medical devices, radiological products, animal drugs used in the production and treatment of food animals, and for establishing maximum limits on such drugs that may be in the tissues of such animals.

14.2.1.3   Environmental Protection Agency (EPA).   The EPA is responsible for approving and governing the use of chemicals used in production of food, both of animal and vegetable origin, and used in or around food processing plants, storage warehouses, food service establishments and retail outlets. Chemicals requiring approval include such things as herbicides, pesticides, insecticides and fungicides. Further, the EPA establishes maximum residue levels (MRLs) for all such chemicals that may appear as residues in food.

The most notable statutes administered by EPA include: Clean Water Act; Safe Drinking Water Act; Resource Conservation and Recovery Act; Comprehensive Environmental Response, Compensation and Liability Act; and the Federal Insecticide, Fungicide and Rodenticide Act. EPA's regulations appear in Title 40 of the CFR.

14.2.2   Other agencies

14.2.2.1   Agriculture Marketing Service (AMS).   AMS, USDA, is responsible for ensuring the safety and wholesomeness of processed eggs and egg products even though FDA has that responsibility for shell (fresh) eggs. AMS carries out its inspection mandate in a manner similar to FSIS, i.e. evaluating the acceptability of facilities and equipment, and assigning agency employees to each plant to ensure compliance with the regulatory requirements for hygiene, and processing. AMS also services the food acquisition components of Department of Defense, and the FNS, USDA. In that role, AMS may write specifications for foods and food products for purchase on contract, or product descriptions for purchase on the open market. The AMS regulations are codified in Title 7 of the CFR.

14.2.2.2   Animal and Plant Health Inspection Service (APHIS).   APHIS, USDA, promotes the health and well being of US citizens through protecting the health of the US animals and plants; ensuring human treatment of animals; eradicating animal and plant pests and diseases; and for animal damage control. APHIS is involved in developing and monitoring voluntary programs for food animal (including bird) producers to reduce, more carefully control or seek elimination of human pathogens from such animals prior to slaughter for use as human food. The APHIS regulations are codified in Title 9 of the CFR.

14.2.2.3   National Marine Fisheries Service (NMFS).   The NMFS, Department of Commerce, fulfills its fish and seafood inspection responsibilities, when requested by processors, who agree to pay a fee for their services of performing inspection. The NMFS's approach is similar to that of FSIS, i.e. evaluating the adequacy of the operator's facilities and equipment, and assigning NMFS employees to the operation to ensure enforcement of their requirements for dressing fish, and for processing into other fishery products. The NMFS's regulations are codified in Title 15 of the CFR.

14.2.2.4   Food and Nutrition Service (FNS).   FNS, USDA, is responsible for the national Food Stamp Program, the School Lunch Program, and for Special Nutrition Programs for certain needy groups within the US population. One significant component of the FNS mission is that of distributing nutrition information to and educating the people they serve. As noted above, FNS relies on AMS in a manner similar to the food acquisition components of the Department of Defense. The FNS regulations are codified in Title 7 of the CFR.

14.2.2.5   Human Nutrition Information Service (HNIS).   HNIS, USDA, is responsible for evaluating the diet of the US population, for formulating recommendations for change, and for preparing information and educational materials to communicate and educate US citizens. The functions and activities of HNIS are codified in Title 7 of the CFR.

14.2.2.6   Agriculture Research Service (ARS).   ARS, USDA, carries out the USDA's very broad research mandate. This includes research projects requested by other USDA agencies relating to fulfillment of their respective missions, and food safety research projects. Projects requested by FSIS include some basic research, but most are for applied research. The functions and activities of ARS are codified in Title 7 of the CFR.

14.2.2.7   Centers for Disease Control and Prevention (CDC).   CDC, USHHS, monitors the nation's human health by identifying threats, tracking problems, conducting investigations and collecting the interpreting data. CDC plays an increasingly important role as a source of data for FSIS and FDA. The functions and activities of CDC are codified in Title 45 of the CFR.

14.2.2.8   Foreign Agriculture Service (FAS).   FAS, USDA, represents the US agriculture community abroad. It collects, analyzes, and disseminates information about global supply and demand, trade trends and emerging market opportunities. They seek to open new markets for agriculture products, improve market access of those already open, and carry out food aid and market-related technical assistance programs. The functions and activities of FAS are codified in Title 7 of the CFR.

14.2.2.9   Office of General Counsel (OGC).   Each department and independent agency within the Executive Branch of Government has a General Counsel. One of the many roles of the OGC is to work with the agencies within each department (or independent agency) to provide legal advice and assistance to agency representatives concerning the enabling statutes under which they function. Because the three main agencies issue regulations, the OGC advice is an integral part of agency business, and good cooperation between the regulatory agency and their OGC is essential to their effectiveness.

14.2.2.10 Office of Management and Budget (OMB). The President's OMB has two major responsibilities: (i) manage the affairs of the Executive Branch (EB) of Government; and (ii) to formulate and submit to Congress the annual budget for the EB. Both functions are carried out in a manner commensurate with the incumbent administration's political philosophies, platforms and promises. The various departments and independent agencies within the EB are obliged to consult and/or obtain the concurrence of OMB on all significant policies, budget initiatives and so forth, prior to their being made public or submitted to the Congress.

14.3 Domestic interests and cooperations

14.3.1 Common interests, philosophies and mechanisms

One common means of interagency cooperation is through informal liaison between employees having common professional interests and/or responsibilities. These are encouraged by agency managers because they provide a continuing awareness across the agencies of general direction, policies under development, organizational and personnel changes, and problems. This produces other intangible benefits such as more creativity, and a broader range of alternatives for addressing needs.

Another means of interagency cooperation is by agency heads periodically meeting to consider major policy issues or initiatives of mutual interest. For example, the Commissioner of FDA and Administrator of FSIS collaborated on the regulations for nutritional labeling of food, and their deputies collaborated several times during development, public hearings, formal solicitation and evaluation of written comments, and considering issues and alternatives for final regulations.

Formal mechanisms used to facilitate cooperation among agencies include Task Forces and Committees, and Memoranda of Understanding (MOU). These may be temporary or semi-permanent, and exist at several organizational levels. FSIS, FDA's Center for Food Safety and Applied Nutrition (CFSAN), the US Army Office of Surgeon General, and NMFS, jointly sponsor the National Advisory Committee for Microbiological Criteria for Foods. An example of an MOU is one between FSIS and FDA for handling of recalls of food products under both agency's jurisdiction in the event of an emergency. In this case, the MOU outlines the responsibilities of each agency, identifies appropriate officials in each agency who would be involved, and prescribes the procedures to be followed when such an emergency arises.

There are other very good examples of cooperation between federal agencies. One is between FSIS, FDA and the EPA on the pesticide data program and the chemical residue monitoring program. Cooperation is facilitated through an Interagency Residue Control Group (NRP), consisting of members from the three agencies. The NRP's functions are:

1. Assisting in identifying and evaluating compounds.
2. Exchanging information on new approvals and uses.
3. Exchanging information on such things as banning of a compound, changes in distribution pattern of a compound, new and altered uses, and new information on the characteristics of residues.
4. Sharing general information on methods for detection, and specific information on such things as improvements in analytical methodology for detection.

In the future, more cooperation between the federal agencies, and more harmonization of their respective regulatory approaches, is needed. Not only is this recognized by the managers of these agencies, but by other bodies. The General Accounting Office (GAO) in 1992, stated that the agencies administering laws posing similar public health risks from food needed even more coordination and cooperation. In fact, the GAO Report concludes that without basic changes to the federal regulatory structure and the existing food safety laws the problems of such things as dissimilar health risks considerations, inefficient use of staff resources, and the occasional duplication of effort, are likely to continue. GAO's recommendation was the creation of single food safety agency that combined the responsibilities of the several existing main agencies (GAO, 1993). Vice President Gore's 1993 report on *Reinventing Government* contained the same recommendation (NPR, 1993).

14.3.2   Rulemaking

FSIS, FDA and EPA are required to follow similar procedures in issuing, amending or repealing regulations or other formal policies, as prescribed in the Administrative Procedures Act (APA), 5 USC 551 *et seq*. This is to allow the public an opportunity to participate in their government's business by offering comments, or submitting data or information for consideration by responsible officials. This process is called rulemaking. The APA also prescribes procedures for public notice before an agency conducts public hearings on an issue to allow interested parties an opportunity to be heard.

The method used to inform the public in the case of rulemaking, the holding of public hearings, etc., is the *Federal Register* (*FR*). The *FR* is a document published every work day by the Government Printing Office (GPO) for the expressed purpose of informing the public of government business, and providing opportunity to participate. Unless a public emergency exists, as defined by the APA and related case law, a comment period of at least 30 days is to be given during which all interested parties may submit comments, data and information to the appropriate agency. The *FR* is available for purchase from the GPO by single issue, or on subscription.

In addition to complying with the APA procedural requirements on rulemaking, the agencies are also obliged to comply with ancillary requirements such as Paperwork Reduction Act (44 USC 3501) and Presidential Executive Orders (EO) such as 136. The Paperwork Reduction Act requires that the Office Management and Budget (OMB) review and approve any new record keeping requirements prior to issuing any regulation containing a record keeping burden.

EO 136 requires the agencies to perform economic and other analyses on regulations that are determined to be significant, and similarly requires review of such regulations by the Office of Management and Budget (OMB). The economic analysis establishes the costs of implementing a new or changed rule versus any monetary benefits to society. If a preliminary determination can be made that the cost is under $100 million, a detailed economic analysis does not need to be completed.

A broad outline of the rulemaking procedure is given below. However, each agency may deviate or change the order based on its needs. In many cases interagency liaison is occurring during the rulemaking process.

1. Identification of a problem or a need that should be addressed through rulemaking.
2. A decision paper for the agency head which explains the problem or need; identifies alternatives; and makes recommendations.
3. If the agency head concurs, the project is assigned to a staff for development.
4. The staff usually forms a multidisciplinary committee to ensure the document is complete and sound.
5. The draft document circulates among key managers of major program areas within the agency for review, comments and clearance. If there are significant changes, the document is recirculated.
6. Review of the document by the Office of General Counsel for legal sufficiency.
7. Submission of the document by the agency head to the Office of Management and Budget (OMB) for review and concurrence with broader governmental goals and objectives.
8. If cleared by OMB, publish in the *FR* for public review and comment.

In most cases, the steps have to be followed through twice: first when preparing and issuing a proposed regulation; and second, when issuing the final regulation (or decision). It should be evident even from the above summarized steps that rulemaking is a very lengthy, involved, and time and resource consuming process. However, the checks and balances help ensure that regulations are not arbitrary; do not conflict with other federal laws; are in society's best interest; and conform to the political philosophies and goals of the incumbent administration.

14.3.3 FSIS and FDA inspection techniques

While the techniques between the two agencies are uniquely different, primarily because of the enabling legislation, several levels and forms of interagency cooperation transpire. This includes something as simple as a telephone call at the lower level of either agency's field organization alerting a representative in the sister agency of something that has been learned that will be useful to their pursuit. It also includes collaboration at the highest managerial level of the two agencies when major policy initiatives are under consideration. The collaboration may include all informal mechanisms as well as formal interchanges.

14.3.3.1 FSIS. Among people who have some understanding of FSIS's activities, they generally view the agency as taking a proactive role in inspecting meat and poultry plants because the agency is involved in all aspects of pre- and post-slaughter and dressing, preparation of parts and cuts of livestock and poultry, and in further processing into other products.

A meat and poultry plant first has to obtain several FSIS approvals prior to starting in business. The initial step is obtaining FSIS approval of the facilities through both a review of blueprints, and an on-site review. This helps assure FSIS of such things as:

1. Proximity to other properties or businesses that might have an adverse affect on products, such as rodent harbors.
2. Suitability of construction materials.
3. Potability of water supply.
4. Adequacy of waste and sewage disposal.
5. Flow of product and movement of people within the facility to minimize cross contamination of products.
6. Adequacy of separation of edible and inedible product areas.
7. Adequacy of employee welfare facilities, including location and number of toilets.
8. The acceptance and location of the equipment.

For information and convenience, FSIS prepares a booklet of the facility requirements, and annually publishes a list of 'accepted' equipment. In addition, another booklet containing non-food chemicals, such as cleaning materials that may be used in meat and poultry plants, is made available to interested parties.

FSIS specialists doing such work are very familiar with publications containing similar information from the other main agencies, and also are acquainted with the responsible personnel in the other agencies.

After acceptance of the plant, FSIS assigns an official number unique to that one plant. The number must appear on all product containers and labeling, and on all carcasses and parts in commerce. FSIS also requires prior approval of labeling for each product to ensure the labels are accurate and truthful, and bear the required features. Finally, plant management is required to submit a 'schedule of operations' to key FSIS line supervisors in order for the agency to know when the presence of inspectors will be needed.

FSIS conducts ante-mortem and post-mortem inspection of all livestock and poultry entering a slaughter facility, and all carcass and bird parts and all processed products entering all other plants. The FSIS employee(s) conducts an ante-mortem inspection to detect animals unfit for human food, or which require special handling; and conducts post-mortem inspection of the every carcass (including poultry) to detect conditions that make them unfit for human food. Animals, carcasses and parts deemed unfit are condemned and removed immediately from the food chain. At meat and poultry plants FSIS employees do daily monitoring of pre-operative sanitary conditions of the facilities and equipment, of operative sanitation practices, and of personal hygiene. Other inspections may include temperature checks of cooked product, formulations (recipes) for correct composition, type and quantity of added chemicals, cooking and cooling procedures followed, handling and packaging procedures, labeling being used, weights of containers, and proper storage of product.

Under the inspection laws, every product leaving a federally inspected meat or poultry plant, whether slaughter or processing, must have been inspected and bear an 'inspected and passed' seal attesting to that fact.

14.3.3.2 FDA's inspection of fish and seafood.   Among the vast scope of FDA responsibilities are those of developing overall policies and procedures governing the safety of fish and seafood. As with other food regulations, FDA carries out its mandate primarily by issuance of regulations and imposition of sanctions against violative product or non-compliant processors. However, as with FSIS, some pre-approvals are required. Plants processing low acid canned food, including seafood, are required to register with the FDA, for example.

Each FDA District Office develops an official establishment list of plants processing seafood in their geographical area. The District Office uses such things as state licenses and registrations of businesses, feedback from investigators, tips from competitors and direct contact by the processor. In addition to monitoring seafood establishments, FDA either conducts sanitation inspection of food services, restaurants and shellfish sanitation programs, or commissions the states to do it.

The FDA employs individual and team investigators to conduct periodic inspections of fish and seafood processing plants. Plant selection is based on the history of compliance, complaints from consumers or other interested parties, and time lapse since the last inspection visit.

14.3.4 Use of Hazard Analysis and Critical Control Point system by the federal agencies

The HACCP system was first used in the mid-sixties by the National Aeronautics and Space Administration in preparing food for the astronauts. Details on the origin and development of the HACCP system is explained in Chapter 1. It was formally presented to the scientific community and general public in 1971 (DHEW, 1972). FDA used HACCP principles in developing and promulgating the regulations in 1973 for thermally processed low acid canned foods. FSIS personnel kept abreast of those changes, and of the ensuing enforcement by FDA. Further application of HACCP principles occurred when FSIS revised and promulgated its regulations for thermally processed meat and poultry products in 1986 and in regulations to ensure adequate preparation of cooked roast beef about the same time. Key FDA officials were kept informed of FSIS's needs and direction in dealing with illnesses from consuming such products due to inadequate cooking.

In late 1980s the consumers, legislators and regulators became concerned about the safety of fish and seafood products. NMFS, Department of Commerce, was given the lead by Congress to develop a model for the new federal inspection program to improve the safety of seafood, and to protect the consumers from mislabeled and unwholesome products. NMFS's role was because of a voluntary inspection program (fee for service) that they had operated for several years and because they had the expertise to do it. The NMFS, after a lengthy study of inspection systems, recommended to the Congress that the HACCP approach should be used to certify fish and seafood as a part of its voluntary inspection program. That has been done and is now available from NMFS on a fee basis. Throughout the process both FDA and FSIS were periodically updated by NMFS representatives.

In 1988, four federal agencies: FSIS, FDA, NMFS and the US Army Office of Surgeon General joined together to fund the National Advisory Committee on Microbiological Criteria for Foods, even though the committee is chartered by the USDA (USDA, 1994). In 1989, the committee endorsed the use of HACCP by the industry and regulatory agencies. The committee's recommendation gave further impetus to and reliance on the effective use of HACCP. The agencies have worked closely to ensure good understanding of each agency's needs and direction.

In 1990, FSIS presented a detailed paper on the use of HACCP in meat and poultry inspection, conducted HACCP workshops to develop generic HACCP models for three products: minimally processed meat and poultry products, cooked sausage and poultry slaughter. FSIS also began testing of HACCP in nine meat and poultry plants. Periodic liaison with FDA, occurred throughout.

FDA in early 1993, announced that all fish and seafood establishments will be required to develop and maintain HACCP systems (DHHS, 1994). Based in part on interagency cooperation, shortly thereafter the Secretary of Agriculture issued a statement that FSIS would mandate the use of HACCP by all federally inspected meat and poultry plants (USDA, 1993).

14.3.5 Cooperation in developing policies and regulations

One exceptional example of cooperation between the federal agencies with regard to development of regulations was with the Nutrition Labeling and Education Act of 1991. This act required FDA, but not FSIS, to develop and propose nutrition labeling policies. However, with a view toward developing USDA regulations for meat and poultry to bring uniformity and consistency to nutritional labeling of all food products, FSIS cooperated with the FDA and jointly conducted nationwide public hearings to assess the needs and solicit opinions from consumers, industry and any interested parties. The FDA and FSIS final regulations were consistent with one another because of the close staff cooperation during the rulemaking process.

The federal agencies also cooperate extensively in cross utilizing information and resources in other areas, such as developing analytical methods for use in laboratories, conducting collaborative studies, information sharing on foodborne illness problems, identifying food safety research needs, and on conducting product recalls.

Another avenue of cooperation between the federal agencies is by jointly asking for evaluations of scientific issues or methods by the National Academy of Sciences (NAS). In 1980 four federal agencies: FSIS, FDA, NMFS and the Department of Defense's (DOD) Army Natick Research and Development Center requested that NAS, National Research Council (NRC) study and formulate general principles for microbiological criteria for foods and food ingredients, and to provide recommendations for a unified, coordinated approach. The NRC conducted the study and published a report entitled *An Evaluation of the Role of Microbiological Criteria for Foods and Food Ingredients* (NRC, 1985). One recommendation was that the four federal agencies establish an ad hoc commission on Microbiological Criteria for Foods (NACMCF). In response to the NRC recommendation, four federal agencies established the National Advisory Committee on Microbiological Criteria for Foods. The Army's Office of Surgeon General assumed DOD's sponsoring role.

The Secretary of Agriculture in consultation with the representatives of the other federal agencies appointed 25 members from academia, consumer organizations, federal agencies and experts from the food industry to serve on the NACMCF. One of the first acts of this Committee was to establish Working Groups (or sub-committees). The working groups were:

1. Hazard Analysis and Critical Control Points.
2. Seafood.
3. Meat and poultry.
4. Handling practices and consumer education.
5. Research.

Representatives from each of the main agencies are members of each of the working groups. This mode of interagency cooperation has contributed immensely to a better understanding of the needs and problems of each agency. Further, because of personnel changes within the agencies, the understanding is always there, and always needs to be furthered.

Since its inception the NACMCF has elaborated and adopted the following documents:

1. Controls and Microbiological Criteria for Ready-To-Eat Refrigerated Foods Containing Cooked, Uncured Meat or Poultry Products Packaged for Extended Shelf Life (NACMCF, 1990a).
2. Microbiological Criteria for Foods: Recommendations on Cooked Ready-To-Eat Shrimp and Crabmeat (NACMCF, 1990b); Microbiological Criteria for Raw Molluscan Shellfish (NACMCF, 1992a).
3. *Listeria monocytogenes* (NACMCF, 1991).
4. *Campylobacter jejuni/coli* (NACMCF, 1993a).
5. Hazard Analysis and Critical Control Point system (NACMCF, 1992b).
6. The Role of Regulatory Agencies and Industry in Hazard Analysis and Critical Control Point system (NACMCF, 1993b).
7. Generic HACCP Model for Raw Beef (NACMCF, 1993b).

The NACMCF'S documents on HACCP provided FSIS and FDA invaluable help in their efforts to promote HACCP among their regulated industries, and NMFS in their offering of HACCP to the seafood industry on the 'fee for service' basis. Many of the NACMCF's recommendations are expected to be incorporated into FSIS and FDA's development of proposed regulations, and especially the seven fundamental principles, and the regulatory agencies responsibilities in monitoring the industry's conformance to HACCP.

The seven fundamental principles of HACCP identified and recommended by the NACMCF are:

- conduct a hazard analysis
- prepare a list of steps in the process where significant hazards occur and describe the preventive measures
- identify the critical control points (CCP)
- establish critical limits for preventive measures associated with each identified CCP
- establish corrective action to be taken when monitoring indicates that there is a deviation from an established critical limits
- establish effective record keeping procedures that document the HACCP system
- establish procedures for verification that the HACCP system is working correctly

In summary, the effectiveness and efficiency of the main federal agencies is enhanced by interagency cooperation on all levels in all forms on a myriad of issues.

14.4 International interests and cooperation

As a preface to anything said in this section or anywhere in this chapter, it must be affirmed in the strongest possible terms that the US interest in harmonization, cooperation and understanding and trade facilitation, does *not* supplant the first and foremost objective of protecting the health of US citizens.

This section makes no attempt to explain the effective efforts of many industry trade groups to facilitate harmonization and trade. Suffice it to say that without such efforts, much less would be accomplished. Because the authors are career employees of FSIS, USDA, the information about meat and poultry will be more extensive than for other foods, including fish and seafood. Because of the international trade interests and specific problems arising therefrom, harmonization of food standards is essential to ensure as a free flow of trade as possible. Further, harmonization of hygiene requirements (which includes processing methods and procedures) is also essential to protect public health.

Ongoing international harmonization efforts can be classified into three broad categories:

1. Bilateral agreements with an individual country, or multilateral agreements with a small group of countries.
2. International agreements.
3. Codex Alimentarius Commission.

14.4.1 Bilateral agreements with an individual country, or multilateral with a small group of countries

In this context, the term 'agreements' might better be characterized as follows:

> Developing an understanding of a country's law and regulations, inspection methods and procedures, and implementing and enforcing all requirements to export or import food products.

Such efforts, usually bilateral, necessarily involve a significant amount of interchange between parties, cooperation and coordination. In many cases the Agricultural Attaches (or other persons with similar duties) in embassies are invaluable in facilitating the flow of information and promoting cooperation.

Changes needed to comply with an importing country's standards and other requirements are almost always represented as being based on credible scientific and technical criteria. However, honest differences arise. Resolution involves a high level of mutual respect, intellectual honesty, and a willingness to discuss and understand. The individuals involved in such activities are not only experts in their respective disciplines, but have an excellent grasp of the protocol involved, and diplomacy needed. The procedures employed by the two main US agencies, FSIS and FDA, differ because their statutory authority differs. Consequently, the procedures are discussed separately.

14.4.1.1 FSIS.

FSIS has a dual role in international trade. The first is to ensure that countries exporting meat and poultry products to the USA have an inspection system at least 'equal to' that of the US system; and second, to aid commodity groups and individual companies in understanding and satisfying the standards and requirements of other countries in order to facilitate export of meat and poultry products to such countries.

In addition to the formal and informal bilateral coordination and cooperation with individual countries, FSIS cooperates in several other ways. The following are examples:

1. The agency conducts training courses for foreign inspection officials to acquaint them with the US inspection system and its underlying principles, and import requirements. However, the participants do not need to be from countries who are, or are interested in exporting to the USA. Many participants are from countries who are interested in establishing and/or upgrading their own inspection systems.
2. The agency provides copies of all laws, regulations, standards and other information to countries interested in qualifying for export of meat and poultry products to the USA. While such activities usually begin

formally it is not uncommon for them to become an increasingly informal interchange between a few individuals in each country.

3. The agency is an active sponsor of and participant in international seminars and conferences, especially major trading partners such as New Zealand, Australia, Mexico and Canada. The topics range from scientific and technical issues relating to inspection and trade to specific exporting/importing problems a country is experiencing with the USA.

Evaluating the 'equal to' status of another country's inspection system for exporting to the USA involves two steps: document review; and on-site review.

Document review involves evaluating a country's laws, inspection regulations and procedures, and other written information that affects the conduct of such a system. In a case where a country's inspection system is found to be deficient, at the country's request, FSIS provides whatever information and assistance that may be needed to help the country conform its documents so they meet US acceptability. When FSIS is satisfied the country's documents will, if implemented and enforced, result in meat and poultry products that are comparable in safety, wholesomeness, standards of composition, and labelling to that produced in a federally inspected plant in the USA, a complementary step is to determine if there are animal or plant diseases in the country that are of concern to the US Animal and Plant Health Inspection Service (APHIS), USDA. If none, FSIS proceeds to step 2. However, if there are qualifications by APHIS, those must be resolved by the country with APHIS before FSIS proceeds to step 2.

The second step involves sending a multidisciplinary technical team to the country to conduct on-site reviews of the inspection system in operation in specific plants from whence product will be exported to the USA: the laboratories used to test product or diagnose disease conditions, including the analytical or diagnostic procedures used; arrangements for training of personnel and course content; and the administrative support system. The team usually consists of a veterinarian, food technologist, chemist, and a compliance officer. After completing the on-site review, officials within the International Programs area of FSIS makes a final decision of the equivalency of the country's inspection system. If accepted by the agency head and key departmental officials, the name of country is published in the *FR* for public information, and for annual codification in the *CFR*.

Once approval of a country for export to the USA has been published in the *FR*, the exporting country's chief inspection official annually provides a formal list of plants that meet all US requirements that may be exporting meat and poultry products to the USA.

All foreign plants exporting to the USA are periodically reviewed by

FSIS experts. This is in addition to the usual inspections of all imported products at time of entry into the USA.

Seeking approval from another country in order to facilitate export of meat, poultry or products thereof, has many similarities to the way the USA approves other countries for exporting to the USA. This is more true among developed countries. Nevertheless, there can be problems.

In the case of the European community, the European Union (EU) establishes and enforces the standards and other requirements for the EU member states. Consequently, when the US inspection system and specifically designated plants are approved for export of pork byproducts to Germany for example, those plants are eligible to export the byproducts to another EU state.

In the case of a couple of developed countries, determining how to qualify meat and poultry products for export; and learning how to retain the qualification over an extended period, can almost be a career-long process for some FSIS personnel.

Facilitating exports to less- or under-developed countries brings other challenges, such as understanding who has the power and authority to make decisions, the basis for such decisions, and something of the type of product the country desires to import. Once some grasp of such issues is obtained, the specific requirements the 'designated authority(ies)' has set forth can be addressed. Some of the basic information is available through the US Department of State, the Foreign Agriculture Service, USDA, and the Agricultural Attaches. In all these activities, as well as more direct liaison with officials in these countries, cooperation and understanding becomes a key component. In the absence of hidden agenda, the efforts migrate toward a free interchange of information that serves in the best interest of both countries, i.e. importer and exporter.

14.4.1.2 FDA.   The FDA recently conducted a survey of its Centers and reported that their international harmonization activities can be classified into the following categories:

1. Training and technical assistance.
2. Hosting and attending international meetings.
3. Preparing and reviewing documents.
4. Conducting reviews in other countries.
5. Reviewing applications for export in the USA.
6. Hosting foreign officials, and explaining the FDA system.
7. Developing international agreements.

Items 1, 2 and 6 consume most of the FDA staff resources.

The concept of 'equivalent to' also exists in the case of seafood imported under the auspices of FDA, although the methods for determining it vary some from that of FSIS.

For many decades the international community has routinely watched the actions of FDA for guidance, and has sought out that agency's expertise which in most respects is the envy of most countries. The FDA is routinely involved in information sharing through international organizations or bilateral agreements. Even though some of these activities such as planning and attending regulatory, scientific, or public health conferences do not directly relate to harmonization or cooperation, such activities do help build an understanding of general as well as specific policy issues and problems, and it helps in communicating and understanding changes in the respective inspection systems.

Bilateral agreements, also called Memoranda of Understanding (MOU, singular and plural) in the FDA community, are frequently used as a means of ensuring that imported products such as seafood are safe, and meet the same standards and requirements as those to which US harvesters and processors are subject to. In the case of seafood, the MOU would include controls over waters from which the seafood is harvested, and the means by which the exporting country will ensure fulfillment of such requirements. FDA conserves staff resources through the use of MOU.

FDA periodically reviews seafood operations covered by an MOU, and periodically inspects shipments of imported seafood, including sampling for laboratory analysis. The results of the visits, inspections and laboratory analysis are retained for future reference and use, much in the same way as for domestic food processors. FDA presently has bilateral agreements (or MOU) with Canada, Republic of Korea, Japan, Iceland and Mexico. Finally, as is the case for FSIS, FDA assists US fish and fishery businesses interested in exporting their products to other countries.

14.4.2 International agreements

Increasing international trade and the evolving global market has continued to drive the need to harmonize standards and requirements for food products in all forms as well as all other industrial commodities. The major reason is the increasing global marketing concepts and practices brought about by modern communications and transportation means, and by the increasing need and desire by various business sectors within the countries to expand their markets. Harmonizing standards and other requirements is the fundamental mechanism for accomplishing such noble objectives, thus allowing business to compete in broader world markets.

There are currently three notable agreements; each, in its own way, fulfills many of the needs to allow open and uninhibited international trade in a myriad of commodities and products. The three are:

1. Canadian Free Trade Agreement (CFTA).
2. North American Free Trade Agreement (NAFTA).
3. General Agreement on Tariffs and Trade (GATT).

14.4.2.1 CFTA. Canada has been a major US trading partner for many years. Over the past several decades the type and volume of all types of products moving between the two countries has continued to increase. With the passing of time, the number of problems and trade barriers seemed to become more burdensome. In the 1980s there was a recognition by government officials in the USA and Canada that, while harmonization of standards and requirements were needed on a more global basis, many of the problems and trade barriers between these two friendly countries could and should be lowered or removed. Further, because of the long and friendly association of the two countries, it was recognized that the objectives could be met more expeditiously than perhaps with other countries, and certainly more than if attempted on a global basis.

Therefore, a major milestone was reached in 1988 with final formal acceptance of the US and Canada Free Trade Agreement (CFTA) by both countries (USCFTA, 1988). In 1993, the USA and Canada signed an arrangement that standardized the *re*-inspection activities each country would subject the other's product to when imported.

While the CFTA extends across a broad range of commodities and industrial products, it certainly includes food products. Even though key officials within the USA and Canadian inspection systems have collaborated closely and frequently for several decades, development of the CFTA required an enormous amount of scientific and technical staff resources in more explicitly deciphering and understanding the differences in the inspection systems, the underlying principles for those differences, and developing a scientifically sound basis for any needed changes in order to accomplish the trade objectives while also ensuring that consumers in both countries receive food that is safe, wholesome, nutritious and adequately labeled.

The 1993 arrangement established permanent working groups on meat and poultry inspection and six other areas. It recognizes and speaks to harmonizing technical requirements and inspection procedures, establishes equivalent accreditation procedures for inspection systems and inspectors, establishes a reciprocal training program that could allow utilizing each other's inspectors for inspection of meat, poultry and fish products.

The CFTA also stipulates that each government will work toward eliminating regulations or standards that are arbitrary or unjustifiable, greater exchange of information, and notifying and consulting during development of regulations prior to their implementation. Finally, it speaks to means by which the two countries may proceed to resolve disputes when they arise.

14.4.2.2 NAFTA. A second major milestone reached in 1993 was formal acceptance by Canada, Mexico, and the USA of the North American Free Trade Agreement (NAFTA). The interests and forces driving NAFTA were essentially the same as those giving rise to the CFTA. Also, as with the CFTA, it covers a very broad range of commodities and industrial products.

As it relates to trade of food products, the NAFTA, as the other formal Agreements discussed herein, uses the terms 'sanitary and phyto-sanitary requirements'. The former is associated with hygienic requirements for foods of animal origin, and the latter applies to foods of vegetable (plant) origin. In both cases, the requirements must be scientifically sound, and must consider the relative risk of public harm. Appropriate and acceptable methods for conducting quantitative risk assessments, and for making qualitative risk management decisions, are areas where good understanding and acceptance of methods exists when considering chemical compounds that may accumulate in animal tissue that is to be consumed. Although the mathematical modeling may not be as sophisticated, it is the same when considering zoonotic diseases. However, the methods for conducting risk analysis relating to food borne pathogens are in embryonic stages. Therefore, this latter area is ripe for cooperation among NAFTA members.

As does the CFTA, the NAFTA contains provisions for resolving trade disputes, and it relates to foods, the mechanisms for dealing with such potentially sticky problems as 'when is the science adequate; and therefore, who is more correct'.

14.4.2.3 GATT.   The agreement with the broadest application and with the greatest trade impact is the GATT. Readers in tune with current food-related international events know that in December 1993, the Uruguay Round of negotiations led to agreement between the negotiating parties on language, i.e. member countries with interests in international trade. Many of the outstanding issues resolved in that last round of negotiations had to do with trade of agriculture products, including food. Because of cultural and socio-economic factors, many difficult problems such as subsidies for certain agricultural products had to be successfully negotiated. Subsidies make it necessary for a country to consider placing higher tariffs on importation of those subsidized agricultural products in order to protect the economic viability of that segment of their agriculture.

As with the bilateral and multilateral agreements mentioned above, the GATT covers a very broad range of commodities and products. It truly is an international agreement directly affecting food, and the regulatory agencies in all participating countries with responsibility for food safety. As it relates to food and food products, the GATT also uses the terms 'sanitary and phyto-sanitary.' Throughout the GATT negotiations the major food regulatory agencies provided scientific and technical assistance to the US Office of Trade Policy, and of course, simultaneously carried on their respective liaisons with professional counterparts in other countries.

These dynamic liaison and supportive activities are forms of cooperation that contribute to a more common understanding of differences in scientific interpretations and inferences, for example. The activities occur on several levels ranging from personal to national in interests, and range from fundamental science to very complex socio-economic and cultural issues.

A critical principle that must be established and adhered to under the GATT is that the 'sanitary and phyto-sanitary requirements' be based on sound science. This is essential to prevent or minimize the adverse affects of artificial trade barriers through tariffs. Yet, in spite of general concurrence that the principle is valid, there will be times when the question of 'when is science sound?' will remain. In cases when actual trade disputes arise due to scientific differences, such disputes will be referred to one of three international bodies as a referee. If the dispute is about animal health, the body involved will be the Office of International Epizootics; if the dispute is about plant health, it will involve the International Plant Protection Convention; and if the dispute is about food safety, it will involve the Codex Alimentarius Commission (see also below).

14.4.3 Codex Alimentarius Commission (CAC)

In the 1960s the CAC was formed and chartered by the Food and Agriculture Organization and the World Health Organization of the United Nations for two purposes. One purpose was that of harmonizing international food standards and hygienic requirements, analytical methods, criteria for evaluating food additives and processing aids, and criteria for evaluating drugs and residues in foods and for setting maximum residue limits for such compounds that find their way into the food supply either intentionally or unintentionally. The second purpose was public health protection. The CAC is based in Rome, Italy.

The CAC's overall governing body is, as the name implies, a commission which is comprised of representatives from member countries. Approximately 150 countries are members. The commission meets every other year, alternating between Rome and Geneva, Switzerland. Issues requiring CAC level consideration between the biannual meetings is handled by an Executive Committee (EC), which meets annually in plenary, but collaborates informally on an ongoing basis. North America has one representative to the EC, which in the past has been shared between the USA and Canada. A Secretariat, also based in Rome, provides the CAC, and the EC, with administrative and managerial support.

The scientific and technical work done under the auspices of the CAC is carried out through several dozen committees. Each committee is comprised of representatives from member countries with an interest in and expertise relating to the committee's function, e.g. analytical methods, standards for sugar and food hygiene requirements.

The activities of organizations like the CAC have spawned several other formal and informal cooperative activities, particularly among friendly nations having common trade interests. For this country's meat and poultry interests, these have typically included Canada, Australia, New Zealand and most recently Mexico; and for countries like The Netherlands with keen interests in milk and dairy products it typically included countries like the UK and France.

All the major US agencies play a significant role in identifying such a key international body (or bodies), and in facilitating the organizational, administrative or procedural changes needed in such a body to ensure competency and credibility. This certainly has been true with the CAC. Over the years the USA has hosted four major CAC Committees, more than any other member country, and has actively participated in all others.

As noted above, the successful operation of the GATT will involve the CAC when food safety disputes arise. The CAC's role in such cases will essentially be that of a scientific or technical referee, evaluating the scientific and/or technical credibility of the arguments of the parties to the dispute. How this will actually work within the CAC framework is unclear at this time.

14.5 Opportunities to increase cooperation

Cooperation will be a critical watch-word, and effecting it a major challenge for government managers and politicians as the USA prepares for success in a more global economy. It will be essential both in the domestic arena as well as on the international scene. The mechanisms are in place. What will be needed is commitment, patience and persistence.

14.5.1 Domestic

It is evident that cooperation among the federal agencies in development of standards and regulations for application within broader US food industry has been heavily influenced by the respective agencies' enabling legislation, their heritage and culture, and the differences among the various sectors of the food industry. Further, the reasons underlying those differences created near insurmountable barriers to full and complete cooperation.

The *Reinvention of Government* initiative led by Vice-President Gore proposes, among many other things, to consolidate all federal government food safety functions in one organizational entity. Because it will require legislation to bring that about, this will present the affected agencies and other interested parties with an opportunity to incorporate other changes into the legislation concerning the means and methods the respective agencies employ to carry out their missions. For example, it would make no sense for a statutory requirement to demand that every chicken be inspected at time of slaughter while every fish is not. Such inconsistencies need to be reconciled, based on public health risk. Similar inconsistencies exist with respect to processing of meat and poultry versus that of fish and seafood; the former requiring daily presence of federal inspectors in the plants while the latter are visited periodically. Under good manufacturing practices and regulatory compliance, it is difficult to justify that a hotdog processing operation must be under the daily supervision of a federal inspector while a cheddar cheese operation only needs to be visited every 3–5 years. A basis does exist for different levels of inspection, but that should rest primarily on risk to public health and not on species or type of food product.

Whether or not the Vice-President's recommendation gains acceptance and is enacted through Congressional legislation remains to be seen. However, in the absence of a single food safety agency envisioned by the Vice-President's report, there is good likelihood that consolidation of the food safety functions now under the jurisdiction of USDA will be brought into a more unified organizational alignment. This would facilitate the 'farm to table' food safety concept.

For more than a decade the Office of Management and Budget (OMB) has functioned within their existing structure in an oversight capacity to not only ensure conformance of government policies with those of an incumbent administration, but to the extent permitted under existing statutes to increase the harmony of policies among the various federal agencies. Because that has worked relatively well, consideration has been given to establishing a more structured and institutionalized means for accomplishing the goals. For example, a permanent oversight committee might be formed under the auspices of the OMB or another appropriate agency. Such a body might extend their oversight to other areas, for example, the federal dollars used by all the agencies for conducting food safety research.

Another major food safety policy area that is emerging is that of microbiological risk assessment. While quantitative risk assessment has been effectively used in the chemical compounds area for nearly three decades, little has been done in the area of microbiological risks. The National Advisory Committee for Microbiological Criteria for Food has recently been requested to consider this area, and make whatever recommendations seemed appropriate (USDA, 1992). A special Working Group of select committee members was formed for this purpose, and periodic meetings are already being held. There is a keen recognition within the food safety federal agencies of the importance and need, and a desire to aggressively move toward microbiological risk assessment. While the agencies may desire to follow a course that will ensure maximum harmonization in evolving policies, the major differences in the enabling food safety statutes will guarantee differences in final outcome among the agencies.

Harmonization and cooperation should not be limited just to policy and regulations. There are notable areas where increased effectiveness and efficiency can be harvested, e.g. personnel support functions, research money, and scientific and technical staff support functions.

The largest expenditure of the main food regulatory agencies is for employee salaries. While USDA has very tentatively explored this in bygone years in a very limited way for intra-departmental employees, in the end nothing substantive materialized and the USDA agencies migrated back to their previous independence. When it comes to inter-departmental employees, even less has been tried.

The present inspection mandates are the epitome of extremes. As noted earlier, FSIS's current mandate is to have daily presence in every meat and poultry processing facility while FDA can visit a fish processing facility at whatever time interval is deemed appropriate, perhaps stretching to once in five years in some cases. Most informed people in and out of government believe the right frequency for inspection visits to such facilities is somewhere between the two extremes, and should be driven primarily by the risk to public health and the operation's history of compliance.

In a more balanced program, what would be so wrong if a federal employee, or a small team, was responsible for inspection of all food operations in a given geographical area? Further, is it not possible that those same people could monitor those facilities for compliance at least with the most fundamental occupational safety and health requirements, and for the environmental requirements?

A second area where significant improvement is achievable is in the expenditure of federal funds, as limited as they are, for food safety research. Little is currently being done to evaluate the needs across the entire foods spectrum, and of course, even less is being done to look at increased efficiencies for conducting the needed research. Food safety is now an 'in vogue' theme. Universities have joined forces in consortia to market their capabilities and share the resources, and in some respects those models appear to have efficiencies that are not being adequately assessed from a national perspective. The university community has a history of establishing reputations around certain themes, for example, Texas A&M with its strong large animal veterinary program. In the foods area, perhaps the government should put more effort into encouraging the university community to create 'centers of excellence' for certain foods and food-related research programs. Does the USA have the economic resources and need for duplication and overlap among universities' research programs?

The third area open for more cooperation is through common utilization of scientific and technical resources the main agencies need. For example, a cadre of microbiologists considering the potential public health hazards of, and means for controlling, *Listeria monocytogenes*, should be able to expand their consideration across all susceptible food products. In addition, a laboratory ought to be able to analyze any food for the residue of a particular chemical compound, not being inhibited by statutory and unnecessary organizational constraints, thereby gaining efficiencies that seem to be unattainable under the present system. In both cases it seems reasonable to infer that efficiencies could also be gained from the number and size of laboratory facilities needed to support a federal food safety program if 'cooperation' was brought to a different level of shared resources.

In the final analysis, there must be a continuing effort not only of harmonization between US federal regulatory agencies, but among international bodies as well.

14.5.2 International

As noted earlier in this chapter, NAFTA has now been formally adopted by the three countries, and agreement on language has now been reached on the GATT. Both hold enormous potential for future international cooperation, but the impact of the GATT, if formally adopted by member countries, will be far greater.

Already planners and policy personnel within the main federal agencies are envisioning a time when the role of organizations like the Codex Alimentarius Commission would function on the international scene in a manner analogous to that of the federal government on the domestic scene. For example, standards for food commodities and products moving in international trade would be established; maximum residue levels permitted in a given food commodity (animal or vegetable) would be established; and, acceptable methods for laboratory analyses would be developed, proven, and adopted. Such actions would presumably reduce or eliminate the need for similar duplicative efforts within each country.

When one considers the difficulty the USA and European Union have encountered in recent years over acceptance and use of growth-promoting hormones in livestock, one quickly realizes not only the barriers to fulfilling such visions and also the enormous need for communications and cooperation. Further, the notion of compromise looms even larger on matters US representatives have heretofore thought inappropriate or undesirable. However, as global trade expands and increases for all other industrial products it is unrealistic to think the same cannot, or should not, occur in the foods area. So it's coming! The challenge for the USA is to remain prepared with the most competent team to play in the international arena. Team members will not only need to be scientific and technical experts in their fields, but skilled communicators, negotiators, and yes, even in some cases salespersons.

14.6 Summary

The USA has many federal, state and local laws designed to ensure the safety of the food supply. The Federal Food and Drug Administration and the Department of Agriculture bear the major responsibility for administering the many laws through varying regulatory systems, but many other agencies at all government levels play significant roles. In the past the agencies involved were affected by three major influences: (i) political; (ii) business sector; and (iii) consumer activists. While the goal of safe food is shared by all three, there are major differences over inspection methods and penalties for violation. Even though those influences will continue as strong as ever, the international influence is rapidly becoming a fourth major factor primarily because of increasing international trade.

As with many other things, the food inspection systems are dynamic and continually in need of change not only in the USA, but worldwide. However, given the web of influences, even in the USA if interagency cooperation was nonexistent the system simply could not function. When one turns from domestic problems and needs to those on the international scene it quickly becomes evident that cooperation is even more crucial. Without cooperation, effective change would be impossible.

Because each US agency and each international trading partner has a different heritage, culture, interests and bureaucratic system, finding a common basis becomes the primary challenge in any attempt to define food inspection systems of the future. For the past few years the HACCP system has been gaining increasing acceptance, and it is very likely to be the only system that will survive the debates among politicians, private business owners, consumerists and government officials. Cooperation has been an essential and integral part of making the system function in the past. However, with the rapidly changing world trade environment, the system for ensuring a safe food supply in the future cannot survive without increased emphasis and effort on cooperation.

References

DHEW (1972) *Proc. of 1971 National Conference on Food Protection*. United States Department of Health, Education and Welfare. US Government Printing Office, Washington, D.C.

DHHS (1994) Proposal to establish procedures for the safe processing and importing of fish and fishery products. Food and Drug Administration, Department of Health and Human Services. Proposed Rule. *Federal Register* **59**(19).

GAO (1993) *Food Safety: A Unified, Risk-Based System Needed to Enhance Food Safety.* General Accounting Office. GAO/T–RCED–97–71. Washington, D.C.

NACMCF (1990a) *Refrigerated Foods Containing Cooked, Uncured Meat or Poultry Products that are Packaged for Extended Refrigerated Shelf Life and that are Ready-to-Eat or Prepared with Little or No Additional Heat Treatment.* National Advisory Committee on Microbiological Criteria for Foods. United States Department of Agriculture, Washington, D.C.

NACMCF (1990b) *Cooked Ready-To-Eat Shrimp, Cooked Ready-To-Eat Crab Meat.* National Advisory Committee on Microbiological Criteria for Foods. United States Department of Agriculture, Washington, D.C.

NACMCF (1991) *Listeria monocytogenes.* The National Advisory Committee on Microbiological Criteria for Foods. *Intl. J. Food Microbiol.* **14**, 185.

NACMCF (1992a) Microbiological criteria for raw molluscan shellfish. The National Advisory Committee on Microbiological Criteria for Foods. *J. Food Prot.* **55**, 463.

NACMCF (1992b) Hazard analysis and critical control point system. The National Advisory Committee on Microbiological Criteria for Foods. *J. Food Microbiol.* **16**, 1.

NACMCF (1993a) *Campylobacter jejuni/coli.* The National Advisory Committee on Microbiological Criteria for Foods. United States Department of Agriculture, Washington, D.C.

NACMCF (1993b) The role of regulatory agencies and industry in hazard analysis and critical control point system. The National Advisory Committee on Microbiological Criteria for Foods. *Intl. J. Food Microbiol.* **21**, 187.

NACMCF (1993c) Generic HACCP for raw beef. The National Advisory Committee on Microbiological Criteria for Foods. *Food Microbiol.* **10**, 449.

NPR (1993) *From Red Tape to Results: Creating a Government that Works Better and Costs Less.* The Report of the National Performance Review. The White House, Washington, D.C.

NRC (1985) *An Evaluation of the Role of Microbiological Criteria for Foods and Food Ingredients.* Subcommittee on Microbiological Criteria, Committee on Food Protection, Food and Nutrition Board, National Research Council. National Academy Press, Washington, D.C.

USCFTA (1988) *United States–Canada Free-Trade Agreement implementation Act of 1988.* Pub. L. No. 100–499. Section 406. United States Government Printing Office, Washington, D.C.

USDA (1992) *Minutes of the Meeting of the National Advisory Committee on Microbiological Criteria for Foods.* United States Department of Agriculture, Washington, D.C.

USDA (1993) *Food Safety Offensives.* News Release No. 0417.93. Office of Public Affairs, News Division, United States Department of Agriculture, Washington, D.C.

USDA (1994) *The National Advisory Committee on Microbiological Criteria for Foods.* *Departmental Regulation No. 104328.* United States Department of Agriculture, Washington, D.C.

Index